Unsung

Heather Hamilton

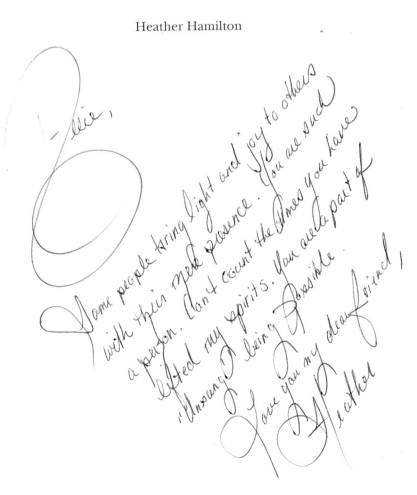

Ellie,

Some people bring light and joy to others with their mere presence. You are such a person. Can't count the times you have lifted my spirits. You are a part of "Unsung" being possible.

Love you my dear friend,

Heather

Unsung

Consultant editor: Lisa Hamilton Johnson
Photographs by: Doug Young

Unsung

ISBN-10: 1470039710
EAN-13: 978-1470039714
Library of Congress Control Number: 2012908522
CreateSpace, North Charleston, SC

Author's note to readers of *Unsung*

When I wrote *Unsung*, several years ago, a memoir about the events leading up to and surrounding the initial onset and subsequent diagnosis of my daughter's mental illness, schizophrenia, I wrote it from memory, from my heart, and from my experience and knowledge at the time. I hope my readers will understand where I felt it was necessary, I changed the names of people and places.

Much has changed in my life since I wrote this memoir. I have lived and loved, lost and learned much more. But *Unsung* is no less meaningful. Any mother, any father, any sibling, relative, friend or loved one of a child or adult living with mental illness, anyone working in the mental health care industry, any psychiatrist, anyone... who has undergone life altering change should read this memoir. *Unsung* has the potential to inspire much needed positive changes in our current mental health care system and in many people's lives... this is my hope.

The passing of time can not change
what happened, only what can happen.

– Heather Hamilton

Statistics regarding *Schizophrenia*

Schizophrenia affects 1% of the total population.

Schizophrenia ranks among the top ten causes of disability in developed countries worldwide.

Schizophrenia, long considered the most chronic, debilitating and costly mental illness, now consumes a total of about $63 billion a year for direct treatment, societal and family costs.

Richard Wyatt, M.D. chief of neuropsychiatry, National Institutes of Mental Health, has said that nearly 30% ($19 billion) of schizophrenia's cost involves direct treatment and the rest is absorbed by other factors – lost time from work for patients and caregivers, social services, and criminal justice resources.

People with schizophrenia have a 50 times higher risk of attempting suicide than the general population.

Suicide is the number one cause of premature death among people with schizophrenia, with an estimated 10 to 13% killing themselves and approximately 40% attempting suicide at least once.

Research expenditures for schizophrenia still lag far behind those of other serious illnesses.

There is no cure.

Source: Schizophrenia.com, 2012, a non profit source of information, support, education

Table of Contents

Acknowledgements

Life is an incredible combination of miracles disguised as simple joys, imagination giving meaning to experience and knowledge, faith in darkness. When you choose in the midst of all the magic, heartache, turbulence, and even tragedy, somewhere in your journey, to be who you are, do what you are meant to do, define yourself rather than let others' expectations direct you, then choosing those who will be with you no matter what is no longer necessary. The process happens simultaneously with living faithfully. I count myself blessed to be able to name a few who have been with me on my incredible journey, who I believe will always be with me.

Guardian Angels

My sister Lisa—*a part of her is Faith in the novel. Faith is the name she should have been given. Her life is a testimony to its healing power. Her love and support, unconditional. Her hands helped make **Unsung** possible.*

My parents. Thank you both for giving me life, great genes, a good sense of humor, a strong heart, a curious mind, and my crooked toes. And for loving and believing in me always.

My best friends. Marlene Gentry, Sherri Altenbach. I could never imagine better friends.

Special thanks to:

Grey Horse Tavern and Ms. Michelle's Urban Gourmet both located in Bayport, New York, for providing locations to photograph the back cover.

Dr. Peter Breggin and Ginger Ross Breggin for their ongoing support.

Wings that Lifted Me

David Stanford for never giving up hope I would publish **Unsung** and for making other dreams come true with me.

Vincent Barone, K.V. Kumar, Mike Dombrowski, Maria Peralta, Patrick O'Neil, Bob Johnson, Whitney Browning, Nancy Martin, Doug Young, Lawson Duncan, Matt Russell, Rich Haberstroh, Pete Carbocci, Sara Carbocci, Dickson Cannon, Brant McAdoo, Mark Mathis, Steve Hart, Jean Noble, Kim Voss, Linda Ringhouse, Kurt vonBartheld, Joseph Regan, Brad Ringhouse, Irene Dougal, Stephen Terry, Anne Winner, Barney Gradman, Priestley Ford, Liz Littlejohn-Barr, Stacy Smith, Kathy Oates Mcleod, Tom and Donna Condra, David Attoe, Mark Mondello, Chuck and Kathy Vetter, Pat Garren, Jamie Bryan, Marge Bryan, Laurie Miller, Sharon Stenger, Catherine Clarke, Jim Morgo, Travis McKeveny.

Wings that Carried Me 'til I found Mine Again

Scott Perricone

Dedication

Where there is great love, there are always miracles.
– Willa Cather

To my daughter Melissa—*chief among my angels, who teaches me every day "the meek will inherit the earth" and whose gentle spirit and loving touch make this world a better place.*

Chapter 1

Voices

Left fist clenched, neck muscles tight, vanilla blonde hair tousled around her angelic face, olive eyes wild, my daughter Ginny hurled her tennis racquet at the fence, crouched down on the court where she and her high-school tennis team were playing a match and screamed toward the sky, "Fuck you, God!"

It was April 3, 2003. We were living in Winter Park, Florida. I'd moved to Winter Park in October of 2002 for a new job and moved Ginny there in January of 2003.

Today, is August 28, 2004, a year and a half later. In that time both of our lives have changed more than most in a lifetime. In that time, I have learned more than I did the entire forty-one years before. Most importantly, I have learned love is the most important element in healing and without it, life is not worth living.

I am sitting in a local bookstore in Asheville, North Carolina, with a strange mixture of feelings, writing my story. On the one hand, I feel very blessed to be able to write it and, on the other hand, I feel more challenged than I have ever been in my life. When my confidence to complete the task fails me and the pages in my notebook taunt me like a marathon I can't possibly run, I listen to my heart, which tells me, "You can't get it wrong. It's the truth."

In August of 2003, the local branch of the waste management company I was working for in Asheville, North Carolina, called Environmental Services, had begun centralizing and downsizing. In the past six months, over two thousand employees and more than a few colleagues and friends of mine had lost their jobs. Though I remained employed, my position as district sales supervisor no longer existed, my life in limbo as they restructured. I decided I needed to find a better opportunity before I no longer had a job.

Along with the inevitable possibility of losing my job, I was also facing the end of my second marriage. And though I believe timing is the mother of change, I know now there were bigger forces at work. Forces that in a matter of a few weeks would gather a lifetime of my decisions and experiences, conceal them amidst my underwear, furniture, and books, and take me on a journey. A journey where I'd need to find the story concealed before I could ever find my way.

I sat down with Ginny and my husband Blake (Ginny's step-dad), who I was separated from but still friends with, and told them, "I think I need to look for work somewhere else."

Ginny was a sophomore attending the same high school where I was once crowned homecoming queen. J.T. Booker High School. To say Ginny was more the scholar and well-rounded person than I was at her age would be an understatement. Think Hillary Clinton and Goldie Hawn as teens and you'll get the picture instantly. In high school I relied heavily on my clearwater view of life, a quirky sense of humor, and what a friend described once as a "nymph like charm capable of disarming the most stubborn case of tight-ass." With these traits, I learned I could win whatever in the tempting sea around me seemed momentarily worth winning. I had—still do— what I like to call a purposeful curiosity about my immediate surroundings and freely admit that formal study for me in high school was a thing to do only when absolutely necessary—a means to an end.

Ginny, by contrast, was fascinated with complexities, with learning for the sake of learning—her taste in books and humor was what my sister Faith would call "eclectic," her social sensibilities more focused on the world than on the typical preoccupations of teenagers. Heavily involved in her school leadership program and their campus and community projects, she also managed a straight-A average and a Southern ranking in tennis, and everything was serious business to her—from the algebraic equations she toiled over every night, determined to ace tests in the one subject for which she had no natural aptitude, to long extra hours on the tennis court with a ball-machine opponent, to home-video plays she wrote, directed, and produced with an enthusiasm and intensity that made me joke with her once, "Your my little Scorsese." The nickname instantly made her frown. "Scorsese's a man, Mommy," she said, scornfully. But then she softened and teased, "Don't you know the names of any women filmmakers?" And then while I blushed and laughed, she rattled off several: "Vyvyan Donner, Ruth Stonehouse, Lule Warrenton," playfully adding herself to the end of the list— "and Ginny Stockinger!"

For her seriousness alone, on most days, though, it would have been oddly easy for strangers to see more of Blake than of me in Ginny, even though they are related, as Ginny said once, "in spirit only."

Blake was an independent video producer, a quietly powerful, soul-searching artist, who eighteen years before I met him fell in love with the Blue Ridge Mountains and the people who lived there and who had made his life's work a communication of their history and culture. Through the years we were married, he struggled mightily to live his dream in the place he loved, while I denied, at every turn, my own colorful ribbon-like essence. Choosing, as my mother had done, to be the glue that held our home and our family together.

Blake listened the way he always listened when he heard me being less than I can be. Eyes cast down, aching to find some way of showing me I had to understand who I was before I could know what I'm to do. While I stood in front of him and Ginny occasionally pacing back and forth, carefully listing the obvious: my concerns for our financial stability, Ginny's education and tennis. I could tell he also felt I was using the job issue as an escape. Another excuse to leave him.

Ginny just listened. Every now and then curling a long strand of her wavy blonde hair around her right index finger, then watching it unwind. When I asked her if she would be okay with moving to Florida, a place I intended to interview for a sales manager's position at another waste management company, she just smiled and asked, "Can we hit outside all the time?"

I laughed. More from relief than humor. Her innocent question the only break I'd had in months from making a series of life-changing decisions.

After we talked, I began reviewing my options. They were few. The job market in Asheville was limited. The chance of my finding a comparable position and salary was not good. A few months before, I'd been listening to the radio, and I remember hearing a disc jockey talking about the plight of women in the work force. She'd done her research.

It seems, in 2002, women in the workforce were making 63 percent of what a man was earning at the same position. Women in the United States making over 60,000 dollars a year accounted for only 6 percent of the workforce. In Western North Carolina only 2.3 percent of the workforce were women in salaried positions making over 60,000 dollars a year. While I was proud to be part of the 2.3 percent, the big picture depressed me, and the realization that I could soon not be a part of the elite group gripped me.

There was my family to consider. Blake and I were getting divorced. We'd been married for eight years—my second marriage, his third, separated once already and the relationship was no longer a marriage but a strained friendship. Ginny and I would need a good support system. My entire family lived in Asheville. My retired parents lived two-hundred yards away in another condominium, and through the years had provided tremendous support for Ginny and for me. Both my brothers, one of whom was Ginny's tennis teacher; my sister Faith, who Ginny and I are very close to; her husband; my brother's wives and children, all lived in Asheville. I'd grown up there, gone to school there, gotten married there, had a child there, bought homes there, worked there.

Ginny seemed to love Asheville. While she had only one good friend, Winnie, she basically had spent her whole life there and though my thoughts of this lovely mountain town are often bittersweet, hers are of the family she loves, a home we used to have on a mountain, her best friend, winning awards at school, get-togethers filled with good food and games. All of that had to be factored in.

There was Ginny's college education to consider. I mentioned Ginny was a Southern ranked tennis player. She was, of course, also state ranked. She would definitely be a top contender for a tennis scholarship to an ACC school, where we'd have in-state tuition. In the year 2000 alone, her lessons, racquets, strings, apparel, tournament entry fees, and travel to tournaments cost 28,000 dollars. While I realized there would be few tennis scholarships that would recoup even half of our investment over the years, I needed any help I could get.

Florida is one of the most competitive states for tennis players. The climate makes it possible for year-round practicing and playing. The number of tennis academies makes it a haven for the development of serious players. Tennis is a household word in Florida. Nearly every home contains a racquet. There are tennis courts in the best sections of towns and the worst sections. There is no better place to learn the game of tennis and no tougher place to compete. Florida would be a good choice for Ginny to improve her game. After all, she was only fifteen. With all the available resources and the weather, she would probably improve at twice the pace.

And there was always the X-factor. My whole life I'd wanted to live near the ocean. Born in the beautiful mountains of Asheville, North Carolina, I was a complete misfit. I knew this instinctively as a child but confirmed it when I saw the ocean for the first time. I was eleven years old, a stranger to the place where I was born, at home for the first time.

Rachel Weichman, a school friend, and her family had taken me with them on one of their many trips to the beach, Myrtle Beach, South Carolina. I remember the smell first, the dense salty mushroomy smell coming from our open car windows as we cruised nearer to the shoreline. Then I remember the first time my feet touched beach, the feel of the sand, warm and soft between my toes. Seeing the ocean for the first time, hearing the waves and their light thunder rolling toward me. Sea and sky touching, with no end to blue.

§

From my seat in the bleachers, I glanced up at the mid afternoon Florida blue sky. It was just another beautiful spring day in Orlando, except my daughter was having a nervous breakdown.

I ran for the gate to Ginny's court as the other parents watched, stunned. Ginny's doubles partner stood next to Ginny cringing. The opponents on the other side of the net giggled nervously. Jodi Andrews, Ginny's coach, joined me at the gate, and we both ran onto the court, speechless.

By the time I reached Ginny, she'd folded herself into a fetal position and was alternately mumbling obscenities I'd never before heard her say and crying. I squatted down beside her in my high heels and tight black tunic dress, but when I reached out to hold her, she shoved me away. I fell backwards on the court to the horror and gasps of the parents watching. My legs spread open, head hitting hard. Ginny was petite like me but strong, and her body was full of rage. I tried not to react to the immediate pain in my head, dug my heels into the court, and scrambled to my feet.

Ginny planted herself on her knees, regal neck craning toward the sky and screamed, "What do you want from me?"

I kept a distance between us this time and said, "It's all right, Ginny. We're going home now. It's okay, honey."

Ginny glared at me and through clenched teeth growled, "I can't take it anymore!"

"I know," I said spontaneously, having no idea what she was saying or what I was saying. "We're going home now, honey," came out. "You don't have to play anymore. It's okay."

I inched my way toward her cautiously. Ginny stood, shoulders slumped, trembling. "I can't take it anymore," she repeated.

Jodi had been collecting Ginny's bag and racquets, and she handed them to me. I slung the bag over my shoulder, grabbed Ginny's racquets, and thanked her.

Jodi asked, "Is there anything I can do? Do you need any help getting her home?"

"No, we'll be fine," I said, responding in a robotic voice I didn't even recognize.

I put my free arm around Ginny, whose body felt both lifeless and heavy, and we began our walk to the car. As we walked past the parents, they stepped back, mumbling things, some of which I could make out. "Can we do anything to help?" "They say she is the best player on the team." "What happened I didn't see it?" "I heard she's been crying at practice." "Where is her father?"

One mother, a single black woman, a teacher at Whispering Pines, whose daughter was a friend of Ginny's on the team and who Ginny rode with to the match, trailed after us. When I'd opened Ginny's car door and made sure she was safely seated, the woman said to me, "I'll get Ginny's book bag. It's in my car."

I waited by the car, keeping a close eye on Ginny, who was now quietly sobbing into her Whispering Pines High School tennis dress. The mother returned quickly with Ginny's bag and handed it to me.

She told me, "Don't you worry now. My Terry had a breakdown about a year ago. It's so hard now on girls. They have so much pressure on them today. Ginny is a beautiful, sweet, intelligent girl. She'll come out of this, you'll see."

I thanked her.

She reached deep into her blue jean jumper pocket and handed me a card. "This is my number," she said. "You need anything, you just call. I got Terry into a Lutheran counseling program through our church, and they have just worked wonders with that child. You call me, and I'll give you the number." She hugged my stiffening body. "You take care now. It's gonna be all right. You just got to believe God doesn't give you anything you can't handle."

I thanked Terry's mother, threw Ginny's book bag and racquets in the back seat of the car, put the card in the glove compartment, and pulled out of the parking lot with no idea where I was going, what we were doing, or that what had just happened would change the rest of our lives.

§

When it gets too painful, when my words come to life, I let little things, things I used to not even notice, comfort me. The sound of the coffee machine in the bookstore café, grinding the daily flavors. The colors of the brightly jacketed books just placed on the shelves marked New Releases. Even the premature Halloween decorations. I let my eyes bounce from one to the other as the different but familiar faces of the employees pass by me smiling.

They've become accustomed to my daily presence in their café, sitting quietly, lost in thought or memory, or rifling through their collection of medical books. I'm a fixture to them now. They, my new friends, whose mere presence encourages me. Without saying it, each of them accepts unconditionally that I am here to write—that I am a writer. It took me forty-two years to figure that out.

Chapter 2

B e s t   M a d e   P l a n s

Ginny's match was played at Carver High School in central Florida. Carver is near an area called College Park. It is a storybook series of quaint neighborhoods sprinkled with bistros, antique shops, local delis, and video stores. The homes in them vary from grand old Southern Colonials to Tudors, and border tiny lakes, fuschia-flowered parks. Many of the bungalows in College Park dating from the 1920s have been renovated into lovely garden cottages. Real estate is pricey.

Browsing through the real estate section of the *Orlando Sentinel*, I'd seen a one-bedroom, one-bath home priced at $220,000. Rentals were equally high. But running through College Park's oak-covered streets is free, and over the past several months had become a favorite pastime of mine.

I turned off a brick street on to a paved one and found myself heading toward I-4, the major interstate through Central Florida. I decided glancing over at Ginny, whose agitation seemed to be building again, that we would go home and I'd formulate a plan from there. Maybe I'd call Maeve, my new best friend, who just happened to be a nurse and who was familiar with the way Ginny had been acting the past few months.

I checked Ginny again. She was chewing on a hangnail, muttering something. I made sure her door was locked then accelerated on to I-4. Traffic was dense as usual. It was Thursday night around 6 p.m. Everyone in Florida was taking I-4 home.

I don't know what happened first. If I heard the passenger door open or I felt the whipping wind, but I do know I screamed and twisting my torso, lunged across Ginny's lap still barely holding onto the steering wheel with my left hand. Our Ford Focus swerved first to the right then slightly over the center line as I grabbed the inside passenger door handle and slammed the door shut. I looked forward for the first time in seconds and saw I was about to rear end the truck in front of me. I hit the brakes and centered myself behind the wheel. Then I yelled, "What in the hell are you trying to do!"

Ginny was crying hysterically now. "Let me go. Let me go. I can't take it anymore! I'm not going to listen to them anymore."

I kept my eyes on the traffic. Hands shaking. Stomach in a vice like grip. Legs cramping.

"You could have gotten us killed!" I yelled. Leave the door alone, Ginny!" I glanced at Ginny's door and saw it was unlocked. "Lock the damned door, Ginny!"

Ginny locked the door. She was sobbing now, and she'd given herself the hiccoughs.

I took a deep breath, trying to keep myself from yelling at her again, signaled, and turned off onto the Winter Park exit. "We're almost home," I told myself. "You can make it."

Winter Park, Florida was our new home. A beautiful little college town whose center is Rollins College, a school known for both its academic excellence as well as sports achievements and whose campus rivals the beauty of any Ivy League schools I've visited.

Even before I'd accepted the sales manager's position with Evergreen in Apopka, Florida, I'd looked at places Ginny and I could live. Apopka would, of course, have been the most convenient and affordable. It was an old farming community, and its many greenhouses gave it an odd charm, but its high school was huge and not noted either for its academics or for its tennis program. I decided that while convenience would have been nice, I could easily endure the longer drive to and from work for Ginny's education and happiness, and the expense—well, I'd manage somehow.

So I chose Winter Park for us—against all advice from my coworkers, who impressed upon me during the interviewing process how terrible the traffic is in central Florida, how miles are no indicator of the time it takes you to travel. Winter Park is fourteen miles from Apopka, and on a good smooth-flowing traffic day, you can make the drive in forty-five minutes. On a bad one, it can take you an hour to an hour and a half, depending on how many accidents have occurred.

But I loved Winter Park and hoped Ginny would learn to like it. How could she not be drawn to the Brady Bunch neighborhoods with their ranch style homes, beautifully cared for yards alive with pastel impatiens, deep green ivy and lime-colored ferns, azalea bushes, and hibiscus blooming everywhere. Her high school, Whispering Pines High School, was nestled into one of these neighborhoods, just a couple of miles from our condominium.

Right next to our complex– not your typical condominium development but rich with the Spanish flavor of warm red brick-tiled roofs, stucco walls, and wrought iron gates opening to tiny gardens, rock and shell pathways— there was a local grocery store, a puppet theater where Ginny could volunteer on weekends, and our gym, where we would work out together.

I'd created a home for us in a place where we were strangers. I'd planted flowers, bought new furniture for every room–letting Ginny choose all of it– placed a welcome mat at our door.

I wanted us to have a new start. I wanted us to find new friends and new hobbies and be happy again. No more talking about divorce, no more worrying about losing a job, stressing out about money, and no more cold weather. We would be living in the sunshine state. Who couldn't be happy?

The answer to that is, of course, my daughter Ginny. I knew before I drove back to Asheville at Christmas time to get Ginny that the transition would not be easy for her. I knew when I was deciding to take the job with Evergreen. I knew her whole life transitions had not been easy for my daughter.

And I had this gut feeling, even though the job with Evergreen was a good one and Ginny seemed quietly supportive and my whole family, who desperately wanted me to stay and settle for some sort of job in Asheville, had rallied behind me, I knew I was making a choice that could work out very badly for Ginny as well as for me.

I felt it. I felt from the beginning that taking a job in Florida and being separated from her, though just temporarily, was not the best choice. I told Blake this one evening as we sat on our deck decorated with over a hundred flower boxes. I'd made cuttings from all my perennials in my mountain home garden and brought them to our condominium, spent hours filling planters so we'd have color every season on our deck.

Blake rocked back and forth in a white wicker rocking chair I'd bought the summer before, while a shock of his black hair fell into his sapphire eyes. He said, "I don't see that you have any choice. You don't have any offers here. You tell me Environmental will eventually get rid of your position. You say there are no jobs here. I just don't get what's so tough about this."

I snapped back, "There are no jobs in Asheville, and you know that as well as I do. But forget that. I was talking about Ginny, Blake. I have a gut feeling that taking this job in Florida will not be a good thing for her."

Blake snorted. "Here we go again with the control factor. Do you really believe you know what Ginny feels? I think she's fine with it." Then he leaned forward. Gently placed one hand on my knee. I cringed. Blake's touch felt both foreign and familiar, and I didn't need any more confusion. He said, "If you'll let me, I'll take good care of her. We'll stay here together. She'll have her own room, her computer, all her things. And, hopefully, a little more freedom. Maybe she'll mature a little, Haley. God knows she could use that."

I didn't answer him. I'd never even considered the possibility of Ginny's staying in our condominium with Blake. Not that I didn't trust him. Blake would never do anything to harm Ginny. In fact, he was a much better father than a husband.

After a few minutes of silence, I said, "I'll have to think about it. Right now, the answer is no. If I take the job, Ginny stays with my parents. She'll be fine there."

Blake scoffed, "Sure. Do they know about this? Have you even asked them?"

He knew I hadn't asked them, that I was just assuming they would want to take care of Ginny.

"No, I didn't ask them." I said. "I've had a few things on my mind lately, like our entire financial future."

Blake quipped, "Which clearly doesn't involve Ginny's welfare."

"Blake," I yelled, "You know it does. You know she is my top priority. You know that is what this whole move is about!"

Blake sat back, folding his strong, calm hands in his lap, and said, "Do I, Haley?"

§

We were home. I pulled into one of the two parking spaces in front of our condominium and breathed a sigh of relief. I told Ginny, "I think I'll call Maeve." Ginny didn't answer.

We both got out of the car. I forgot her book bag. She forgot her tennis bag and racquets. Except for the plan to call Maeve, I still had no idea what we were doing. We walked together up the short rock and shell pathway to our house. I noticed my potted plants on our small patio needed watering. I'd watered them that morning before taking Ginny to school, but Florida heat can cause even the most resilient flowers and shrubs to wilt. The marigolds were bowing over atop shriveled African Heather and the white impatiens looked as though they could not be revived. I knew they could be though. Just a splash of water over each pot and they'd all be refreshed and ready to face another day. I marveled every day at the ease with which these delicate creatures could be restored, even as I stood with my despondent daughter having no idea how I might restore her will to live. Mind in tact. Body as healthy as a horse. Suddenly without the strength to open the door.

§

I will never forget the first morning I woke up in my new home in Florida. It was October 19, 2002, around 7 a.m. I slid off my air mattress, glancing at my clock, and immediately began rummaging through the boxes in my bedroom for a sweatshirt. I was going for my first early morning walk around my new home. Pajama shorts and top still on, I found a fluffy cotton-hooded Environmental sweatshirt, slipped it over my head, stepped into my running shoes, tied them quickly, and headed out the front door. The early morning humidity covered me like a blanket. I looked down at my sweatshirt and laughed out loud. It was mid-October, and I didn't need to wear a sweatshirt. And even though I didn't know a soul or even what direction to take around the grounds of my new community, I felt the sun was shining just for me.

Chapter 3

S i n k i n g ,   D i v i n g ,   F l o a t i n g

I turned the key in the lock and Ginny and I entered our condominium one by one. She immediately ran up the stairs to her bedroom. I'd given Ginny the master bedroom and bath in our two-bedroom condo, thinking that is what a teenager wants most. Her own space. I had to practically force her to decorate it. In Asheville, she'd picked out the furniture. A light beech wood with Victorian curves on the head and footboard of the bed and a huge dresser with mirrors. I'd had the furniture in place when she arrived in January, but I thought she would want to decorate her own room, so I left that up to her. But after she had lived in it for two weeks without unpacking the first box from Asheville, I began to make suggestions. Finally, when Ginny didn't respond to me at all, I began picking things out to decorate with and bringing them home daily for her approval. Glow in the dark stars for her ceiling. Pink and white starry curtains. Stained-glass butterflies. Ginny loves fairies, and I'd bought her some at Christmas. One was in the form of a nightlight. I set all of these things out. I'd bought a matching purple and pink bedspread and pillows and, in the end, after I'd spent an entire Saturday afternoon decorating while Ginny sat on the bed studying, she looked up at me and said, "It looks nice, Mom. This should be your room."

But the room was still hers, and I listened now for what she might be doing in there among the stars and the fairies I'd been so hopeful she would love. No sound. I called to her, "Ginny, what are you doing?"

She shot back, "I'm getting a shower. I feel gross."

Okay, I thought, that sounded normal. This was the first normal thing she'd said or done in the past couple of hours and it came as a great relief.

Slumping down on our over-stuffed sectional sofa, I picked up my cell phone and called Maeve. She was probably still at work. Maeve was a workaholic. I'd met her in October at my hairdresser's, just a couple of weeks after I'd moved to Florida. It turns out not only did we go to the same hairdresser, but we lived in the same complex. Maeve is a nurse, but at the time I met her, she had just relocated for a job as the manager of a senior health home care company. Her company had relocated her from Jacksonville. She'd had to sell her waterfront home and boat, give away her dogs, and leave a man she was falling in love with. We bonded instantly, sipping coffee and having our hair foiled.

We were both in our early forties. Both working single moms. Both had been married more than once, and both had experienced a fair amount of change in a very short period of time because of new jobs and moves to central Florida.

I felt blessed to have met this babbly Irish-Italian woman, whose soft sparkly eyes reminded me of pale green glass and whose bright childlike smiles could charm even the most hardened soul. Maeve was a gift to me. The first best girlfriend I'd had since the eleventh grade. And Ginny loved her.

She answered, "Hey, babe, what's up?"

I cleared my throat, "Hey, listen, I don't want to hit you with all this at one time, but...um...Ginny kind of freaked out at her tennis match today."

"She what? What happened?"

I heard the shower upstairs blasting out sheets of water, and I propped my feet on the coffee table. "She threw her racquet down on the court and started screaming obscenities. I had to take her off the court."

Maeve protested, "Ginny doesn't even cuss! Oh, honey, I'm so sorry. But I told you you needed to get her help. I told you something is very wrong."

And all of a sudden it hit me. Everything hit me. The past three months of coming home from work and finding Ginny in her bedroom closet, sitting in the dark, the sudden outbursts of tears at the breakfast and dinner table, the one-sided conversations in the car, waiting for Ginny to respond to anything I said, and taking her to the school counselor, then finally scheduling her an appointment with the counseling service my company provided.

I started crying, "I know. I know. I have a counseling appointment scheduled for her tomorrow. She's going to see someone tomorrow."

"Tomorrow may be too late," Maeve said matter-of-factly. "I think you should take her to the hospital now. I'll meet you there."

My heart started pounding, and I could feel this large vein in my forehead popping out. "What hospital? What are they going to do?"

"You should take her to Willow Pond. That is closest. It's small and clean, and she'll get to see someone quicker."

"I don't know," I said, and suddenly feeling it wasn't okay to leave Ginny alone. I got up and climbed up the stairs to her room. "I'll call you back. I want to talk to Ginny first. And thanks, Maeve. I know you are trying to help. I just have to make sure I'm doing the right thing."

"Ginny needs help, babe. I've been telling you that for months. Call me back when you decide what you guys are doing, but she needs help."

"Okay," I said. "I will. I love you."

"I love you, too," Maeve said, and I clicked the phone off, placing it in its holder on my belt.

I found Ginny dressing. She was no longer crying or mumbling, so I decided we could talk.

"Ginny, Maeve thinks maybe we should go to the hospital."

Ginny didn't answer; she just kept slipping into her blue terry cloth sweat suit.

"What do you think? Are you feeling better?"

She answered, "I'm hungry. Can we get a veggie burger?"

This is good, I thought. She's hungry. There is no need to go to the hospital. This is just a bad day. She's tired and hungry and having a bad day. She needs a veggie burger, not a doctor.

"Okay, honey," I said, feeling some of the weight lifting from my shoulders. "Let's go get a veggie burger, then maybe you'll feel better."

I started walking toward Ginny to hug her, but she stuck out two fists. "Don't come near me!" she screamed. "They'll get you too!"

My stomach cramped this time, but I kept inching past the bed toward her. "It's okay, honey. I'm the only one here. No one is going to get either one of us." When I reached her, I pressed Ginny's fists together, then lowered her arms to her sides. She collapsed on her bed sobbing. I sat down next to her and cradled her head in my lap.

"I want it to stop, Mommy. Please make it stop."

"Shhh," I said stroking her arm. "It's all right. Everything is going to be all right." But I knew then that I couldn't handle this anymore. Ginny needed more help than I could give her. She was hurting beyond a mother's help. The strong arbor of hope I'd built within the past few months to deal with her struggle to adjust to our new life was caving in. It was becoming very clear to me I could not love Ginny out of this. And though I'd been assured by more than one peer of mine who'd survived relocation that Ginny's behavior was completely normal for a teenaged girl, I was beginning to see it was not. This was no ordinary depression. My daughter needed help.

I grabbed my cell phone and punched in the code I'd set for the counseling agency. A nurse answered on the third ring, and I explained to her briefly who I was, my company's name—that I had a daughter who had an appointment scheduled for tomorrow, but that I felt like she was having a nervous breakdown and I didn't know what to do.

The nurse's voice sounded like warm bath water feels. She calmed me with her every word, quietly asking questions about Ginny, our move, what had happened during the day. I answered them all, eager to help, eager to get help. Then she asked if she could speak to Ginny, who seemed to have calmed down, so I agreed and handed her the cell phone.

Ginny took the phone and sat up on the bed. I had the volume at the highest level because at work I sometimes can't hear over the noise of the trucks—so I could hear the nurse.

"Ginny, I hear you are having a really tough day, what's happening, honey?"

Ginny started crying. "I want them to stop. I am not going to take it anymore!"

"What do you want to stop, Ginny?"

"The voices!" Ginny screamed. "I want the voices to stop!"

It was the first time I had ever heard her use the words "the voices." My daughter was hearing voices. And she was telling a complete stranger. After months of my asking her what was the matter, what could I do, why was she so quiet, why wouldn't she talk, what was bothering her—I find out by listening to her tell a stranger: she hears voices.

The nurse answered, "Ginny, I want you to try to calm down. It's okay, honey. Ginny, are you listening to me?"

Ginny nodded, then mumbled, "Yes."

"Ginny," the nurse continued, "You need to know you are not the only one who hears voices. There are a lot of people who hear voices. We have medications now that can make the voices go away. You want them to go away, don't you, Ginny?"

Ginny answered, "Yes."

"Okay, honey, I want you to answer just a few questions for me okay, and then we'll see about getting you some help."

"Okay."

"Ginny, have you ever thought since the voices have been bothering you that you might want to commit suicide?"

"Yes." Ginny answered, without having to think. Then she added without a pause, "That's what I'm going to do. I'm going to get rid of them."

"But, Ginny, remember you don't need to do that because we can help you. There is medicine that will get rid of the voices. Now, when you thought about getting rid of the voices, did you have a plan?"

"Yes. I'm going to take some pills and chemicals. I'm going to swallow some pills and chemicals."

My stomach turned inside out. I broke into a cold sweat. My teeth started to chatter. I couldn't believe what I was hearing.

"But there is no need for you to take any pills now, Ginny. Remember, you are not the only one who hears voices, and there are lots of ways to help you. Okay?"

Ginny didn't answer.

"Ginny, have you ever seen anything? I mean when you hear the voices, do you see anything unusual while they are talking to you?"

Ginny began sobbing and holding the side of her head. "Yes. Yes. I saw flames and people screaming and burning and, she gulped then cried out, "and I couldn't help them!" Ginny fell over into my lap crying hysterically. I picked up the phone.

The nurse said, "Ms. Robbins, Are you there? Ms. Robbins?"

I answered, "I'm here. I need to go. You've upset Ginny terribly."

The nurse's voice lost all its warmth and she told me firmly without pausing, "Ms. Robbins, your daughter needs medical attention immediately. You need to take her to the nearest emergency room and tell them what you've told me. The doctors will know what to do, but you need to take her immediately before she harms you or herself or both."

I couldn't believe what I was hearing. "Don't you say that." I measured my words. "Don't-you-dare. My daughter would never hurt me or herself."

"*Never* is a big word, Ms. Robbins," the nurse said. "We try not to apply it to real life. I suggest you get your daughter to the hospital immediately, or what you say may never happen just might."

I took a deep breath then answered, "I don't need you to tell me what my daughter will do. I called for your help, not threats. Jesus Christ. What is the matter with you? What kind of counseling service is this?" And I pushed the end button hard with my thumb.

For a while, we just lay there on the bed, Ginny crying, soft sobs building to hysterical ones, then back down again. We lay across each other, and I could feel her heart. It was a strong healthy athletic heart. And I had thought before today, even when she was depressed, one filled with love and joy. But now, now I felt in just the last few moments so much of what was in Ginny's mind and heart was being exposed, and the more that was exposed, the less I knew about her, about us, about anything.

It was dark outside now. The glow in the dark stars on her ceiling shone. Ginny reached out for my hand. "I want to go to the hospital, Mommy. But I want a veggie burger first.

"Anything," I answered and kissed her on the forehead, "anything you want."

"Can we go to Burger King?"

I smiled at the simplicity of her question, at the fact that, yes, this was something I could do, and I said, holding her head, "Yeah, we can. I'm betting they don't have veggie burgers in the emergency room."

No matter what we have gone through in Ginny's life, I have always tried to find humor in every situation. And always Ginny has laughed, but Ginny wasn't laughing as we lay there on her bed, and it occurred to me that I hadn't heard her laugh for weeks.

§

I left Florida, August 27 of 2004, three weeks after it had been hit by Charlie, the worst hurricane to make land in central Florida in over a decade. At the time, I had no idea it would be hit by three more storms in the weeks to follow. Even Asheville, mountain cradled Asheville, did not escape Frances and Ivan and Jeanne. And by the first week in October, both of the places I call home had been declared disasters several times.

It's all connected. Our lives to nature, nature to our lives. Everywhere I go, my internal storm is reflected by the effects of external ones: broken limbs, broken hearts, too much water—all night cries. I hear people talking, waiting in line at the grocery store or sitting in the bookstore café sipping coffee. It's almost always about the storms: how they lost power for weeks, had to throw out all their two-for-the-price-of-one gallons of ice-cream, lost a tree, had damage to their fence. And way worse. The ones whose silences are longer than their conversations. The ones who'd lost homes and loved ones.

Two years ago, if anyone I loved had had to live through such storms, I would have been deeply affected. Immersed myself in the shared disaster. Been a part of rescue and clean up efforts. But today, after surviving two years of back-to-back storms in my own life, I know I have to be more selective with my energy. Choosing to find a raft I can float on, rather than swimming around picking up broken remnants. And always saving my strength for the next time I must tread water. For years the undisputed treading-water champion of my neighborhood pool, I have learned how to float.

I have so many beautiful memories of me and Ginny and water. And one faith-affirming one.

Ginny was three years old. We were living in Hickory, North Carolina, where her father, John, had taken a job as the tennis pro at a local country club. It was past mid-summer. One of the many horrifically humid evenings we spent at the club. This particular one at a cocktail party by the pool, where the members children were allowed to swim while the adults drank.

I thought it was a horrible idea from the start. And the minute we received the invitation, I told John I didn't want anything to do with it. But John had no choice about attending the poorly conceived events of his wealthy membership, and he wanted my company.

So I conceded. Packed Ginny's "swimmies," towel, and a change of clothes in her pink elephant bag, dressed myself in a t-strapped crème lace cocktail dress that gave me confidence, took John's hand, and we headed for the party.

Though I refused to drink anything alcoholic while I was supervising Ginny swimming, I was downing bottles of water in the mid-August, ninety-degree heat, and after about an hour at the party found myself desperate for a restroom. I called to John, who was standing a few feet away with his back to me and Ginny, talking with some of the club members, and mouthed that I needed to go to the bathroom, motioning to him to come sit on the side of the pool right next to where Ginny was happily spinning around in the water, held up only by her bright yellow "swimmies," one of those wonderful inventions that children usually see as an annoying hindrance to their movement (I had been waiting, in fact, for Ginny to issue her usual command: "Deez off!"). And I had as much confidence in them as the air it took to fill the plastic, which was next to none.

John excused himself and walked over to me, looking a little annoyed. I said, "I'm sorry, honey, but I have to go to the bathroom. Will you please watch her?"

John looked down at me and Ginny and said, "I have been watching her and I'll continue to watch her. Now will you stop making such a big scene and just go? You know I'm capable of seeing and talking at the same time."

I got up from where I was sitting on the side of the pool. Gently pulled the hem of my dress down, rolled my eyes at John and told him quietly but angrily, "Well, excuse me if I was a little concerned about our daughter who cannot swim being supervised by a bunch of intoxicated adults."

John stared back at me and said through clenched teeth, "You've made your point. Just go. You're embarrassing me."

So I went, looking over my shoulder at Ginny until I reached the locker room, then rushing down a back hall. Peeing at the speed of light. Washing my hands and literally running back out to the pool to find Ginny—nowhere. Her bright yellow swimmies floating on the water. And John was on the other side of the pool from where I'd left him, talking to more club members.

My feet felt like lead weights as I stepped up to the edge of the pool where I'd left Ginny and cast a desparate look into the water to see my daughter just beneath me struggling on the bottom of the pool to breathe underwater.

I dove in. In three feet of water where no diving is allowed. I dove in, narrowly missing hitting my head on the pole by the pool stairs, my right shoulder painfully banging the metal rail. In seconds I had Ginny in my arms under water. And within a minute in my arms out of the water. Heart to my heart.

After much coughing and spitting and then a wonderful life-affirming sound of her crying, I remember most holding her face in my hands. Ginny's eyes on mine. And her words then as now touching prophesy.

She said, "You try to save me."

Chapter 4

What You Don't Know

After we picked up some veggie burgers at Burger King, we met Maeve at the hospital. When I forgot to call her back, she called me and said she'd meet us there. Maeve is one of those people you can rely on.

Willow Pond is a relatively small hospital, tucked into one of the Brady Bunch neighborhoods in Winter Park. I'd passed by it probably fifty times on my daily runs. It was just minutes from our condominium and Ginny's high school.

Surrounded by oaks and dogwoods, perfectly trimmed hedges, and land-scaped parking lots filled with Mercedes Benz, Jaguars, and Lexuses, it seems much less foreboding than most hospitals. At least it did that evening to me, as I kept trying to convince myself —*this isn't so bad…we're going to go in there, get some help, and Ginny will be better by morning.*

Maeve was already in the emergency room waiting room when Ginny and I walked in. She must have rushed home from work to change, because she was wearing a blue halter top and low-cut jeans, and she'd fixed her mid-length highlighted shag in the wispy-sexy style she wore when she went to Duffy's, the local Irish pub.

She walked over to us, smelling like honeysuckle and clean sheets in her four-inch heeled sandals. She hugged Ginny, then kissed me on the cheek. "Hey," Maeve said in her joking voice, green eyes twinkling. "What the hell kind of place is this to meet?"

I forced a laugh. She looked at me, then at the reception desk. "You need to get her checked in; there's a few in front of you. They'll give you the paperwork. I'm gonna go outside for a second. I need a smoke." Then she pulled me close to her and whispered," Johnny's here. Remember that paramedic I told you I met last weekend at Duffy's? He's here. Outside."

I nodded. "Okay, well let me get her situated and fill out the stuff."

"Okay, babe," she said and squeezed my arm as she headed toward the automatic door: "I'm right outside if you need me."

I waved to Maeve, then turned to Ginny, who asked, "Where is Maeve going?"

"To smoke, honey. Come on. Let's get you a seat and I'll check you in." I found two seats together near the water fountain, and Ginny sat down.

Willow Pond is a clean cheerfully decorated hospital. The lobby décor is surprisingly up to date, with geometric designs and a profusion of bold, bright colors. The chairs are a mix or lime green, purple, and rust—the paintings, eclectic.

I walked up to the receptionist to sign Ginny in. She checked the roster on the clipboard. "Are you the patient?"

"No," I answered. "I'm here...we're here...it's my daughter who has the...um...who needs to see someone."

The young olive-skinned nurse rolled her large brown eyes and asked, "What seems to be the problem?"

I wish I knew, I thought. But I said, "My daughter is hearing voices and it is really upsetting her to the point she is talking about committing suicide. A counselor advised me to bring her here."

The nurse's eyes seemed to have gotten bigger. She cleared her throat. "Who is her psychiatrist?"

I suppose that would be a normal assumption to make. If you tell someone your daughter is hearing voices and is suicidal, why wouldn't the person assume mental illness, assume previous treatment by a psychiatrist. But I was new to this nightmare and continued to be alternately angered and hurt and frustrated by it.

I leveled my small green—what I've been told often—intelligent eyes to her innocent brown ones and said, "My daughter doesn't have a psychiatrist." Then I mustered whatever dignity I had left and said in a voice the entire lobby full of patients could hear, "This just happened. Before we moved to Florida, my daughter was perfectly normal."

The nurse nodded. "I understand. If you will just fill out the paperwork, someone will be right with you."

I grabbed the clipboard of forms and attached pen and said, "Thank you."

I walked over to Ginny and sat down. She hadn't moved from her seat by the water fountain and was staring blankly in front of her. I began the arduous task of filling out the paperwork.

Here's what I want to know. Who makes these forms? Is it the hospital? The insurance companies, a committee with members from both? Is the IRS involved? The CIA? Because it doesn't feel like giving reasonable information necessary for identification; it feels like an interrogation. Question after question. Page after page—culminating in a list of diseases and conditions I never knew existed, and you're supposed to respond with reason while you're having a crisis. And every blank you fill makes you feel you are revealing something you probably shouldn't or something you don't really know well enough to be signing your name to as if it were irrefutable truth—your family's medical history, for instance.

I have a pretty good memory. Some ex's would claim painfully good. But I don't really know whether anyone on either side of my family ever had asthma. Maybe someone did. I didn't want to be dishonest or misinform someone about a condition that might affect my daughter's current health but.... The next time I have an emergency... what? What will I do? Who keeps the family's medical history? Who can research it in an emergency?

And speaking of emergencies, isn't it interesting what constitutes one? Clearly, my view of this differs from a number of people's. I glanced around me as I continued to check boxes and fill blanks. Across from us, sitting on one of the rust chairs there was a large man who by the size of his stomach appeared to have swallowed a medicine ball. This, however, was not his emergency. His left ankle, which he'd propped up on a nearby coffee table, had been wrapped with an ace bandage, apparently by a two-year old. The man had an annoying cough that made the medicine ball in his stomach bounce up and down.

What did I know? Maybe he was in for a variety of conditions. The poorly wrapped ankle, the medicine ball stomach, and the annoying cough. But whatever his trouble, his emergency was evidently not top priority. Nor was ours. We would both wait at least until forms were complete.

Maeve blew back in and knelt down before us. Her large tanned breasts heaving up and down. She squealed. "He asked me out! Johnny asked me out!"

"Terrific," I said sarcastically. Then showing her the six pages of forms, I asked, "Is this crap really necessary?"

Maeve stood up, "Yeah. It is. It's a pain, but it is." She switched gears back to her love life. "He's taking me to Barking Stars. It's a bar downtown, I think. He says it's really fun. They have a piano and people sing and play and, oh, great martinis. He says to get the sour apple one."

I rolled my eyes. "Yeh, right. Do they deliver?"

Maeve laughed. "You're ridiculous, but I love you." She turned to Ginny, who was still staring blankly into space. "Hey, you wanna go find a snack machine? I'll treat. Anything you want." Ginny stood up listlessly, "Sure," she said.

"Don't go too far," I warned, as they started down the hall to the right of us. I pointed to the clipboard of forms, "I'm turning this in and they could call us."

Maeve winked at me, "Trust me. It'll be awhile."

Maeve was right. Apparently, emergency rooms are run much like fast food restaurants. You come in, take a number, and wait your turn. Suicidal behavior does not take precedence over badly wrapped ankles.

§

It occurs to me now, although I don't remember thinking this at any time on the evening at Willow Pond, that the night in the emergency room in Winter Park was only the third time I'd been in an emergency room in my entire life—and Ginny's first.

I come from a family of abnormal healthiness. There's a statement. But it's true. In my life to date, and I hate to put this out there because it's like cursing someone, which I don't believe in, but…in my life time, my father has been ill once. He's eighty-nine, and as I said before I'm forty-three. I'm not kidding.

He had vertigo. I wasn't born yet. Okay, he's also had quadruple bypass surgery for blocked arteries, but I don't consider that an illness. It was an effect of years of unnecessary worry, which, yes, clogged his arteries and so on and so forth, but all said and done after seventy years of worrying, one day we had a huge fight, I threw a waste basket at him, and he told me he might die and I'd regret what I'd done. The remark was cause for concern. I'd never heard my father say he might die. I called the doctor.

All his life my father has lived well. He's a vegetarian. He doesn't drink. He married the right woman. He is an athlete. He exercises every day—walks, plays tennis, even works out on weights still. He didn't retire from his job as Asheville Community Theater's director until he was sixty-eight. He worked most of his life seven days a week. He fathered four children and now has four grandchildren. My father is about living, not dying. However, most of his life he did one thing wrong. This, not illness, landed him in the hospital. My father nearly worried himself to death.

He learned from his mistake, though, and that is why he is alive today. He was not ill. He made bad choices. There is never a reason to worry. There is never a reason to conjure up something bad that does not exist. He knows that now.

So back to my point. I have not spent much time in hospitals, nor has anyone in my family. Hospitals make me very uncomfortable. In my family if you are even going to the doctor, you are probably dying. In my family, doctors are a last resort.

Maeve, on the other hand, has spent a good deal of her life working in hospitals. Words like *triage* and *catheter* are a regular part of her vocabulary as coffee is part of mine. And I couldn't be more grateful. For Maeve and anyone else who has chosen or will choose a medical profession, you are much needed and greatly outnumbered by men with medicine ball stomachs who can't take care of themselves, never mind others.

§

I handed the nurse the clipboard with my insurance card and sat back down. Maeve and Ginny returned, Ginny munching on a bag of pretzels. They sat down on seats next to me.

Maeve half whispered to me, covering her mouth with one hand, "She seems really bad. Totally out of it. Has she been crying?"

I nodded.

Maeve whispered, "They'll probably give her something to calm her down."

"Whatever," I said. "Drugging her isn't the answer. We need to figure out what's wrong."

Maeve spoke in a normal voice. "Honey, I told you, she is depressed. Anyone can see that. And now she's delusional. She told me she's seeing things."

I put my hand over my face. "Yeh, I know. She said that earlier."

Maeve took my hands and placed them in hers. "It's okay. We're here now. We should have been here weeks ago, but we're here now. Then she

30

dropped my hands and sat up straight. "Oh, fuck me running." This was one of Maeve's favorite expressions.

"What?" I said.

"I can't go out with Johnny. I'm leaving tomorrow to help my parents move."

"Tomorrow?" I said. "Since when? I thought you weren't going until next week." Maeve's parents were moving from their home in West Virginia to Texas to live near one of her sisters.

"I talked to Dad today, and he sounded terrible. He said Mom didn't know how to pack and they needed to have a garage sale. He said the movers would be there on Wednesday, and they didn't have anything done."

"So, you're going.... When are you leaving?"

"Tonight," she said. "Well, I was before you called. Tomorrow now. Tomorrow morning."

"Did you ask off?"

Maeve rolled her eyes. She hated her boss. Or rather her boss hated Maeve. Anyway, Maeve's work situation had not been good since the day she took the sales manager's job, and it didn't appear to be improving.

"You mean, did I call the bitch? No, I did not. But she'll never know. She never works on Friday. I have everything done. The office looks great. I've already made the schedule out for next week. She has my business plan. I'm covered. 'Course the bitch will probably fire me anyway, but there's nothing I can do about that. It's family first for us from now on." Maeve put her right hand up for me to high five. I slapped it. "Yeh," Maeve said, "No more corporate bullshit. You can pay us baby, but you can't own us."

I smiled. Maeve's defiant attitude was a welcome change from my own, which seemed to be becoming more and more repressed as Ginny's depression worsened and I felt the increasing need for medical insurance and financial stability.

Maeve jumped up. "I've got to try to catch Johnny before he leaves." She looked at me for approval. "Do you think he'll be pissed? What should I say?"

"Tell him the truth," I said.

She curled her full lips into a pout. "I don't want to get into the whole thing about Mom and Dad." Then she perked up and winked at me, pointing her fingers at me like a gun. "Remember, girl, the less they know, the better," she shot out.

"Then tell him some of the truth," I said. You're half blonde by way of chemicals and foil, and you forgot you are leaving tomorrow, but you'll think about him every minute of the day while you're gone...when your brain is working."

Maeve laughed. "If you weren't so funny, I'd kick your ass."

She walked outside to find Johnny.

"Go ahead," I mumbled, "Everyone else has."

§

Ginny finished her pretzels, walked over to the trash can and threw the bag away. When she came back, she said, "Let's go home. I'm tired."

I looked up at her, touching one of her hands. 'I wish we could, baby, but every time I think you are going to be all right, you start having a rough time again. We're here now. Let's just wait a little bit more, so we can see the doctor. Then we'll go home. I promise."

Ginny sat back down as a tired nurse opened the door to the emergency room and mispronounced my daughter's name. "Ginny Stackhanger?"

We both stood up and walked to the door. "It's Stockinger," I said. "No one gets it right."

She smiled and handed me my insurance card. "Stockinger?"

"Yes," I said. "That's it. You remember that now because in fifty years, if you're still here, you might have another one."

The nurse giggled and said to Ginny, "Your mom's funny."

Ginny nodded, "It's how she survives."

Another moment of clarity from the supposedly "mentally ill one." No one could have said it better. I absolutely have had to use some humor as a means for survival. It usually works.

I think it's the smells in a hospital that have the worst effect on me. The garish mixture of ordinary life and preventatives of death. Tuna casserole, heating in the nurses' station microwave, some overworked nurse's supper. Disinfectants, new plastic bags, blood, urine, and vomit.

Machines lined every wall of every hall we walked down. Tall ones, wide ones, all painted cream or grey—with monitors or scales or wires decorating their tops and sides. The nurses we passed were dressed in a variety of multi-colored printed scrubs, but all of them smelled like they'd just come out of a dryer filled with sheets of Bounce. Their white shoes were speckled with either urine or blood or both, and they squeaked past us on the linoleum waxed floors.

The barely curtained rooms hid nothing. That particular night, exposing a middle-aged man throwing up, a teenager having convulsions after an over-dose, a woman six or seven months pregnant, going into premature labor.

Ginny reached out for my hand and gripped it. The nurse forced a smile.

"We are putting you back here," she said, as she escorted us to a fairly well burlap-curtained room at the end of the unit. "This is our best room," she whispered to me. "Maybe she won't be scared back here." I thanked her.

When we'd entered the room and she'd closed the curtain behind us, the nurse spoke to Ginny. "You can lie down on the bed if you're tired. Another nurse will be in soon to check your vital signs."

I asked, "Can you tell my friend where we are? She's a beautiful blonde and she'll be out in the lobby. Her name is Maeve."

"Certainly I will," she said.

I thanked her again, and she left the room.

Ginny sat down on the bed, and though there were two chairs on either side of a small desk by the bed, I sat on the bed with her.

She looked exhausted. Deep circles had formed under her eyes that now looked bloodshot.

I said, "You can lie down, honey. I'll sit in the chair."

Ginny said nothing but folded herself into my lap. She felt warm, and I was glad to have her close to me.

Like most hospitals, Willow Pond is air conditioned to the point of refrigerating its patients. I knew if I looked in the mirror my nose would be bright red and my lips blue. Ginny was like a blanket to me.

The nurse swooshed back the curtain and entered our small space. He was short and chubby, dressed in mint green scrubs and his black hair was neatly jelled. His skin was as fair as Snow White's, making me wonder if he'd ever left the hospital.

He stuck out his hand to me, which I thought was odd, but I shook it anyway, and he said, "Mrs. Stockinger, is it?"

"Robbins," I said. Ms. Robbins. My daughter is the Stockinger. Ginny Stockinger."

"Sorry," he said quickly. "I just assumed, never should do that anymore." He paused. "Is there a Mr. Stockinger, or...um...I mean, a Mr. Robbins— Ginny's father or your husband with you?" He was blushing now.

"No," I said. "Just Ginny. One patient at a time."

He chuckled. "I'm Peter, Mrs....I mean Ms. Robbins. I'm going to do a little check on Ginny's vitals, and then we want to run some tests."

"What kind of tests?" I asked.

He pulled on his stethoscope, which was hanging from his white, short thick neck and looked at the chart he was carrying.

"Well, it looks like we are getting blood and urine samples and...um...a cat scan. Nothing to be alarmed about. Just like to take a look at the whole picture." He forced a smile at Ginny, who was half-way sitting up. "Ginny, can I get you to come over here and sit in this chair while I get your temperature and vitals?"

Ginny nodded and scooted off the bed into the chair.

Peter took her temperature and blood pressure and pulse and wrote down the results.

"Okay, then, everything seems fine. All done here." He popped up out of the chair he was sitting in. "I'm going to go get the residential counselor and then I believe we'll take Ginny for her tests."

I asked, "Would it be possible to get a blanket? It's freezing in here."

Peter nodded. "I'll see. We might even have some warm ones."

"Great," I said.

As he was leaving, Maeve pulled back the curtain. "Hey, guys." She walked over to Ginny. "You have a great room!"

"Yeh," I said, "Just a notch below the Ritz Carlton but what are you gonna do? I didn't make a reservation."

Maeve laughed. "You screwball" she said and she tousled Ginny's hair. "Your mom is a nut."

"Yeh," I said, "certifiable." I bounced my fists on the bed and said, "I want my own room. Damn it. I'm crazy too."

Ginny frowned. Maeve stifled a laugh.

"I'm sorry, honey," I apologized half-heartedly. "You know I don't think you're crazy. I may be. But you certainly aren't."

Ginny was still frowning.

Maeve broke the tension. "I could use some coffee. How about you, babe? I know where I can get us some. I've got connections. I know the keeper of the coffee."

"You talked me into it," I said, then added, "And see if you can find any liquor to put in it."

Maeve laughed. "The only alcohol we'll find here is rubbing alcohol."

"I'll pass," I said, "at least for now. But check with me later."

Maeve laughed again and pulled back the curtain. "I'm off on a coffee run then. Need anything, Ginny?"

Ginny shook her head, and Maeve stepped out. She started to draw the curtain again to give us some privacy.

"Hey wait," I said. "What did you say to Johnny?"

Maeve pulled the curtain around her face like a scarf and smiled at me. "What you told me to say, of course. Then I kissed him on the cheek."

"So, now we'll never know whether it was my beautifully chosen words or your passionate kiss that stole his heart."

Maeve winked, "I think it was both. We're a great combination."

I blew her a kiss, but she had already dropped the curtain, which she forgot to close this time and was walking away. "Hurry back with the coffee I'm fading!"

"No worries," she called without turning back and worked it, as only Maeve could, past a group of young doctors walking down the hall.

Ginny crawled back on to the bed and this time lay down. I scooted closer to the foot to give her more room.

The residential counselor appeared from behind the curtain. She was a small middle-aged woman with cheap permanent black dye in her hair, wearing cat-eye glasses with rhinestones on them. Her scrubs had a jungle pattern on them. She smiled like someone was pulling her mouth with strings—first at me, then at Ginny. Her breath smelled like cherry Halls cough drops.

"Hi, Ginny, I'm Marjorie." She sat down in the chair closest to the bed with her chart and pen. "I'm just going to ask you a few little questions and then we need to get some samples from you." She looked up at me. "Is that okay, mom?"

"That's fine," I said.

"Now, Ginny," Marjorie began, "can you tell me why you think you are here?"

At first Ginny didn't answer, and my jaw began to tighten at the thought of trying to explain the unexplainable, of having to intervene. As the silence permeated the room and all I could hear were the names of doctors being called over the monitor, I decided someone had to answer jungle woman or she would never go away.

I said, "She had a breakdown today when she was playing tennis for her school."

Marjorie brightened. "Oh, you're a tennis player?"

Ginny frowned. "I shouldn't have screamed and caused a big scene. They'll say it's her fault."

Marjorie shifted in her seat. "Ginny, why did you scream?"

Ginny didn't answer.

Marjorie asked again, "Ginny? Was there a reason for you to scream?"

Ginny nodded. "Yes," she said, "I was hearing the voices. All day. They got really bad when I was playing. I just couldn't take it."

Marjorie was making notes. "And are you hearing them now?"

Ginny stared into her lap. "Yes."

"Can you tell me how many voices you are hearing?"

Ginny mumbled something I couldn't understand.

I asked her, "Is it one or two or three? Just tell us, honey. I mean if you're hearing them, you know how many."

Ginny stared at the wall to the left of the curtain and said, "Shut up."

Then she said to Marjorie, "I don't know. There are a lot." She paused, then added, "I'm not hearing them anymore, though. It's better now." She looked up at me. "Can we go now?" she asked.

I tried to smile. "They need to run some tests, honey. Then we can go."

Marjorie looked up at me. "How long has she been hearing the voices?"

I realized at once—I had no idea. The fact was—I'd just learned she was hearing them at all. "I don't know," I answered, in a trancelike state. Then I turned to Ginny. "Ginny, when was the first time you heard the voices?"

"In October," she answered.

I swallowed hard. That was when I'd left her for Florida. It was exactly when I left. All of my premonitions had come true. My taking the job in Florida was not a good choice for Ginny. In fact, it appeared to have driven her crazy.

I said to the nurse, as if she could understand, "That is when I left." Then I corrected myself, realizing she had no idea what I was talking about. "That is when I took a job in Florida and moved. Ginny was living in North Carolina, finishing her school semester. I thought that was the best thing, in case the job didn't work out. I wanted her life to go on as smoothly as possible. But before, before that, we've only ever been apart one time since she was born longer than two days. We were apart for three days once when I got married the second time."

Marjorie had stopped writing, and she looked at me. "Well, that's a um... that is...." She switched her attention to Ginny, who was staring at her. "You love each other very much. That is evident. I…um….” She adjusted her cat glasses. “I can’t say I’ve been with my kids that much. They kind of have done their own thing since birth.” She laughed heartily, then became serious, glancing at me, then back at Ginny. “And sometimes that’s good. To be independent. You know we all have to grow up someday and sometimes taking a few steps independently along the way is a good thing.” She stared at me. “I’m sure you love your daughter very much, but letting go just a little bit might be a good thing for both of you to work on… in the future.”

Ginny, who had been sitting at the head of the bed the entire conversation, scooted to the foot where I was and put her head in my lap. I began stroking her head. I could see how tired Ginny was, and I said, “Do you have any more questions for us, or can we get the samples? She is getting very tired.”

Marjorie stood up. “Certainly. No, I’m finished. I might come back later to check on her, but for now, we’ll just get the samples.” She gave me a long stare. “You have a very sweet daughter. I hope everything works out.” She patted my shoulder with one hand and disappeared behind the curtain.

Chapter 5

M i s s t e p

Margaret Mahler (May 10, 1897 – October 2, 1985) was a Hungarian physician, who later became interested in psychiatry. Margaret discovered through her research of families with schizophrenics that there was a constant correlation between their existence and the presence of a very controlling mother.

These are the findings of one woman. This is one piece of research. But it is one that rings true to me. Like any caring parent, I am realizing daily how much even a shred of truth about the way you've taken care of your child can hurt.

I don't know how life would be for Ginny or me had I married different men or not married at all. I only know what I did do and why. All my life, I've been attracted to men who are quiet, romantic, fiercely independent dreamers. My first husband, John, Ginny's father, is no exception. Nor is my second, Blake.

I have always believed the single-most important thing to any man is his freedom: to play, work, hunt, fish, spend money, drive cars too fast, work on them all day, love, and dream. And I never took away either of my husbands' freedom. Realizing, too late with both men, that while my recognition of their needs was very intuitive and my unconditional respect more than admirable, I left no room for balance. In either of my marriages. Or in my relationship with my daughter. Unconsciously and unwittingly making myself all encompassing mother, friend, lover—whatever or whoever was missing. Very often, I became both my daughter's voice and her ear.

You may have already guessed whose dreams we followed over the years, but if you haven't it was John's first and then Blake's. In very different ways, Ginny and I both gave our lives to these men and their dreams. I believed in both, beyond faith and hope. Ginny believed in them because I did. I know in my mind and in my heart that my single biggest hope in marrying both men was to make Ginny's life better—fuller, healthier, happier. The road to hell is paved with good intentions.

§

Maeve appeared, nudging the curtain back with her bare shoulders, holding two tiny cups of coffee-machine coffee. "Sorry," she said to me," this is all I could find. They were out at the nurses' station. Not even any rubbing alcohol to put in there." She giggled, handing me the Lilliputian cup.

I took it. "Thanks. I don't know whose more tired, me or Ginny." I took a sip. The coffee, which Maeve had fixed with creamer I never drink, tasked like sweet bitter paper. I squinched my nose.

Maeve joked, "Good, huh? Hey, be thankful. It's gonna give us a boost."

"I'd rather have a red bull," I said.

"Yeh, well, they were fresh out of that at the nurses' station. I can get you some red blood if you'd prefer."

I stuck my tongue out at Maeve. "Gross. You're gross!" I took another sip, then said, "Listen, this place may seem like home to you. Things like blood and pee and vomit everywhere normal, but for the rest of us civilians, it's pretty gross, I'm telling you. Pretty damn gross."

Ginny, who had moved back to the head of the bed and was sitting up, snickered. I smiled back at her, then reached over to tickle her. "Tell, Maeve, sweetie. Isn't this a gross place?"

Ginny just snickered again.

Maeve raised one eyebrow at me. "It's life, babe. And you'd better get used to it."

"What?" I said. "Being in a hospital. Thanks, but no thanks. As soon as we get these tests, we're outa here. And I mean outa here! Like don't let the door hit you in the ass outa here!"

Ginny laughed.

Maeve sipped her coffee and lifted both eyebrows. "We'll see about that," she said.

We both gulped our small cups of coffee down. Maeve set our empty cups on the side table.

The curtain moved and another nurse appeared. This one was a man dressed in light blue scrubs. His almond shaped eyes matched the color of his uniform. His face was thin and angular, very European, but he spoke with a Midwestern accent, very pleasant, no offensive vowel sounds, rising or descending inflections.

He smiled at both Ginny and me, then Maeve; briefly studied the chart he was holding; and seated himself closest to Ginny, who was still sitting at the head of the bed.

He glanced at Maeve, then at me. "So which one of you is Ginny's mother?"

Before I could answer, Maeve said, "Well, I'd love to take credit, but...." She pointed at me. "That's the mom."

I smiled first at the nurse, then at Ginny, who appeared not to have heard Maeve.

"Yes, I said. Ginny is mine." Then smiling again at her, added, "The love of my life."

The nurse cleared his throat. "Well, okay, then." He looked at me. "I'm sorry to make you repeat information you have already given. I know it must seem like you're having to say the same thing over and over, but we just want to make sure we have all the facts so we can figure out what will be best for Ginny."

I stared back at him. "I trust you'll involve me in that process."

"Oh, of course, of course we will, Mrs. Um...."

"Robbins," I said. "Ms. Robbins."

"Right, and I'm sorry I didn't introduce myself. I'm Lyle. It's good to meet you." Lyle straightened himself in the chair.

Gesturing to Maeve, I said, "And this is Maeve, Lyle. Maeve is my best friend. And," I added, "She's a nurse."

Maeve smiled. "Yeh, Lyle, you'll have to make sure you dot all your i's and cross all your t's. I'll be watching you."

Lyle forced a smile. Maeve seemed to have frightened him. She had that effect on some men. In fact, I'd only ever seen men have one of two reactions to Maeve. Either she scared them or she charmed their pants off. Nothing in between.

Lyle turned to Ginny. "Okay, then, Ginny. I seem to have trained eyes on me, so I'll try to do my best here. Can you tell me why you are here?"

Ginny did not look at Lyle or answer him.

I said, "She's hearing voices. They got bad enough today, she had a...I don't know what you call it, but...like a breakdown...."

Maeve inserted, "Manic episode."

I continued, "It was...she was very upset, and then she talked about a plan to commit suicide if she couldn't stop them. That's when I brought her here."

Lyle raised one eyebrow and wrote something, then he looked up at me. "When was she talking about committing suicide?"

"Tonight," I said, "when we got home from her match. She had a breakdown during a high school tennis match she was playing in, and I took her home."

"I see," Lyle said. Then he addressed Ginny again. "Ginny, how long have you been hearing voices?"

Ginny answered, "Since October."

Lyle wrote something down. "And how many voices are you hearing?" he asked.

"I don't know," Ginny snapped back.

"Okay," Lyle said. "That's okay, um. Sometimes it's hard when something as confusing as this is happening to you to know exactly what's going on." He paused, then said quietly to Ginny, "I'm sure it's been very frightening for you."

Ginny nodded her head and began crying.

Lyle turned to me. "Do you remember, prior to October, her ever mentioning hearing voices?"

"No." I shook my head. "I never heard about them at all until today."

Lyle looked confused. "So today is the first time you've realized Ginny is hearing voices, and she's been hearing them for six months?"

I immediately became defensive. "I moved to Florida in October. Ginny was living with my parents in Asheville. I called every night, e-mailed every day. I went home at Thanksgiving to visit. Ginny seemed like she missed me. And I missed her. That was all. No hearing of voices—or none that I was told about. When she got to Florida, she started crying all the time. She'd shut herself up in the closet and wouldn't talk to me. She didn't care anymore how she looked. And yes, I've noticed something is wrong. I've been worried sick about it. But I've just been trying to surround her with my love and support and our friends' love and support. She goes to a nice school. She plays on the tennis team. She's making good grades. I thought she was going to be okay. That we'd get through this."

Lyle answered, "Of course. Of course you did," as though he understood; and then, as if he didn't understand anything, asked, "Now, why did you move to Florida?"

I rolled my eyes. "For a job. I got a job as a regional sales manager at a waste management company.

Maeve said, "It's a good job."

Lyle said, "And so you moved here, then moved Ginny here. Any family here?"

Maeve raised her hand. "Me."

Lyle seemed annoyed. "But you're not really family?"

Maeve said, "No, just chosen. Sometimes that's all women like us have. We have to do what we have to do to take care of our kids."

Lyle said, "I understand. My sister is a single mom. I'm sure it is no fun."

Maeve smiled. "Oh, we still have fun." She winked at Ginny. "Don't we, Ginny?"

Ginny smiled at Maeve.

Lyle asked me. "Any family history of mental illness?"

I was struck dumb by the question. During the past three months of Ginny's depressed behavior, I had not thought even once about mental illness. Not even today when she talked about voices. But I knew there was a history.

"Ginny's uncle has some problems," I said. "Her dad's brother—but there has never really been any formal diagnosis of his condition. They don't know whether his behavior is...whether he acts the way he does because of the drugs he's been given or whether it's something genetic."

"I see," Lyle said. He had been writing as I talked, and he continued making notes as he asked, "How old is Ginny's uncle?"

"Forty-one," I said, "same age I am."

Lyle looked up. "You look thirty-one."

I forced a smile. "It's all this peaceful living."

Maeve laughed. "You nut," she said. She turned to Lyle. "She's not right, but you'll get used to it."

Lyle stood up. "Okay, well, um...Ms. Robbins, Ginny..." He didn't acknowledge Maeve. "I'm going to take Ginny for a couple of tests and then we'll be right back. One of you should probably stay in the room. We don't want to lose our room, but someone can go for coffee. There's a machine down the hall."

I told him, "Thank you. We found it."

Ginny scooted off the bed. Lyle began to usher her out of the room.

I stood up and stopped them. "Can I go with her?"

Lyle smiled. "That won't be necessary," he said. "Ginny will be fine. I'll have her back shortly." And they were weaving their way through the most recently stretchered patients, past the nurses station.

Maeve put her hand on my shoulder. "What are you going to do about work?" she asked.

I sat back down on the bed. "I haven't even thought about it."

"Are you going tomorrow?"

"I don't know. We'll have to see what happens. I have a feeling this is going to be a long night, and then tomorrow I need to take Ginny to her counseling appointment. And I can't leave her alone. I don't know what I'm going to do. I don't know what I can say at work that won't alarm anyone."

"Didn't you say you called your company's counseling service to make the appointment?"

"Yeh, I did...why?"

"Then they already know you have a problem. I'm sure management was told."

"They can't do that. The service is confidential."

Maeve lifted her eyebrows. "Sure it is."

"Well..." I let out a sigh. "I can't do anything about it now," I said. "I mean, I can call Richard and say Ginny isn't feeling well, but that is going to sound really lame. I don't know."

Maeve said. "Tell him you have to go out of town. Family emergency. Someone isn't well. Hey, it's true, you know. You have a family emergency."

"Yeh," I nodded. "I do.... Okay, I'll call Richard and I'll leave a message. This way, it doesn't hit him tomorrow."

"Good. I think that's good. And just act calm. Don't say anything about Ginny."

"Okay," I said. "I'll do it."

Maeve opened the curtain. "I need a smoke. Can I bring you anything?"

"No," I said—then changed my mind, suddenly noticing again how cold I was. "Try to find some blankets. I'm freezing."

§

It was ironic—the whole situation we were in. While I described Maeve as a workaholic—having put herself through college while working full-time, working two jobs at a time when she was in the reserves, running million-dollar companies—since Ginny was born, I've made almost every career decision based entirely on what I felt would be best for Ginny. All but one. My decision to take the sales manager's job in Florida. And even in that decision, which was partly in the interest of my own future, I had Ginny's welfare in mind. I reasoned that she needed a place where she could train all year. Private tennis lessons. A place to exercise daily. I wanted her to be well dressed, to have a home she'd be proud to bring her friends to, to have enough money we could enjoy our vacations from school and work together. She'd soon want a car, and she'd soon need money for college, even with the scholarships she'd surely get. I knew all this would be possible, if I took the job with Evergreen.

As I have said before, even with those important factors in mind, I wondered, from the moment I got the offer, if it would be the best choice for Ginny in other ways. But after weighing the financial benefits, after listening to close friends who assured me Ginny was clearly old enough to accept the fact that I needed to progress in my career and that promotion was not possible in Asheville, after gaining my family's support, I went against my gut.

And now here I was sitting in a hospital—my daughter apparently hurt beyond any reasoning person's ability to comprehend—waiting for the inevitable verdict: I was yet another in the new wave of mothers who'd chosen her career over her family, who believed she could have it all, who was trying desperately to climb the corporate ladder, to live a man's dream.

And yet, nothing could be further from the truth. I'm far from a superwoman. A hard, smart worker—yes. Dependable and creative—yes. I've brought both optimism and energy to the companies I've worked for, and at every job, I've been known for my loyalty. More than anything, I've been interested in building community more than building a resume. But this last aspiration, in my mind, describes a woman's dream of career—not a man's. And still, it's what has accounted for my success. And everywhere I've worked people have known that my daughter's well-being was my top priority and, if they have not always understood that devotion—most of them being men or women who have chosen career over family—they have, at least, accepted it. That is, until Evergreen.

Don't misunderstand me. I would never suggest that the Fortune 200 companies I worked for in a male-dominated industry were terribly sensitive to my plight as a single mom. They just respected me as a valued employee and, I guess, hoped my personal life would not interfere with my responsibilities.

I'll say to, that at my own personal expense, I never let my life outside of work interfere with my productiveness on the job. The first two years I worked for Environmental, I took one day off. On that day, I closed on our condominium, sold our mountain home, and moved. Never skipping a beat, never asking one favor.

When I moved to Florida, I arrived on a Friday evening in mid October, unpacked myself that weekend, arrived at work at 7:30 the following Monday morning, and never stopped working from dawn to well after dark every day until I flew back to Asheville to be with Ginny and my family at Thanksgiving.

Late evening get-togethers with Maeve at Duffy's were my only reprieve from the not uncommon twelve-hour day. My weekends were spent preparing a training program the company didn't have, reports that had never been generated, and attending civic and community events Evergreen had never been represented at.

In return, I was given an office with one malfunctioning computer, an uninviting small desk and brown chair, a few inadequate shelves, a poorly trained sales staff, and no support from management or operations. No one in the building I worked in ever asked if I needed any help with my relocation. In fact, human feeling in the place seemed to match the coldness of my office environment precisely. No one made any effort to welcome me, not even the offer of a lunch or a drink after work. All had homes and family in Florida, except me.

I had to plead for two days to make the ten hour trip to Asheville to pack up my daughter and move her to Florida. I finally got the okay at noon on Christmas Eve. I was so upset and concerned Ginny would think I wasn't coming and I would ruin our family's tradition of Christmas Eve dinner, I drove over eighty from Winter Park to Asheville. Ginny was waiting with open arms—the first I had seen in weeks.

While I was working at Evergreen, dozens of male management figures signed on with the company. They took days off from work to furnish their homes, find doctors, make sure their children were settled in school, their boats properly moored. I was never allotted so much as an hour to get a new driver's license.

If not for Maeve, her love and friendship and optimism and understanding, I probably would have cracked up. I thank God for her every day, for all she gave me during one of the most difficult times in my life. If the nurse had known Maeve, he would not have dismissed the hand she raised to his question about family in Florida. She *was* family.

And so I should probably say more of Maeve, much more. But where to begin? Maybe with Duffy's, because this place I went with Maeve in our few hours of leisure became an emblem of a sort. Some moments now when I feel most disconnected from everything, I go back there in memory to this bar where we became friends.

Maeve and I have a great deal in common, but I'm not the seasoned traveler she is. My move to Florida was the first one I had ever made in my life by myself. Maeve has lived all over the United States, traveled around the world. By the time I met her she was an old hand at moving herself.

Before I met Maeve, I'd probably been in a handful of bars—altogether maybe twenty times in my life. I'd been married twice for a total of fifteen years, but I'd lived with my first husband, marriage included, for fifteen, so basically I'd had two relationships with men in twenty-three years. Maeve knew more about bars than I knew about my college major. She'd even been a bartender once. She had also been married more than twice, but her marriages did not last as long as mine, and the truth is, she'd probably been with more men in one week than I've been with in a lifetime.

When she took me to Duffy's, her favorite bar in Winter Park, for the first time, all of what I've just told you became immediately apparent. Maeve was in control, and I was lost. She glided from barstool to barstool, flirting with the regulars, ordering drinks I'd never heard of, and swearing like a sailor.

It was a new world to me. The dark-wooded, low-lit, smoke-filled Duffy's—a world where the regulars seemed more like characters on a t.v. show than real people, their lives somehow removed from the goings on of the outside world.

There is a warmth about Duffy's that I can feel still, though I can't explain it. The atmosphere with its rustic wood tables, wooden floors worn with dancing, and tarnished brass just makes you feel comfortable. Like you can't hurt anything there and nothing can hurt you.

Duffy's owner, Patrick, is one of the kindest men you'll ever meet. It is his personality that you feel when you come in the place. Patrick is, of course, Irish, and every night he manages to bring in the best musicians around. They play to the wee hours of the morning, while locals and Rollins students gorge themselves on traditional Irish fare—shepherd's pie, Irish stew— washing it down with beer after beer, until they have filled their empty souls with Patrick's world of comfort so they can face what waits for them outside.

I loved my nights at Duffy's with Maeve and Patrick and all who came there. Before Ginny arrived, this was my family life. And if you had told me when I was living in Asheville that when I moved to Florida I'd spend most of my evenings while waiting for my daughter with a wild eyed Irish Catholic girl in an Irish pub, talking and dancing with the regulars and that they would become a family to me—my home away from home—I'd have scoffed and said, "I don't frequent bars and I can assure you I never will."

Now, I'm just thankful Duffy's was there. And I'm thankful for all the regulars who were so kind to me. And for Patrick and, of course, for Maeve. As it turned out, I had very little to dance about during most of my time in Florida, but I danced at Duffy's.

§

Ginny and I both love to dance. She is, and always will be, my favorite partner. And prior to my moving to Florida, my pre-Duffy's days, she was my only
dancing partner.

From the time Ginny was born until I moved to Florida, I never went
out dancing. There are numerous reasons for this. And while I have since
learned you can never dance enough and that you should always make time
to dance, when Ginny was born, the single most significant event in my life, I
decided I would give up anything to be with her. Including one of my favorite
things—going out dancing. At the time, it seemed like the thing to do. And
through the years, never caused me a moment of remorse. So, even though
all the adults I worked and socialized with seemed to think I was being unrea-
sonable, denying my own needs in favor of my daughter's, my dancing shoes
stayed in the closet.

Not that I didn't dance. I danced all the time. Tore the livingroom floor
up when they played "Saturday Night Fever" on the oldies station. Tapped my
feet on the floorboards in the car to my favorite country songs.

And Ginny and I danced. Together. From the time she was able to walk.

Our first dance floor was the huge deck off the back of our first house.
I'd bring Ginny home from the tennis club where I'd worked all day as John's
assistant, get supper going, sauces simmering, chicken baking in the oven,
then take Ginny's tiny hands in one of mine and guide her to the deck. It
was right off our den where we kept our stereo and if I cracked the sliding glass door slightly open, we could hear the music without disturbing our
neighbors.

Except for one night. When we definitely disturbed the neighbors.

I'd had a long day. A very long day, helping John teach clinics, run the
pro shop, take care of Ginny, brush the courts. When Ginny and I got home,
I headed straight for the refrigerator. Pulled out a chilled bottle of chardonnay, uncorked it and poured a generous plastic cup full. Then I turned on
the stereo, put some toys out for Ginny to play with and started supper. Once
the meal was well under way, I grabbed Ginny and my half-finished cup of
wine and we headed for the deck.

And while Barry White groaned, "Calm me Down," as only Barry White can do, and the summer sun pinked the evening sky, Ginny and I bumped and grinded away. Ginny's tiny bottom bouncing off my calves, my waist swaying into her head, both of us laughing like we had the secret to life, until we looked up and found our neighbors standing in our yard, watching our version of American bandstand.

They were a retired married couple, Wynonna and C.B. Wonderful. Salt of the earth, give you the shirt off their backs kind of people.

And...dyed-in-the-wool Baptists.

Wynonna walked closer to our deck, which was only a couple of feet off the ground and leaned over toward Ginny. Her cat-eyed glasses, hanging from a strand of pearls around her neck, fell forward as she patted Ginny on the head and said, "And what are we up to tonight?"

Ginny giggled, spinning around in a circle and told Wynonna, "Dancing. I'm dancing." Then she looked up at me and added for good measure, "And mommy is drinking. Giggle juice."

Chapter 6

Disbelief and Unheard Prayers

I called my general manager, Richard, and left a message on his cell phone, saying I wouldn't be in the next day. I tried to sound calm. I didn't mention Ginny, and I said I would check my messages.

Ginny and Lyle returned. Ginny was dragging her feet. She lay down on the bed the minute they entered the room.

I asked Lyle, "Everything go okay?"

"Fine. She's just tired," he assured me. "We still need to get the cat scan, though. That's next. She can rest for a few minutes until the nurse comes."

I thanked Lyle and he left. For the first time all evening I looked at the clock on the side table. It was 11:30 p.m. We'd been in the emergency room for over three hours, and I was exhausted.

I pulled a sheet up over Ginny. She mumbled, "I love you, mommy." I sat down on the side of the bed, holding on to her.

Maeve pulled the curtain back. "What's the good word?"

I didn't sit up. "They're coming back for a cat scan," I said.

"I thought they had already done that."

"No," I said. "Just urine and blood samples, I guess. Then we graduate to a cat scan."

Maeve laughed. "I saw Johnny again. But he's going home now."

I sat up. "You should go with him... not home, but you guys could go for a drink. This place is ridiculous. I could have tested twenty patients by now and diagnosed all of them. At the rate we're going, we'll be here all night. You should go for a drink with Johnny. Then go home and get some rest. You've got a long drive tomorrow."

"No worries," Maeve said, sitting down in one of the chairs. "I'm not leaving you."

I smiled. "Thank you. You know I hate it here."

Maeve nodded. "I know," she said.

This time two new nurses appeared with a stretcher. They arranged Ginny on the stretcher as if she could not be told how to position herself, strapped her in and told me she was going for a cat scan.

Maeve, who had forgotten my request for blankets until now, went on a hunt for them when I said again how cold I was. As soon as she stepped out, I collapsed on the bed. I must have fallen into one of those light sleeps when it feels like you're still awake because the next thing I felt was the comfort of being covered gently in something straight out of a clothes dryer. Maeve had done better than just blankets; they were warmed blankets. I was too tired to ask how she'd worked that magic. "Thank you, Maeve," I mouthed. "Thank you."

Maeve put her hand on my shoulder. "Try to rest, babe," she said. And I closed my eyes as she stood beside me.

Ginny arrived a few minutes later, and when the nurses had gone, switching off the light as they left, we curled up in the bed together, drawing the blankets around us, Maeve comfortingly close by in a chair. Hours passed by as we all slept, waking only occasionally to the sound of a monitor or a patient's cries.

When the curtain moved again, I jumped. The light from the room outside was bright, but my watch said it was 4:30 a.m. Our newest visitor was a doctor. He was a short, dark-haired man with wire-rimmed glasses. He was wearing a white lab jacket over a blue button down shirt and khaki pants. His nametag said *Dr. Brewer*.

I sat up and tried to fluff up the back of my flattened hair. My mouth tasted sour from the hospital coffee, and I was suddenly conscious of how bad my breath would smell. I halfway covered my mouth and said, "Hello."

Dr. Brewer walked over to the side of the bed and said, "Ms. Robbins?"

I smiled. "You're the only one who's gotten that right."

He smiled back, then glanced at Ginny, who was still asleep. "I have the results of her cat scan."

I sat up straighter, holding my breath.

"There is nothing to indicate any brain damage. No abnormalities whatsoever."

I let go of my breath. "Thank god," I said.

"We don't know, Ms. Robbins," he continued, "and it is too early to tell exactly what is causing the voices Ginny is hearing."

Maeve seemed to wake up hearing this. She shifted a little in her chair, but did not interrupt the doctor.

He said, "We've arranged for Ginny to go to our crisis unit until she can be stabilized. This will be better for Ginny and for you."

"What? Go where? What are you talking about?" I wasn't asking him, I was demanding; what he'd said of Ginny's test results and what he had "arranged" to do with her did not coincide and how he felt his decision was "better" for us was incomprehensible.

"Willow Pond," the doctor continued calmly, apparently unruffled by my reaction, "has a behavioral unit at our south location. It is the best one in the state. Ginny will be safe there until we can stabilize her."

I glanced frantically at Maeve, who seemed to be taking the information in stride, then back at the doctor. "I can assure you," I told him, trying to keep my voice steady, "that my daughter is going nowhere without my permission. And certainly not to a psychiatric hospital." I reached over and patted Ginny on one of her legs. "Come on, honey, wake up. We're going home."

Maeve was standing now, and I stood too. Ginny rolled over. I put my arms around her and whispered, "Come on, honey, you need to wake up. We're going home."

My legs were shaking now, and I felt sick.

Dr. Brewer was saying, "Ms. Robbins, I don't think you understand. There is a law in Florida…the Baker Act, which enables law enforcement officials and doctors to hospitalize the mentally ill who may be a threat to themselves or others."

"Oh my God!" One of my knees gave way, and I fought to stand up. I turned to face the doctor. "You people are crazy here!" I screamed. "You will *never* take my daughter from me! Do you understand me—*Never!*" I got right up in his face. "My daughter is not the crazy one here, and if you think I'm going to leave her in your care, you're sadly mistaken. What the hell kind of place is this? My daughter is going through a tough time because we moved here to a strange place, away from our home and friends and family. But I had no idea just how strange a place it is until now. I came here for help. I came here trusting my daughter could get some help, and now you're trying to lock her up? Over my dead body! And believe me, I have no intention of staying here one more minute, much less dying here!"

Ginny was sitting up now. She scooted off the bed groggily, and Maeve walked over to one side of Ginny to steady her.

The doctor looked startled. He spoke very quietly. "I'm going to go check a few things, Ms. Robbins," he said. "I suggest you stay put. We are trying to help you and your daughter, and we need your cooperation—but trust me, even if we don't get it, Ginny will be taken to the unit."

I had been holding onto Ginny, but I let go and stepped in front of the doctor. "You do whatever you need to do. But my daughter isn't going anywhere without me. I don't give a damn about your crazy laws. I'm her mother. I have sole custody of her. No one is taking my daughter from me. Not the state of Florida, not you, not anyone. You got that!"

The doctor sidestepped toward the curtain. "I'm trying to do what is best, Ms. Robbins. We have laws and they need to be followed. Now, if you will simply cooperate with us this whole process will be much easier."

"What process?" I demanded. "You said the law is for the mentally ill. Are you telling me my daughter is mentally ill?"

Dr. Brewer cleared his throat. "I am trying to help your daughter."

I demanded again, "Are you saying my daughter is mentally ill?"

Dr. Brewer didn't answer.

"If you are 'Baker Acting' my daughter, that's what you are saying, isn't it?"

"Well, I…"

"Are you, or are you not saying my daughter is mentally ill? After you just told me that her cat scan indicates she has no brain damage, no abnormalities; after she's lived a completely normal life all her life, you are telling me you are 'Baker Acting' her? I want you to say it. Go ahead. Say what you are insinuating. Because when you do, when you call my daughter mentally ill, and I'm standing here with two witnesses and you try to 'Baker Act' her, I am going to sue you for every dime you've ever made and there isn't a lawyer in America who wouldn't be happy to take my case. Now, you go ahead, Dr. Brewer. Go ahead. Tell me one more time you are 'Baker Acting' Ginny. Tell me my daughter is mentally ill. Give me your soon-to-be newsworthy one-evening diagnosis. Because I swear to you, if I have anything to do with it, it will be the last one you'll give."

Dr. Brewer glanced at Maeve and Ginny, then lowered his eyes to the floor. "Very well," he said, "if that's what you want. If you don't wish for Ginny to receive the treatment I feel she needs, you may go. I won't stop you."

I grabbed Ginny's hand. "You're damn right you won't. You are so damn right." Maeve had hold of Ginny's other hand, and the three of us seemed to understand together that there wouldn't be another instant of delay. I felt Ginny's hand tighten as the three of us paraded out of the emergency room, past the nurses station, past the half-curtained rooms, past the meal carts stacked with dirty dishes and half-filled trays.

Maeve knew the hospital, and she turned us left just outside of the emergency waiting area, guiding us to a back exit. We were walking as fast as we could without losing hold of each other, when suddenly Maeve burst into laughter, then Ginny, then me. Ginny's pace slowed and I slowed to match her, but Maeve pulled us on. "Don't slow down now. We gotta get out of here."

I shot back, "They can't do anything to her now."

Maeve was still laughing. "I'm not worried about Ginny. It's you they're gonna try to lock up. You lune bird."

"What?" I said. "I thought I was great. I might even think about law school. I did a great job defending Ginny."

"Okay, I'll admit. You can make a pretty strong argument. But aren't you supposed to plead insanity to get off? I mean you were saying how we're normal."

"Yeh." I looked at Maeve then winked at Ginny. "But we know better. Hey, I got the job done."

"Speaking of jobs," Maeve said. "If I get fired and have to apply here for work, I'm gonna pretend I don't know you."

"And I'm going to tell them you are my much older sister."

Maeve laughed. "You bitch!" she said joking.

"Hey? It takes one to know one," I said.

Maeve and Ginny and I laughed again as the electronic exit doors opened in front of us. We stepped outside into the early morning air, and the smell of gardenias enveloped us. For a moment, my only thought was—it's a new day.

§

When we got to our cars, Maeve suggested we go for breakfast, and I suddenly realized while I'd gotten Ginny dinner I hadn't eaten since breakfast yesterday. I was starved.

We agreed on Denny's, where Maeve could order her favorite: eggs over My hami. We followed Maeve there.

Ginny ate a huge plate of pancakes and toast and hashbrowns, as if she hadn't eaten in a year.

We sat in the booth at the back of the restaurant. Only two other couples were eating. It was 5:15 in the morning.

Maeve asked me, "Did you call Jake?" And I realized for the first time since I'd met Jake four months ago that I hadn't thought about him all day.

"No," I said.

Maeve took a sip of coffee, then asked, "Are you going to?"

"Yeh," I said. "Yeh, I will." I looked at Ginny, whose head was buried in her breakfast. "We'll talk about it later."

Maeve started to scoot out of the booth. "Well, I need the little girls' room. Wanna come?" she asked me, obviously wanting to talk about it now.

I glanced at Ginny, then put one arm around her. "Honey, Maeve and I need to go to the bathroom. Are you going to be all right?"

Ginny, mouth full of pancakes, nodded, swallowed twice, then spoke. "I'm fine," she said, "go ahead."

I didn't want to leave her, but I wanted to make sure Maeve didn't do anything when she got on the road, like call Jake before I talked to him. She was bad about doing things like that, thinking she was being helpful.

We walked into the women's restroom and I said, "I don't want to leave her for more than a minute, but I need to tell you something. I don't want Jake to know anything until I talk to him, okay?"

"Sure, honey," Maeve said, closing the door to her stall. "I wouldn't think of telling him. I was just asking if you were going to call him. I mean I assumed you would."

"I will," I said. "I am." I was standing at the long counter of sinks, staring into the mirror at my deeply circled eyes. I started to cry. I was in love with Jake, and the thought of complicating our very new relationship and possibly losing him frightened me beyond words.

Maeve flushed the toilet and came out of the stall. "Hey, it's okay, honey." She put an arm around me. "I didn't mean to make you cry. I just think he should know what you're going through. I mean, he should want to know."

I snatched a paper towel from the dispenser and wiped my running nose. "I know. I'm just scared. I mean, I really...with everything that's been happening, I really didn't think about him. I mean, I always think about him...

you know, I always think about him, but not today or yesterday, and now I don't know what to say to him."

Maeve looked at me in the mirror. "You have to tell him the truth, honey. He'll understand."

"Oh sure," I said, lips trembling. "Sure he will." I raised my right hand, my index finger at the mirror. "Strike one. He's dating a woman twelve years older than he is." I stuck up my middle finger. "Strike two. She's a two-time divorcee." I stuck up my ring finger. "Strike three. She has a teenaged daughter who is hearing voices." I cocked my thumb and motioned like an umpire. "She's outta here." I slammed my hand on the counter and cried harder.

Maeve turned my shaking body toward her and hugged me while I sobbed. "Hey, it's going to be okay. Give him a chance. I'm sure he'll understand. And..." She held me at arms length. "if he doesn't, fuck him...no." She smiled, wiping a tear from my cheek. "Don't fuck him." I'll switch teams and you can fuck me." I hugged Maeve. We hugged each other. And I laughed through my tears.

§

After we finished breakfast, Maeve went to her condominium to pack and begin her trip north. Ginny and I went home to sleep. We collapsed into my bed, slept in the clothes we were wearing, me holding Ginny the way I did when she was a baby.

It hit me just before I drifted into a dream that we had not said prayers together, a nightly ritual, which up to that point we'd never missed.

Ginny and I had cowritten our nightly prayer years ago when she was old enough to compose. Three. We changed it twice in twelve years. Once to include Blake and a friend named Carla, who came into our lives as quickly as she left, bringing the gift of her daughter's friendship to Ginny and a tornado of warmth and fun for me. And one after Jake came into our lives.

It goes like this—

God bless mommy and daddy and grandmother and granddaddy and Blake and Jake and crazy Carla. And all the living creatures. Never let any harm come to them.

We sing the end part. It goes—

Dream weavers, nothing but good dreams...for my baby.

Then we kiss and say together, "Lollypopland."

Just like that. We prayed. Never missed a night. Until *never* had no meaning for either of us.

Chapter 7

L a w ,   L i e s ,   a n d   C o n s e q u e n c e s

Another day of writing for hours in the café. As I sit here in the comfort of my new home away from home, it occurs to me that there was a lot going on beyond the curtained room Maeve, Ginny, and I slept in that night in the hospital. A doctor, several nurses, and a residential counselor were busily planning to destroy my daughter's life:

She said she would kill herself. She's definitely suicidal.

The mother is a problem. But we have no proof Ginny's ill. She did come here voluntarily.

It doesn't matter. She needs to be confined. Did you see that stare? Worse I've ever seen.

Yeh. Definitely. Have to "Baker Act" her.

What about the mother?

I'll deal with her.

There is a saying I think applies beautifully here. "God save me from those who try to protect me."

Though in the next few days and weeks I would hear the term *Baker Act* more than my own name, I did not actually research it until a month ago. Jobless now, living back in my hometown with my parents and daughter, I began doing the research I should have done months before. On laws, regulations, mental illness, and drugs.

The Baker Act is the Florida law covering both voluntary and involuntary treatment of the mentally ill. It was created more than thirty years ago: Chapter 394 of the Florida Statutes, known also as the Florida Mental Health Act.

Florida law encourages people with mental illnesses to seek treatment voluntarily and to choose the type of treatment needed. But Florida recognizes that some people with mental illnesses may need to be involuntarily admitted for evaluation and treatment.

The Baker Act outlines a bill of rights for the person who is mentally ill, provides a system of due process for the person receiving services in a designated mental health facility, and creates a system of community-based acute care services.

A receiving facility must ensure that persons receive needed services in the least restrictive setting and in the least intrusive manner. Consequently, receiving facilities must ensure that persons are not inappropriately admitted to community or state hospitals. Under the Baker Act, no one can be admitted to a state hospital without first being screened by a community mental health center or clinic, which must certify that state hospital admission is the most appropriate placement for the individual.

Up until June 30, 2004, Baker Act regulations allowed police, mental health professionals, or judges to arrange temporary confinement of people who present a danger to themselves or others. They must be examined within seventy-two hours and released if it is determined they no longer present a threat and will not suffer neglect.

Governor Jeb Bush signed Baker Act reform into law June 30, 2004. The law will allow court-ordered outpatient treatment for people with severe mental illnesses, like schizophrenia and bipolar disorder, who have a history of non-compliance combined with either repeated Baker Act admissions or serious violence. As of January 2005, Florida will be one of forty-two states with assisted outpatient treatment.

It should be noted that Florida's Sheriff's Association led the effort to reform the Baker Act to keep those who are too ill to know they need help from getting trapped in the revolving door of short term hospitalizations, incarcerations, victimization, and violence.

I believe it would not take a rocket scientist to figure out Ginny did not fall into the category of someone who needed to be Baker Acted. And though I refuse to spend time worrying about the past or what I truly have no control over, I am paralyzed at times by the thought of what might have happened to Ginny that night if I had not been there. Not that what did happen is anything I feel good about, but without me, the reality is my daughter, who was in a strange place surrounded by nothing but strangers while she was having the worst day of her life, could have been whisked away by policemen to a mental hospital because of one doctor's and a few nurses' misguided use of a poorly conceived law.

As for the medications that both the counselor and the doctor promised would make the voices go away: well, they do something quite different. This I now know. What I do not know is if it is the pharmaceutical companies' greed, government regulation, the doctors' lack of research and knowledge, or just the pervasive need of the American public to do what is most convenient that keeps this myth alive.

So I keep searching, and I keep coming back to the voices in favor of believing that most of us are sane until someone convinces us we aren't. Writing about the role that GAP (The Group for the Advancement of Psychiatry) has played in the world of psychiatry, Dr. Peter Breggin notes, **"They publish a 'Fact Sheet' to help psychiatrists sell themselves to the public."**[1] Breggin cites GAP's estimates of Americans afflicted with various mental, emotional, and developmental problems, and says, "These estimates add up to 59.5 million Americans...more than enough to keep busy a mere forty thousand psychiatrists."[2] Breggin adds, "Perhaps not having added up its own figures, GAP estimates that a mere one in five Americans need psychiatric treatment; but that's 20 percent of the population or approximately fifty million Americans"[3] I have to wonder if most of them are taking drugs they were told would make the voices go away.

Here's what the drugs called neuroleptics *do* do. "Neuroleptics have their main impact," according to Peter Breggin M.D. and David Cohen, Ph.D, "by blunting the highest functions of the brain in the frontal lobes and the closely connected basil ganglia. They can also impair the reticular activating or 'energizing' system of the brain. These impairments result in relative degrees of apathy, indifference, emotional blandness, conformity, and submissiveness, as well as reduction in all verbalizations, including complaints or protests. It is no exaggeration to call this effect a chemical lobotomy." [4]

Chapter 8

A c c e p t a n c e

We slept for four hours. I woke up first. Ginny woke up when I got up to go to the bathroom. I asked her if she was getting a shower. She said, "Yes." I told her I was getting one too. I asked her how she felt…if the voices were still bothering her. She said, "No, I'm fine."

White water from the showerhead covered me with warmth. It felt wonderful. Anything to do with a normal routine seemed wonderful now. My bar of Camay smelled more like roses than fragrant soap. My lace antique rose shower curtain seemed lovelier than it ever had. I started to sing, something I do to lift my spirit. Choosing one of my father's favorite songs from the musical *Oklahoma,* I smoothed the light pink bar of soup over my breasts. "Oh what a beautiful morning, oh what a beautiful day. I've got a beautiful feeling, everything's going my way."

That's when I heard Ginny. Her bathroom was directly above mine, and she was screaming. I pulled back the shower curtain, jumped out of the tub, without grabbing a towel or turning off the water, and ran upstairs.

I found Ginny naked, sitting on the toilet seat in her bathroom, shower on full blast, light off. She was crying hysterically, holding her face in her hands.

I turned the light on and went to her, kneeling down and encircling her with my arms. "What is it, baby? What happened?"

"It's them," she screamed. "They're here. I've got to get out of here."

I said calmly, "I'm the only one who is here, honey." I tried to smooth her hair. "And I won't let anything happen to you," I said.

"You can't, Mommy," she protested. "You can't keep them away. They won't let you."

"Shh…shhhh, it's okay, Ginny," I said. "No one is going to get you. I'm here I will never leave you."

Ginny sat straight up. "I don't feel safe here," she said. "I want to go."

I took her red, tear-streaked face in my hands. "Where do you want to go, honey?" I asked.

"I want to go to the hospital," she said. "I want them to make the voices go away."

The bathroom was fogging up from the hot shower water that was still running. Goose bumps were rising all over my skin. I stood quickly, reached up and turned the water off. Then I wrapped a towel around Ginny and one around myself. "Are you sure you want to go to the hospital, honey?"

"Yes," she said, matter-of-factly.

"Ginny," I tried to explain, "if we go to the hospital and voluntarily admit you, you'll have to stay. You just can't change your mind. They won't let you. Once you go in, you won't be let out until they think you are well."

"Okay," she said. She seemed resigned.

"Are you sure you want to go?"

"Yes," she answered. "I'll pack after I shower."

I was staring into the fogged up mirror, not believing what I was hearing.

"Mommy," Ginny said. "Will you stay in here while I shower?"

"Yes," I said. "I'll be right here."

§

While Ginny packed, I called Willow Pond. After a couple of conversations with nurses, someone found Ginny's paperwork. I was told we didn't have to go back to the emergency room. We could come straight to South admissions center for the Behavioral Unit. Then I was given directions.

Ginny and I ate breakfast at her favorite place—IHOP. I talked very little. I kept staring out the huge window to my left, across the street at a mechanic's shop. Their big red and white sign read *Technician Magician*. Jake worked there, and so did Ted, another friend of Maeve's I met at Duffy's.

The regulars called Ted "TT," short for Technician Ted. Ted drinks rum and coke like water, has a child's smile and heart, and the kindest brown eyes I've ever seen. He's Italian, my dancing partner at Duffy's—the best dancer I've danced with in years. One of eight boys. And the woman he loves most, his mother, died.

Maeve, Jake, and I spent many Sundays together at my condominium while Ted cooked his mother's sauce in the same pot she had cooked in. Ted would call me first thing Sunday morning, checking to see if I had parsley, bread crumbs, the right kind of cheese. Then he'd go shopping. He'd arrive an hour later with pot in one hand and bags full of meets, neckbones, his favorite hard cheeses, garlic, onions, and tomatoes, cradled in his other arm. I'd fix him a captain and coke, turn some music on, and Ted was in heaven.

On these Sundays, Maeve, Jake, and I would hang out at the pool. Jake loves to swim. Maeve loves the sun. I just loved being with both of them.

Ted would come out to visit when all his carefully chosen ingredients were in the sauce, but he'd go back in every fifteen minutes, checking the temperature, adjusting it, tasting the sauce, adjusting it, and pouring himself more rum.

We talked about everything. Our childhoods, parts of cars, the traffic in Florida, movies we loved. On these afternoons, I became famous for my "meaning of life" questions, which Jake, Maeve, and Ted all answered thoughtfully.

Ginny seemed to love our Sunday afternoons. She'd stand on her head in the pool, lifting her long legs up above the water, then come up for air, squealing like a child. "Did you see that one, Mommy?"

Jake would throw tennis balls with her. Maeve made Crystal Lite lemonade for all of us, and she'd bring every tanning lotion and sunscreen known to mankind in her beach bag and remind all of us to keep reapplying.

We'd talk and play, swim and sun for hours, until the incredibly rich aroma of Ted's sauce drove us inside to eat.

I remember thinking one night as we all sat at my candlelit dining table, dipping French bread into Ted's sauce and sipping red wine, "This is our family now. Ginny and I have a new family." I'd glance over at Ginny drinking her ice water, eyes bright and clear, and say to myself, "She'll be okay. We'll make it. We have people who love us here. That's all that matters."

§

My cell phone rang. It was the admissions center asking when we were planning to arrive. They'd told me earlier we could come any time before 2 p.m. It was just noon, but the woman who called said we needed to get there as soon as possible. We'd have a lot of paperwork to fill out. And Ginny would have to be interviewed.

A lot of paperwork was no exaggeration. It took me over an hour to fill out the forms. Then we waited an hour to see a counselor. Then he interviewed Ginny for an hour. Then he interviewed us both for another hour. When it was over, I wondered if I didn't need to check myself in.

The counselor walked us up the tree-lined pathway, past a pond, to the Behavioral Unit, and Ginny checked in. They searched her bag first and discarded most of what she'd packed, handing it back to me in a wad. It turns out we really didn't know how to pack for a psychiatric hospital.

I hope you never will have to know, but just in case—Don't pack any belts, any clothes with zippers or hooks; no shoes with ties or buckles; no toiletries except shampoo, soap, a brush with soft bristles, a regular toothbrush (nothing with batteries) and toothpaste; tampons or pads, if necessary. Hair ribbons are not permitted.

The charge nurse reviewed with me the visitation procedures, which amounted to three two-hour evening sessions a week, one of which would be taken up with a group meeting, then a couple of hours Saturday and Sunday afternoon. Call times varied, according to allotted privileges, but the basic schedule included one call every evening during one designated half-hour and one in the morning. That was it.

I did not get to meet Ginny's doctor, and I was not shown her room. When I asked if Ginny would be able to get full vegetarian meals and snacks, I was told she would. I hugged Ginny and kissed her. She felt lifeless in my arms. I wanted to talk to her and hold her in my arms, but I was ushered out by a nurse, who told me it was past visiting hours and Ginny needed to eat dinner with the others.

§

As I was walking out of the unit, my phone rang. It was Jake.

When I heard his voice, I dropped the bundle of Ginny's things and put my hand to my mouth to muffle a cry. Except for those few minutes in the bathroom at Denny's with Maeve, I'd kept the tears inside up to this point. But hearing his voice made my defenses start to crumble. I wanted more than anything for him to hold me.

"Hey," he said. "Why didn't you call me?"

"I'm sorry," I choked out, "um…I've been kind of busy."

"What's wrong?" Jake asked. That's how it is with us. I can hear what Jake is feeling in his voice. And he can hear what I'm feeling no matter what I say. I hadn't answered, so he said, "What's the matter?"

I was still trying not to cry. I said, "Ginny had kind of a nervous break-down yesterday, during her tennis match at Carver. I took her to the emergency room, but, anyway, long story short, we had to come here where I am now…to Willow Pond, South, the Behavioral Unit. They are going to run some tests and try to get her some medication that will help her." I had gathered Ginny's things from where I dropped them and was walking toward the parking lot, and I held my breath waiting for Jake's answer. I'd said more than I wanted to. I'd done just what I didn't want to do—I'd hit him with everything at once. I could only hope for the best now, and expect the worst.

But instead of sounding distant, Jake sounded hurt and a little mad. "Why didn't you call me?"

I wanted to laugh and cry and hug Jake and thank God all at once.

I said, "I was scared, Jake. I thought maybe it would be asking too much. I mean getting you involved in this."

"I am involved," he said firmly.

I smiled. "I know you are."

"Anyway," Jake's voice sounded lighter, "it probably wouldn't have been such a good idea for you to call me."

My heart skipped a beat. "Oh?" I said.

"Yeh, not about Ginny, no, I kinda screwed up last night."

"Oh?" I said again, even more concerned.

"Yeh, I cut my finger up. Actually almost sliced it off."

"What?" I was at my car now and I balanced Ginny's rebundled things against the back door, opened the door, dropped them into the seat.

"It was stupid," Jake said.

"What happened? Did you do it at work?"

"No," he said, "I wasn't working…"

I pushed Ginny's bundle across to the passenger side to make room for me to sit, fell into the driver's seat and pulled my legs in, shifting the phone quickly to my right ear.

"Me and Ted and a bunch of the guys were having a few beers after work. You know like we always do, just standing around. Well, I had a few too many, and I decided to do this trick with a beer bottle and I nearly cut my ring finger off."

"Honey," I moaned. "Who took you to the hospital?"

"I didn't go to the hospital. Ted took me to the walk-in place over on Lee Road. Then he went to the titty bar next door."

"He didn't stay with you?" I closed the car door and started the engine, backed out of the space, and started moving slowly toward the entrance, not wanting to get to the road until Jake had finished his story.

"It didn't matter. He came back," Jake said. "Took me back to the shop to get my car."

"Oh, honey," I said. "I'm so sorry. Please don't drink like that anymore."

"I know. It was stupid. I told you. But the one guy did a crappy job sewing me up. I was bleeding everywhere, and this other doctor came in, saw it, and redid the stitches. I bet I lost a pint of blood."

"You didn't go to work today, did you?"

"I had to," Jake said, "have to, you know that. It was my own damn fault. I'm just gonna have to work around it."

"Do you have any pain medicine?"

"I need to go pick up my prescriptions. I'm out of the samples they gave me and I need gauze and…where are you?"

"I'm on my way home," I said. "I just left the hospital."

"Come here," he said. "We'll go get the stuff later."

"Okay," I said. "I'll be right there…and Jake…"

"What?"

"Thank you."

"For what?" he said.

"You know," I said. "I love you."

"I know," he said and hung up.

Though we had met just months before Ginny's breakdown and were just beginning to fall in love, the truth is, the fact that Jake lived with me through the most difficult time of my life, bonded us more than most married couples. And the life-changing events we've experienced together have made us closer than some couples who've spent a lifetime together.

Chapter 9

Steppin' Out and Falling

Jake and I met on December 20, 2002 at Duffys. For months afterwards, when I told friends and family about meeting him, I would begin by saying, "I don't usually meet men at bars." Or, "Neither of us frequent bars but...." Finally, after I'd watched enough of them react with a mixture of skepticism and disgust, I stopped explaining and justifying. When "Where did you meet?" came up, I answered simply, "In a bar."

It was an unusual December night in central Florida. The temperature had dropped rapidly from the time I got in my car at work around 6 p.m. to drive home and an hour later when I arrived. My patio thermometer read 48 degrees. I shivered and quickly closed the front door behind me.

I knew I'd have to dig through my closet to find a sweater. I'd left most of my warm clothes behind in Asheville, trying to make the best use of the small space in my car during the move and figuring from what I'd been told that it rarely gets to freezing in central Florida.

It turns out that so-called "winter" was the coldest locals had experienced in years. There were actually two nights in January of 2003 that temperatures dropped below freezing.

In my bedroom, I slipped off my dress and shoes. Maeve called a second later while I was rooting through my closet for a sweater.

"Hey, babe, what's up?" she asked, in her usual cheerful upbeat tone.

"I'm looking for a sweater," I said, shivering in my underwear. "I'm freezing. Didn't you tell me this is the Sunshine State?" I spotted one of my favorite sweaters I'd forgotten I'd packed and smiled, pulling it off the hanger.

Maeve laughed. "You're a wimp," she said. "Hey, we going to Duffy's?"

I frowned. I really didn't want to go to Duffy's. I'd had a stressful day at work. I was PMS-ing. I just wanted to put on my favorite pink angora sweater, pull on my grey sweatpants, order a pizza to be delivered, and watch a movie.

"You go ahead without me," I said. "I don't really feel that great, and I don't want to spoil your fun." I opened my dresser and pulled out my grey sweats, while Maeve began her Duffy's campaign.

"Oh, come on. Just take a hot shower and fix your hair. You'll feel better. You can come over here and get ready. We'll get ready together. I'll fix your hair. Come on. Let me do your hair. You will look fabulous, dahling."

I pulled my sweat pants on. Resolved not to give in. "That's so sweet," I said. "I would love for you to do my hair. Just not tonight. Tonight, I don't care what I look like."

I knew Maeve was pouting. I set the phone down for a second, pulled my sweater on , then picked it back up.

"Come on, honey," she pleaded. "You're going to be leaving for Asheville in a few days and Nathan is flying in (Nathan is her son), and we won't have any girl time. Come on now. It's Christmas. This can be my early Christmas present."

I moaned, "Maeve, I can't. I really don't feel like it. I can't drink when I'm PMSing. You know that. My tolerance will be zero. And I don't want to be around a bunch of other people who will be drinking. I'm not in a good mood. I'll just bring everybody down. I mean, it's Christmas, Maeve. God, I don't even have a tree. You don't have a tree. I *never* don't have a tree. Our kids aren't here. It isn't snowing. I'm just...look...I don't feel like it. Maybe tomorrow night I'll feel better."

"You know what you always say?" Maeve was digging deep. She was not letting me off the hook.

"What?" I asked flopping onto my bed.

"Nothing is promised, that is why you live each day like it's your last."

I snorted, "Yeh, well, I hope this one isn't my last. It would be a hell of a way to end it. Bloated, depressed. Stranded in palm tree land at Christmas."

Maeve laughed. "So we're stranded. Let's make the best of it. I hear the natives have a local bar where we can drown our sorrows."

I laughed, having suddenly decided that my need to stay at home was not worth upsetting Maeve. "Remember, you promised to fix my hair," I said.

"Promise."

"Can I come over?"

"I have a glass of Chardonnay waiting."

"I love you."

"Me too, you. See you in a minute. Oh, and by the way. I am going to decorate."

"What?"

"This weekend. I'm going to make this place look like Christmas for Nathan."

I laughed. "Okay. I feel better already. I can't wait to help. Just don't make me string popcorn."

Maeve laughed. "Get over here. It's getting late."

"Okay, be there in a sec. And don't say I didn't warn you about the hair. It looks like hell. You better be able to work miracles."

"No worries," Maeve said.

§

Maeve did work miracles. She not only fixed my hair as pretty as I've ever seen it—wispy and soft, shiny and sexy—she lifted my spirits.

When I walked in to her beautifully furnished condo, Maeve was playing Christmas music. Crème-vanilla scented candles lit the living room, and she handed me a chilled glass filled with my favorite Chardonnay and kissed me on the cheek. Then she laughed at my sweater. "You are not wearing that sweater," she said. "Where did you get that thing?"

I was a little hurt but defiant. "I love this sweater," I said. Then I remembered the main reason I loved it. "Know what Ginny calls it?"

"No, what does Ginny call it?" Maeve asked.

I smiled at the memory of Ginny's sweet voice and imagination. "She calls it my fuzzynutter."

Maeve burst into laughter. "Your what?"

"My fuzzynutter."

"God," Maeve said. "Ted won't believe this thing." She touched the puffy sleeves. "It looks like cotton candy." Maeve laughed again.

"All right. Enough about my sweater. You need to fix my hair. I see yours already looks beautiful as usual. And so do you."

Maeve smiled. She did look beautiful. She was wearing a burgundy blouse with a matching choker and a pair of her favorite jeans. Her earrings were long bangles of crimson and brass, which looked stunning next to her bronze skin.

I figured she must have gotten home early from work and been fixing herself ever since. She'd straightened her hair with this gell that made the highlights glisten. It looked beautiful.

And after she'd worked on me for half an hour, so did I. My favorite tight jeans and pink sweater turned out to be just the backdrop for my hair and make-up. She matched the tones of blush, shadow, and gloss perfectly to the shades of my sweater. When the Christmas music ran out, she played Wynonna Judd instead of her usual Pearl Jam, knowing country is my favorite. And she refilled my wine glass twice until I protested, then she pouted, "You're not driving. What do you care?"

"Believe me," I said, "I care. And you should too. I get one more glass of wine in me, and you'll be bombarded all night with my 'questions on life.' The only break you'll get is if Ted dances with me and if I don't stop, we'll be dancing on the tables."

Maeve laughed. We were sitting on her bed, make-up spread over the coverlet. She'd just finished applying my lip gloss and she held my face in her hands. "Perfect," she said. "You look like an angel."

I added, "An angel in a fuzzynutter."

Maeve laughed again. "You're a nut all right," she said.

Together we blew out the candles, turned off Wynonna, and headed for Duffy's.

Duffy's was packed. Decorated to the hilt and packed. Bubble lights, snaked around garlands of plastic pine, lined the windowsills. Red-velvet ribboned wreaths hung from the thick wooden beams. There was a tree in every room. In the front where the stage was and the band of the night was playing "You are the sunshine of my life" as we walked in, there was a six-foot pine encircled with white lights and macramé angels. Each of the side rooms had smaller trees with multicolored lights and tiny beer cans on them. On the bar at the center of the pub, there was an old ceramic Christmas tree, just like ones my grandmother used to make. It was painted a forest green and lit with tiny pink lights. There was a chip out of one side.

Garlands hung from mirror to brass lamp. Red candles draped with fresh holly decorated every table. We found Patrick by the fireplace wearing Santa's hat and delicately placing cards in the employees' stockings.

Ted was standing beside his usual table in his Technician Magician uniform.

He hailed us the minute he saw us. "Hey, the angels are here," he said, smiling his beautiful smile.

Maeve and I walked over to Ted and hugged him together. He ordered us drinks, chardonnay for me and white zinfandel for Maeve.

We held them up for a toast. Ted spoke. "To the two most beautiful women I know," he said. "Let the party begin."

Maeve and I smiled and toasted. Maeve kissed Ted on the cheek. Then Jake appeared.

He was wearing a Technician Magician uniform and was flanked by two other Technician Magicians.

Ted introduced them all to us. Jake, then Larry, then Troy.

Jake smiled at me. Maeve and I were standing side by side, but Jake smiled only at me. His gently receding blondish-brown hair revealed his pale blue eyes, handsomely chiseled features, and movie star's smile. Jake has classic good looks. Like Paul Newman and James Dean. Melt your heart, make your knees shake good looks.

I blushed and noticed Maeve watching me out of the corner of her eye, frowning.

After we'd been introduced, Larry and Troy headed to the bar. Jake stayed and moved beside me. He was drinking a beer and he asked me if I needed anything.

"All set," I said, pointing to my unfinished glass of wine I'd set down on the table.

We talked about where we were from. Jake—Jake Welch—had lived in Florida since he was thirteen, but before that in Switzerland, Canada, and even a brief stint in West Virginia, where Maeve was from. His dad had worked for the government, something to do with programming computers. Jake is the oldest of three boys. His mother and father are divorced. His father remarried.

He told me all about Switzerland, riding motorcycles through the orange groves in central Florida as a teenager, how he likes to hunt with his best friend, Brent.

I told him I'd been a creative writing major in college, that my whole family was involved in theater, how I'd grown up performing and writing. I talked about Ginny, how much I love her and missed her, that she was a straight-A student and Southern ranked tennis player and that she would be moving to Florida in a few weeks.

I asked him about his job. He said he'd been a mechanic ever since he graduated from high school. He said his car crapped out on him one day on the way home from high school, and he was stuck on the side of the road not knowing how to fix it. He said he decided right then and there that he would never be in that predicament again. That's when he started working on cars.

He said he was going to junior college at night and that he wanted to go on from there to the University of Central Florida when he graduated.

I told him getting a college education was important. That a lot of people didn't see how my creative writing major translated into my sales manager's job at the garbage company, but I did. I said, "If you can communicate well, you can sell and manage better than most."

I danced a few times with Ted, who kept walking over and nudging me, saying, " "Hey, you gonna miss another good song?" I danced with him reluctantly, while Jake stood at the table, never taking his eyes off me.

Maeve cornered me in the bathroom once, but other than that I spent the whole evening with Jake, and I couldn't have been happier.

"Did you see his smile?" I asked Maeve while we were in the bathroom. I was looking in the mirror, applying more gloss. "And those eyes. I love his blue eyes. They're like the ocean. They're like...they calm me." I half squealed.

Maeve laughed. "Yeh, you seem pretty calm." Then she muttered, "Not."

"Hey," I said, turning to face her. "Give me a break, okay? We've been coming here practically every night for two months, and you know I've never met anyone I was even remotely interested in...as more than a friend, I mean." I looked back into the mirror, smoothed the gloss with my lips.

"So," Maeve said, "you pick a mechanic? A twenty-some-year-old mechanic? Come on, girl. Get over it. You need to get away from him."

I was surprised Maeve wasn't happy for me and a little hurt. I faced her again and asked, "Why?"

Maeve stepped back, put her hands over her mouth like a megaphone, and sounded in a deep voice, "Jerk alert, jerk alert, warning all vulnerable females, there is a jerk in the building, and if you are suffering from a bad case of PMS and too much white wine, you may not be able to identify him."

I laughed. As much as I didn't want to, I laughed. Then I protested, "You don't know Jake's a jerk."

She smiled. "Jake, jerk. See, they're interchangeable. Ergo, my point." Maeve opened the door. "Ted says he's a jerk." We were back in the bar walking toward Jake and Ted.

I rolled my eyes. "Ted's being overprotective. Tell him I'm a big girl and I can handle myself."

Maeve put her arm around me. "I'll do no such thing." She stuck out her index finger. "One, you're not a big girl, and two (she raised her middle finger), you must be drunk, 'cause you've been staring at a grease monkey all night like you got stars in your eyes and shit for brains."

I laughed. Maeve stopped talking. We were back at Ted's table with Ted and Jake. I didn't mean to, but I was staring at Jake again. He blushed this time. Maeve snapped her fingers in front of our faces. "Snap out of it," she said. And Jake and I both laughed nervously.

The band was playing "Stand By Me," and Ted asked me to dance. It was a slow dance, so Ted held me in his arms. I could feel Jake's eyes on me, and I pulled back. Ted looked confused and hurt. He said, "Hey, what's up with you and Jake? You two meet like a couple of hours ago and then badabeem, badabum, you're inseparable?"

I didn't answer Ted, and I tried not to look into his eyes.

"Hey, what's up? You can tell me."

I held Ted closer, but I was looking past him over his shoulder. "No comment," I said.

Ted sighed. "Yeh, that's okay. I know you baby. You just watch yourself, all right?" Ted held me at arms length. "Those Florida boys are not nice. Trust me."

"What?" I protested. "We're just talking."

Ted held me again, moving me slowly in a tight circle. "You keep it that way, just talking. If that son of a bitch ever tries messing with anything, I'll kill him."

Troy and Larry needed to go, and Jake volunteered to take them back to their cars at the shop. But not before he asked me to dance for the first time all night.

It's funny. How two people can be great dancers but they don't dance well together, and then two people can just be good dancers but they move together like one, or two people can just have incredible chemistry and fit. Ted and I dance together like we are one. Jake and I fit.

I will never forget how it felt. The first time in his arms. I've forgotten the song we danced to. What time it was. Who was on the floor with us. But I'll never forget how he felt and what he said. He said he liked my fuzzy sweater.

When the dance was over, Jake asked me to ride with him to the shop. Maeve protested, but I went with him anyway. After we'd dropped off Larry and Troy, he drove me back to Duffy's. I'd promised Maeve I'd come back. We never left each other. It was our pact.

Jake parked in the back lot of Duffy's, shut the car off, and scooted toward me. I'd been wondering all night what it would be like to kiss him. Not true. I'd actually been betting myself it would be wonderful. I've always believed you can sense when you meet a guy whether or not he's a good kisser.

But there in his car, with Jake so close, I was getting scared and a little defensive. I couldn't stop thinking. What if Ted was right and he was a jerk who just wanted one thing? What if he was just trying to see how far he could get? What if he had a girlfriend his age he hadn't told me about? What in the hell was I doing worrying about a twenty-nine year old mechanic I just met and had next to nothing in common with?

I looked at Jake. "You know this isn't going to work out."

"What?" Jake asked, innocently slipping his strong right arm around me gently.

"You and me," I said, trying to be sincere, but avoiding his eyes. Jake didn't move, but started stroking my arm. "I'm too old for you, you know,"

I said. "I'm forty-one years old. Maeve doesn't tell guys her age, I mean she doesn't make a habit of it. She says it shouldn't matter, but...."

Jake interrupted. "It doesn't." He leaned over and softly kissed me on the cheek.

"It does matter," I protested weakly. "We're from different generations. You don't even know who the Beatles are."

"Sure I do," he said smiling. "They're all over the place. In the trees." He kissed me again, this time on the forehead. "On the ground."

I pushed him away gently. "Stop, you goof. Okay, you may know who the Beatles are, but you don't know their names."

Jake kissed me once more, on the lips. Then he said, "How about Paul?"

"That's one," I said. "So you know one."

He kissed me again on the lips. "Then there's John."

"Okay, two," I said indifferently.

He kissed me again, this time with his tongue. "And Ringo."

I laughed a little. "Lucky," I said.

"No, there's no Lucky," Jake said. "But I do remember a George."

I laughed and mumbled, "I give."

Jake cradled my head in his hands, laying me down underneath him, turned my lips to meet his. Then he covered me with his lips. He kissed me like he was making love for the first time, gently prodding, then slowly guiding himself deeper and deeper inside me.

When we walked back into the pub, I was glowing. But I'd made up my mind to spend time with Ted and Maeve. I needed time away from Jake. He was making my head spin. I felt like I was forgetting who I was.

Maeve and Ted spotted us immediately. Jake went to the bar to get a beer. Ted asked me to dance. Then Maeve asked me to dance. While they both took turns spinning me around the floor, I felt dizzy. When I couldn't see Jake, and Ted had gone to the restroom, I grabbed Maeve and told her we needed to go—out the back way. She grabbed her purse, and we ducked out the kitchen entrance.

We ran to Maeve's white Toyota Celica convertible, laughing, and jumped in. Maeve started the car and rolled down her window. And there was Jake, poking his head in through her window. Maeve and I both jumped and screamed. In one fell swoop, Jake quickly and deftly shifted Maeve's car into neutral and shut the engine off. He smiled at Maeve.

Maeve looked furious. Jake shifted his stare to me. "What did you do that for?"

I cleared my throat. I felt like my heart was going to pop out of my sweater. I told him, "I was…um…it's late. We need to get home." I looked at Maeve for reassurance.

Maeve frowned again and turned the car back on, shifting into first. "Yeh, lover boy. It's late. Past your bedtime."

Jake smiled, but he seemed hurt. He said to me, "Can I call you?"

I nodded. "Sure…um. I've got a new number. I don't even know it yet. Ted's got it, though. Ask him."

Jake seemed disappointed. "Don't you have a business card? A work number? Anything? I want to take you dancing. There's a country western bar called Cowboys. I want to take you there."

I smiled. "Okay. Just ask Ted for my number. He'll give it to you."

Jake was leaning into the car. Maeve was revving the engine. "Okay," she said to me. "We about done here, sweetcakes?"

I winked at Jake. "Yeh, we're done."

Maeve revved the engine again. Jake stepped back.

He said, "Night, Haley."

Maeve squealed her tires pulling out of the parking lot. I yelled, "Good night, Jake."

Maeve turned to me. "What was that? I thought you were trying to get away from him?"

Then she shifted gears and smiled, saying, "Ted doesn't have your number."

I laughed. "I know he doesn't."

Then Maeve laughed too. "Smooth," she said. "That's my girl. Now you're coming to your senses."

I turned the radio up. Maeve had some rock station on I hated. They were playing some god-awful song by Smashed Pumpkins. It was pounding in my ears. But it was better than talking to her about Jake. Not that I didn't want to talk about him. I wanted to shout from the rooftops, "I love Jake." But I just kept listening to the Smashed Pumpkins, thinking about the Beatles and how I could get Jake my number without Ted and Maeve finding out.

And while I did not actually shout "I love you, Jake" from the rooftops or tell Maeve what I was feeling, I did call Ginny the next day to tell her about Jake. But before I'd said one word about meeting him, even before I mentioned his name—separated for months by distance and what was going on in our lives—Ginny knew the tone of my voice. I said four words when she answered the phone and not one about Jake, told her, "I love you, baby." And Ginny told me, "You're in love. I want to meet him."

And a month later, she did meet Jake. When I picked Ginny up from school that day, I could tell she'd had a good day. Or at least better than usual. She was smiling when I drove up to her tennis practice. And she even talked to me on the way home about her match the next day.

I saw it as a sign things were getting better. That Ginny was adjusting to her new home and her new school. And I decided it would be a good time for her to meet Jake.

So I called him up. Invited him to supper. He seemed really glad I called, kidding that he was getting worried I didn't want Ginny to meet him.

Ginny and I danced around each other in the kitchen, snapping the tips off green beans, slicing carrots, and singing with Shania, "Any man of mine, better walk the line….," while Jake crept up behind me, stealing bites of beans and carrots and crunching them in my ear.

After we ate, Jake got a call from his brother in California. He walked outside on the patio to talk to him, while Ginny and I cleared the dishes off the table.

After I made certain Jake was outside and the door to the patio was shut, I cornered Ginny in the kitchen. Wide-eyed with anticipation, hands clasped to my chest, I asked her, "What do you think?"

Ginny stared back at me. Like her eyes were digging into my soul and said very simply, "Be careful."

I was crushed. My excitement zapped like a happy little bug fried by white light. And all I could manage to say was, "What?"

Ginny continued carefully measuring her words, leveling her eyes to mine, telling me in no uncertain terms, "He grew up too fast."

I breathed a sigh of relief. Not only was she not producing one of her typical revelations, she wasn't telling me a thing I didn't already know about Jake.

Ginny paid no attention to my sighing and went right on speaking to me as if she were my mother and I was marrying Jake. She told me, "He will try to protect you."

I just smiled. "There are worse things," I said.

"No," Ginny told me unequivocally. "Not for you."

I was undaunted, shrugging my shoulders and teasing Ginny in a child-like voice, "And what will I do?" I asked her.

Ginny shot back, "You will try to escape."

I laughed. "I wouldn't be too sure about that, sweetie," I told her. "I told you I am big-time in love. Hopelessly devoted. The whole nine yards."

Ginny ducked her head and stared at the floor. She said simply, "I know."

I continued teasing her, "So," I said. "What will Jake do when I try to escape? Will he try to escape too?"

Ginny looked up again. "No," she said quietly. "He won't leave you."

"And," I said, "so what does happen to me and Jake?"

Ginny looked away. Out our kitchen window. Toward a light over the dark path leading away from our home. She said in a distant voice, "He will learn to let you fly."

She stood very still for a few moments, while I stared at her pained profile. Until she began to cry. I stepped toward her, arms wide open, and she folded herself into me. I said, "What, honey? What is it? Do you not like Jake?"

"No," Ginny mumbled into my shoulder, then said, "I like him a lot."

I patted her on the back and said, "What then?"

Ginny stepped back, wiping her eyes. She said, "It's just so hard. Here I thought we would have this whole life together, just you and me from now on and what do I know?" Ginny rubbed her eyes again. "I mean it's obvious God sent him to you. That you are made for each other. And..." Ginny was crying again, "and how happy he makes you." She cried harder then suddenly tightened her jaw, pursed her lips like a fist, and staring straight at me blurted out," Where is *my* happiness?" Then she broke into large aching sobs, while I circled her with my arms.

I held her tight for over a minute. Then said, "Right here. With me. It is you and me forever, Ginny. I will always be with you."

Ginny kept crying. Holding on to me and crying. She didn't say a word for what seemed like minutes. Then she whispered. "You can't. You can't be with me forever," then stepped back and looked me in the eyes. "You think you can, but you can't, mommy. You can't make my happiness. I have to find it on my own."

It was a conversation not unlike many we'd had through the years. In restaurants, eating lunch before one of Ginny's matches, sitting on our sofa stuffing down pizza on a Friday night, or sitting on a park bench watching birds fly. With both of us trading perspective. Me, as the daughter, Ginny as the mother, me as the mother, Ginny as the child. It was our little dance. And we did it so well, I never thought it would stop. Couldn't imagine a time when we would no longer know how to move together.

Ginny and I were still standing in the kitchen, both crying now, holding on to each other, when Jake appeared in the hallway, propping himself up with his right arm at the entrance to the kitchen. He cocked his head sideways like a puppy and said, "Hey, what's the matter with my girls? I leave for a few minutes and you fall apart?"

I needed to laugh, so I did. And Ginny tried to smile. We pulled away from each other and began wiping our faces with our sleeves. I told Jake, "We just missed you."

Jake smiled and walked toward us, grabbing us both into a bear hug. He told us, "No need for that. I will never leave you." Then he stepped back, his eyes brightening and said, "But I do think we should all go bowling."

Ginny perked up and asked, "Can we, mommy?"

But before I could even consider Jake's suggestion or her questions, "Ginny's smile had turned into a frown. She stared down at her feet and said, "Forget it. I can't. I've got a ton of American history."

I looked at Jake who seemed very disappointed. Then back at Ginny, who was still frowning, and in the most cheerful voice I could muster said, "Okay, so we don't go bowling tonight, but…" I smiled right at Ginny, "I bet if we're good and promise not to cry anymore, the handsome man standing in our kitchen might just get us some ice cream."

I looked over at Jake, who was smiling back and noticed Ginny smiling too. Jake bolted for the front door, but just before he opened it, he winked at both of us, bowed low, and said, "Ladies, I am at your service and will take orders…from both of you."

Ginny and I both laughed.

It was another thing I loved about Jake. His flare for being entertaining. I had literally grown up in the world of theater, surrounded by actors my entire life, none of whom had Jake's natural abilities—his sense of timing, his way of making people laugh.

Chapter 10

A p r i l   S h o w e r

I realized after I'd been circling the neighborhoods of College Park and Winter Park for half an hour wondering what Ginny might be doing, how she was feeling, what was happening on the unit—that I should have asked Jake what was the quickest way to get to his place from the hospital and written the directions down. Jake is great with directions. Not just in a place where he grew up. Anywhere. He knows geography, his right form his left—north, south, east, and west. He pays attention to signs, landmarks, names of roads, and he has an excellent memory.

I remember selectively the color of the leaves on the trees I pass. The type of window on a house I like. The sound of a child's laughter. The smell of my mother's pumpkin bread baking. The way the gerber daisy's petals feel brushing against my face.

I have no sense of direction. No idea whether I'm going north, south, east or west. I forget names of roads as quickly as they are told to me. Maps are like pieces of ancient Sanskrit. And most of the time I'm not altogether certain which is right and which is left.

I thought about calling Jake, but then finally I recognized a street near the duplex he lived in. There was a house on it painted bright pink. That's how I remembered which way to go. Drive past the pink house, turn toward the fire hydrant; the big oak tree will be on the other side of the road and you're there. Simple.

Sometimes I would drive Jake crazy with my selective memory, and he would demand, "How can you be a sales manager over four divisions of a Fortune 200 company and not be able to follow directions? How do you get around?"

"I ask directions," I would answer.

"But you can't follow them?" he would protest.

"Then I ask again."

§

I pulled into Jake's driveway and checked my rearview mirror to see what I looked like. I needed lip gloss, so I put a little on, then I got out of my car and walked up to the front door of Jake's white brick house. I knocked loudly once.

Jake yelled, "It's open!"

I walked in to the living room and shut the door. Jake was standing in his uniform next to the couch. He looked annoyed. My eyes went to his bandage immediately; it was dirty with grease.

"Where the hell have you been?" he demanded.

I walked over to him, dropping my purse off on a chair, put my arms around his neck and kissed him while he tried to turn away. "Jake," I protested.

"I've been waiting for you forever," he said. "What took you so long?" Then he added in a disgusted tone, "Don't tell me. You got lost." I glanced at the floor. "I knew it," he said. "You know I live all of three streets from the hospital?"

I didn't say anything. I wasn't in any mood to be criticized, and I was too tired to fight. Jake must have seen how hurt I was because he put his arms around me. "How's Ginny?" he asked.

I buried my face in his shirt, which smelled like gasoline. "I don't know," I said. "I miss her already." Then I started to cry and Jake held me. We stood there for a long time just holding each other.

After a while, Jake stepped back and showed me his bandaged left hand. "Look at this crap," he said. "It's ridiculous. I can't do anything with this on."

I wiped my tears on the sleeve of my shirt and got mascara on one of the white cuffs.

Jake said, "I need to take this thing off, but I can't until we get more gauze and antibiotics. I'm gonna get a shower."

"Okay," I said, dropping down on the couch.

Jake leaned over and kissed me on the forehead. He said, "Can you help me get my clothes off?"

I laughed at this. "Now there's an offer I'm not gonna refuse."

Jake smiled. "Don't laugh. This is ridiculous. Remind me never to drink again."

I pulled Jake's shirt up with both hands and covered his chest with kisses." "I don't know," I said, "I kinda like this."

Jake pushed me away gently and unbuckled his belt with his right hand. "Come on. I'm injured."

I unzipped his pants. "Yes," I said. "And don't you worry. I am going to take good care of the patient." I smoothed my hand up and down his penis.

Jake groaned. "Cut it out. I need to get a shower. You keep that up and you're going to get a shower."

I laughed and pulled his pants and boxers down at the same time. "Okay," I said. "Suit yourself. I'll leave you alone…after I get you undressed." I helped Jake unbutton his shirt.

"I didn't say leave me alone," he said. "Just let me get a shower first." Then he kissed me on the top of my head. He kicked off his shoes and pulled off his socks, scooped up his dirty clothes in his right hand, and walked naked into his bedroom. I followed him to the door and watched him throw the clothes in a heap in the corner. Then he disappeared into the bathroom.

I leaned against the frame of the bedroom door. In a minute, I heard the shower running. Then I heard Jake calling me.

"Hey, come here," he said. "I need you."

I slipped off my high-heeled sandals and walked down the hall into the bathroom. Jake pulled back the shower curtain. Water was dripping from every part of his muscular body as the shower head pulsed on his chest. He was holding a bar of Irish Spring soap in his right hand and he handed it to me. "I need you to wash me," he said.

I took the slippery bar of soap, trying to figure out how I would manage without getting soaked. At first I sat down on the side of the tub and leaned into the shower. Carefully soaping Jake's private parts. But I was getting very wet, very quickly, and Jake was getting very hard. And before I could formulate a better plan, Jake lifted me into the shower with his strong right arm and started trying to unbutton my pants. He was kissing me hard, pressing his swollen cock into me. I slipped out of my pants and thong. Jake started tugging on my shirt. I pulled it off, unsnapping my bra. He ran his tongue up and down my neck. Then kissed me on the lips. He pulled me closer to him and then gently pushed my head down until my mouth was near his penis. I dropped the soap and held him, taking his penis in my mouth and teasing him with my tongue for a few long seconds, then gently encircling his balls in my left hand, pulling down on them ever so slightly, while my right hand stroked his penis up one side, over the top, then down the other. Jake groaned. I kept this up for a minute until his thighs were trembling, then went down on him. Jake was moaning now. He pushed my head down a little more. When he did this he was in my throat, and I kept praying I wouldn't gag, that I could hold on until he came. Then I remembered what he loves, so while I sucked on him hard and long—with my left index finger, I started stroking the little smooth place behind his balls, "his spot". He exploded into my mouth, groaning and moaning at the same time.

Jake came in my mouth for what seemed like minutes. Then he pulled me up with his right arm and held me like a strong boy who'd just picked up a porcelain doll and whose mother was telling him, "Be careful, you could break her."

§

I look back now on all the times Jake and I have spent together, and I know that many who read this memoir will feel I could have been doing something more constructive with my time. I should have been doing more research about what was the matter with Ginny. I could have been finding better ways to treat her.

So let me be the first to say I didn't get it right—but also—here's what I learned, and I'm still learning, and I hope what I've learned helps others. I know this personally. I would never have survived the past two years without Jake, and while I will accept criticism, I won't apologize. Or try to justify the time I spent with him because from our time together, I know this—loving is never wrong.

§

After we ate dinner and picked up Jake's prescriptions, I spent the night with him. He wrapped me in a favorite afghan his aunt had crocheted for him and held me in his arms. I cried most of the night. And when I wasn't crying, I was fighting the urge to drive to the hospital and bring Ginny home.

I kept picturing her in some hospital room, alone, with nothing but bare walls to look at, lying on a cot, clutching the purple teddy bear I'd given her.

Jake kept trying to comfort me. He told me he'd get a ladder and climb up to her window, jimmy the lock, figure a way to get her attention without anyone else catching on, carry her back down to me. While most men I know couldn't even think of something so dramatic, never mind be able to pull it off, the reality is Jake was completely capable of making his plan work, and though I wanted Ginny home, I knew better than to encourage him.

I thanked him and kissed him on the forehead. Watched him close his beautiful blue eyes to dream, while mine remained wide awake all night long.

Chapter 11

S t a r v i n g

Visiting hours at the Behavioral Unit were from 1 p.m. to 3 p.m. on Saturday. I arrived at 12:30. I did not want to be late. First, I had to be admitted to the parking lot by speaking Ginny's patient number into the intercom system. Once I was inside the building, I had to give her name and patient number to the receptionist, then wait in the downstairs lobby. There I had three options. I could sit down on the plastic furniture, stand and stare at the plain brick walls, or do both at the same time. I chose to stand and stare.

I was surprised more parents weren't visiting. Only two other mothers were waiting with me, and there were fifteen kids in the unit. But there was constant traffic through the lobby. I found out later the admittance door for the adult psych ward was on the first floor to the right of the reception desk.

One o'clock came and passed. By ten minutes after one, I was getting upset. I asked the large woman dressed in blue behind the desk, "Could I go up now? Visiting hours are supposed to start at 1 o'clock."

She motioned with her chubby hand for me to wait. Then she picked up her black phone and called the psych ward. She asked, "Are you ready for the visitors yet?" She listened for an answer. After a few seconds, she said, "All right. I'll tell them. Only one is asking," she added. Then looked on the sign in sheet. "It's Robbins. Stockinger's mom." She listened to something else then said, "Okay," and hung up.

The big lady in blue said to me, "You'll have to wait a few more minutes. They were late getting back from crafts and a few of them need to get their medication."

"Oh," I said. "Thank you." And I sat down on the nearest plastic couch.

At 1:30, we were told we could go upstairs. By then two other mothers had arrived, and we walked together up the long steep lobby stairs. We opened the heavy wood door at the top of the stairs. One of the mothers walked over to the intercom on the right wall next to the door to the psych ward. She said she was there to see her daughter and told her name. I followed her lead, the other mother followed me.

There was a loud buzzing noise and when we heard it, the first mother pushed the door open and walked into the unit—and the rest of us followed.

Yesterday, when Ginny was admitted, I'd paid little attention to our surroundings. I kept desperately hoping some miracle would occur, that Ginny would suddenly snap back into herself, but when I saw she wasn't going to do that, I clung to her, trying to listen to the nurse, who was telling about their policies and procedures. When I couldn't meet with Ginny's doctor and they wouldn't show me her room, I became even more anxious, and all I was focusing on was holding Ginny. I didn't feel anymore as though we were voluntarily admitting her, but as though she was being taken away from me by force.

Today, I was paying attention. I noticed the walls of the unit were painted a peaceful light blue with forest scenes all over them, a rushing waterfall, birds in flight. The furniture that lined the walls looked new. It was leather. Blue leather, with fruitwood framing. The dark blue, mauve and green carpet had no padding, but it was clean.

The nurses' station was down the entrance hall to the right. The center part of it was open, with a semi-circular counter the nurses worked behind, and both sides were closed off by walls with doors.

The group therapy room and one classroom were directly centered at the end of the main entrance hall, and the patients' rooms and bathrooms were located to the right and left.

I wandered down the main hall, anxiously searching for Ginny, and I found her sitting on a couch outside the classroom, trying to hold her head up. Her fair skin was paler than I'd ever seen it. Her olive eyes deeply circled and the pupils dilated, looking like small dark moons. She was wearing one of her sweatsuits and some socks, and she had draped a thin cotton blanket around her.

When I reached out to hug her, she did not move or put her arms around me.

I started to cry. "Ginny, honey, are you okay?"

Other kids in the unit walked by us, most dressed in pajama-like pants and shirts and wearing slippers, all looking like zombies.

Ginny said, as if she were asleep, "I'm tired, Mommy."

I sat down beside her, still holding on. "Can Mommy get you anything?"

Ginny shook her head, then placed it in my lap.

I cleared my throat and tried to fight back more tears. "They said you had crafts." My voice was shaking. "How did that go?"

Ginny did not answer me, but reached for one of my hands and held it. Her hand felt like ice.

"Ginny," I said. "How was crafts?"

She said in a voice I wouldn't recognize as my daughter's, a drugged and hypnotic voice, "I couldn't go. I was too sleepy." Then buried her head in my lap.

I wanted to scream and cry at the same time. I kept thinking, "What in the hell are they doing to my daughter?" And, "I've got to get her out of here."

Ginny mumbled, "Can you bring me some food? I haven't eaten since yesterday with you."

I leaned over closer to her. "They didn't feed you?"

A nurse passing by gave me a dirty look.

"Ginny?" I asked her, "they aren't feeding you? They told me you would be able to get three vegetarian meals a day...and snacks. And I specifically told them you don't eat cheese or eggs!" My face was turning red I was so angry. "Didn't they ask why you weren't eating? Didn't they ask if they could get you something else?"

"They told me I'm anorexic. Or bulemic. I don't remember. I told the admissions couselor about the time in the ninth grade where I was afraid of getting too fat and she wrote it down. Now they are saying I'm not eating on purpose."

Every nerve in my body was tensing. I really thought I was going to scream or hit someone, preferably the next nurse who walked by.

I ran the palm of my hand over Ginny's back and said, "I'll get you food, honey. Don't you worry. And I'm going to straighten this out. You will eat if I have to hold a gun to someone's head."

"Mommy?" Ginny looked desperate. "Can you get me something now?"

I was heartsick. The clock on the nurses' station read 2 p.m. If I left to get Ginny food, I'd be away for her whole visiting hour. I said, "If I go, I won't be able to visit."

Ginny put her head in my lap again. "I'm really hungry, Mommy. That medicine is making me sick."

I knew I had to go. I said, "I'll go get you something, sweetheart. But I'm going to speak to the nurses first. This is ridiculous—you not eating for twenty-four hours."

Ginny sat back up. "Can you get me a veggie burger with fries?"

I smiled and held her face in my hands. "Yes. I'll go right now. Are you going to be okay here?"

Ginny nodded.

I stood up. Ginny lay down on the couch. I hugged her and pulled the blanket over her socks. "I'll be right back," I said. "I promise."

Ginny shut her eyes.

§

And I was off. On a mission. To find food for my daughter and feed her. A basic instinct of every mother.

But from the time I stopped breast-feeding Ginny, when she was a year old until that moment in the crisis unit, it had always been not so much instinct or part of my daily routine as an ongoing challenge.

I remember telling her father when I stopped breast feeding and began feeding Ginny formula from the bottles, my life turning into a constant series of sterilizing or warming events, "I hate this." We were standing in our kitchen, John holding Ginny while I prepared another bottle. "Number one," I said, "this formula stinks." I stuck the can up to John's nose. "Smell it," I demanded. John winced and squinched his nose. Then I said, "See? It does stink! I know I wouldn't drink it. God. Who invented this stuff? I know it wasn't a mother. Or a baby. And what kind of name is that for something you eat? Formula?" I rolled my eyes, while John stood patiently beside me, holding Ginny, waiting for my tirade to end. "Oh yeh, right," I said. "Can't you just see it? Some adult in a fast-food restaurant ordering lunch. Going— 'no, I'll pass on the burger and fries. I'll take some of that Formula instead.'"

John said calmly, "She can hear you, you know. She can hear the tone in your voice. I think she's getting used to the stuff, but if you keep going on about how bad it tastes, I bet she won't take it at all. Then what are you going to do?"

I stared up at him. "I don't know," I said. "But I'll think of something. Better than formula. Trust me."

And I did think of something. I basically fixed gourmet meals for my daughter from the time she was a year and a half on. Vegetarian gourmet meals. Because Ginny won't eat food with eyes. And she doesn't eat cheese or eggs either.

Even her school lunch, which I fixed every day, was kicked up a notch from the usual fare conscientious parents sent—tempeh-avacado sandwiches, homemade peanut butter and banana, marinated tofu, fruit and carrots with her favorite terra chips. Never any junk. No processed foods. Always with a handwritten note on a napkin. Something I knew would make her smile. Like "I love you crazy" or "Smooch, Goochers, I miss you!" or "You are my sunshine…." From her first week of school, I never missed a day making her lunch or writing her a note.

One year, when Ginny was in the sixth grade, one of her teachers wrote me a note. She asked me if I'd be willing to have a meeting with some of the mothers. Teach them how to feed and care for their children. And another time when I was entertaining Ginny's brownie troupe at our home on the mountain, fixing each of them the snack of their choice, I remember one little blonde waif of a girl named Katie whispering in my ear, "You make me feel special." I hugged her tiny body and smiled through tears.

When Ginny started playing tennis tournaments, I had another challenge on my hands. Her eating healthfully on the road. At least at home I knew all the places to shop. And I had my own kitchen to cook in. But traveling to tournaments was different. And it was then I learned the fine art of preparing food that could be stored and still taste good. I think I could teach a course— How to Eat Like You're at Home When You're on the Road. By Ginny's tournament days, she had heard the story of my early rantings on baby food dozens of times, and when I told her once the thing about teaching a course, she said without missing a beat, singing the last word to me, "Yeh, and I'll bet it wouldn't include the use of… Formuuulaaaa!"

When I passed the nurses' station, there was no one in it, but when I pressed the button for approval to exit, a nurse's voice came over the intercom.

102

I told the voice, in a clipped tone I usually reserved for work, "This is Ms. Robbins, Ginny's mom. I'm leaving to get her some food. She hasn't eaten in twenty-four hours, and I want to speak to whoever is in charge of the meals."

There was a long pause, then I heard the nurse's voice. "You may leave, Ms. Robbins, but if you come back after 3 p.m., you will not be admitted."

I wasn't about to waste any more time arguing; I would deal with getting back in to give Ginny her food—after visiting hours if necessary— when the time came, so speaking to an intercom, I said, "Fine!" And the hand behind the voice buzzed me out of the ward.

I drove as fast as I could to the nearest Burger King, but the traffic was bad, as usual. Still I managed to get back at 2:35. A nurse let me back into the unit, and I marched down the hall toward Ginny, who was still lying on the couch. A tall nurse dressed in white scrubs stopped me. She said, "You can't bring food in here without prior approval."

I looked up and glared at her almost black eyes. "I told the nurse on duty I was going to get my daughter food," I said, "She has not eaten in twenty-four hours!"

The nurse cleared her throat. "I will make an exception this once, but you can't do this again. It upsets the other patients." Then she said," I'm going to have to inspect the contents of the bag."

I gave her the Burger King bag and said, "I told another nurse I want to speak with whoever is in charge of the meals after I visit with my daughter. And, actually, I also want to speak to whoever is giving her medication. I want to know what she is taking because I know it's too much. She looks like a zombie!"

The nurse had finished inspecting the bag, and she handed it back to me. "I'll make a note, Ms. Robbins, but I can't promise anything. Your daughter's doctor is in charge of her medication dosage, and he isn't here."

"Who *is* her doctor?" I asked. "I haven't even met him yet!"

The nurse said, "It's Doctor Traynor. He is a very busy man. But I will make a note you would like to speak with him, and I'm sure he'll call you. He's a very good doctor."

I rolled my eyes. "I certainly hope so," I said. Then I walked quickly toward Ginny, who just then stood up and opened her arms to me. We hugged and then settled together on the couch while she ate in silence. I watched her devour in minutes the two veggie burgers and large order of french fries I'd brought, which I thought might be too much food, and I watched with a strange kind of despairing relief, knowing she was getting some nourishment now but wondering how long she'd have to go before her next meal. When she'd finished, she wiped her mouth, hugged me and lay back down.

I said, "I'm going to speak to them about your food and medication, Ginny."

She nodded. "Okay, mommy, thank you," she said in a small voice, absent of feeling. In five minutes, she was asleep in my lap, having said nothing else, and in five more minutes, a voice came over the intercom, telling the parents visiting hours were over.

When I first told my sister Faith that Ginny was having trouble of the kind parents pray their children will be spared and that I couldn't tell her yet exactly where things were going for us because I didn't have any idea—which was the truth, Faith seemed to know intuitively that I'd be needing something out of the ordinary to keep going. She sent me a box of letters Ginny had written her—almost three months of them, composed while Faith was away at school. On top of the box, she taped a short note, remarkable as much for what it didn't say as for what it did, because my sister is not known for brevity, as she is the first to admit. She'd written simply, "These are yours more than mine."

For a few days, I read hungrily, looking for—I don't know what exactly— consolation, absolution, clues? And then I read just to hear my daughter's voice speaking to me again. Because Faith was right—the letters were written for me, almost as if my daughter had some hint of the time that was coming, though there was nothing of that in her words beyond what any reasoning person would call coincidence.

I have finished the box now and am starting over. Each letter is like feeling my daughter's gentle arms around me when she used to slip up behind me at the kitchen sink and gather me in and whisper gentle, funny things, like "How can a mommy be so tiny?"

She loved surprising me, and I know now that I could read these letters she wrote my sister for the rest of my life and never find any foreshadowing of the days we have since lived—most especially of a day I am about to describe, when in much less time than I was in labor with my daughter but with much greater pain than I endured at her birth, Ginny's world and mine began to turn in ways I wake to be startled by again and again.

I wanted to tell Ginny I loved her. That everything would be all right. But a nurse came by and ordered her to get up to go to group therapy, and I spent the last few minutes with her, wiping what in happier times we used to call "sleepies" from her eyes, kissing her cheek and steadying her as she stood up to join the other children headed toward the therapy room. I asked if I could bring her anything. She whispered, "Slippers." I nodded. She wasn't looking at me, but I couldn't voice even a simple word of acknowledgement that I'd bring what she requested—I was mute with feelings I couldn't have begun to name at that moment even if there had been someone to listen.

I hugged and kissed her again, then let her go.

Almost the moment I turned from Ginny, anger restored the urge to speak, and I headed for the nurses' station, thinking some inspiration would hit me, that I'd find some way of telling the staff they needed to pay more attention to the details of taking care of my daughter. "Or I'll take care of them," I thought, knowing that was exactly what I couldn't say.

There were two nurses working. The tall one with the black eyes, whose name tag read Maria and a short blonde one with hazel eyes whose tag read Heidi. I leaned over the counter. "Excuse me," I said. "I'm Ms. Robbins, Ginny's mother. I need to speak to someone about her meals and medication." I looked from one nurse to the other, trying to signal respect for both.

Maria raised her thick eyebrows. "It's after visiting hours, Ms. Robbins," she said. But Heidi was giving me a sympathetic gaze, so I turned all my attention to her. "I know," I said, in an apologetic voice, and I know you are very busy, but I want to help everyone understand about my daughter's diet. Yesterday I was so nervous about learning the policies and procedures, I didn't explain very well what she eats."

Maria put down the chart she was working on and stepped toward the counter. She told me in a very firm, reprimanding tone, "Ms. Robbins, I'm not sure what you told the staff yesterday. After we spoke in the hall, I reviewed the nurse's notes from the previous day, and I found nothing to indicate Ginny has any special dietary needs."

I tried to interrupt Maria. "But, I…"

She cut me off. "What you need to understand is we are not running a restaurant here. This is a hospital, Ms. Robbins. For acute mental patients."

The words hit me like stones I didn't see coming. Or like unwelcome words of acknowledgement after I knew the facts. I swallowed hard and said, "I realize that. I…I just want…my daughter…to be able to eat, and…" My voice was trembling now, and I could feel the tears welling up in my eyes. "I'm willing to help in any way. I don't, we don't expect special treatment. I know it must be hard for you taking care of all these children. But I…if you'd just let me help. I don't think we'll have a problem. If you've got a refrigerator and a microwave, I can bring things she can eat that are hardly any trouble to fix. She can even fix them. See, it's just I know you say you have vegetarian meals, but my daughter doesn't eat cheese or eggs, and it's hard for her. I mean she was starving today. She's used to the meals I fix. She's used to me taking care of her." I looked at Heidi, who seemed genuinely concerned. "Please," I said to her, "I don't want to cause trouble. I just want to make sure Ginny has good food." I was crying now. "I'm her mother, and she…she… I've always…that's what I do. I make sure she eats right and is safe and I…" My nose was running and Heidi grabbed me a tissue from the box on the counter and handed it to me. "I don't want to cause trouble. I just want to take care of my daughter."

Heidi said, "I think we can work that out. I don't see why you can't bring Ginny food." Maria was raising her eyebrows again, but Heidi continued. "We've got a little space in the refrigerator and freezer. She can use that."

Maria said, "You need to understand. We are making an exception, and you do not need to tell the other patients."

"Oh, I do understand," I said. "And I won't. I promise you. I understand completely. I just want Ginny to be well and happy. I won't cause any trouble."

Heidi smiled. "Ginny seems like a very sweet girl, Ms. Robbins. I see where she gets it from."

Again I thought I would cry. Until that moment I had not realized how starved I was for some sign of kindness from the people on whom Ginny was depending, but I fought to stay composed. "Thank you," I said to Heidi, then turned to Maria. "Will you ask Dr. Traynor to call me about her medication? Ginny has never taken any drugs. We don't even take aspirin. She's an athlete. I just think maybe he doesn't know this and…um…. I really need to speak with him about her medication. It's just too much. Will you have him call me?"

Maria looked as though she was going to either refuse or reprimand me again, but all she said was, "I'll give him the message."

I thanked Maria and Heidi. Then I walked down the hall glancing back at the therapy room, trying to see Ginny. But the heavy door had thick glass; what I could see were just shapes of people. None familiar. None that would answer even the smallest part of my need for one more glimpse of my gentle girl. My painter of rainbows, my dancer in gazebos, my comforter of small creatures was somewhere still within the range of my voice if I had shouted, but the windows of the room were covered with charts and I was being buzzed out.

When I drove back to Jake's that night, I told him what had happened. He said I should have called him to bring the veggie burgers. I said they wouldn't let him in. Only immediate family were allowed to visit the patients. Jake considered this for a minute, chewing his bottom lip, then asked, "What are they hiding?"

Chapter 12

Call It the Way It Is

It is mid-October in Asheville. The leaves on the maples, oaks, and dogwoods are changing colors. The bookstore is getting busier. Customers come in wearing sweaters and blowing their noses.

Ginny is studying to take the GED. She has decided not to go back to high school. She also plans to take the SAT and apply to several colleges with good tennis programs, maybe even try for a scholarship. Most days, I am hopeful because I must be.

On Mondays, Tuesdays, and Thursdays, we take spinning classes together, and before dinner every evening we walk. It is on these walks I've learned what she remembers of her days in the unit.

"Do you remember..." I ask her as we walk, holding hands down a long mountain dirt road that leads to a stable in the woods. "Do you remember how the shower in your bathroom was leaking and the floor was flooded?"

Ginny nods. "Oh yeh," she says. "It wasn't so bad, though. We got towels and put them down on the floor to soak it up. I got April to help me. She was my roommate then. But then a nurse told us we were creating too much laundry."

"What if you'd gotten up at night and slipped on the wet floor?" I asked her. "Did they think about that? You know, I said that to them when you showed me the floor, and I complained to the nurses on duty."

"I know," Ginny said, looking up at the tall thin pines that line each side of the road and tower above us. "I think they just didn't have enough money to fix things or something. That's what Eric said. He said they never paid him the right amount."

"What?" I said. "They have to pay the employees for the hours they've worked. I mean, they could get in really big trouble."

"I don't know," she said. "He told me it was a private hospital and that they controlled pretty much the whole system in central Florida and did pretty much what they wanted to do. He said his check was always wrong. That he was always getting cheated hours he'd worked. He complained, but he said it never did any good. He said he loved the kids so much, he'd volunteer if he could, but he needed a paying job."

"That's awful," I said. "Eric seemed like a very nice person to me. I have no idea why they weren't paying him or fixing the plumbing. Do you know your stay there cost over 30,000 dollars?"

Ginny frowned. "Boy, that was a waste of money. Wow, that could have bought a lot of tennis lessons."

"Yeh," I said. But I was thinking about her long speech on the hospital. Speeches of that length had never seemed remarkable to me before Ginny's illness. Now, when she was able to speak a paragraph without pause, I marveled.

We walked for a little while in silence, which I don't mind now. Because of these new bursts of fluent speech, I've even started to relax enough to believe the longer periods of silence won't last. This is a leap of faith for me.

For the past year and a half, conversations with Ginny have been rare, and even now with my renewed faith and hope, they still seem like jewels.

A silencing combination of hearing multiple voices—what she has now described to me as over twenty at a time—dealing with depression of the kind that makes getting out of bed, brushing your teeth, taking a shower seem pointless, and anxiety that would make your skin crawl if you sat too long with it, mind racing from one nightmare to the next, has kept Ginny from talking. Not just to me, to anyone.

Before I moved to Florida, ever since she learned to talk, we spent whole days and countless nights doing just that.

My daughter was not only my daughter, she was my friend, and I, hers. We shared everything. Now, she is still the love of my life and my friend, but I don't take one moment we share, one thought, one memory, one word—and certainly not a sustained conversation—for granted. Before the onset of her illness, I never imagined a time when we wouldn't be able to talk. Now, midway through my life, halfway up a mountain I took for a hill, I can see clear to the bottom of "anything is possible."

But there was once a time, actually, still, most of our life together, when "anything is possible" meant—means—hope, gave—gives—us both energy and strength.

Not only do my daughter and I look alike, same small features, same smile, same curly hair, we both love to write and direct and act. From the time she was in the first grade, Ginny began writing plays and scripts for the videos she shot. She'd cast her plays and videos with the neighborhood children, her dog—Mr. Bojangles—or, worse case scenario, anyone who happened by (our mailman, the garbage men, the pizza delivery person), directing them all with very firm gestures, commanding them to perform as if they were paid professionals.

I'd stand nearby in our kitchen, listening, fixing the cast members' iced teas, paper plates filled with snickerdoodles or homemade chex mix, distributing the goodies whenever Ginny gave them a break. And sometimes, when

I thought she could take it, giving her just a little advice, like, "I don't think you should be so hard on them. I think they're just doing this for fun."

Ginny would frown. Turn on me immediately and say, "Well, that's their problem. A job's a job, and if they can't take theirs seriously then they shouldn't do it at all."

She'd handwrite copies of her scripts, sometimes twenty pages long, with illustrations. One time she stayed up all night, making ten copies of a twenty-page script, even one for Mr. Bojangles. At rehearsal the next day, with bags under her eight-year-old eyes, she placed Mr. Bojangles script under his paws and told him, in front of all the neighborhood children, completely serious, hands on her hips, grim look on her face, "That's yours. I stayed up all night making you a script, so don't mess it up."

Mr. Bojangles cocked his head sideways and looked up at Ginny. You could tell he knew she meant business. And, in fact, he did nail all his entrances and exits. Because when he wasn't acting in Ginny's productions, he was the recipient of Ginny's generous love, as much love as a dog could ever dream of, and as Ginny was fond of telling me and Blake when we questioned something Mr.Bojangles was doing, "He's not stupid, you know."

Chapter 13

B a t t l e f i e l d s

On Sunday, my visit with Ginny in the unit was even more discouraging. She fell asleep five times in two hours. I heard the words *schizophrenic* and *bipolar* used a dozen times in reference to her behavior. And her doctor did not even leave a message for me, no response at all to my request to speak with him.

After I visited Ginny, I spent the rest of the afternoon at Jake's, retrieving work-related voice mails, responding to them, and calling my reps to catch up on their Friday. None of them seemed to know what was happening with Ginny, seemed totally caught up with their own struggles to stategize against our competitors' lowballing, meet with the demands of decision makers without losing big contracts, and pacify the clients constantly violating restrictions while honking for more service than they'd had at the outset— so I helped them with their problems and said nothing about mine.

Jake and I went out for sushi at a tiny restaurant on Park Avenue in Winter Park. It was one of our favorite places. Jake drank a lot of sake and wound up singing while I drove us home.

Jake is not a good singer, but he's a natural songwriter. And when he drinks a lot, he spontaneously makes up rhyming lyrics to the songs playing on the radio, then he sings them off key at the top of his lungs. That night he was singing to Tim McGraw's "She's My Kind of Rain." Only Jake's version goes, "She drives me insane."

When we got back to his house, he fell asleep in less than an hour. I was actually glad. I needed to plan for the work week, to organize my thoughts and my days. I needed to pull myself together.

When I'd filled in my planner for two weeks, thought of every possible scenario I could encounter my first day back and generally exhausted myself, I got ready for bed and lay down next to Jake.

He turned toward me and mumbled, "Did you lock the door?"

I reminded him he'd locked and dead bolted it when we got home.

He said, "Good. That's what you should do. You should always keep your door locked. Your problem is you trust people."

On my way to work the next morning, I called the number Heidi had given me for Dr. Traynor five times. I got his answering machine three times and left three different messages. Twice, I hung up. The third message I left went something like this: "Dr. Traynor, this is Ginny Stockinger's mother, Haley Robbins. I've already left two messages for you and I have yet to get a return phone call. I don't know what you've been told or seen on any paperwork regarding what I do for a living, but I'm a sales manager for a waste management company. When our customers call me, and I get an average of about forty calls a day, it is about their garbage, not their children. And every day I return every one of their calls and try to help them. I'm calling you about my daughter, Dr. Traynor. The most precious human being in the world to me. And apparently you can't take one minute out of your day to return my phone call. I don't know who you have to answer to other than your patients, who are at your mercy, but I can assure you that if I ever did my job the way you do yours daily, I'd be fired on the spot. No questions asked. Now you tell me, Dr. Traynor, which is more important—picking up someon'e garbage or saving a life? I'm thinking with the way I do my job and the way you do yours, maybe we should switch. I'm certain I couldn't be any less caring."

When I arrived at work at 7:45, no one seemed to know anything about what Ginny had been through. Everyone, however, was in a panic because the CEO of the company had decided to pay us a "surprise visit" on his way to our south Florida operation.

Before Ginny's breakdown and subsequent hospitalization, before any of the events of the past few days, I might have been panicked too. It's funny how we have to experience actual crisis before we know what one is.

My regional sales manager, Andy, was already in the office when I arrived. He'd flown in on a red-eye. He told me about the abrupt calling of the managers' meeting.

I remained calm, asking him what he'd like me to present. I told him I assumed we'd just stick with the general business plan we'd made in January for all four divisions.

Andy seemed nervous, very unsure of himself and me, and rather than agreeing with me, he began formulating a presentation on the spot and asking me to type it up.

Then Richard, the general manager over operations and sales appeared in my doorway. He told me we'd be presenting our general business plan together and that I'd simply need to present the sales portion when it was my turn.

But when he left, Andy insisted we finish what we had started. So together we worked feverishly for the next two hours, pulling up numbers and organizing data. Even creating a whole new strategy, me wondering the entire time if this would not be viewed as a conflict of interests.

To understand a bit more how conflicted I was about Andy's plan, you must know part of Evergreen's structure was such that as sales manager for central Florida, I was forced to answer to two bosses at the same time. Richard was the general manager over operations and sales for central Florida. Andy was the Southeast regional sales manager.

The meeting was held at 11 that morning in the conference room. Richard introduced his staff to the CEO of the company, Hal, and he moved forward with the general business plan, talking about last year's Ebit (earnings before interest or taxes) vs. this year's Ebit, last year's budget vs. this year's budget, the goals we'd outlined, and the steps we would take to achieve them. Each step contained a specific time line. He wrapped up with saying he had full confidence in his team, but oddly he didn't ask one of us to speak. I assumed we were finished.

Then Andy spoke up and said how I'd be giving the sales presentation after lunch. There was some murmuring, but mostly people were just glad to get out of their chairs and stand up, and the focus shifted to where we'd go to eat.

I tried to be pleasant at lunch, sat at the table with the CEO and several of our staff. It turns out Hal is a runner as well, and we shared a few race stories. When we were returning to the office and I was alone, I checked my messages. No calls from the doctor, and I realized I had missed the morning call time to speak with Ginny.

Walking back into the meeting I remember feeling exhausted—less than mediocre as a mother, a sales manager, and a person. Part of the problem was I had an instinct that what I was presenting was not only superfluous but also unwelcome— turns out my instincts about the presentation were dead right.

After thirty strained minutes of presenting what Andy and I had put together in a very hurried fashion, there was silence in the room.

Then Hal leaned forward in his chair and stared directly at me. He said, "I could not be more disappointed. I came here to see what progress this team has been making. We have quite an investment in central Florida as I'd hoped this team realized. But what I've found is—this isn't a team at all. Hell, you all aren't even on the same page." He paused, and then fired at me. "Are you even working for this company? I feel I need to ask you that, because after that presentation, I don't want to assume anything. It seems the general business plan I thought you all worked on—that was submitted to me in print in January and today by Richard—is not your plan at all. That you have a wholly different plan, which seems at best disorganized and at worst ridiculous. I mean, you tell me. Whose team are you on, Haley?"

"Yours sir," I responded.

Hal scoffed, "Not mine, Haley. It's not my team. It's Evergreen's team. No, don't suck up to me after what you've done."

I was speechless. Humiliated, furious, frustrated beyond belief, but still—ever the optimist—waiting for Andy to speak up. I was sure he would explain that he was the one who insisted I make a separate presentation and then apologize for his misguidance, but there we sat in silence for what seemed like five minutes. Then Richard said, "Well, if you have no further comments or questions for us, Hal, I think we all need to get back to work. Are we all set here?"

Hal nodded and the meeting was adjourned.

Later that day, when Hal had gone, I was told by numerous regional and local staff members that Hal is famous for pulling such scenes. I was also told Andy should never have advised me to make a separate presentation apart from the business plan. Every member of the staff who was in the meeting—except Andy—came by my office to express how genuinely sorry for me they were. But I felt no comfort.

I felt numb. I could not have cried if it had been considered acceptable behavior. And of course it never would have been.

I worked the rest of the day on government bids, helped two of my reps with proposals they were writing, and updated the data base. And, as usual, I returned phone calls from angry customers we hadn't "picked up."

Andy never came back in to my office. And just as I hadn't known he was arriving, I didn't know he left. I worked until 7 p.m., and as I was locking up, Jake called. Everyone else had gone home at 5 o'clock and the sound of the phone startled me.

"Hey," I said.

"Straw," he answered. It was our standard exchange at the end of a work day, and it felt like a pillow to me now.

"When you coming over?" he asked.

"Soon," I said. "I'm leaving now."

"Hurry up," he said. "It's Ted's birthday tomorrow; we need to get him something."

"Okay," I said, "but I'm really tired, honey, and I'm hungry."

"I'll fix you something," he said, "after we get Ted's present."

"Okay," I said. "I love you."

"How's Ginny?" Jake asked.

"I didn't get to call her. We had a manager's meeting. The CEO was here today."

"Did you get a raise?" he joked.

I couldn't bear to tell Jake what had really happened. Not then anyway. So I said, "No...um...just business as usual."

Jake was silent for a long moment. I thought he sensed something was wrong, but if he did, he decided not to press me. When he spoke, he said, "Bastards. They don't appreciate you enough." Then he dropped the whole thing in favor of his current preoccupation about Ted's gift. "Okay," he said. "Well, get here as soon as you can. I want to get him a special kind of lighter, and the store's gonna be closed if you don't hurry."

"I'll be there in a minute," I said.

Jake snapped, "You're thirty minutes from here if you told me the truth that you just left."

I was tired. I didn't want to argue, so I said, "It's an expression, Jake."

"Yeh," he said. "Well, express your ass over here, right now!" And he hung up.

118

Chapter 14

A n y   P o r t   i n   t h e   S t o r m

The store where Jake thought we could buy Ted's lighter had gone out of business, but he found another place to buy it. As Jake snaked in and out of the traffic on I-4, my thoughts were on Ginny. Monday was not a visiting day at the unit, but I was looking forward to talking with her on the phone at the appointed "night call time." At the instant the time arrived, I interrupted Jake's running commentary on where else we could look for Ted's lighter, eagerly dialing the number at the unit. The attendant on duty told me that patient number 10461 was already in bed. He said he could not wake her up. What else…what else could go wrong that day?

I held the phone to my ear long after the attendant had hung up, willing a connection I couldn't make. I'd spent fourteen years never apart for more than three days from my daughter, and now I was being denied the privilege of speaking to her by a complete stranger.

At 9 o'clock that evening, Dr. Traynor finally called. Jake was in the kitchen fixing me manicotti. I was lying on the sofa, pillow propped behind my head, heels kicked off, sipping a glass of wine.

Dr. Traynor said, "Ms. Robbins?"

"Yes," I answered.

He said, "This is Dr. Traynor. I want to apologize for not getting back to you sooner. I appreciate your message…"

I interrupted. "Which one?" I asked.

Dr Traynor laughed. "That's good…um." He cleared his throat. "I can see you are a force to be reckoned with."

I didn't answer him.

"But, um, you're right. I should return all my calls. It's just that…well, it's not possible with my case load."

I really didn't want to hear him plead not guilty, so I said, "Let me get right to the point, Dr. Traynor. I certainly don't want to waste any more of your precious time. I apologize if what I'm about to say is repetitive, but the communication between you, the nursing staff at the unit, and me has been so poor, I feel I need to start from the beginning. First of all, my daughter is not mentally ill. She had a nervous breakdown one time in her life due to the stress she has been under with our move to Florida. She is a wonderful, creative human being with a good mind and a huge heart. She is not a juvenile delinquent, as I gather from all of the searching of belongings at check-in many of the children in the unit are. Prior to coming to the unit, she had never taken drugs. She does not drink. She does not smoke. She has never been a behavior problem. In fact, she was in a leadership program back at her old school in North Carolina. Now, I don't know what is going on in that place where I unfortunately took her to be treated for a breakdown, but in two day's time, I can't even recognize my daughter. She looks like a zombie. And the nurses are calling her schizophrenic and bipolar. I want you to know, Dr. Traynor, that if this continues, I will take my daughter out of that unit. I brought her in. And I will take her out. And no one will stop me."

I looked up to find Jake standing in the entrance to the living room, sipping his iced tea and listening.

Dr. Traynor cleared his throat. "Well, first of all, thank you for sharing more about Ginny. She is a very sweet little girl but very quiet. I'm glad to learn more about her, though she did tell me she was a tennis player."

"Is one," I corrected him. "A very good one."

"I'm sure she is," Dr. Traynor answered, while Jake stepped back into the kitchen. I could hear the oven door opening and smell the manicotti baking. It smelled like tomatoes, mozzarella, and basil melting together—and something else. Like someone cared about me. I closed my eyes and was grateful for the moment.

Dr. Traynor continued, "The truth is, Ms. Robbins, I have high hopes for your daughter. I've got her on a few different medications that I hope will stabilize her and from that point on, I think there is a chance she could be just fine. I really believe, as you've indicated, Ginny's condition may be partially due to some of the current stress in her life—the move, I mean—and her subsequent depression. I'm treating her with this in mind. My hope is we'll see some good results from the course of medication, but we must let the medication run its course. Now I've instructed the nurses to review the medications and the dosage levels with you just as you requested. And, of course, when and if I do make necessary changes in her treatment, you will be notified. Now, can I do anything else for you, Ms. Robbins?"

"Yes," I answered.

"What is that?" Dr. Traynor asked, obviously trying not to sound impatient.

"I'd like to meet you—in person. I really.... I mean, I can't believe so much of what has happened in these past few days, but most of all that I'm letting someone take care of my daughter whom I've never even met. It's just... this isn't the way I am. None of this is like me. I can't let you take care of my daughter when I haven't even met you. I mean, would you? Would you let someone you'd never met take care of your children?"

Dr Traynor cleared his throat again. "You make a good point, Ms. Robbins. And I can see how much you care about your daughter. She's very lucky to have you. But...um...I don't want to make promises I can't keep. Let me check my schedule, and someone will get back to you."

I could hear in Dr. Traynor's voice that he was not going to give me any more than that, so I said, "Thank you. And thank you for calling me back."

"Oh, you're welcome, Ms. Robbins." Dr. Traynor sounded relieved. He added, "You know my daughters are swimmers. Doesn't sound like they are on the level Ginny is with her tennis, but they enjoy it."

"That's nice," I said, trying to act like he was just another parent but utterly uninterested in searching for something more meaningful to say to this man who was engaging in social niceties while feeding my daughter mind-altering drugs. Finally—for Ginny, not for him—I added unenthusiastically, "I think it's important for kids to be involved in sports." That, at least, was truthful, though I could have cared less if it made him feel I'd accepted him or his idea of treating Ginny. I hadn't.

"Oh, absolutely— it's so important," he agreed. "Well, good night, Ms. Robbins."

"Good night, Dr. Traynor," I said, with my last ounce of civility.

Jake came back into the living room. He was carrying several cardboard boxes—some jewel size, a few shoebox size, and some shirt size with newspapers stacked on top.

He had a roll of tape ringed around his fingers and a pair of scissors.

"What's all that for?" I asked.

Jake knelt down on the floor in front of me, neatly arranging his supplies. Then he sat down, crossing his legs. "I'm wrapping Ted's present," he said, pulling the lighter from his shirt pocket.

I didn't say anything.

Jake chose the smallest box he had, a slender watch case with a dark blue silver embossed top. He smiled, tore a piece of newspaper off a page near his feet and wrapped the lighter in it. Then he placed it in the box. It fit perfectly and he smiled again. Then he glanced up at me.

"What?" he said, realizing I'd been staring at him. "You've never wrapped a small present in bigger boxes? But before I could answer, he said, "No I guess you don't know anything about little pleasures. Miss Regional Sales Manager."

I protested, "That is not true. And you know it."

Jake smiled, choosing a shoe-size box. "I know," he said. "I just like to make you mad."

I kicked him lightly with my toes, and he laughed. "Quit it," he said. "Pick on someone your own size."

In a few minutes, Jake had finished his masterpiece, and he took it into the kitchen, setting it on the table. Then he stood back from it admiring his creation. "Now," he said, to no one in particular, "this is what gift giving is all about. Not the gift. But the surprise. It's the element of surprise that we all need."

I thought of Jake's harshness earlier that day and compared it to the care he was taking with my dinner and the playfulness of the last few minutes, his insight far beyond his experience in life, and sighed.

Then I heard the key turning in the front door and I knew it was Ray, Jake's roommate, home from work. Ray is a big boy of a man with a baby face and the most beautiful curly brown hair I've ever seen. He's a musician at heart and a phone salesman by day. He'd be gone from the apartment many nights in a row, playing with a band or partying with friends, then he'd show up hung over or stoned, swearing he was going to change. Jake and I actually saw very little of him, but when we did spend time together, I loved being with Ray.

Jake and I would be sitting in the living room watching t.v., and Ray would wander in from his bedroom. He'd pick up on of his guitars, sit down beside me and strum a few chords. Then he'd drop his glasses down on his nose and give me his best Elvis impression. "I wrote this for you, baby," he'd say, breaking into some romantic chorus filled with highs and lows and all the angst between them. When he'd finished, I would applaud wildly, and Ray would jump off the sofa, thanking me Elvis style. "Thank you. Thank you very much." Then, Ray style, he'd stick out his tongue, flip me a bird, and say, "Don't even think I really care about you."

But Ray did care about me. And the last day we spent together, when Jake was out of sight, he told me "Take care of yourself, girl." Saying without saying he didn't believe Jake was going to.

Ray walked in and shut the front door. He winked at me, then called out to Jake in a feminine voice, "Honey, I'm home."

Jake wheeled around the corner of the kitchen with his hands on his hips, faking a frown. In his own best feminine voice, he said, "Well, you're late, dinner's burned, and I'm on the rag."

Ray laughed and Jake burst out laughing too. It was a routine I'd grown accustomed to. But I liked their Irish accent routines better.

Ray walked into the kitchen. I slid off the sofa and joined them. Jake pulled the oven door open again to check the manicotti.

Ray teased, "Look at lover boy being domestic." Then he broke into his falsetto, singing, "Here comes the bride...."

Jake let go of the oven door. It slammed shut. He turned on one heel to face Ray, and gritting his teeth said, "You wanna sing soprano for the rest of your life, you keep that up."

Ray laughed in his face and Jake broke into laughter too. He dropped one of his wrists and said in an effeminate voice, "Okay, sweet britches, I'll leave you two alone." He batted his eyelashes at Jake, then headed for his bedroom, throwing kisses.

Jake said, "Yeh, you'll think sweet britches when I give you a wedgie."

Ray squealed from his bedroom, "Oh, you beast!"

Jake laughed. Then he took the manicotti out of the oven and shut it off. He asked me, "Fix me some more iced tea?"

I groaned. "Baby, I'm starved," I said, "can I....," but before I could ask him if I could get a bite to eat first, he turned on me and said, "That's nice. I fix you dinner and you can't even pour me a glass of tea?"

I protested, "I thought you meant *fix* it, like a whole pitcher."

Jake rolled his eyes. "You know I don't let you fix my tea. You don't make it right."

I didn't say anything. My head was aching with hunger. I couldn't even remember what he had wanted in the first place.

"Forget it," Jake said and stomped off to his bedroom, slamming the door behind him. I set my empty wine glass down and ran after him.

I found Jake lying on his side on the bed with his back to me, holding his pillow over his head. I shut the door and kneeled down beside him on the bed, putting my arms around him. I said, "Honey, I didn't mean to make you mad. Thank you for fixing me dinner. I'll go get your tea, right now, okay?"

But Jake didn't answer me or move.

"Honey," I said. "Jake? Please don't be mad. I could feel my face getting warm and the tears coming. I said, "I had such a long day, baby. I miss Ginny so much, and I'm just tired and hungry." I slipped my hands down around his small waist. "Jake?" I was crying now. "Jake, don't be mad."

Then I could hear Jake chuckling into the pillow. Suddenly he threw his pillow aside, grabbing me in his arms and pulling me to him. He said, "I got you!"

"Stop it!" I protested, trying to break loose. "Don't scare me like that!" I started crying again. Jake tried to hold my face in his hands but I turned away. "Don't" I said. He kissed me softly on the cheek. Then he pulled me into his chest. "I got you," he whispered, as if I were dangling from a ledge.

Jake's left hand was still completely bandaged from his accident, but he handled me easily. Before I knew it my skirt was up around my waist and my panties were on the floor. And before I could take another breath, Jake was in me.

I started to tell him, "Let's wait until we eat," but before I could, Jake was finding new ways to fill me, and I wasn't hungry anymore.

Chapter 15

F o r   B e t t e r   a n d   F o r   W o r s e

Ginny has grown to love Beethoven. Really all classical music. But Beethoven is her favorite composer. I watch her eyes as she listens to his various symphonies. They seem to change from light to dark depending on the rhythms and sounds she is hearing. Her face becomes more relaxed. I wonder how much research if any has been done on the healing effect of music for those who hear voices. Then a voice comes to me which tells me there has been research done about stimulants other than drugs. Very thorough research by one man. A lone runner in his field. A trailblazer only a few have had the heart, sense, and guts to follow.

In his book *Toxic Psychiatry* Peter R. Breggin writes, "The thought processes that get labeled schizophrenia require higher mental function and therefore a relatively in tact brain. No matter how bizarre the ideas may seem, they necessitate symbolic and often abstract thinking. That's why lobotomy 'works': the damage to the higher mental centers smashes the capacity to express existential pain and anguish." He adds, **"It's also why the most potent psychiatric drugs and shock treatment have their effect."** [5]

Here's what I wonder. Is it possible Beethoven's music is helping Ginny come back to life? That after all the negative effects the drugs have had on her, literally dulling her senses and ability to express herself, she is reaching out to Beethoven to communicate what she cannot? That her doctor and counselor and I poke and prod, day in and day out, trying to get her to respond to us, to life, and after all is said and done, it is Beethoven who reaches my daughter. His light enduring touch, the key.

§

It was Tuesday, April 8, 2003. Ginny had been in the unit four days. She'd missed two days of school and two days of tennis already, and I knew I needed to call Whispering Pines and tell them something; I just didn't know what.

I called on my hour drive into work that morning. It turns out, I needed nearly an hour to navigate their voice-mail system. I was given quite a variety of options to choose from, different departments, different reason codes: one for sickness, one for tardiness, one for transfers, one for withdrawals, one for doctors' appointments, one for early dismissals, one for field trips—everything but nervous breakdowns. No code for that, I'm afraid. No code if your child is absent due to the fact that he or she is in a behavioral unit. But, as I later found out, the school certainly could have used one.

A growing number of kids at Whispering Pines are spending time in the unit and many are on medication. When I finally reached Ginny's school counselor, she told me I was not to worry about Ginny's falling behind in her schoolwork, because the school and the behavioral unit have a program in place for students like Ginny. She said Ginny would be attending classes at the unit and receiving credit for her work, so when she returned to school, she would not have the additional pressure of catching up. The counselor went on to say how successful the program had been on reducing stress level associated with these students returning to their regular school schedules and once again assured me I did not need to fill out any paperwork or communicate with Ginny's teachers or coach—that everything would be taken care of.

I thanked the counselor at least three times and hung up, breathing a sigh of relief. It never occurred to me until I began my research at the bookstore how disturbing the information she gave me is. That there are so many kids at this one school with mental problems they have a joint educational system set up with a behavioral unit? That a normal day for the school nurse at Whispering Pines didn't so much involve treating flu bugs, cuts and scrapes, and an occasional broken bone, but administering drugs to all the mental patients? Unbelievable. But true.

At work, everyone had recovered from the CEO's visit. It was business as usual, picking up garbage. Once again, I felt relieved that a bit of weight had been lifted. I'd spent the night before, while Jake slept peacefully beside me, wide awake, once again, this time worrying about my job. A couple of times he did wake. Mostly because he could feel my arrow-tense body when he tried to curve into me. He put one of his large hands on my hips and turned me to him. Then mumbled, "Come here. Where have you been?" kissing me gently, then falling back to sleep.

The truth is, having learned from my father's experience, I'm not a worrier. In fact, most of my friends and family would say I could stand to worry a little more than I do. But mostly I think I've got some convincing arguments against worrying at all. And the fact remains, I almost never worry.

That night after the CEO's visit was a notable exception. I truly felt after Hal had blasted me in the meeting and Richard hadn't spoken to me after and Andy had escaped without a word, that my job must be on the line. And I never needed to keep a job more. I had no idea what the total cost of Ginny's hospitalization would be or her emergency care, but I knew it would be expensive and that I desperately needed the insurance my company provided.

I didn't know it then, but I was in for another shock when I checked my mail at the condo on Thursday. Just a week after I'd taken Ginny to the emergency room at Willow Pond, the bill from them for what my insurance didn't cover arrived—3,800 dollars. I dropped to my knees at the mailbox. What I didn't know was that was only the beginning. That Ginny's medical care costs for the next six months would soar to 60,000 dollars, only part of which my company's insurance would pay. And that part I would literally have to beg for.

Over the weekend, I'd brought some clothes and shoes over to Jake's. His place had become home to me. I even hated spending the little time I spent at my condo gathering outfits for the week.

The new home I'd tried to create for Ginny and me was filled with ghosts now. I'd walk into the bathroom and hear Ginny's screams or I'd go to get something out of her closet, something she'd asked me to bring to the unit and see her sitting in the floor like she used to, crying.

After Ginny told me she didn't feel safe there, it would never feel like home again. My only home was with Jake.

I'd created a shopping and delivery routine for Ginny's meal requests. I shopped at the grocery store by Jake's, which was also close to the hospital, and I delivered nearly a week's groceries during Sunday's visiting hours. Most of the vegetarian items were small and neatly packaged, so her food only took up one shelf in the refrigerator.

The staff was cooperating with me about using their refrigerator and freezer, and they were even taking extra time to help Ginny fix meals she could eat. As odd as this may sound, Ginny and I had developed a new way of life. She was living in a behavioral unit. I was living with Jake. We both had found a way to survive.

By mid-afternoon on Tuesday, I was beginning to feel grounded again, like things were under control. My top salesperson, Carson, had sold a huge front-load account. My inside sales rep, Marlene, had gotten caught up on all the entries into our data base, and my sales coordinator, Brianna, had scheduled several promising networking events for potential business later in the week. Things were looking up.

Tuesday night was a visiting night, so I was excited about getting to see Ginny. I'd talked to Jake, and he was planning to work a little later, so I could visit with Ginny and Jake and I could have dinner together later. Everything was fine I told myself.

Then my cell phone rang. It was the main number of the unit. I was sitting in my office alone, and I quickly got up to shut the door. The call was from Hope, a counselor who'd been assigned to work with Ginny. Sometimes when I think back on those days, I can't help but wonder at all of the ironies—the whole idea of Hope calling me. Just what I needed. Or so I thought.

She asked if I could meet with her when I came for my visit that night, and though I was eager to learn anything I could from those who were working with Ginny and to help them with whatever I could, I was disappointed, even irritated, that such sessions had to be scheduled during visiting time with my daughter. After all, I hadn't gotten to speak with Ginny or see her the whole day before, so in slightly different words, I told Hope this. I asked her if I couldn't come another day, like tomorrow, when there were no visiting hours.

Hope's response was curt, her tone business-like—with no promise at all. Her words sounded like they were being typed rather than spoken. She said to me, "Ms. Robbins, do you want to cooperate with us or not? I am trying to communicate with both your daughter and you, but if you don't have time for me, I'll just work with the other thirty parents Dr. Traynor wants me to see."

"No," I said, my stomach twisting with sudden alarm. "No, I'm sorry. I…um…I just miss my daughter, and I know how important it is to her that we spend time together. That's all. I didn't mean to be difficult. And thank you, thank you," I heard myself saying in a voice that sounded like a coward of a stranger, for wanting nothing more, I reminded myself, than to see my child. But I kept it up, "Thank you, Hope, for working with her," I said. " Thank you. I'll be there at 6:30 this evening, and we can talk, just…um…if you can make sure I get to see Ginny too…for a little while?" I added, not believing I made the request into a question that sounded like an apology.

"Certainly," Ms. Robbins. "That won't be a problem," said Hope in a tone that clearly told me it would be. "So, we'll see you at 6:30 then?" she asked, as if she thought I might change my mind.

"Yes, I'll be there. I'll be there," I reassured her.

My meeting with Hope, could I not have predicted it?—was a disaster. I think the fact that I'd initially tried to reschedule our meeting was preying on her mind, and it didn't help that I was completely agitated going into the conference.

Even after Dr. Traynor had assured me the staff would go over Ginny's medications with me, when I arrived that evening, I had to request once again that they do so. And when they did, they rushed through the names of the drugs, their purpose, and the dosages, as though I had a medical degree in psychiatry. The review went something like this.

Ms. Robbins, Dr. Traynor currently has Ginny on three types of medication. The first is Clonapin, which basically is a drug used to calm her, make her less anxious. She is also taking Paxil, which he hopes will stabilize her moods and help with depression, and then there is the Seroquil. This medicine is an anti-psychotic. It is used to treat the voices. Let's see (a glance at Ginny's chart)...dosage levels right now are... it looks like 1200 milligrams a day—that is, administered in the evening—of the Seroquil. Then in the morning she gets...60 milligrams of the Paxil and 20 of the Clonapin.

"I see," I said, seeing nothing, but hearing loudly the words "which he hopes..." the doctor "hopes," not that Paxil *will* stabilize, but that "he hopes...." But I knew it would be futile to point out the thing about hope, so instead, I said, "And for how long will this continue?"

"Until Dr. Traynor changes her dosage levels," was the response delivered in a tone that said *what other possible answer to that question could any reasoning person have anticipated!* What essentially they had said, it occurs to me now, is *the dosage will remain the same until it changes.*

But at that moment all I knew was that I was determined not to be intimidated. "Well," I said, "Isn't this a lot of medication? I mean, wasn't this just for like the initial crisis stage?"

"Dr. Traynor will be the judge of that, Ms. Robbins," was the quick response, delivered mechanically, as if the speaker had practiced.

I wasn't going to let it go that easily though, and I'd done some practice myself. "What research has there been into the use of these medications in treating children?"

This time the answer sounded less programmed—there was more than a hint of offense: "Ms. Robbins, Dr. Traynor is a board-certified, highly qualified doctor, who is recognized as one of the foremost authorities on mental illness in the country. If you have any more questions about the course of treatment for your daughter, you will need to speak with him!"

§

But I already had answers to my questions. At the time I didn't know any more than I'd been told about the medications, but I knew about language. If you are certain of an outcome, you don't use the word "hope" in speaking of it. Not "the doctor *hopes* Paxil will," but Paxil *will*. In a word added or left out there is often a universe of difference. Briefly, the answer to my question about the medication levels being excessive was and is "Yes." And no. No— none of the medications Ginny was being given have been tested for their specific effects on children.

In his book *Toxic Psychiatry*, Peter Breggin, M.D. writes of the Federal Drug Administration's action and stance on psychiatric treatments,

> In general, the FDA has done little to monitor or control the use of psychiatric technologies or to highlight their damaging effects. Mostly the FDA lends authority to the use of psychiatric drugs by approving them, and in the case of psychosurgery, it gives tacit legitimacy by not even investigating it. The public is lulled into believing that regulatory agencies are busy at work protecting them. Furthermore, as we've seen in regard to Prozac and Zanax, FDA approval of a drug misleads the public into thinking that thousands of patients have been tested in controlled studies for months or years, when in reality a few hundred are tested for a few weeks. Example: The FDA controlled trials for Clozaril [a drug another psychiatrist later suggested for Ginny's treatment], an extremely brain-disabling and sometimes life-threatening drug, lasted only six weeks.[6]

My reading on this subject further revealed that to date, there have been no tests or trials done on children under the age of sixteen using any of the drugs that have been prescribed for Ginny's treatment. The more I read, the more disturbing the picture becomes. Of the paradoxically impotent power of the American Psychiatric Association, Dr. Breggin writes that it " **represents more than thirty five thousand of the approximately forty-thousand American psychiatrists.**"[7] The drug companies provide the backbone of financial support for APA and for most of organized psychiatry." [8] Breggin writes, "according to its annual reports published each Ocotober in the American Journal of Psychiatry ,15 to 20 % of APA's total revenue has come from drug company advertising." [9]

Sometimes when I'm reading, I am conscious of my eyes being painfully dry from a habit developed during my first days of research in the bookstore— not only did I read for long periods without blinking but also found myself, when I couldn't bear another word, suddenly feeling how wide my eyes had grown, the lids unnaturally pulled back, brows raised in a way that must have made me appear bedeviled to anyone who might be looking at me. And sometimes, when I couldn't read another sentence, I'd close my eyes and berate myself for being even half a second among the naïve believers in a medical profession in which doctors simply could not be influenced by anything other than the need to heal. Forgetting the obvious—that doctors are human and that the need for money is powerful.

I guess it is that every profession has its share of unscrupulous people, another share of silent people who recognize the wrong but can't summon the courage to speak against it, and those like Dr. Breggin—unfortunately in a small minority—who will speak whatever the cost. In *Toxic Psychiatry*, Dr. Breggin recaptures, in one passage, a debate he participated in.

On April 17, 1987 (ironically the year Ginny was born), Dr. Breggin appeared on the Oprah Winfrey Show. He was debating Dr. Fink, at the time president-elect of APA, which was drug-company funded. The debate was another of those wide-eyed moments of reading for me and well worth writing down:

Dr. Breggin: Millions of dollars are being pumped through the Psychiatric Association by the drug companies.

Dr. Fink: No. I can't deny that we get millions of dollars of support from the drug companies.

Dr. Breggin:Your scientific meetings are funded by the drug companies.

Dr. Fink: I don't—that's irrelevant. That's irrelevant.[10]

"I think not, Dr. Fink," I said out loud, as I wrote the word *irrelevant* the second time. And then, noticing someone nearby staring, to myself I said, *I think there has rarely been any circumstance so relevant. Love your name, though. Know you didn't choose it, but I "Fink" it chose you.* So many ironies...

§

I met with Hope in "the classroom" at the unit while Ginny waited on the sofa outside. I sat in one of the students' chairs—Hope, at the teacher's desk.

Hope is a pretty woman with long dishwater blonde hair, multiple pierced ears, and an athletic build. She was sporting some sort of tattoo on her chest, exposed by her loosely fitting white smock. I couldn't make out what it was without staring at her breasts, so I decided to live with the mystery.

Hope is a very intense person, who took to grinding her pretty white teeth and shifting the position of her jaw whenever she seemed uncomfortable with my answers.

We talked a little about Ginny's breakdown, but fairly quickly she shifted into telling me Ginny was having a good deal of difficulty with school. She said she was falling asleep during her classes and that the teacher was requesting, on a regular basis, she be removed from the room.

Hope then forged ahead to ask me if I'd started thinking about the process I'd have to go through to qualify Ginny as disabled and finally spoke briefly about two educational programs Florida offers for those who simply can't return to school.

I was trying to be patient. I kept telling myself, "This woman is young. It's her job. She doesn't know Ginny. It's not her fault."

But I looked up at one point and saw Ginny staring through the window at me. Her large open innocent eyes saying, "Stick up for me, Mom! Tell her who I am." And so I did.

I let Hope know who Ginny is—a bright, beautiful, imaginative, sensitive child, who had difficulty adjusting to a huge move away from all she knew and loved. Then I said, "There is no way, no chance in hell you are going to talk me into believing my daughter is disabled. You don't even know her. I've been with her all my life. You've met with her a couple of times in two days."

Hope cleared her throat. "Ms. Robbins, can I be frank with you?"

"Absolutely," I said. "I don't have any problem with the truth. It's this place that does. It's this place that is putting labels on my daughter."

"Ms. Robbins," Hope interrupted, "I've worked with a lot of children since I've been here at the unit. Fifty a month, six hundred a year, eighteen hundred in the past three years, and I've never seen a case as bad as your daughter's. She is...non-responsive."

I stood up and shoved my chair aside. "You want a response? I'll give you a response." I stepped toward her, gritting my teeth. "You and that doctor you work for are drugging my child. You are not helping take care of her as you should, you are not treating her as it's your job to do, you are simply drugging my child. In massive amounts. Amounts an adult couldn't tolerate. And then, I pointed my index finger at her, "You have the nerve to report to me she is the worst case you've seen in years. What was it you said—'unresponsive'?" I was standing over Hope by now. Fists planted on her desk. "How about we go to the nursing station and pick up a few bottles of Ginny's pills? Then I give you some. My treat. No charge. And after a few hours, why don't we chart how responsive you are? You know? Just for comparison's sake!"

I was leaning toward Hope now, and she was pushing her chair farther back. Wide-eyed, she said, "There is no need for us to do that Ms. Robbins. You need to calm down. Now, I will record your concerns about Ginny's medication and dosage and present them to Dr. Traynor, and he will take it from there."

I smiled. "Not up for taking the medication you're so eager to cram down my daughter's throat?"

Hope looked past me as she spoke. "That is hardly necessary," Ms. Robbins. "I am not the one who needs help."

I stared straight into Hope's eyes and told her, "That is debatable."

Outside the classroom, I found Ginny waiting for me on the couch, staring blankly down the entrance hall. I covered her with my arms, praying she had not heard Hope or me. And that she would stop hearing the voices. That I would somehow figure out a way to truly help her. Praying.

If I had a clearer vision or maybe just a better view, I could tell you how much of what I've lived was coincidence and how much fate. But I don't. So I'll just put it out there and leave it for you to decide.

I was born with the ability to express myself—underwater, playing charades, in front of an audience of thousands, behind the wheel of my car, on a stage, in the bedroom—I have no trouble letting anyone know how I feel or telling myself.

When I was a teenager, I used to stand in front of my mirror—for hours—having imaginary conversations, with boyfriends, girlfriends, teachers, Bobby Sherman, Robert Redford. Robert Redford once asked me to dinner. Yes, he did. At least that's what I heard. From the mirror.

Anyway, the point is, I have no trouble expesing anything, which is good, because for the past year and a half I've spent whole days defining my daughter to others. At the unit—telling the staff who she is. Past her breakdown and medication. When she is whole. How she knows what you are made of by the sound of your voice. Trusts the sun and the sunmaker, her dog Mr. Bojangles, more than those certified to treat her. Comes here to me and this world by way of a message from the sunmaker, that we need to change. Feel our strengths instead of imagining our weaknesses.

§

My daughter can express herself too—when she trusts. And unlike me, with a Grand Canyon of emotions, her expression always fits. Feels like a favorite pair of slippers. Here's one of my favorite of her expressions.

Dear Aunt Faith,

The stars are so close on the mountain tonight, I told Mommy I might be able to reach one for her. Mommy said it was sweet of me to think of giving her a star but that maybe it was best to leave the stars in heaven. When I asked her why, she said that we were lucky because we had so much light in our lives, but that there were lots of places on earth where people needed all the stars God put in the sky.

Thank you for sending me Sophie's World for my birthday. Ive read nearly a hundred pages already. It's fun reading about someone my age who likes to think about things as much as I do. I love the way the philosopher sends Sophie letters with questions. I love thinking about the questions: "Who are you? Where does the world come from? What does it take to live a good life? Do you believe in Fate?" 10 I wonder what you think about those things since you are a real philosopher. Mommy says you won't have time to write me back now because

138

you are studying so hard, but maybe when you get back from Pennsylvania we can talk?

Tomorrow, my friend Winnie is coming over. I've already planned what we're going to do. First we'll be writing a play about two friends who get angry with each other but then realize they love each other too much to be angry. Then we'll jump on the trampoline until we get so tired our legs are wobbly and we laugh and fall down together. When I'm by myself on the trampoline, I like to jump and spread my legs and arms out wide like I'm hugging the whole world. Anyway, then I'll tell Winnie about the book you sent, and I know she'll ask to read it too, so I'll run in the house and get it and we'll lie on the trampoline with the tops of our heads together, like we've done forever, and we'll take turns reading chapters to each other. I won't mind to hear the part I've already read again.

I play tennis almost every day. I'm getting pretty good. I know I am, partly because Mommy says so but mostly because for a long time I couldn't hit the ball where I wanted to and now I can. Do you ever wonder about when people first are able to speak another language without thinking about it□well, that is, without having to plan every word? Anyway, I was thinking maybe there's a time like that when you learn a sport too, and your body sort of starts to think by itself. I don't actually remember when tennis started to get like that for me, but it's amazing to think about when Mommy used to toss the balls to me really soft and sometimes I'd miss, and now I can hit a ball coming really hard, like Daddy can hit it, and put it anywhere in the court. I hope I don't sound like

I'm bragging. I don't mean too. I just think it's amazing and kind of mysterious what a person's body can do.

I miss you. Mommy says when you come home from school in August, we can have a big party. She's planted lots of flowers that you'll love. Sometimes Mommy and I walk together around the yard holding hands, and she tells me the names of everything she's planted. Sometimes I remember the names, but mostly I love to walk with her and listen to her talk. Mommy's a character. She can always make people laugh, even when they're sad. I called out to her just now and asked her to tell me some of the flower names again, and she called back and said: "Bachelor's button, sweet William, nasturtium, fox glove, lily of the valley." I guess you know how much she loves her flowers. As much as I like writing plays!

Maybe when you come back, Winnie and I will have the play about friends ready and we can put it on for everyone.

Don't worry about writing me back. I know about having to study hard. School is wonderful, but sometimes people don't understand that you have to spend a lot of time on homework. Winnie gets mad sometimes when I tell her she can't come over because I've got to study. But right now it's summer, of course, and I'm giving myself a little time to rest.

I'll write again soon. I'm glad Mommy told me to leave that star. Maybe you are looking at it right now. Wouldn't that be amazing?

Love,

Ginny

Chapter 16

R i d i n g   W a v e s

I spent so much time on the phone after Ginny was hospitalized that it began to feel like all I did was return messages from family, friends, Ginny's coach, the unit staff, the insurance company, and my reps. My only break in this routine was the time I spent with Jake.

He would take me on a motorcycle ride or to a movie I wanted to see. He'd find a new restaurant we hadn't been to or call up Brent and his fiancée Lisa and we'd go over to their place to play Scrabble. I thought many times during those days about how scared I'd been that when Jake found out about Ginny he would leave me. When the real truth is, he was by my side always.

Maeve came back a week after she left, bringing more bad news. Among her many accomplishments Maeve is a captain in the army reserves, and while she was helping her parents pack and move to Texas, she'd gotten "the call." She didn't have specific orders yet, but she knew she was going to have to serve sometime in the very near future, either in Iraq or the States.

My new home no longer felt like home, and my new family was falling apart. Ginny wasn't with me, and I felt we were both at the mercy of her caregivers in whom I had no faith. Maeve was leaving. The world was at war. I'd never been one for enumerating losses, but during Maeve's call, I had this sudden memory of a line from a poem Faith told me had haunted her forever. "The center cannot hold..." this poet says, describing a world gone awry.

But during Maeve's call, I could also see Maeve and me in our happiest hours together and was reminded, through those recollections of our friendship, how much my whole philosophy of life centered on gathering everything I could from the precious beautiful moments offered us. Long before the catastrophies of Winter Park; in fact, long before Ginny was born, I was a person who believed with all her heart in the idea of *carpe diem*. And so it was that in spite of Maeve's news, I turned to the moment. She was back, and there would be Sauce Sunday to look forward to. And even a simple joy like that was a tremendous comfort.

In fact, Maeve hadn't been home for more than two hours before Ted was calling to make plans, and I brightened a little. I knew it wouldn't be the same without Ginny, and I would have to leave the group for visiting hours and come back, but we'd make the best of the time we had together. That was what those days were about for all of us. Making the best of what we had.

Ted came over around noon on Sunday and started the sauce. Then Jake arrived. Maeve followed. Jake and Maeve headed for the pool, and I drove to the hospital.

Ginny was more awake than usual and we had a good visit. She'd painted me a butterfly in her craft class, and I hugged her and held it to my heart.

By the time I got back to my condo, it smelled like Ted's sauce, and Ted, Jake, and Maeve looked sauced as well. Maeve had brought over a couple of coolers of beer and by the time I arrived, they were into the second cooler. I slipped into a bathing suit and joined them by the pool. As soon as I rounded the privacy fence between the back of my condo and the pool, Maeve saw me. She grabbed the bottle of Chardonnay she'd brought for me, waving the bottle in the air and doing a little dance of greeting as she poured me a plastic cup full. "Hey babe," she sang, "we've been missing you!"

Ted and Maeve and I sat on the edge of the pool with our drinks while Jake swam around in circles, popping up every now and then to splash me whenever he thought I was getting too serious.

Maeve asked, "So how was she today?"

Jake had swum to the edge of the pool near us to rest. He propped his elbow on a rim of tile, to hold his bandaged hand in the air—the chlorine must have soaked into the gauze because he was wincing as he looked at me, or else he was anticipating I'd get gloomy trying to answer Maeve's question. His other hand was half way under water and cocked, ready to splash me.

I scolded him. "You should probably not even have had that hand in the water and you certainly shouldn't be splashing me."

Jake deliberately dipped his good hand deeper into the water and splashed me. Ted and Maeve and Jake all laughed. I stood up. "Jake!" I said.

"Don't tell me what to do, and you won't get splashed," Jake said.

I sat back down, dangling my feet near him.

"Don't tell me what to do?" I said. "Oh my god, you sound like a little boy."

Jake moved closer to me, positioning himself between my legs and grabbing my thighs. He dropped his voice about an octave and said, "I'm a big boy and you know it." Then he moved in closer and started kissing me. Maeve laughed even louder. Then she said, "Oh stop it you two…." And when Jake kept kissing me… "Oh, my god. It's too early for that."

"Get a room," Ted jeered.

Then Jake and I stopped kissing and started laughing. He was holding my neck with both hands.

"Don't splash me again," I told him with mock anger.

"Oh yeh?" Jake said. "What if I do? What if I accidentally…just a little bit…." Jake dipped his left hand in the water, flicking water on me, "what then?"

I stared straight into the blue of his eyes. "Honey," I said, "Nothing is an accident with you."

Jake blushed and smiled.

Ted coughed and managed to say, "I don't know about that. Have you checked his hand out lately?"

Maeve laughed. Jake's smile turned to a frown.

I defended Jake. "Cheap shot," I said. "Two more and you're out."

"What?" Ted said, throwing up his hands. "Hey, you can't kick the cook out."

"All right," I said, laughing. "Don't make me choose between the boyfriend and the cook."

Jake winked at me. "I got your cooking right here."

Maeve said, "That's it. Jake wins. He's the boyfriend and the cook. You're out, Ted."

And we all laughed.

I hadn't forgotten Maeve's question, and I started to tell them about Ginny's butterfly, but then I felt a little breath of a breeze brush my chest and arms, and looking up, I noticed the leaves of the live oaks beyond the terrace of the pool stirring and had the sudden memory of Ginny in a dance recital when she was four—the light on her long skirt, her face intent with her effort, maybe too intent for one so young, and suddenly the laughter seemed a thing out of place and the time not right to share a treasure of that kind.

I woke from the memory to hear Jake talking us into getting in the pool. I dropped in, giving the memory up to the cool water. Jake raced me across the pool, and when I lost badly, Maeve tried to make me feel better by complimenting my style. Ted and Jake threw one of Ginny's huge plastic multicolored beach balls back and forth until Jake's good hand was tired.

Later, after showers and dry clothes, we ate in candlelight to the music of Natalie Cole, which Jake put on just for me, and while we were listening to her, I started asking my "famous questions," as Maeve called them.

I started with, "What is the ideal woman?" asking no one in particular.

Ted leaned forward and poured more wine in my glass. "Be more specific," he said.

"Okay," I said. "I mean, if you had to describe the qualities you admire, respect, and love most in a woman, what would they be?"

Maeve interrupted. "Can I choose a man?"

I laughed. "Yes. Yes you can," I said. "But I'm going to describe the perfect woman."

Ted growled, "Yeowza, all right, you go girl."

Jake laughed.

"Okay," Ted said, rubbing his hands together, "the perfect woman. Geeza wheeza. I gotta go with a blonde."

"Yep, gotta go with blonde." Jake agreed.

"And small, petite," Ted said, "I don't want any Anna Nicole Smith. She needs to be smart and honest and just…you know…a good person. Like my mom. Now that would be the perfect woman for me."

"What color eyes?" I asked, taking a sip of wine.

"Brown," Ted answered. "Can't trust blue or green."

Jake, Maeve, and I chimed in all at once, "Thanks."

Ted laughed. "No, no, I mean, I trust you guys. You guys are fine, but I just don't trust a woman, I mean, for me, that doesn't have brown eyes."

"Okay," I said, setting down my glass and turning to Jake, "What about you, honey, the perfect woman?"

Jake stuck both hands up in the air, "How dumb do you think I am?"

Ted and Maeve both laughed.

Jake put his hands down. "Skip me. I can't win on this one."

Ted mumbled, "I'm thinking you already lost."

Jake looked at him. "What?" he said.

"No, man, I'm just saying it's simple," Ted explained. "Your beautiful woman asks you who the perfect woman is for you—it's her, stupid. That's what you should have said."

Jake didn't say anything. He picked up his beer and took a long drink. Then he belched loudly, smiled, and announced, "The perfect woman for me is Brittney Spears, and if she walked through that front door right now, I'd ask her to marry me."

Ted frowned, "Yeh, well, you'd be asking the wrong woman, cause Brittney is a stupid, badly made-up overgrown girl. You, my boy, have an angel." Ted winked at me, then lifted his glass to toast the moment, and Maeve and I joined him.

Maeve said, "Here, here. To our angel of a host." The three of us toasted again, while Jake sat in silence.

Later that night, when we were in bed, Jake was not so silent. "Why'd you do that?" he asked me in his most annoyed tone. "Why do you have to analyze everything?"

"What?" I said, "What are you talking about?"

"We were having a perfectly good time," Jake said, "and you had to go and ruin it."

I was staring at the ceiling in Jake's room. "I was just having fun," I said. "Let it go."

"No," Jake said, turning to face me. "I won't let it go. You set me up. You made me look bad and you did it on purpose."

"Jake," I protested, turning toward him. "I had no idea what you would answer. How can that be setting you up?"

"Well, it is." Jake chewed a fingernail off and spit it out. "Or it was," he said. "You did. And by the way," he added, in a smug tone, "I was going to say you, until you made me so mad.... I swear I could...."

"You could what?" I asked innocently.

Jake looked at me. The blue in his eyes was turning slightly darker, which I have learned means his defenses are weakening. So I put a hand on his boxers. At first, he flinched, but then, instinctively, he moved closer to me, as I smoothed my hand over his bulging penis.

"You could what?" I teased, kissing him gently.

Jake groaned and kissed me hard. "I could tear you up, which is what I'm gonna do right now."

Like most men, Jake is fond of using testosterone packed words like "fuck" and "screw." This latest phrase, "tear you up" was a variation on the others. I've learned to live with them all. The truth is, no matter what Jake says, what he does, is make love.

At first, I protested a little. But my protests weren't real and Jake knew it. He slipped out of his boxers, then cradling me in his arms, turned my naked body over and mounted me. His baby skin covered me like the pillow part of a band-aid, while he parted me with his fingers. Jake guided his stiff penis into my soft folds, and when I started to come, he kissed my cheek while I shivered from his heat. The way he touches me inside out.

Jake smelled clean, like his soap. And he blew soft breaths into the hollow of my neck. We were so close, it was like we were one person, moving gently up and down. As if we were lying on a raft in the ocean, just past the breaking waves.

I was going to tell him how much I love him…that no man has ever gotten to me the way he does, but he found my spot again, and all I could do was moan, my heart in my throat.

Chapter 17

No   Choice

Go figure. The thing I was dreading most when I moved to central Florida—driving to and from work—became my solace. In the morning, Jake would kiss me good-bye, then drive away to the shop, and I would head for my favorite stop—Dunkin Donuts. There, I'd order my usual, a sour crème cake donut and black coffee, then I'd turn on my favorite country music station, press my foot down on the accelerator, and relax.   I had fourteen miles of central Florida traffic to sort out my life.

    In the midst of those nightmarish days, I'd find beauty in that drive. It isn't hard to do in central Florida, easily one of the most beautiful places in this country to live. There is green everywhere. All year round. Available to every aching or joy-filled heart in every imaginable shape, shade, and size– from the giant Loblolly pines with their high thick crowns of drooping branches to the lush ground cover of liriope. It is hard for me to pick what I love most about this place, but I believe it would be its green. Everywhere– kissing you with hope. Never giving you a chance not to want to live.

The place where I was born and now live, Asheville, North Carolina, is definitely not green all year round, though my sister Faith has often told me I'm not fair in my descriptions. "Look at that row of holly trees and tell me what gives them their unique hollyness," she said to me one oddly warm January day when Ginny was a baby and we were strolling her, in a carriage my mother had saved from my childhood, around the neighborhood where Faith and I grew up.

Faith spoke in her best "philosopher's voice"—a voice so gentle and sad even in anger that Ginny told me once, "You feel like you accidently wore sneakers to a church wedding if you disagree with her, Mommy." Ginny was right, but it didn't keep me from answering Faith back.

"I can tell you what doesn't give them their 'hollyness' and that's living here in a place where it rains and snows on the same day." So then Faith started to catalogue the beauties of our hometown. "What about all those magnificent magnolias on Haw Creek highway, and the white pines on the bank above our old house, and the rhododendron and laurel? You said you love the laurel."

I might as well talk to the wind as try to tell Faith why I don't like Asheville. I'll admit the hollies are beautiful, but the truth is there is probably that one row in all of Asheville amidst whole forests of huge oaks. In winter the long bare branches of these skinny giants spread like ganglia everywhere into skies that in an hour can turn from a haunting thin veil of chalky blue to smoky scud to violent amber. Faith's "magnificent magnolias" are scraggily even in summer and the pines are mostly trunk, having been brutalized by immemorial winters of winds in the Blue Ridge. And the rhododendron and laurel are almost entirely phenomena of wealthy neighborhoods and the forests along the Parkway, which I have the legs and lungs to run through and enjoy but which most of the city's residents never see. But Asheville is and will probably always be Faith's heaven on earth, so whenever she starts her lists of what she says I don't see, which I really do see…just differently, I've learned just to agree with her.

What I know for certain of Asheville is this: even within a day, its colors will change dramatically. In my lifetime, I've witnessed a deep snow in May and my brother wearing his bathing suit trunks on Christmas. And I have learned to count on nothing in Asheville. Except change.

Famous writers and artists have flocked to this place through the years. Here, facing the natural angst in their own sensitive souls and the adversity caused by so many abrupt changes in nature, they hone their skills, producing creations that simply don't happen in a place where it's always green. In one way, my sister Faith seems an anomaly in Asheville. Steady. No lover of change, she admits she has not had much adversity in her life. But there is this odd weight-of-the-world aura about her, like she feels guilty for her own good fortune. And wants to take on the burdens of others—everyone and everything, from the lives of her philosophy students to the bees that buzz in a space beneath her bedroom window every summer, "flying valiantly on wings too small to support their bodies," Faith says. "They make a home in the wall of our house," she told me one year, "and even though their constant drilling can't be good for the frame of the window and makes a bigger and bigger stain on the siding every summer, I won't let them come to harm—they are so intent on making a place for themselves."

When I remember my past two years living in Winter Park, I think of how peaceful this part of Florida is. How, no matter what, I could count on the sun shining and green surrounding me every day and what a blessing that was. How I'm not at all certain I could have survived, when Ginny's trouble began, living in a place where it snows in May.

I needed to make some more decisions and on those long drives to work, I found myself working through some of the hardest choices I've ever faced. Though I felt I could not even consider qualifying Ginny as disabled, I needed to think about how I would care for her once she came home.

Of course, there was always the option of us moving back to Asheville, a familiar place where we'd be surrounded by the love our family and friends, something Faith pointed out to me at least once a week after she found out about Ginny.

But I had many loves in Florida now, and as much as a garden needs light and water, I needed to find a way to stay in our new home and keep trying to build a new life. I reasoned I could get Ginny a part-time caretaker, someone who would pick her up from school, help her with her homework, make sure she took her medication, and was safe. It would have to be a nurse or someone at least with some sort of background in mental illness, but surely I could find that.

If we went home to Asheville, I'd lose my job and my insurance, and I'd be leaving Jake, so I quickly ruled that out. For the next two mornings on my drives to work I stayed on my cell phone, collecting information from the local available resources and my insurance company about in-home care. What I found was discouraging. My insurance company would pay up to a hundred dollars a day for in-home care by a licensed professional for only ninety days. When I checked on the current hourly rates for licensed health care professionals, I found the range to be from eighty to one hundred dollars an hour. It was time to find another option.

That is when I thought of John, Ginny's father. I had, of course, called John and told him about Ginny– what she was going through, what *we* were going through– and he'd offered to help in any way he could.

The reality was that John lived in San Francisco. He was working on a start-up company, and the funding he received irregularly from investors had to go back into the business. He was living on a very limited income with no financial means to help us.

But when I called him again and told him I hadn't been able to find any feasible alternatives for Ginny, he said he could come to Winter Park and help with her care, so I talked with Ginny and after rethinking all the options that weren't really options for anyone in my income bracket, I decided to ask Jake if it would bother him—actually, I asked if he thought he could live with John's moving in with me and Ginny for awhile to help out. Jake said it was fine. And once again, I felt we would all be all right. That all those I loved were trying to help me and Ginny and that if we worked together, Ginny would get better.

So John began making plans immediately to move to Florida. First he had to convince his business partners and investors that he could still play an active role in the company. Then he had to pack and make moving as well as storage arrangements. Then there was the little matter of a three-thousand-mile drive with his cocker spaniel Mischief, aptly named, as I was forewarned and would soon see first-hand.

John told me he would be on the road in a month. I knew then I'd have to come up with an interim plan for when Ginny was released from the hospital, but at least I was making some progress.

When I stopped by Duffy's that night to tell Maeve and Ted about John's coming, they were less than enthusiastic. Maeve got quiet. Ted asked if I'd talked with Jake about it. I told him Jake had said it was fine. Ted rolled his eyes and jiggled the ice in his rum and coke significantly.

"What?" I said. "He said it was fine."

Ted lifted his eyebrows. "What was he gonna say? I mean he knows you are trying to do what is best for Ginny by having her father come. But wait until..."

I must have looked anxious, because Maeve cut in and tried to soften Ted's skepticism. "He oughta know it's the only way she can care for Ginny and still keep her job. I mean, is Jake gonna quit his job to stay home with Ginny? What options does she have?"

"I know, I know..." Ted said, but his tone said what he knew had nothing to do with my need but with Jake's. He took a generous drink of his rum and coke, and then said matter-of-factly, "*I* know she's doing what's best, but you gotta face it guys. I mean, an ex-husband living with you? Come on. What guy is gonna put up with that?"

"What are you saying?" I asked Ted, as if I didn't know.

"I'm saying I hope it's not for long, cause I think Jake is just being nice for now—maybe he's even thinking it won't really happen. I mean I really don't think he wants your ex-husband living with you. That's what I'm saying."

Maeve seemed to have exhausted her supply of support in her brief defense because she was nodding now, and as soon as Ted finished, she said, "No guy I know would like it." I could feel my mouth quivering, something I'd rarely experienced and something Maeve had never seen, which is probably why she compromised and added, "But hey, I mean it's up to you, babe. You can just lay down the law. When hubby comes, just tell him, 'This is temporary. I'm doing what I think is best for Ginny. But eventually,' Maeve said, pausing briefly as she planned my speech to John for me, 'actually—as soon as possible—if you're going to stay and help, then you need to get your own place."

I had gotten the lip quiver thing under control by the end of Maeve's advice, and now all I wanted was someone to say things would work out. So I said, "That's good. I will. I'll tell him that."

But Ted wasn't finished. He pointed the rim of his rum and coke at me and said, "And you better start thinking about how you and Jake are gonna be together through all this. You got your daughter and ex-husband living with you; he's got a roommate… I'm telling you, it's not gonna be easy and…"

Maeve was looking at Ted now as if to signal him that I had been advised and he'd said enough. "If he loves her, it won't matter," Maeve said, protectively.

Ted looked right back at Maeve, undeterred by her eyes or her words. "Yeh," he said, "well, we'll see, won't we? I mean a lot don't matter when it doesn't matter. If you know what I mean."

Maeve and I both looked at each other in the same instant, puzzled as we often were by Ted's sudden riddles; then simultaneously, we said, "What?"

Ted rolled his eyes, as if anyone with good sense would have recognized what he just offered as something profound. But he reluctantly explained, "I'm just saying, everything's fine as long as no one rocks the boat. Doesn't matter if the boat's sides are not high enough or it's not the most comfortable ride or there's a good hole or two in it. But you start rocking it, and watch who bails. You know? It's like ex-husband in…boat's rockin' big time…lookout!…boyfriend overboard."

156

Maeve started giggling midway through Ted's analogy, and by the time he'd got to "ex-husband in," she was laughing loud enough to draw attention from people across the room. When she caught her breath, she said, "Thank you, Dr. Kinsey…or should I thank the bartender? I'm not sure who's talking here, you from some former life or your drink."

"Who's Dr. Kinsey?" said Ted, looking genuinely bewildered.

"I rest my case," said Maeve.

Then we all laughed. Ted and Maeve loudly—me, enough to keep from crying.

Chapter 18

Circle   of   Pain

Thursday night was group therapy night at the unit. It was a time for patients and their parents to come together and learn from each other in what the staff at the unit had described as "a controlled, nurturing setting."

This week would mark my second group therapy session with Ginny. I practically had to drag her to the meeting room. Last week, there'd been just a few of us at the meeting, apparently a week when there were more discharges than check-ins, and the counselor in charge kept focusing on Ginny. She must have asked Ginny three questions to every one she asked the others. At one point, I had to plead with Ginny to answer her, and when she didn't, I told the counselor Ginny had had enough questions for the evening.

But tonight we walked into the room and it was crowded with parents and patients. Ginny trailed behind me, gripping my right hand. I was so intensely aware of the pressure of her hand that it took me a moment to register a wet stinging sensation on the back of my neck. I turned around to find Andrew—who I had seen on other occasions and who had informed me he was the youngest patient in the unit—shooting spit wads at me through a straw. When he saw the disgust that I made no effort to hide, he laughed like a hyena, then screamed, "Gotcha, Ginny's mom!" I turned away from him and kept walking, pulling Ginny with me.

As we walked away from Andrew, the counselor whose tag read *Geena* reprimanded him. "Andrew, I told you never to do that again. Now go sit in the corner and take a time out." I didn't notice if Andrew obeyed, but I could hear his hyena laugh and then a fair impersonation of the counselor.

Meanwhile, I could see that more parents were squeezing themselves into the room and it was apparent no one had taken much trouble with arrangements to accommodate the crowd. Chairs that had probably been left from some other meeting were in a clutter in the middle of the room and there weren't enough for the patients, let alone the visiting parents. I was wondering if anything would be done when Geena finally requested that we get chairs that were against the walls and arrange those with the others into a circle.

Ginny sat down, ignoring the nurse's instructions. I looked at her, but her head had already dropped forward, her chin touching her chest—a picture that was becoming more familiar to me each day. I thought briefly of calling her, but I felt suddenly tired as if all the energy I could summon would have to go into moving a few chairs. So I did that, awkwardly dragging them into what was becoming, with help from a few other parents, the semblance of a circle.

When the circle had been formed and everyone was seated, Geena called the session to order. She said we would be working on self-love, as well as loving others.

Marcus, a young man with midnight black skin, orange tinted hair in tight braids close to his scalp, and a gap between his front teeth, laughed loudly. Geena told Marcus his laughter was not helpful, which seemed to make him laugh more. Then Marcus's mother, an ample black woman, wearing a pants suit something close to the tinting of her son's hair, turned to Marcus and said, "You shut up, boy, you hear me?– or I'm gonna whoop your black ass right here in front of all these white folks. Then we see who be laughing… mmhm, we see fo' sure."

So much for the nurturing, I thought. I looked around to see the reactions to Marcus's mother, but it seemed that each person in the room was inhabiting some other world; eyes were turned to the ceiling or the floor or to points in the distant corners of the room, as if no one had heard anything more than they were accustomed to, and it occurred to me then that maybe most were accustomed to much worse than Marcus's mother could deliver in a single speech.

Geena was asking us to introduce ourselves, and this did seem to bring a few pairs of eyes to focus on her. Some were hostile, some frightened, some sad, some vacant, some just bone weary. But everyone managed an introduction, after which Geena started around the circle asking her self-love question.

Now I knew how Jake felt about my questions. It was payback time, and I could feel myself begin to resist any answers, begin to formulate how I could appear cooperative and still keep from showing any of myself to this group of strangers for whom I had been unable to develop any feeling other than the vaguest sort of despair.

Geena began with a lanky thin teenaged girl with long chestnut hair and pale blue eyes. Her name was Natalie. Natalie was wearing plaid pajama bottoms and a man's white undershirt with no bra. When she finally spoke, she sounded like there was gravel in her throat.

Geena prompted, "Okay, Natalie, we'll begin with you tonight. Natalie, I want you to share with the group something you love about yourself. Or a couple of things. How ever many you would like."

Natalie said nothing. After a few moments, she stared at her mother, a tall thin woman who occupied the chair beside her but who did not seem connected with her daughter in any way other than that her eyes were the same pale blue. She had a scar on her left cheek. She did not respond to Natalie's staring. She, herself, stared at the school clock on the canary yellow wall in front of her with that look I said earlier made me feel people here were not really here at all.

Geena prompted Natalie again, "Now I know this isn't easy Natalie. We don't like to talk about ourselves, but just give it a try. Tell me something you love about yourself."

Natalie was still staring at her mother, and she seemed to be speaking to her when she finally mumbled in her gravely voice, "I like how I can hide from people."

Natalie's mother shifted her slender hips and smoothed a wrinkle out of her jeans. Her face seemed to be tightening with each word her daughter spoke.

Natalie finally looked away from her mother and up at the ceiling. Then she continued. "They don't even know it. They think I'm there but I'm not."

At this, Natalie's mother pursed her lips tightly, her jaw grew rigged and her chin pocked with anger. She frowned deeply. She did not look at her daughter, but suddenly released her lips and pulled them back so that her teeth were bared. She said, "We know where you are. You're here again for the second damn time in three months. It's no mystery, Natalie. We can all see where you are."

Natalie frowned just like her mother. "Shut up," she told her in an angry voice, her face still toward the ceiling.

Geena interrupted. "Mrs. Smith, if you would please wait until I ask you to speak. You will get a chance to speak, I promise, but right now, I would just like Natalie to answer."

Natalie's mother nodded, but the corner of her mouth nearest her daughter turned up into a smirk that said she had dismissed Natalie out of contempt and everyone else present as too stupid to see the games she had figured out her daughter was playing.

Geena said, "Natalie why do you love hiding from people?"

Natalie dug her socked feet into the carpet and stared at them. She said, "Cause…I don't know." She twisted in her seat. "Cause, then I'm in control. I don't like other people, 'specially my mom, trying to control me."

"Okay," Geena said softly. That is certainly understandable. I think we all feel that at one time or another. Okay, then, well, I hope we can talk about this more later, Natalie, but since we have so many participating tonight, and I want to thank all you parents once again for taking the time to come, I think maybe we'd better move along to the next question."

Geena adjusted her flowered smock over her huge hips, then asked Natalie, "And what is something you love about your mom?"

I glanced at Ginny, who was sitting beside me staring blankly in front of her, as though she were in a trance.

Natalie said, "I can't think of anything."

Her mother put her head in her hands.

"Well..." Gina said. She cleared her throat. "I know you've had a long day, Natalie, and..."

Natalie's mother picked her head up, interrupting Geena. "This day's no longer than any other we've had. She can't think of anything she loves about me 'cause she don't think about anybody but herself."

Natalie stood up and pushed the chair behind her. It tipped and fell. Then she yelled, "There is nothing I love about my mom." She glanced at Geena, then stared back at her mother. "I was gonna save it 'til later, but you asked for it. I hate you, you bitch!"

Ginny swallowed hard. She was still staring blankly, but she took my hand and held it as if she'd never let go of it.

"All right," Geena said, standing up and walking over to Natalie, whose mother was crying now. "I want you to calm down Natalie. We'll talk about this later." She took Natalie over to another empty seat away from the one she'd turned over and away from her mother. She gently placed Natalie in the chair then walked over and set the tipped chair back on its legs.

"Okay, Mrs. Smith," Geena said, returning to her seat. "I would like for you to tell the group something you love about yourself then something you love about Natalie, and we'll move on."

Natalie's mother was still crying but somehow trying to swallow her sobs, which made them sound strange. The mother sitting next to her, handed Natalie's mother a tissue from her purse and Natalie's mother blew her running nose. Then she stared at the floor and spoke in a childlike voice. "I love my chocolate chip cookies," she said, a smile creeping across her lips. "They're real good. My brother Jed says, 'the best in the world.'" Then she began to cry again. Between sobs, she said, "And I love Natalie when she was a baby...when I could hold her...and she...she would smile at me. Doctors say they can't smile 'til after three months...." Here she broke down completely and cried in little jerks of breath for at least a minute. Then she said through sniffles and ragged breathing, "But Natalie...she smiled at me...when she was born."

Natalie's mother rocked back and forth in her chair, sobbing without restraint now. Then suddenly she stopped rocking and sobbing. She closed her eyes and spoke slowly and comfortingly, as if she was trying to convince herself more than us. "She knew I was her mama.... She knew."

I had been lost for these long moments in Natalie's mother's grief, but then I felt a pressure against my right arm and looked to find Ginny's face turned up to mine. Her eyes were open wide, and all I remember of the rest of the evening was how she seemed in that moment at once very young and very tired of her life.

§

Another night with no sleep. Finally slipping out of Jake's bed, tiptoeing over to my purse and digging quietly through it for one of Ginny's letters.

Jake waking immediately. I think with him it's not so much that he's a light sleeper as he has really keen senses. Half-asleep, feeling instantly when I'd left his side.

He propped himself up on his elbows and stared straight at me, crouching over my purse at the foot of the bed.

He said, "What are you doing?"

I whispered apologetically, "I'm sorry, honey. I can't sleep. I was just going to get one of Ginny's letters and go into the livingroom and read. I thought you were asleep."

Jake frowned. "I was." He ran one hand over his forehead, then motioned me toward him. He said, "Come here. Get back in bed."

I put the letter I'd found back in my purse and crawled up on the bed, back into Jake, who cupped my whole body into his chest, nesting his chin on my head. He kissed my hair, then told me, "You have to sleep." Kissing my neck, he said, "I know you think you can go 24-7…but you can't…." He kissed my cheek, adding "or even if you can, you shouldn't." Jake held me closer. "It'll all be there tomorrow, you know, for you to sort out. Just try to get some sleep for now. You need to rest not read." He kissed the top of my head. "That's your problem, you know. You pack way too much into that little head of yours."

"I know," I whispered, while Jake tenderly fingered my breasts, then turned me into him. I kissed his lips first, then his chest, circling his small nipples with my tongue, while Jake put his hands on my shoulders and gently pushed me down to his cock.

I had just started to take him in my hand and my mouth when he said softly, "You don't have to…you know…if you don't want to."

I looked up at Jake, at the man who was my waking dream through so many sleepless nights and told him without blinking, "I always want you."

§

The next morning, after Jake kissed me goodbye and left for work, I curled up in the covers with Ginny's letter. No matter where I was, finding a way to start my day with her voice.

Dear Aunt Faith,

It is so hot here. Beach hot in the mountains. You wouldn't believe it. Mommy is so happy. She loves heat. Says our pool is as warm as bathwater. Blake told her to read the thermometer on the side of the pool, which he pointed out read 72 degrees. He said the man at the pool store said a normal temperature for an outdoor pool is 87 degrees. Mommy just laughed and splashed me before she did a flip underwater. When she came back up for air, she told Blake we're both mermaids. I laughed, but Blake kind of frowned. He told her, "Yeh, right. Frozen mermaids."

Mommy says she's going to buy a fountain for us. Plant it in the middle of the pool so we can swim under its spray. I told her Winnie and I would love that.

We went on another hike today. Up our mountain. Mommy loves to go hiking. Blake says she was born in a ballgown and hiking boots. I thought that was pretty good. For a man.

Anyway, she took me to her secret place today. You have to straddle a stream to get to it. Climb over mossy rocks the size of big clouds, that feel old and soft like elephants' ears. But when you do, if you can, without falling and killing yourself, you get to rest on this bed of fallen leaves. Look up through the tree branches at the hawks' wings knifing through a big chunk of blue sky.

Mommy says it's a place fairies know to land but that she just stumbled on it trying to get through a long day.

I think sometimes Mommy gives up too much for me and Blake. Then she goes looking for it. On the mountain. Mommy loves the mountain. She told me once "It's a heartbeat of earth." I don't know. I love to hear Mommy talk, but sometimes it makes me really sad. It's like God made a mistake. Put the moon's voice inside of Mommy and Mommy's innocence inside the moon. Sometimes when I get up at night I see her standing out on the deck looking up at it. Like she knows what she lost. And who she lost it to.

Oops. Gotta go. Mommy's calling me to set the table. She fixed my favorite vegetarian chili. I'd save you some, but it would probably go bad.

Love,

Ginny

Chapter 19

F r i e n d s   a n d   L o v e r s

Jake and I had long passed the beginning stage of our relationship, the stage where you share only the good parts of your past, hoping neither of you will ever discover the parts that can cause love to die.

But we had learned our soft spots. And we handled them with care. That's what happens when you love someone. You're not so eager to judge a part of yourself.

In the beginning, Jake and I were just like everybody else, every new couple. He had to hear how I'd written a novel, starred in plays, won a couple marathons, thought I was a really good sales manager. And I had to hear about how Jake's first car was a Porsche, how he put his little brother through college, that he can kayake and surf, knows the roads of central Florida like the back of his hand, can take apart any car made and put it back together again so it will run better.

After awhile, though, a few months of days and nights together, you see a few rough spots. You try not to notice them at first. Then you just try not to focus on them. But unless you're not looking or listening at all, unless neither of you ever moves or opens your mouth, you're bound to know they're there. And that they are the test.

One of the rough spots has to do with my percentage of body fat. How it can't quite absorb two glasses of white wine. That's right. I might be able to manage four sales divisions of a Fortune 200 company, but get more than two glasses of chardonnay in me and I'm dancing on table tops with strangers.

Jake has witnessed this more than once. And, in this case, he doesn't ignore it. Just plants himself at a table near mine until he thinks I might fall. Then calmly saunters over to me, loops his fingers into my belt hops and lifts me into his arms, while all the men in the room boo him and yell things like, "Hey, let her go! What do you care if she breaks her neck? You just want a piece of her ass."

Meantime, I've saved more than one woman in central Florida. From the wrath of Jake. He may have the patience to take apart any car made and put it back together, but when it comes to being tailgated, especially by a woman, Jake goes ballistic. I tell him calmly. "Honey, they don't mean to do it." Putting one hand on his thigh and rubbing it, I say, "Driving is just not important to most women. It's just a way of getting from one place to the other. How we do it is immaterial."

While Jake and I were busy learning we'd rather spend time together than with anyone else, Maeve and Ted were becoming inseparable. They spent nearly every night together, drinking, at Duffy's.

Ted was a regular. Maeve, the pub celebrity. She'd quit the manager's job when she received her tentative orders and taken a job as a nurse at Willow Pond. But no one a Duffy's thought of Maeve as a nurse. At Duffy's, Maeve was Captain O'Neil, ready to go to war, commanding unconditional respect and support from the regulars.

And Maeve was ready to go to war. Always. I remember one night at Duffy's together, before I met Jake, when one of the regulars was egging her on to show us how many push-ups she could do. At that point in the evening,

Maeve had had two glasses of wine, three beers, and two shots with three different kinds of liquor and red bull. I'd had my standard two glasses of chardonnay and three glasses of water with lemon and was laughing loudly at nothing funny, cheering her on.

But Maeve didn't need any encouragement. Seconds after all the regulars began egging her on, she hit the floor— calves tight, butt tensed, boobs hanging out of her halter top, red-faced but still smiling—and proceeded to do fifty push-ups. Men's push-ups. The big-boy kind. With no cheating. No knees on the floor, feet-crossed, no elbows caving. Fifty push-ups.

I can do five. Stone sober. Arms shaking. Butt quivering. Five. On a good day.

Maeve still called, every day. Usually when she hoped I was taking a lunch break. If I was in a meeting or working on reports, she'd leave me a message.

"Hey, babe, it's me. Tell them you have to pee. It's the law of averages. Make like hay to the restroom and call me. Jesus! Don't they let you eat lunch? (I could hear Maeve exhaling smoke.) Tell them you're dying. That you feel it coming on. Fifty years from now. But you need to prepare. Ah hell, tell'em I said to go fuck off. What kind of a regional sales manager doesn't get to a take a lunch break? Call me!"

The answer to Maeve's question was, of course, me. I did one of three things during my lunch hours at Evergreen: answered phone calls from irate customers we had not picked up, filled out reports and price modules for senior management, or submitted bids that would be trashed upon receipt due to our inability to recycle or provide any competitive numbers on disposal.

But at the end of my days, on my way home, when I did have a chance to call Maeve back, she always wanted the same thing. For me to join her and Ted at Duffy's for a drink. And when I would try to explain to her that between my job and visiting hours at the unit, I didn't have much free time and the little time I did have I wanted to spend with Jake, she would just blow her cigarette smoke into the receiver and tell me, "Whatever."

It was odd. How in the beginning of our friendship, I thought Maeve and I had so much in common. Sort of prided myself on seeing the similarities others couldn't.

For instance, Jake. Who saw Maeve as an overdominating, desperate to find a man, envious of my position at work and my relationship with him, and irresponsible mother (this last observation after he'd seen her watch her son Nathan drink himself sick on several occasions).

The truth lies (now there's an oxymoron)…anyway…the truth lies somewhere in between what people think and what they feel. Based mostly in the present—what is currently going on in their lives.

Jake was right on a number of points about Maeve. And though I'm about to describe why, I'd like you to consider first that right is not always quite right when the one who's "right" judges another to be wrong mostly on factors out of their control. As Jake did with Maeve.

While Maeve had held numerous powerful positions with large companies, her current job as a nurse, arguably one of the most physically and emotionally challenging ones there is, was not comparable to mine. Whether most people realize it or not, working in the waste management industry, managing people and the environment, is one of the most dangerous and difficult jobs there is. You deal daily with the operation of heavy equipment, hauling a variety of substances—some very heavy, like concrete; some life-theatening, like friable asbestos; some sharp, like glass and wire; and some unknown, like needles from diabetics or drug users, babies people didn't want and have thrown in dumpsters. If you're in management, all of that means trying to keep your drivers from getting hurt or killed, your customers from doing what could endanger the public and themselves, and owners from getting sued ten different ways. That is, you must manage people—everyone from the Spanish-speaking immigrant with a fourth-grade education and just enough English to order some fast food with a lot of pointing at pictures to a recent college graduate who thinks he can make six figures his first year in

172

sales to acres and acres of landfills, toxic gases, and the treatment of water. And revenue—millions of dollars of revenue. And the goals—to make millions more, no matter how inadequate your resources are or how miserable the condition of the economy. Add that to being a woman manager in a totally male-dominated industry, a creative writing major in a business whose substance is numbers—numbers of roll-offs, front-loaders, rear-feed hoppers, compactors, balers, hoists (where the average price of a used industrial waste truck is more than a veteran public school teacher's yearly salary in my home-town), an imaginative thinker managing in a world of logic and strategy. Add all those things together and you have untold stress. And the reality of my life day to day.

Back to comparisons and Jake's having it half-right. Maeve and I are both single working mothers, but our children are very different people. Her son did, in fact, have a deep affection for alcohol. And he was not mentally ill. Nor was he living with his mother. And more than likely would never require full-time care. He was simply a young man, sewing his very common oats in the wildest way he could imagine. Drinking liquor all night long at any pub he could find. He would never inherit the earth, though he'd do a lot of vomiting on it. And though Maeve wasn't much of an example for anyone when she was drinking, what I could see that Jake couldn't and what Maeve surely understood is that one word of reprimand from her would simply have meant that Nathan would have drunk elsewhere after telling her where to go.

And as far as Maeve's relationship with men versus mine with Jake, well, Jake was talking about apples and oranges. Also about something that is both unfair and true. The truth is, I am incredibly lucky. The truth is, I come from love. I come from two people who love each other deeply. And that has made all the difference in my life. So no matter what sort of challenges I have had in relationships, or will have with Jake, I will always feel loved. Maeve, on the other hand, comes from a home many would view as a glimpse of hell. And so she does not love like I do, will never trust like I can. And therefore will probably not ever be in a lifetime relationship.

And though I know some people can and do overcome similar circumstances, go on to lead perfectly normal lives, surrounding themselves with love, the fact that Maeve was halfway through a not so normal one with no true love in sight did not bode well. And though I am a firm believer in the transforming powers of the human spirit, I know all the indicators of a broken one. And I've never seen excessive drinking and smoking transform anyone. At least not into someone she would want to be. Could be—like Maeve, minus her little brush with hell.

All said and done, it was becoming more obvious every day that my new family was falling apart.

Ted did his best to keep our little foursome together. Asking Jake at work if he wanted to meet us at Duffy's. And Jake would immediately walk outside the shop and call me, demanding, "Did you say you were going to Duffy's with them without calling me?"

And I would just sigh. Explain the whole thing about Maeve calling me and me telling her I wanted to spend time with Jake and after I'd finished there'd be a moment of silence. Then Jake would say, between clenched teeth and the distant sounds of compressed air tools, "I don't trust...either of them. They are...two of the most...manipulating people...I've ever met. Plus..." he would add, the clank of a metal tool on concrete punctuating his favorite observation, "They are both drunks."

It was ironic. That the place that had brought us all together was now separating us. How if it hadn't been for Maeve, and one cold December night inside at Duffy's, Jake and I might never have met.

But I didn't talk to Jake about this. We weren't there yet. Where you talk about how you can't stand the thought you might never have met. Where you both say how it felt when you first met. Where you say whether you think it was coincidence or fate or something beyond explaining. And where you tell what it all means to you.

Ted did tell me once, after several Captain 'n cokes, that the night Jake and I met, Jake had simply asked him, "Who's the blonde?"

When Ted looked at both Maeve and me and answered, "Which one?" he said Jake smirked and said, "Yeh, right." Then Ted said he told Jake I was a good friend, and he got this feeling if he hadn't, Jake would have told him he was planning to fuck my brains out.

I told Ted, "But he didn't. He didn't say that."

"No," Ted said. "But he thought it. Trust me, that was all he was thinking about."

Over a year and a half later, I still don't know what Jake felt when he met me. And it isn't that I don't care or that I'm afraid of the answer, it's just that I don't want whatever the answer is to alter the meaning of that night for me.

Before that night, before I met Jake, I'd thought I was in love, and I'd had my heart broken. I'd danced with strangers and shared vows that were supposed to link me to a man for life. I'd had friends turn into lovers and lovers turn into friends. And what I hadn't lived of love, I'd heard or read about. But I never had that shaking, lump-in-the-throat, fast-heart-beat feeling you get when you meet the person you know you must always have known—who is more than lover or friend, who must for all time have been the intended one.

When I came back to Asheville, Faith asked me to hear one of Glen's school concerts. To close the program, his students performed a piece called "Amor de Mi Alma" (Love of My Soul). Whoever wrote that song must have known a love like mine for Jake. And so the meaning of that night at Duffy's for me is that I had that feeling for the first time. And nothing Jake or Ted could tell me would add to that. And certainly not that Jake might just have wanted "to fuck my brains out."

Chapter 20

Parallel Parking

So Jake and I had passed the stage where you just share selected parts of yourself and your life. With the one exception of that night of our meeting at Duffy's, we pretty much had the past and the present covered. But as far as the future went, well, we just hadn't talked about it. We didn't say we couldn't talk about it. There were no rules spoken or understood. We just didn't. Until one day.

We'd spent the morning eating breakfast at Frankie's, a local diner, then calling Ginny. Visiting hours at the unit weren't until later. Jake and I took turns talking to her, and she seemed to be having a good start to the day.

Jake kidded with her about my driving and actually got her to laugh as I'd seen him do before, even during her deepest depression.

After breakfast, Jake had tried to teach me how to parallel park—again. It was a lesson he was determined I would learn. And not just how to, but how to in three turns of the wheel.

During his first attempts, after I had revealed one day that I would drive ten blocks to avoid parallel parking, I would protest, "Why are you making such a big deal out of this? I've never had a traffic violation or accident in my life. And it's obvious I've gotten along fine without being able to parallel park. It's also pretty clear I wasn't given the best gross or fine motor skills, so why do you expect me to drive like I'm Jeff Gordon?"

"I expect you to be able to parallel park any time you need to," was Jake's economical response. I don't think he was even listening to me when I told him how hard it is to answer a cell phone, apply lip gloss, sing to your favorite song, and park at the same time. "I try, Jake," I said. "God knows I try."

"Try harder," was all Jake would say.

So we were off again that day to downtown Winter Park, where I had first revealed my inadequacy, to learn the fine art of parallel parking.

"The trick," Jake told me, "is to focus. You don't make a move without thinking about what you're doing."

I rolled my eyes. "Oh, great," I said. "You want me to drive just the opposite of the way I live."

Jake laughed. "You said it, I didn't." Then he got this very serious determined expression on his face. "Okay, now just listen to me. You can do this. And don't give me that thing about being a woman. My mom's a great driver. She can drive circles around me."

I rolled my eyes again. "Okay, well can't you just consider yourself lucky? You already have one woman in your life who can drive."

Jake didn't smile. "No," he said. "Now come on. Quit avoiding the task at hand. Pull up to the other car's door handle, just like I showed you."

So I did. Then I tried hard to focus on backing up straight, then cutting to the left, then straightening the wheel out and pulling forward.

Jake said nothing while I was driving. When I shifted into park, he opened his door, glanced down at the curb, then shut it. He looked over at me smiling. "All right," he said. "Better."

When we got out, I couldn't help noticing the car was perfectly straight, centered exactly in the middle of the space, tires just inches from the curb. But I didn't say a word. About how Jake's idea of "better" is my idea of "perfect." Just smiled from the inside out and put my whole hand in the palm of his.

That afternoon, after we'd made love, Jake was toweling me off. He was gently running the plush towel over the insides of my thighs when I told him, "Jake, we need to talk."

Jake looked up and once again proved to be atypical of all the men I've known who do one thing and one thing only when you say that to them—run for the door as fast as they can. Of course, I have to give myself credit for my timing. And experience. Jake was in no position to run for the door. That aside, he didn't have the look of someone who would run if he could, and, more than that, his voice was a tender combination of care and concern when he said, "What's the matter?"

I opened my arms to him, and he scooted up beside me, resting his head on my breasts.

"Honey," I said, "This is hard for me to talk about. I want you to know that. For a lot of reasons. One is, I'm not really sure what I want. All this we're going through with Ginny, well, it's confusing enough. Never mind the fact that I'm really not doing what I believe I'm best at and... okay...I just have to say it. Just know I'm saying this and I may...I just may be formulating an escape. Not on purpose. Not from you. But just... you know...sometimes people do one thing to keep from doing what they should do."

Jake nudged his face into one of my breasts and teethed it lightly. Then he said, "How far are you from getting to the point?"

"Jake!" I protested sitting up a little. "Don't kid around— I'm serious. I'm trying to tell you something important."

"Yeh," he said. "I know. I just want to know if half an hour from now you're still gonna be trying 'cause if you are, let me go to the bathroom first."

I laughed a little. "All right. No— Don't go. I like you there. Here. I'm gonna finish. I promise."

Jake said, "Okay. Finish. Or come get a golden shower."

"You are so gross," I said.

Jake kissed my breast. "Yeh, and you love it."

"Okay," I said, taking a deep breath, then letting it out. "I might someday, not now, not even soon…well, sooner than later, because you know I'm not like twenty anymore…but…"

Jake rolled his eyes. "Please get to the point."

"Okay, okay. I might want to have another baby."

I paused to see what Jake would say, but he was happily sucking away. So I continued. "Not now, not even soon. Just someday, and my doctor says, well, she says, I am perfectly healthy and you are young and we should start thinking about it and um trying—in like two years. She said if we want one, we really shouldn't wait any longer than that."

Jake had stopped sucking and he wasn't saying anything. So I said, "I probably shouldn't have said anything. I'm probably scaring you to death. But I…I have to say it. I mean if I figure out this isn't some kind of way I'm trying to escape what I'm supposed to do, and the feeling just grows and I really want to have another baby, the only person I ever want to do that with is…you."

I kissed the top of Jake's head. His fine hair feels just like a baby's and it made me cry. Jake turned over then scooted up beside me. He looked right into my eyes, brushing my tears away. "What?" he said. "Why are you crying? You don't see me running, do you?"

I caught my breath. "Are you okay with that?" I asked, shaking.

"With what?" Jake asked, kissing me on the forehead.

"With having a baby with me. Someday. Maybe."

Jake would not take his eyes off me. I thought the blue in them would color the green in mine. He slipped his hands into my hair while he kissed me slowly and long, drawing every part of me into him. His hands moved tenderly from the curls in my hair to my shoulders, then to my breasts, which he cupped as if they could break. He inched his tongue down my neck to the soft place just at the base, then he brushed my chest with kisses and moved from one breast to the other, sucking each nipple as if it might give up a secret. Then he fingered me until he found my spot, which he touched, lightly and quickly with his index finger until I came— a steady sinewy stream of white flowing from me into Jake's hand.

I could feel his cock rubbing against my thigh. It was hot and hard and restless.

I kissed the top of his head and asked him, "Honey, what do you want?"

Jake lifted his head. His eyes met mine. He said, "I'll give you three guesses...and the first two don't count."

Chapter 21

Holidays

It will be Halloween in ten days, Ginny's favorite holiday. When she was a child, even up until I moved to Florida, we'd decorate for it as much as most people do for Christmas. We'd pick up Ginny's best friend Winnie, bring her to the house, and the two of them would rummage through our big closet, searching for the full cardboard boxes marked Halloween Stuff.

They'd pull out strands of jack-o-lantern lights, a black plastic spider web with a large purple and green rubber spider attached to it, a scarecrow Ginny made from a paper bag when she was seven, purple ghost garlands, miniature electric haunted houses, and two stuffed black cats. Then they'd go to work transforming our home into their version of a freak show.

A couple of nights before Halloween, we'd drive to the Farmer's market and pick out pumpkins of all shapes and sizes, then invite the neighbors over. We were famous for our pumpkin-carving parties. Complete with apple bobbing contests and blind-fold walks through our house of horrors. We even provided all the costumes. And the neighborhood kids would run for our chest of them. After they'd picked out their favorite ones, they'd head outside to jump on our trampoline. Capes flying in the air. Little hearts pounding under superman suits.

One Halloween, Winnie couldn't come, so I created a Cher costume—bought this long black fall, heavy black mascara, eyeliner, bright red lipstick, and a skin-tight leopard suit and Ginny dressed as Sonny in hippie hair, a mustache, and a big plastic nose. When Ginny would ring the doorbell at each house, I'd burst into "Now, everybody, have you heard, he's gonna buy me a mockingbird…" and she'd stand behind me giggling. After about the tenth house, Ginny told me, "You're a real ham, you know?"

I laughed out loud. "You have no idea," I told her. "You should have seen me as a teenager." Ginny rolled her eyes and said, "Daddy says you're worse now."

I stopped and faced her, hands on my leopard-skin hips. "Would you rather me be one of those moms shaped like a pumpkin who wears big bulky white sweatshirts with ghosts and 'Boo!' embroidered on the front of them and stands at the door saying to the trick-or-treaters, 'Oh, now isn't that the sweetest thing you've ever seen,' no matter what they're wearing?"

Ginny laughed. "No, mommy. No," she said. "I guess it's just a little scary how much your version of being a mom matches Cher's."

§

This year she is dressing up as a clown, and we are handing out candy together. We bought a multi-colored wig and red-white-and-blue face make-up for her to wear. And, of course, a rubber nose, and I'm just going to be me.

Last year, her last Halloween in Florida, I let her go out trick or treating—mostly because she seemed to want to go, and excitement had become something rare for her. I went with her because by then, all the kids at Whispering Pines were aware of Ginny's problems and she had no friends.

She wanted to be a doctor, so I found a first aid kit in the baby department at Walmart for her. The whole thing was made out of terry cloth, complete with a stethoscope and pill bottles. Ginny loved the kit. And we walked hand in hand through the Brady Bunch neighborhood of Winter Park, me believing once again that everything was going to be okay. Not the okay I'd hoped for. One where Ginny would spend Halloween with her new friends in Florida. At a party. Or a sleepover. Come home afterwards and tell me who was in love with whom, what the hottest shade of nail polish is, or how one of her friends had corn-rowed her hair. Not that kind of okay. But one where she wasn't reeling from the voices in her head. Trying to hurt herself. Or forgetting she ever loved Halloween.

It was another beautiful night in Florida. Whispering Pines had a football game at home, and we could hear their band playing the "Star Spangled Banner." Stars peaked through the looming oaks that hovered over every street we walked, and little children sprung out from behind their parents, lighting the night with color and laughter.

We met one woman who'd lived in her home since she was a child. Her parents sold it to her husband. "My husband passed away last year," she told us. "I live here with my sister now."

She handed Ginny a handful of snickers, while she talked about her husband. "He loved Halloween," she said. "Why he used to come home early from work just to make sure the house was all lit up for the kids. He'd string lights from here to kingdom come. Nearly killed himself falling off a ladder. A couple of times." She laughed softly, as the green in her tiny eyes lit up. "God, I miss him," she said, then looked up at Ginny. "You be smart. Marry a good man like I did, and your life will be full."

Ginny thanked the woman with emerald eyes, and we walked down her driveway. When we got to the edge of it, Ginny said to me. "Jake won't die on you, will he?" And for some reason, I laughed until I cried.

I continued to try to meet with Dr. Traynor, some days making four or five phone calls to his office, then to the unit. Dr. Traynor never returned my calls.

Occasionally, during visiting hours, I would hear Hope or one of the staff members say he was actually in the building. Under other circumstances, I might have been amused by the staff's hushed reports of his presence; they spoke almost like he'd suddenly taken a notion to haunt the place. But what was haunting me was not funny at all. That I'd never even seen the man who was treating my daughter, who had Ginny's life in his hands—a doctor who, in fact, was no more substantial to me than a ghost.

Easter came. I made Ginny a small tree out of pastel colored wire with a basket for the base. On the delicate wire, I hung plastic eggs in her favorite colors, with treasures I thought she would love. I'd cut out tiny pictures of her best friend, her dad, and me and placed them inside the eggs. I bought her a tiny lady bug pin for good luck. I picked out her favorite flavors of jelly beans and filled the basket with them.

When I brought the tree to the unit, Ginny greeted me with a hug and then squealed when she saw my gift. She hadn't even gotten to see what was inside the eggs, but she seemed as happy as I'd ever seen her. Silently, I was thanking God while I hugged my daughter in the entrance way to the unit.

But suddenly, when my head was buried in Ginny's shoulder, Maria walked up behind us and seized the tree, which was dangling from my right hand. "She can't have that now," Maria barked at us. "We're doing baskets later." Then she inspected the tree closer, spinning it around in her large fat hands. Its tiny wire branches shook and its brightly colored eggs wobbled. Maria said, "I'm not sure she can have it at all, but I'll see." Then she stared directly down at me. "Ms. Robbins, you know there are not supposed to be any sharp objects in the unit."

I bowed my head. "Yes, I know…but I just…. I just wasn't thinking about the wire. Please let her have the eggs…later, I mean, when you do the baskets."

I looked at Ginny, whose smile and energy had faded completely. She was tugging me listlessly toward the nearest couch.

186

"I'm sorry," I told Maria. "We, um, Easter is very special to us. I used to have Easter egg hunts at our mountain home and invite all of my family and friends."

Maria looked uninterested standing in the hall clutching Ginny's Easter egg tree.

But, I continued, "Ginny and I made up games like our chalk drawing contest. The children got to draw pictures all over our driveway with Ginny's big bucket of colored chalks. They searched for the hidden eggs in my gardens, the woods, our house, then jumped on the trampoline. Every year I made a huge feast and...."

Ginny added in a tiny childlike voice, "Bunny cake."

"Yes!" I said, smiling at Ginny, who was staring at the floor. "Yes, I made Bunny cakes! Every year a different one."

Maria stepped toward the nursing station, carelessly swinging Ginny's tree against one of her huge hips. One of the eggs fell off—the orange one. Ginny got down on her hands and knees and crawled to it. She picked it up and opened it. It was the one with a picture of her best friend Winnie inside. Ginny smiled at the tiny face. "Thank you, mommy," she said as I kneeled down beside her. We hugged.

"Happy Easter," I whispered in her ear.

"Happy Easter to you too, mommy," she said.

Chapter 22

S p i r i t   C r u s h e r s

It seemed every visiting day, one of the patients was discharged, and Ginny had begun to ask when she could go home. Since she had wanted to come to the unit— and until now seemed never to entertain the idea that there might be a better place for her— I took her new question as a sign that something had changed enough that she could at least imagine herself leaving, and of course I missed her more than I would an arm, so I began to ask about when she'd be released.

I started by asking Hope every day, then questioning the staff if Dr. Traynor had mentioned when she could go home. Of course, John and I had been making plans daily for his arrival, and I'd even asked Richard if I could bring Ginny to work for a few days if her release from the hospital and John's coming to stay with her didn't time out, and amazingly, he hadn't balked; in fact, he was as close to generous as anyone had been at work since the whole ordeal began.

But right away, Hope let me know that until Dr. Traynor could begin reducing Ginny's medication, he would definitely not consider releasing her.

When I asked Hope when she thought that might be, she said she had no idea.

The staff had kept me updated on Ginny's medication, which was clearly not being reduced, and though my own desperate hope for Ginny to come back to me and to herself made me think her asking about leaving was a sign of improvement, most visits the change I saw was not a change between the day of her admittance and the first time she asked about leaving, but the harrowing change that hit me all over again every time I came to visit—the difference between Ginny in the unit and Ginny in her days of jumping with abandon on trampolines, of hitting her two-handed backhand for winners that left her opponents laughing in awe, of drawing pictures that made people ask if she planned to major in art, of holding snails and lightning bugs on her fingers with a reverence most reserve for church.... My first glimpse of my daughter on each visit to the unit was a moment I could never prepare for, any more than I could prepare for the strangeness of most of our hours together there.

There were evenings during my visits when she'd laugh hysterically for minutes at a time, then burst into tears. There were times when she couldn't hold her head up. She could never carry on a conversation. Not even a simple one about the weather or what she was wearing. When she spoke her voice was usually flat and the words were often preceded or followed by a sudden movement of her hand slapping at her thigh, a motion I had never seen until those days in the unit but one I have watched by now a thousand times. Her face was mostly without expression, her eyes usually vacant. Her questions about leaving, like so much of what she said, had a parroted tone I had not wanted to acknowledge at first, as if she had memorized words she had heard another child speak to a parent, having vaguely sensed that something similar was expected of her. So my optimism about Ginny's coming hope disappeared as quickly as it had appeared, and before I could even absorb the feeling of more lost hope, I was faced with yet another challenge.

In my sessions with Hope and the other counselors, they began asking questions about our personal life. Some were puzzling, some disturbing, some outrageous. I had no idea at the time these questions were based on delusions Ginny was recounting to them as if they were truth. It was only much later I learned that the medication Ginny was taking actually causes hallucinations. Why the staff didn't know is a question that still needs to be answered.

§

Since coming back to Asheville, I have stood in the bookstore in front of the shelves labeled Psychiatry until I feel my legs begin to numb, reading until the words blur. I go to sleep and wake up asking myself what I might have done for Ginny had I known in Florida what I know now, and as I read, the sentences seem to lengthen with longings as keen as I have ever known [oh, Ginny, look at me once more instead of through me, beyond me]. I have never been one to dwell on the past, but the scenes of my daughter when she was still whole come to me unbidden in the pages of a book that tells of unconscionable behavior among "normal" people, people entrusted with the mental help of others. There are passages of Peter Breggin's *Toxic Psychiatry* in which it seems to me he is writing out of the memory of Ginny's brightest hours to illuminate the darkening path of psychiatric practice. As I read, I see my daughter as she was before any of the treatment.

"The American Psychiatric Association's governing body," according to Breggin, "made a conscious decision to rely more heavily on drug company funding for its activities..."[11] [jump high on the trampoline, Ginny, as you did on the mountain, arms and legs outstretched in joy— the afternoon, your dress, your squeals of delight, spun gold]. "and that decision," Breggin explains, "most likely influenced individual doctors to line up as well for the handouts"[12] [oh read to me again, Ginny, with breathless, holy anticipation for the hundredth time from *Caddie Woodlawn, The Summer of the Swans, Twenty-One Balloons, Number the Stars*]. Dr. Breggin says, "In the early 1970s APA was in financial trouble..."[13] [laugh again, Ginny, at the antics of your puppy Mr. Bojangles]. Breggin writes, "In general, psychiatry was losing badly in the competition with psychologists, social workers, counselors, family therapists, and other medical professionals who charge lower fees for psychotherapy patients."[14] [Paint me a picture of lady bugs, and let the colors say how much you love life]. Breggin notes, "At the same time, psychiatry was coming under increasing criticism about psychosurgery, electroshock..."[15] [Ginny, let me see you dance again, hold joy in your eyes] "and the newly publicized drug-induced disease, tardive dyskenesia" [16] .

How could I not have known what Breggin knew—that the APA Task Force to Study the Impact of the Potential Loss of Pharmaceutical Support appointed in response to increasing concern about lack of professionalism and conflicts of interest in the field of psychiatry by its very title suggested the fear that independence from the drug companies would mean the loss of 'lifeblood' support for APA programs[17].

Of his grave concern about the training of those in the medical profession Dr.Breggin writes, "Recently, while teaching a seminar at a mental hospital, I asked the assembled psychiatrists, psychologists, social workers and nurses if their recent training had dealt at all with the issue of caring about or loving their patients in the process of helping them heal. Among the fifty participants, only one person, a nurse, raised her hand." [18]

Waiting for Ginny in the lobby of the treatment center in Asheville where she visits weekly with her new counselor, I was in an area with a tight grouping of chairs and a table and a gaunt-looking woman and what I assumed must be her teenaged daughter were sitting next to me.

A counselor came out of the back treatment rooms with a boy who appeared to be about ten going on fifty. He had dark circles under both eyes. The counselor walked over to the woman and girl and handed the woman a slip of paper. "Dr. Dreggs wrote him a new prescription," she said. "He thinks maybe this one will work a little better."

The woman put the piece of paper in her purse and said, "I hope it doesn't keep him from sleeping. That last one kept him up all the time."

"Oh," said the counselor, whose face looked genuinely concerned, "Well, if it does, you call us immediately." The counselor put her arm around the boy. "We don't want Andrew missing his sleep." She rubbed his head.

The woman smiled, then pointed to the girl, "How about Nisa?" she asked.

"I've lost the piece of paper with her next appointment on it."

The counselor said, "I'll go get another one and put both their appointments on it. How's that?"

The woman smiled. "That'd be good," she said as the counselor headed for the office.

Then the woman looked over at me and said, "He's manic depressive like his daddy, and she's bipolar." Then she laughed half-heartedly. "They keep me busy."

I said, "I'm sure." Then, trying to be comforting, I added, "This seems like a good place. The doctors and counselors seem to really care."

She agreed. "Oh, yeh. Yeh, they do. We been coming here for ten years. My two oldest came here too. And my husband. He's dead now." She paused, shifted in her chair, brushing something off her jeans. Her children stared at the ceiling. "Killed hisself two years ago this month," she said. Then she smiled as if remembering something. "Funny, he was doing so good. They'd just switched him to a new medication, and his mama and I both thought he was doing good." Then she added, "All my kids took after him. They're all on something or other."

I didn't know what to say, but I said, "I'm sorry."

"Oh," she said, "Don't be. I don't know what we'd do without the drugs. I thank God for NAMI helping me get 'em. Are you a member?"

"No," I said.

She laughed. "Listen at me. I don't even know what you're here for and I'm asking you if you're a member. That was pretty stupid."

I smiled and said, "That's okay." Then I added, "I'm here for my daughter."

"Oh," she said, "Well, if you need anything…I mean help getting medication, figuring out what type of disease she has—anything, NAMI—it'll help you. Want me to write it down for you?"

"No," I told her, "it's an unusual name. I'll remember it." Then I asked, "Did they help you with your husband?"

"Oh yes," she said. "He is a vet, you know—was, and he was all messed up from the war, that first Gulf thing. We didn't know what all was the matter with him, but NAMI told us. Come to find out he had five different mental diseases, which they tried to help us treat."

I said, "I'm so sorry. I'm glad you and your children are all right." Then I looked over at the boy and the girl, who had both fallen asleep in their chairs at 10:15 in the morning.

The woman glanced at them too, then smiled. "Yeh, well, they're good as long as they get their medication. No trouble at all." She nudged her daughter. "Come on sleepy head. We'll have to go here in a minute when she brings me your appointments. You two can sleep in the car."

I knew NAMI well by then, of course. Breggin talks at length about the organization and its advocacy of drugs and other biopsychiatric treatments. On one of my days at the bookstore, I sat for an hour staring at a page where he describes NAMI, the National Alliance for the Mentally Ill. **"Like the APA and its local branches, NAMI and some of its state organizations actively solicit and obtain support money from the drug companies."[19]**

Listening to this woman whose whole family had been diagnosed incompetent to function without drugs, I had reached into my purse and pulled out a notepad where I'd copied the strongest passage. I'd had an impulse to give it to her, and what came to me in that moment was something Faith said once about how people have so few answers, know so very little about the questions that matter most, and mostly they are frightened so they pretend they know. I don't know exactly why I didn't put my notes in the hand of the vet's wife and ask her to read them as soon as she could, call *me* to talk if she wanted to. Nothing is simple. I'm learning every day that in one way or another, we are all responsible for the way things are. When the woman got her new appointments and left, I sat reading again what I had found in the bookstore and before I had finished, I made myself a promise that if I saw her again, I'd do two things—ask her name and read to her the words I had almost memorized:

> [NAMI] and its state affiliates consider all severe psychosocial disorders to be biochemical in origin and advocate lobotomy, electroshock,

and drugs. It resists the growing movement of psychiatric survivors and supports of patients'rights in general.

APA and NIMH (the National Institute for Mental Health) work hand in glove with NAMI. They lobby Congress together and meet the press together. NAMI leaders have direct access to the leadership of APA and NIMH, and they help plan national campaigns on behalf of biopsychiatry. NAMI recently published a letter it received from outgoing NIMH director Lewis Judd in which he spoke of the "dedication and shared purpose which has forged a unique and strong relationship and collaboration between NAMI and NIMH. With no apparent awareness of the inappropriateness of handing a federal agency over to a self-serving parent lobbying group, Judd declared, "NIMH, in a very meaningful sense, is NAMI's institute." He then went on to repeat their shared but wholly unproven credo: "During the last 15 years, we have unequivocally established that mental illnesses are brain-related disorders, which often involve strong genetic influences." The public's false impression of breakthroughs in biological psychiatry is based on the repetition of these unfounded slogans. [20]

"We have unequivocally established...." – Faith was right: mostly we are frightened, so we pretend we know without a doubt.

A sentence from Breggin's book comes to me at odd times now—peeling vegetables in my parents' kitchen, walking with Ginny in the neighborhood: "As I finished my college career," he writes, "I was already interested in psychiatric reform. I had barely an inkling of the forces within human nature, society, and psychiatry itself that would make reform in psychiatry seem beyond reach."[21]

When the nursing staff and counselors at the unit weren't calling me to come in and listen to their notes on Ginny's delusions, they were harping on the fact that she has an uncle with a history of problems. Though Ginny's doctor had given no formal diagnosis, the staff continued during the course of our conversations to label Ginny not only schizophrenic but bipolar, which all of the other patients' parents had told me was the same diagnosis their children were given. Here's a thought. Maybe it's contagious. Not schizophrenia and bipoar disorder, but the mental health community's illness. The kind that makes a person condemn a child to a lifetime of legal drug use and increasingly abnormal behavior rather than try to make their life better.

And just as troubling to me was the response from the staff when I brought up time and time again how I felt the basis for Ginny's illness was my initial separation from her, that my moving was too much for her to take. As often as I made that observation, I was told, "This would have happened anyway, Ms. Robbins. It could have happened when she left for college or during some other life-changing event. But it definitely would have happened. You shouldn't blame yourself."

What no one seemed to understand either was that I wasn't interested in placing blame. What I wanted was the truth. Because I believe truth and love are all that matter. If the truth is that taking the job with Evergreen and moving to Florida caused my daughter to break down, then Ginny and I needed... need to face that...together. Look at the choice and how it ultimately hurt her, so we can understand each other and ourselves better—so we could...can forgive and move on.

There were two things I could count on during this period of my life: the medical bills pouring in and my sister Faith's e-mails.

Faith is a poet. A doe-eyed, child-like, smiling, tiny-boned, plump-hearted poet. And a philosophy teacher by profession. She is also an artist and a musician, a wonderful cook, a loving wife, and the closest friend I have. Whatever was going on in her life, she never failed to write me, and I looked forward to her e-mails more than I did the sun rising.

We'd tell each other jokes laced with memories from our past, our childhood, our home and family. I'd ask her for advice about how to handle situations at work, and though she doesn't have any experience in the world of business, she has a sense of what people need to hear, and she could always find just the right chord for me to play so my staff would listen.

I would tell Faith things about me and Jake I could never share with Maeve because I knew she would hear what I was feeling. Always her response would be a mixture of truth and hope and blood. If she ever expressed doubt, she measured it out with generous assurances that I would find my way.

We are very different people, my sister and I. But we came from the same place. And when she answers me, it's like she knows how I was formed. What parts of my mother's womb were too small to hold me. How I strained to get out into this world. And how I will always find a way to break free from anyone or anything that tries to contain me.

Ginny knows this too. Everything that can't be figured out about me, my daughter knows. Though she may have it tucked away for now, buried in a cosmic display of life-transforming events, if you get close enough to her, listen to her smile, hear the way she holds my hand, you can figure it out. Who we both are. How strong our connection is.

Dear Aunt Faith,

There is a chance I might run for class president this year. I'm thinking about it. Mommy says she'll help me make posters. Maybe you can too.

She has this kind of crazy idea. I don't know. See what you think. She says we should make a poster with a hole in it big enough for me to stick my face through. She said below my face the poster should read, "I am who I say I am." I don't know. I mean, I get it, but some of the other kids might not.

Here's what I'm going to do if I get elected. I'm going to make a rule nobody can hurt anybody on purpose. I'll be honest about it. I mean, I'll say it was God's idea first. But how I had to make it a rule so the class would follow it.

What do you think?

Hey, did you know we live in a galaxy called the Milky Way? That is so neat! I told mommy I can never eat another one of those candy bars. It would be like I was eating our world.

Mommy says she'll eat my share for me. But I know she's just kidding. Mommy would never eat the world. Sometimes I think it's the other way around. That the world is eating her.

I've got a fort now. And a slide. And monkey bars. Mommy can cross them three at a time. You should see her. She climbs up one side, sticks her butt way out, bends her knees low, grabs the first bar and then swings way out like she's flying. Only at the last minute her hands hook metal.

I've never seen anything like it. She has the shortest arms of any grown up I've ever seen. And the longest reach ever. Like she's halfway between heaven and earth.

Blake told her the monkey bars were supposed to be for me. But Mommy just laughed at him. She told him, "Go ahead. Try to pull me off. I'll just swing from the trees." I tried not to laugh, but I couldn't help it.

Sometimes I'm sorry for Blake. I think he thinks if he loves Mommy enough, she'll be normal.

Gotta go. Mommy's calling. She found this lake at the top of the mountain, we're not supposed to swim in. She says because it's in a private community.

But last week, when we went on a hike up the mountain, Mommy made friends with this nice man who is the security guard. He says mommy and I can swim anytime. So we're going now. Before Blake gets home. I'll write more later.

Love,

Ginny

Chapter 23

D r e a m s

Thought by wish, day by night, Jake and I began to dream together. We didn't make a big production of it like some couples do. Publicly "ooing" and "ahh-ing" at cars and boats and houses, arms around each other, faces aglow, saying things like, "Oh, it's perfect. You like it, too? It's meant to be. We're meant to be." Followed by Hollywood images of his lifting and spinning her round and round and setting her down breathless, and eyes meeting for a long time, and then lips. Not Jake and me. It was more like we'd slip each other dreams when it was just us, alone.

We'd be driving to dinner, Jake instinctively turning the volume up on the songs I love and changing the station when the music didn't fit our mood. There was a rhythm we both felt, and we let our minds and hearts travel in it, listening to the words of our favorite songs.

I'd be humming along quietly to a song I liked, traveling to one of my dreams when it would end, and I'd turn toward Jake slipping him a piece of it. There was my dream of living in a log cabin surrounded by thick woods, spending my days writing and gardening, my nights cooking and making love to Jake. Jake would listen to my dream. Then he'd tell me how he'd love to have a place in West Virginia, where it's less expensive to live, life is simple, and he could hunt and fish all day.

I'd tell him, "I could live there."

He'd add, "In a log cabin."

I'd say, "Of course."

He'd smile. "With me."

I'd say, "Only with you."

Like that. No oo's or ahh's. No big production of hugs and kisses. Just exploring "what if's" and molding them into "could be's." We weren't consciously building a life together—past, present, future, and dreams. It was just happening. And that's how I knew it was real.

Turns out, it was very lucky for me I had Jake to dream with then. Because so many of my dreams, dreams all mothers have for their children were fading.

Whether we work or stay at home, there are dreams all mothers share. We all want our children to live happy, healthy lives. We want them to do well in their studies and whatever they choose for themselves beyond that—sports, music, art. We want them to go to good schools, get good jobs, have a sense of civic duty, live their own dreams. And along with that are the smaller dreams—that they'll learn how to drive and be safe drivers, that they'll understand it's expensive to rear a child and try to help out, and even smaller than those, that they'll be accepted by other children, have sleepovers, be invited to parties and proms.

I had all these dreams for Ginny. But after her breakdown, one by one, I began to let go of all of them. If you are taking medications like Ginny's, you may not drive a car—in fact, if you go out, you need someone's hand in yours when you cross the street. Any social setting, including a classroom, is not a dream but a nightmare. You have no concept of what a carton of milk and a sandwich costs, let alone a month's groceries, utilities, and rent. It is not a matter of ignorance or insensitivity; it is a matter of synapses and cells that no longer do a person's bidding; it is a matter of living in a world apart; it is a matter for philosophers to consider, unless they are mothers, for then the questions are unbearable—when does a child cease to be herself? In those days, Ginny was lucky if a classmate even spoke to her, and if she remembered to tell me of anyone reaching out, no matter how small the gesture, I found myself almost absurdly grateful, as if a simple exchange of hellos were something to be congratulated.

Prior to her breakdown, Ginny had been a young woman with an understanding of life beyond her years, an athlete who knew the challenges and rewards of daily training and practice. She had a gift of humor and compassion. Loved to read and draw. She could hold her own in a family of performers. After her breakdown, a good visiting hour with her involved Ginny's actually speaking and being able to walk the halls of the unit—though not necessarily at the same time. The dosage she was being given of the drug Seroquil alone, I would later find out, is the highest amount that might be prescribed for an adult with severely psychotic behavior.

Even with Maeve's and my job, my commitment to be with Ginny any time I was allowed, and my relationship with Jake, Maeve and I managed to carve out a few special days together. One of those we spent at my favorite place—the beach.

Maeve knew I'd only been to the beach once since I'd moved to Florida. That was with Jake and Ted, and we really didn't go specifically to the beach. We went to a bikefest, which was at Daytona beach, and after Ted and Jake had looked at all the bikes they wanted to see, we wound our way through the narrow streets to the place where pavement met sand.

It was night by then, a cool spring night—the ocean blueing to black. I stood there on the beach facing the ocean, my hair blowing in the salty breeze, with Jake's arms around me, thinking, "I want to spend the rest of my life with the ocean in front of me and Jake by my side."

Ted stood next to us in the sand, looking at me, my head on Jake's shoulder. He said, "You really haven't been to the beach since you got here?"

I smiled back at him, then sighed. "Nope," I said. "Not until now."

Jake held me tighter.

Ted said, "That's a shame, baby." I smiled again as I watched another wave breaking, listening to the unforgettable symphony of water reaching for sky then falling heavily to the earth.

Jake said, "You know we're seventy percent water." Then putting his chin on my cheek, he added, "We all began our lives surrounded by water." He kissed me where his chin had been resting. "That's why you love it here," he said, "it's a part of you."

Ted scoffed, "Yeh, well this sand's becoming a part of my shoes and I hate sand in my shoes." He picked up one foot and shook his pant leg, watching the sand fall off his shoe.

I looked up at Jake, who whispered to me, "Guess we better go."

I kissed him. "Thank you for bringing me here," I said.

Jake kissed me back. "Thank you for being here," he said.

When I told Maeve about us going to the bikefest and how much it meant to me that Jake insisted I get to see the ocean, she groaned. "Yeh, real sweet. You spend your whole life in the mountains where you don't belong, then you come here to be at the ocean, where you've dreamed of living, and you barely get to catch a glimpse of it because your boyfriend is more interested in looking at motorcycles than in what you love. Real special."

"That's not how it was," I protested, as Maeve pressed the accelerator toward the floor, driving us toward Cocoa Beach.

"That's how it *is*, baby," she told me. "You just don't want to admit it."

We had the top down on Maeve's convertible, and after days upon weeks upon months of being confined in my windowless office for hours on end, I was breathing in all the fresh air I could while Maeve was on her eighth cigarette, sucking in nicotine like it was her mother's milk.

We'd made a pact on Monday, no matter what, we were taking a personal day on Friday. We weren't saying what we were doing, we were just submitting the paperwork on Monday, then packing for our day at the beach. I didn't even tell Jake. In fact, we didn't tell Jake or Ted.

After what seemed like an endless week, Friday finally came and with it an anticipation that seemed to be pulling at me physically as I woke up and stretched up into those delicious moments when dark is beginning to give itself up to daybreak. And when the thought of Ginny hit me squarely in the chest as it did every morning, I said audibly, "No, I won't. I can't. Not today." But still I lay back down for a few moments, seeing Ginny in the days when she moved effortlessly, and I had to remind myself, as I did so often, that if I didn't claim some respite from sorrow, I would soon be of no use to my daughter or anyone.

Maeve picked me up at seven, in the peach light of an early morning that promised to become another beautiful spring day in central Florida. She drove us to Frankie's, across the street from our condos. She was quiet, smiling but not speaking when I got in the car and saying nothing on the short drive, which was rare for Maeve. I guessed she was in as much need of this day as I was, and so I decided to be quiet too, as rare for me as for her. I remember that stillness now and the thought that came to me in it—we all need healing, which comes sometimes in ways we do not anticipate.

Frankie's is family owned and the first place I ate breakfast in Winter Park. The cooks there are all married to the waitresses, so you know if they don't get it right the first time, they'll be doing it again and catching an earful at the same time.

Glenda, with her Dolly Parton hair and New York accent, was my regular waitress. She could just look at me and know what I wanted. She'd still ask to be polite, but she knew.

Today, she said, "It's one egg scrambled with swiss cheese, white toast buttered, and a side of bacon?"

I smiled, "You got it." It's good to have someone know what you need.

Maeve ordered some omelet she thought would fit her Atkins' diet, with no grits or hashbrowns or toast. Maeve was always fighting her weight. She stayed on some kind of a diet. First, it was the Beach diet, then it was the cabbage soup diet, then Atkins. It killed me to watch her focusing so much effort on what she could and could not eat.

I love good food. I just can't eat the large portions usually served and frankly I'm pretty horrified how many people can eat what's brought to the table and then wind up ordering more. My gut tells me it isn't about their wanting or needing more food. Something else is missing. I had started to do variations on the themes of missing and healing, when Glenda returned with our coffee and ice water. She said to Maeve, who hadn't spoken yet except to order her food, "Why don't you just eat whatever she does? It looks good on her."

Maeve rolled her eyes, which were rapidly losing some of their sparkle. "She could eat a chocolate house and it'd 'look good on her,'" Maeve said, the disgust more than evident. "And I could have a crumb of it and it would look like I ate the whole damn thing."

Glenda laughed. "Hey," she said winking at Maeve. "Don't worry. Men like women with a little meat on their bones."

Maeve frowned. "She doesn't have any trouble there, either—believe me. A lot of men love tiny women. It's a power trip for them." Maeve sipped her coffee. Then she said, "Men love to dominate women. But, hey, don't ask me." Maeve put her hands up, then pointed at me. "She's the one with the boyfriend." Clearly Maeve's unusual period of silence had ended and I was glad. Sparring with Maeve was a considerable part of the fun of being with her. And I knew she was anticipating my comeback, which was part of the delight of delivering.

So I protested her boyfriend remark. "Generalizations are never accurate. Every man is different. And..." I added, seeing Maeve's satisfaction was getting a rise out of me, "Size doesn't matter."

Glenda clucked her tongue and walked away as Maeve burst into laughter. "Oh yeh?" she said. "That's not what you said about Jake."

"Shut up," I told her with mock seriousness, as I worked hard not to laugh. I could feel my face turning a deep red.

Maeve was still laughing, but she managed to form and O with her lips and mouthed, "Ah can't get ma mouwf around it."

I was laughing now too. "Shut up!" I said, "God, I'm never telling you anything again." But I could feel the tension that had already collected in my muscles that morning, giving way to our familiar teasing, and suddenly I remembered something Ginny saying when she was no more than eight or nine years old. "God has a sense of humor, don't you think, Mommy?"

"Yes," I said.

Maeve looked at me and cocked her head to the side, and I realized I'd answered Ginny aloud. "You okay, babe?" Maeve asked.

"I am." I said. And I meant it. It wasn't the first time Maeve had embarrassed me in a public place about a private matter. And it wouldn't be the last. But what dawned on me in that moment was that embarrassment isn't all bad. Sometimes it can teach you humility, remind you to laugh at yourself. But here's the real thing you can learn from it, if you'll let yourself: what doesn't matter as much as you might have thought or what should matter more. And then, just as important, sometimes it can spark a memory that is worth every bit of the momentary discomfort, whether you learn anything or not.

At Frankie's I was a regular. Before Ginny was in the unit, we ate pancakes there every Saturday. Before I drove to work Monday through Friday, I ate breakfast there. At Frankie's I was a mother and a business woman. Except when I was with Maeve. She had this unique way of bringing out the side of me that I realized more and more was part of my ability to hang on through the worst life could dish out. There is plenty of sadness in life; but there is laughter too, and often times the two can come together in remarkable ways.

Chapter 24

A D a y i n t h e S u n

At Cocoa Beach, we unloaded the car, then set up for the day. We brought lounge chairs and beach towels, two coolers, one with spirits (I love that word) and one with water. A beach umbrella. A radio. Maeve's bag of spritzers and oils. Sunglasses. A frizbee. Magazines. And our cell phones.

When we were situated in our chairs, Maeve decided to call Ted. I protested, but she'd already pressed in the code for Technician Magician. Jake answered. Maeve was holding up the phone so I could hear his voice. She looked delighted and winked at me. Giggling under her breath, she said, "Hey, lover boy, guess who has your woman?" She kept holding the phone out so I could hear.

Jake chuckled, "Ah, let me see. Is it a blonde broad with big boobs?"

Maeve laughed. "You got it, baby."

"Where the hell are you?" Jake asked. "I can barely hear you."

Maeve laughed again. "Cocoa Beach, baby. I kidnapped your woman and took her to the beach." Maeve winked at me again. "And she's laying here naked, winking at guys."

I grabbed the phone protesting, "I am not!" But Maeve took it out of my hand.

I could hear Jake calling Ted and laughing. He said to Maeve, "Well, tell her to find me some women."

I frowned. Maeve was still laughing.

She said, "We just called to tell you boys while your sweating your buns off working on cars, we'll be soaking our buns in the sun."

Jake said, "Let me speak to Haley."

Maeve handed me the cell phone. I said, "Hey."

Jake said, "Straw." Then he added, "Don't burn those cute buns."

I laughed. "I wish you were here," I told him, while Maeve mimicked me and then stuck her index finger down her throat.

"I love you," I said.

Jake grunted. "How come you didn't tell me you were going?"

"It was a last minute thing," I lied, regretting it the moment I said it. "We both need a break."

"Yeh," he said joking, "Well, when you come home tonight *I'll* break you."

My face turned red. Maeve rolled her eyes.

"Jake?" I asked, "You're not mad are you?"

Jake chuckled. "No," he said. "Have a good time."

I started to give Maeve back her phone, but I heard Jake and held on to it.

"Not too good a time, though," he said, "without me."

I smiled, "I won't," I told him. "I love you."

I gave the phone back to Maeve who held it between us again while Jake asked her, "Hey, what's she wearing?"

Maeve answered, "I told you—nothing." She winked at me again. Then she said to Jake, "What's it to you?"

Jake insisted, "Which one is it?"

Maeve smiled. "It's a thong. The black one."

I heard Jake groan. Then he said. "I told her not to wear that in public."

Maeve protested. "Don't worry. There are no thong police here. She's fine."

Jake said, "Yeh, well you remind your little buddy in crime, the thong police is right here waiting for her when she comes home tonight."

Maeve laughed. "Okay, big daddy," she said. "I'll tell her. Gotta go. It's been too much fun."

I could hear Ted in the background yelling, "Wait!" But Maeve hit the end button She gave me a disgusted look and said, "Don't you ever get tired of his shit?"

I was putting more lotion on my thonged buns. I decided I didn't want to be in trouble with Jake and have burned buns.

I told Maeve, "It's not like that. You think it's a challenge for me to put up with Jake, but the truth is I love him just the way he is."

Maeve turned on to her back and shut her eyes. "Well, I just don't get it," she said. "You know he has no freakin' idea how much you carry on your shoulders. Anything about how much you need a break. And he treats you like a child."

I lay down on my stomach. Buns to the sun. I turned my face toward Maeve. "He treats me like I'm a woman," I said.

"Yeh, right," Maeve said. "I'm gonna get a tape recorder for you and plant it in his car. Maybe when you play back the recordings, you'll hear the truth. He is so full of himself it's sickening." Maeve leaned over her chair and took a sip from her water bottle. Then she said, "He is so damn lucky to have you it isn't even funny. And there you are with your 'I hope I didn't make you mad, honey. Let me bend over a little further.'" Maeve brushed sand from her calves.

I laughed. "You're ricidulous. Listen, it works for us and that is all that matters. I see other sides to Jake that you and Ted never see, you know. He is very sweet to me. He's just, I don't know, I guess, old fashioned. No, traditional. I don't know. He just likes things a certain way. Like he's the man, and he's in charge. And that's fine with me."

Maeve put her hands to her throat, pretending to choke herself. "Oh, god, here we go. Barefoot and pregnant. Rolling back forty years of bra burning."

I laughed. "You know that's not true. You know how my life is. Five days a week. Grinding it out in my office—doing budgets, working price modules, analyzing reports and preparing for meetings." I wiped a line of sweat running down the back of my right thigh. "I see the guys come in off the nesi routes at 5 and 6 at night, after they started their day at 3:30 a.m. They tell me about their days slinging trash in the ninety degree heat. How they didn't get any lunch. How their stomachs and knees ache." I squirmed a little, as the heat seemed to be pressing into my lower back like an iron on cloth. "Meantime, the men in mangagement sit behind mahogany desks in their air-conditioned offices, penciling in another vacation on their calendars. And the hell of it, Maeve," I said, propping myself up on my elbows, "is that I'm one of them now. I've joined the ranks of the bullshitters."

Maeve wiped sweat from under her belly ring and said, "Yeh, well, let's not forget. They pay more for bullshitters. And I can't remember when you had a vacation."

Maeve was right about vacations, and I'd learned quickly that it's truth about women in management having to work twice as hard as men to prove they had as much value, but I didn't want to be comforted at the moment. "Yeh, well at least when I was in sales, when I was out on the streets," I said, "I felt like I was helping the guys who made it all happen. You know I'd make sure they had good clearance, that they didn't have blind backs or tight spots. That the trash wasn't so heavy it'd break the forks or cause them to get a ticket. But now, now I'm so damn far away from the trash, I can't even smell it. I'm not picking up trash, I'm generating it. And it makes me sick. I used to love my job, but now... Now, I'm calling the shots from a glass tower. I'm the one I used to stand at the watercooler and make jokes about with my drivers. I'm the freakin taskmaster who's forgotten what the task is."

Maeve frowned. "Yeh, well you're preachin' to the choir, babe, and trust me, Jake doesn't understand. He doesn't have a fuckin' clue what you do."

I shook my head, then laid it back down facing Maeve. "He does too," I said. "He knows all about it. And he listens when I tell him about my days." I swiped at a line of sweat forming on my stomach." I remember this one time I was describing how frustrated I was with our operations manager. How he used to sit in our weekly managers' meetings and talk about the cost of temp labor. And how my team needed to generate more sales so we could better absorb the costs of it." I rolled my eyes, while a little boy in front of me kicked sand at part of his crumbling castle. "Anyway, right there in the moment, a second after I told Jake the problem, with no experience whatsoever in the waste management industry, he came up with a solution."

Maeve lifted her head and smirked. "Oh, yeh? And what theory did your big-balled mechanic come up with...which by the way I'm sure would only work in theory."

I sat up frowning. "You're wrong. It would have worked in practice. If our operations manager was smart enough to implement it." I pulled at the band on the bottom of my suit to see if I was burning. "But," I sighed, "he isn't. I could write down verbatim Jake's detailed plan for back up when drivers are late, sick, injured, fired, or when they retire. One that would stand the test of time and work every day. Cut costs. Free up time. And the ops manager we have probably couldn't even read it, never mind make use of it. But..." I said, putting my head down for a second, then facing Maeve again. "You know, sometimes you really surprise me." I lay back down. "I would never pick you to judge someone by what they do."

Maeve turned over to face me while a flock of seagulls flew over our heads and a mother screamed at her son—a little boy maybe six or seven—who was wading into the water past his waist. Squinting at me, Maeve said, "You know I'm not judging Jake's being a mechanic."

I laughed at this. "Oh, right," I said. Then you won't mind if I perform a little memory test with you?"

Maeve looked confused but she answered, "What? About what?"

"Oh, let me see," I said, licking my lips. "How about I recall a few of the names you've called him. Which..." I lowered my chin, "I'm certain were just terms of affection, not meant to show *any* disrespect." Maeve frowned but didn't stop me. "How about 'big-balled' or 'grease monkey'?"

Maeve frowned deeper, then said, "Say whatever you want. I have no problem with what Jake does for a living. I'm talking about what kind of man he is."

"Oh," I said. "So I guess I should be happy you don't care he's a mechanic but you don't think he's a good man?"

"I didn't say that," Maeve said, wiping sweat from under her eyes. "I just don't think he's the right man for you...." She paused, trying to gauge the effect of what she wanted to try next. Then she said, "Like the thong thing. You know he doesn't say things like that because he cares about you, babe. He says it because he's a control freak. And that is a scary match for you because you couldn't be more eager to please."

I sat up, swinging my feet over the side of the chair and taking a sip from my water bottle. "So what am I guilty of here? Wanting to make Jake happy?"

"No, you're guilty of bad decision making. He is not the right guy for you, babe. Trust me."

"I just... I don't get it," I told Maeve, shaking my head. "If you were serious about someone. I would... I would never dog 'em. I wouldn't sit there and criticize them every chance I got. I mean, if I didn't like them, I wouldn't lie about it, but you know, in the end, I'd say to myself, 'it's her decision.' Unless I thought he would hurt you. Now, that's different."

Maeve sat up and planted her feat in the sand just inches from mine. She stared straight at me. "Yeh, it is. And that's what I think Jake will do. I really think he could hurt you, babe. And I love you. I just don't want to see you get hurt."

"But see," I said, "That makes no sense. I mean, I know you think I'm out of his league. You've said it dozens of times before. If that's true, why would you think he would hurt me. If you really believe that, why wouldn't you think I'll hurt him?"

"Cause I know you. You won't hurt him. You'll never hurt him. You love him. But, babe, he doesn't even know who you are. I hear you telling people about him, you know. You act like he's some kind of a world traveler, when the reality is since he was a teenager, he's spent his life living like any other average lower middle class guy in central Florida. He can't even appreciate what he has 'cause he doesn't know what he has. I mean, yeh, I'll give him credit—he saw you were beautiful. Picked you out of the crowd. Like any fool could. But beyond that, baby, he doesn't appreciate the first thing about you. Not your spirit, your talent, your discipline, your experience—nothing. I see him, you know, when we're out— checking some girl out half our age with probably half your IQ, none of your talent or discipline, or spirit, and certainly no devotion like the kind you have for his sorry ass. He thinks I don't see him, but I do."

I laughed. "All men do that. Hell, if he didn't do that, I'd think he wasn't a man. No, I'm sorry. If that's all you got on him—that he looks at other women—he can stay guilty as charged, and I'll still love him."

"That's not all, babe. I can tell he doesn't get you. He doesn't."

"Well," I told Maeve, "I'm not sure how fair that is. I'm not real easy to 'get.' And if you want to know the truth, I think other than Ginny and Faith, Jake probably 'gets' me better than anyone."

"Okay, I give up," Maeve said. Then she said, "You know what?"

"What?" I said.

"Nothing would make me happier than to be wrong about him. For Ted and me to both be wrong. For Jake to be a really good man who 'gets' you and loves you and won't leave you." Maeve stared straight into my eyes, took a deep breath and continued, measuring her words as though she had a bagful to choose from but had decided to be very selective about which ones she would give me. "I hope, babe, I really hope he isn't stringing you along… getting whatever he needs or wants right now, while your beautiful little heart is banking on forever. I hope to God that isn't what's happening." She took another breath. Tears welling in her sunlit eyes. "See, Jake and I are more alike than you think. We both have 'walk away' dads. And …." Maeve was crying now, two large tears running down her cheeks, "…and we both hurt from this…*will* hurt…." Her shoulders were shaking now and her breaths came shallow and sharp. "...the rest of our lives," she managed to get out, after a long effort at control. Then she wiped at her cheeks, using both hands and looking up to keep more tears from spilling, then down again almost instantly her eyes blinking from the sun. "Oh, what the hell," she said, "if you don't mind I'm just gonna cry."

I smiled and nodded and noticed that her tears had stopped.

"Anyway," she said, sniffing and brushing her hair away from her face, "the *truth* is...." She paused for a second and frowned, then gave me a little half smile, cocking her head and looking at me as if I'd said something—"God, did you hear that? I'm starting to sound like you...." She breathed out the beginning of a laugh, and I started to laugh too, but she spoke quickly to stop both of us. "Hell, whatever...," she continued, "your favorite saying works here—and 'the truth *is*,' babe, history repeats itself. I've spent a lot of time in my own life walking away from men who loved me...walking away before they could leave me. See, that's what happens when you get hurt really bad by someone who is always supposed to be there for you. You live your life in fear. Never really trusting or believing anyone who loves you. And...." Maeve dropped her head, lowering her voice to a child's whisper and raising her eyebrows. "You become what you hate," she said. "It sounds crazy, I know." She closed her eyes and the tears started again. "Believe me, I know." She cried silently for a little while and when I touched her on the arm to comfort her she pulled away and shook her head. Then she opened her eyes and looked at me. "It happens," she said. Every day. History repeats itself."

"Oh, my God," I said, reaching over then and squeezing Maeve arm. "Stop this," I said. "Stop this right now. We're here to have a good time, not to dig up our pasts. *You* are gonna be fine. *Jake* is gonna be fine." I sat up straight, smiled big, and tossed my hair back. Then I leaned toward Maeve. "You've given yourself hamster eyes," I said. Maeve didn't smile. "Don't worry," I sang, "be happy."

Maeve rested her elbows just above her knees and dropped her head again, covering her face with her hands. I couldn't tell if she was still crying, so I kept singing the same words over again, tapping a rhythm on her arm and then on the top of her head until she finally couldn't keep from laughing. Her shoulders started to shake, and then she lifted her head and laughed out loud, grabbing my arms, bouncing me up and down on my chair a little as she laughed. Then catching her breath, she said, "No! No! We should sing your song," and she burst into, "Stand by your man…."

I laughed. "Ya think. Think I could do Tammy's song?" I was still bouncing even though Maeve had let my arms go.

She'd stopped laughing and was looking at me as if she couldn't believe I'd asked the question. She said, "Babe, you *are* Tammy's song."

Chapter 25

P a s t ,   P r e s e n t ,   F u t u r e

People's voices soften at the beach, or maybe I just hear the contrast between the high pitch of the gulls and the resonance of the human voice. I'm certain—no trick of sound or light in this case—that they move differently. It doesn't seem to matter what age people are, they act like children when they are at the beach. Their steps are lighter, quicker—their bodies more elastic. They laugh more and longer. And their faces seem calm like they are sleeping, only you can see they are wide awake.

Maeve and I lay in the sun, turning from one side to the other, re-basting ourselves with lotion every half and hour, until noon, when she announced she was starved.

"Atkins omelette didn't quite do it for you?" I kidded.

Maeve laughed. "Shut up and put your shorts on. There's a great café somewhere over to our left I think. They've got the best sandwiches in the world and I'm celebrating. To hell with Atkins." She paused, dropping her sunglasses down on her nose. "Well, at least for today," she said.

Maeve was right. The sandwiches were wonderful. I had one with crab cakes and a dill mayonnaise, and she had one with smoked white fish and a light marmalade spread. I drank chardonnay and she drank white zinfandel, and we considered splitting a piece of key lime pie but finally passed, making a small concession to good judgment.

After we'd eaten, I asked Maeve if we could go for a walk and she thought that was a wonderful idea. We headed back to our campsite and slipped off our shorts, then rubbed sunscreen on each other's shoulders and backs and headed south down the beach.

The tide had just gone back out, so we had plenty of sand to walk on, but we chose to stay close to the water, hopping over jelly fish and skirting the sharp shells.

Maeve was wearing her light shimmery-blue bikini with her silver belly-button ring and silver hoop earrings. I had made a move to put on a beach wrap in deference to Jake, but Maeve had immediately given me a look of warning. I thought she might give me another lecture, too, but she just said, "You were born to wear pearls and a black thong, babe."

As we walked down the beach, men and boys alike stared at us, and I decided it was a toss up between the discomfort of their ogling and Maeve's inevitable harassment about Jake if I'd covered up. Maeve was obviously enjoying the sizing up enough for both of us.

When she wasn't encouraging the attention we were getting, we talked about our lives before we met—beginning with childhood, a time we agreed seemed sometimes far away and sometimes like yesterday. We remembered games we played as kids. Maeve's favorite was dodgeball, mine was hopscotch. But we both liked Red Rover and shared funny stories about trying to break through some fat kid's arms.

I asked Maeve about being at war because I loved to hear her tell war stories. This time, though, she talked about her hair. Mine is naturally curly and hers is straight, but we also both have our hair foiled, so we share an appreciation for trying to grow out very delicate damaged hair.

Maeve began, "Here's a story of sacrificing hair in the service of our country."

I smiled. I knew this would be a gem.

Maeve said, "I'd been trying to grow my hair out for over a year and a half, just barely trimming it every month to keep the ends healthy when I got my orders for Kuwait. I didn't think about it at first. I mean, I knew in the past I'd had to cut it, but I don't know…. I was fighting with Doug, and my mom and Dad were upset I was going to war again and my hair wasn't on my mind." She laughed. "But boy it was when I got there. There'd been an infestation of lice throughout the whole camp, and they weren't letting anyone in with hair. So…." Maeve sighed, remembering. "Anyway," she continued in a moment, "my beautiful long hair I'd spent over a year growing got chopped off in about one minute."

"Oh," I said, groaning. "You must have been dying while they were cutting it."

"Maeve tilted her head up like she was thinking. "No," she said. "Actually, it bothers me more thinking about it now. Because when it was happening… well, let's just say losing the hair beat the alternative."

"Oh god, I know," I said. "Lice! How gross! I remember when Ginny used to come home and hold out a notice from school—'Dear Parent… head lice has been detected on several children, etc. etc.' I would freak out. Every time. I just never got used to it. We'd go get that special shampoo and wash everything we owned and steam clean the carpets and furniture. The first time, before I knew better, I threw out more than I want to think about. And even after I learned, I always had an impulse just to pitch everything the minute I saw the note. Ginny developed a routine of coming in the door on 'note days' saying 'Mommy, get the lice soap, spare the furniture.'"

Maeve laughed. "That kid has an awesome sense of humor, but youda been one hell of a nurse—the first thing's a compliment, by the way, and the second…well, not so much."

I hopped gingerly over another jelly fish, protesting with as much dignity as I could manage in the air, "I'll have you know I was a nurse!" I said.

Maeve looked at me puzzled, then she giggled, sensing something afoot. "When?" she asked.

I struggled to maintain seriousness. "I was Nurse Flynn," I said, "in my high school's production *of One Flew Over The Cookoo's Nest!*"

Maeve laughed out loud, then said, "And that wasn't even the good part. Why didn't you get Ratchet?"

"I know," I said with a tone of regret. I hated to say the next part because I knew Maeve would tease me unmercifully, but it was that or lie because I knew she wouldn't let it drop. "That's the part I wanted," I said, "but my drama teacher said I was...too pretty."

"Ooohh," Maeve said, her voice already taking on a tone of mock sympathy. She stuck her bottom lip out, pretending to pout, and said, "Poor pitiful you. Too pretty to be a mean old nurse."

"Stop it!" I said, shoving Maeve a little. "I didn't say it, he did."

Maeve countered, "You didn't have to say it. It's obvious. Yeh, well, what a life. Cursed with being too pretty."

"Oh, shut up," I joked. "Like you're not some sight for sore eyes." And it dawned on me, looking at Maeve's generous Grecian-urn curves, how many forms beauty takes and how I wasn't kidding when I said I'd have given up my particular type of prettiness up for a chance to do a character role.

Maeve was laughing. "Where do you get sayings like that—'sight for sore eyes'? Sometimes I think there's an eighty year old mountain hillbilly housed somewhere in that little head of yours."

I laughed. "Yep, Grandma. Thar sure is." Then I started singing and slapping one knee, "Yee, haw, thank God I'm a country...."

Maeve's laughter rode up over my singing, and she shoved me toward the water saying. "Shut up, you nut. *You* may have a man, but I'm still trying to attract one."

I lost my balance then, and in trying to keep me from falling, Maeve lost hers. We went down together, laughing, and as we tried to help each other up, we fell again. Then the laughter got to be that kind you can't control, the kind you beg the other person to stop because her laughter makes you laugh more, and you can't breath. And in one way, though the laughter starts to hurt and you know it's up to God whether either of you can ever stop, one part of you wants it to go on because you feel it's bringing you close to some truth that you'll surely see if you don't die first.

I didn't know it then, but that would be the last day Maeve and I would spend at the beach together. I'm glad I didn't know it. Typical Maeve style, she'd tucked a camera away in her purse, and the whole day she kept asking our beach towel neighbors and passers by to take pictures of us. So I have those. And the memories of our walk on the beach, hours of lying in the sun in that comfortable silence only true friends share. The time we walked out into the ocean holding hands until the waves broke us apart. How we let them carry us out until we found bigger ones to dive into and how we dove into them until our eyes stung with salt and our noses were running.

It was a day I will always remember. One of the few when I totally forgot about how much trash needs to be picked up or what I needed to bring to Ginny at the unit. It was a day of peace.

§

Ginny loves the beach. The ocean. The waves. Wind and water breezing over her.

Sometimes, when I was waiting for visiting hours to begin, I'd shut my eyes, hear her laughing while John's father held her up by her tiny arms, wading just a little bit into the waves of Mauii.

Ginny was two. And in love, like me, with a place we only got to visit. The beach. Any beach. This time, we spent a week in paradise, at one of the nicest hotels on the island in a penthouse suite.

John's father is a salesman. A very good salesman. And he decided to take one of his bonuses and spend it all on a vacation in Hawaii for his whole family. So for one week in our lives, Ginny and John and I lived like kings and queens. Actually, looking back on it, probably better.

We dined in a restuaruant with tables on an island. The waiters canoed you to your table. The island was surrounded by a pool fed by a waterfall with a cave beneath it. Couples swam around us, kissing and laughing, then headed for the cave only to return moments later, glowing with their secret.

We gourged ourselves on the island's fruit: banana-colored pinapples, soft as marshmallows, sweet as heaven, mangoes the shades of sunset, then indulged in African lobsters, finally feeding each other mouthfuls of fresh coconut cream pie—Ginny imitating us, using her hands as spoons and offering us all bites.

Later, at the luaii, we dressed Ginny in a tropical bathing suit, necklaced her with shells, and tied a little grass skirt around her waist. She ran around the tiki torch-lit grounds squealing, "Catch me, Mommy! Catch me!" while I chased after my nymph in green.

Now, when we take our evening walks, I call up memories like these for Ginny, then watch, as her still mostly solemn expression slowly transforms into her face as a child. Happy. Mischievous. Full of life.

And I wonder…. What studies have been done using memory as a tool for transformation. I've done enough research to know through the years it has been used as a major tool in both analysis and counseling. But I wonder, still, how much it is being used to help those who hear voices—if at all. I've found no books, not even a chapter on the subject.

I know Ginny's doctors and counselors don't use it, choosing instead in their meetings with Ginny to focus entirely on the present. What voices she is hearing now. How many. Whether or not there are hallucinations with them. If she's had any more thoughts of suicide. Then, based on whatever she tells them and their fear of another attempt, they prescribe medication. Medication that can and will, unless I can make my appeal strong enough, eventually end memory. When memory is gone, Ginny and all those who hear voices will be left with one thing—to live with them.

I don't get it. I just don't get it. Call me uneducated on the subject. Lacking the knowledge and experience I would need to understand these methods. Questions about the voices. About suicide. Then drugs and more drugs.

Call me stupid. But just let me ask this—why would anyone treat an illness of the mind by focusing on what is not real? Give voices, delusions, hallucination, and fear more power. Make them seem real. Why? I don't get it. I just don't get it.

But I know this. When I take Ginny to places in her past, a lifetime of real and meaningful moments, she tells me she does not hear the voices then. And what could that be except that then they did not exist? But she did. Without them. Alive and happy in a world where she could have sound and silence at will. And no voices except the real ones. The ones that spoke love.

Just one mother's observation. Based on a lifetime of knowing—my daughter.

Chapter 26

B a b y ' s   B r e a t h

Weeks into Ginny's stay at the unit, I noticed the accusations about our home life dwindled and then one day stopped altogether. Maybe it had become obvious even to the most judgmental of the staff how much I love my child and how unlikely it would have been I would ever let any harm come to her. But, whatever the reason, I could feel the change of heart almost like a touch the day a shy boy named Peter saw me coming down the hall and forgot who he was for an instant, calling out boldly, "Here come the Poem Lady." Hope laughed and three of the other nurses stopped what they were doing and Peter got shy again, but everyone started gathering around, obviously to see what I had up my sleeve that day.

Some days it was a new song for group therapy. Some days it was braiding hair—for whoever wanted a braid or a lesson in braiding. Some days it was the poems I brought for all the children, the thing that had earned me a title from shy Peter. That day I had an idea for a game, but I just stood for a few moments realizing how the little acts of kindness can accumulate so that people you have known for a short time, relatively, begin to act as if they'd always known you. I'm guessing more than a few had noticed that I'd never missed a visiting day. One child, I recalled, even told me once, "I've seen you more in one week than I've seen my daddy my whole life." Another moment when it was hard for me to separate my feeling of joy and sadness.

But there was one thing that was very clear to me the more time I spent with the children at the unit. And though I have no medical degree or any type of certification whatsoever in the mental health field, all of my senses are still in tact, and that is all anyone would need to realize every one of these children had been misdiagnosed. All being treated for broken minds, when it was clear it was their hearts that had been broken.

And here's my mind-blowing revelation. Coming years before the majority of mental health experts will admit to the truth of it. Antipsychotics do not treat or heal broken hearts. They will not enhance the lives of sensitive souls. And they will never be the answer for the most gentle spirits on this earth to cope with living in this world.

Years ago, actually decades ago, Dr. Peter Breggin found a way to help heal these rare human beings with compassion and tenderness and an eagerness to learn from them "what hurts" so he could help them feel better. But tragically Dr. Breggin proved to be the exception in his field. And, as a result, through the years many with mental illness have either killed themselves or spent a lifetime trying to.

I can't help recalling our evening in the emergency room. The night of Ginny's breakdown. And her catscan results. Clean. No abnormatlities whatsoever. And no apparent consciousness either, in fact, an obvious denial—in Ginny's doctors and counselors—of a bigger picture. Bigger than anything organic. As big as the soul. Bigger. A spirit being crushed by this world.

When I am not so angry about this willed ignorance that I can't see straight, I envision things. Like a court order, some sort of mandate for all of the psychiatrists in America, demanding they go back to school and to residencies, where they would be required to learn what it is they are supposed to be doing for a living. To study the human heart and mind and to make connections. Talk to those who are ill. And most importantly—listen to them.

It won't be easy for them, I know. Going back to school. Having to study so hard. But probably easier than it was for my daughter to take five accelerated learning classes for college-bound high school students stoked up on 1200 milligrams of Seroquil prescribed by none other than her psychiatrist. Payback is hell.

Well, so much for my ideas about progress. How we might better treat and try to heal the mentally ill. And why should anyone care? Because the pharmaceutical companies are all over it. Yes, siree. We can all just sit back and relax and feel completely safe just knowing how they are helping treat and cure those with mental illness.

For instance—our military. It's not enough the men and women fighting to protect our country are risking their lives every day. No. Now they are being subjected to the suggestion from the makers of Paxil that any depression or anxiety they feel due to being at war can be treated by taking this drug. Never mind that there have been countless deaths involved in the use and discontinuation of the use of it. Yes, this is true. Our military is now being treated with Paxil. Some of the bravest men and women in our country, risking their lives for us and not even realizing they have a double threat in their lives now. Whatever war they are currently fighting for us and Paxil.

More "cutting edge" from the pharmaceutical companies and the mental health community. You no longer have to bother with taking pills. Trying to stick to a schedule of daily dosages. You can get a shot. That's right. A whole month's dosage of drugs entering your body in one shot. Let's see now, what would you call that—progressive thinking? Convenient? How about destructive? One look in the eyes of someone on a shotfull of the medication kids got in the unit where Ginny stayed, and you could have seen—anyone could see who could bear to look. Something had happened without a doubt. But nothing to do with healing at all. Every day I grew more certain that whatever the difficulties outside for Ginny, the unit was not the place for her to be.

So while I sang songs or played games or braided hair or read poems every time I visited, I also asked every time I left when Ginny would be released.

And I was repeatedly told, in no uncertain terms, by the same nurses who had mellowed in other respects, "Those orders will come from Dr. Traynor, and he hasn't said anything about releasing Ginny."

Yet in spite of the staff's pessimism and my ongoing doubts, Ginny did seem finally to be improving a little—something I learned later was in the nature of her illness, brief periods even, when if you hadn't known Ginny before, you might not have known anything was the matter with her. She made presents for me every craft class. A jewelry box, a wind chime, a ceramic heart. And she'd been elected "president of the unit," which I later discovered was a dubious honor given to the child who'd been there the longest, but which also, in fairness to Ginny, did carry with it responsibility—assigning the other patients daily duties and keeping records of who had and who had not done their jobs. Ginny seemed eager to be useful. It was this eagerness, in fact, that seemed to me at the time the clearest sign of improvement—a return of pleasure in outcomes.

Meantime, the medical bills continued to jam my mailbox, and I had begun the impossible task of trying to pay them. With the high rent on the condo, my car payment, living expenses, and credit card bills, I kept coming up short to the tune of about a thousand dollars a week, listening to voicemail after voicemail from threatening creditors. I was operating now on promises.

But I was not worried.

My contract had stated I'd get a bonus in April based on the year-end reports, basically on our ebit. The contract did not say the bonus was discretionary, which I probably should have realized, given the elusive character of ebit, but for me a contract has always meant word of honor, and a promise has always been a promise to me.

Anyway, the last week in April I was called into the controller's office. I thought he was going to tell me the date for our monthly business review had changed or ask me why my reps' cell bills were so high—something fairly routine. But he didn't ask me anything. He just told me no one was getting a bonus. Period. No warning. No debate. No discussion.

When I had my first minute alone, the full force of the controller's news hit me and with it the realization of how I'd been counting on that bonus to pay medical bills. I couldn't help hearing Jake's voice in my head. Over and over again. Telling me, "You trust people too much."

Willow Pond was relentless. They would call every day, sometimes two times a day when not even thirty days had passed since Ginny's first bills were generated. And the calls were not reminders, they were threats.

So I chose to pay the medical bills, just as I'm sure they'd hoped. And then, of course, the rent came due, then the car payment, then the credit cards, and the nightmare had only begun.

Where Maeve and I lived at Terra Cotta Villages, there was something constantly the matter with our units. We paid some of the highest rent in Winter Park and lived with mold, leaking ceilings, faulty plumbing, occasional air conditioning. Cockroaches thrived because the exterminators came infrequently—some months not at all. The saying "you can't judge a book by its cover" could never have been more aptly applied. On the outside, Terra Cotta looked like a neighborhood of luxury condominiums, but after we'd lived there for a few months, we both knew what it was—a seventeen-year-old development, poorly maintained and barely managed.

Maeve and I tag teamed on calling the management with our ongoing list of problems, almost never receiving a return phone call or any service. There were no apologies for their shortcomings and no thanks for our patience, but when Maeve needed a temporary extension on her lease, they told her, "That's just not possible. We never make exceptions."

I didn't ask anyone for help, didn't even tell anyone I was under stress. I just kept going to work every day, doing my job, visiting Ginny, and willing myself to believe things would get better. It was and is my way. If I'd even thought to discuss with anyone what I felt when I learned there would be no bonus, I'm not sure what I would have said—maybe that it was the closest I had ever been to losing all perspective.

Looking back on it all now, I know that my judgement was affected by that final blow from Evergreen. If I had it to do again, I'd tell the collectors from Willow Pond I'd pay them as I could. I'd not have let them threaten me about my credit or my daughter's welfare. Ironically, paying the medical bills did not safeguard anything for me, and it occurred to me even then that as soon as my check to Willow Pond's bill collectors cleared, they would just find someone else to call.

§

One non-visiting night, Jake and I decided to go look at new cars. Jake hated my Ford Focus. He thought it was both cheap and unsafe. It made no difference to him that I didn't really choose it, that it was part of a former company's program to reduce costs—he just wanted me to get rid of it.

I'm thinking of a good comparison. Something he owned and used that would have affected me in the same way. It's like this I guess: Jake's a mechanic—he loves well-built cars, trucks, and motorcycles; I'm a writer—I love well-crafted poems, stories, and plays. I suppose it would have driven me crazy if Jake spent his free time reading dime store novels.

But he didn't. And I *did* drive a cheap car. So cheap it drove Jake crazy, so we went to look for a new one, one that was safe and better built, and one that Jake approved of—I guess, beyond safety— on some aesthetic grounds of the relationship between design and motion and power that will probably always remain a mystery to me.

I wanted a Mustang. I'd always wanted a Mustang. So we looked at Mustangs for hours until I couldn't justify their cost.

We spent the night wandering around different car lots, Jake giving advice to the uninformed, overzealous, fast-talking salespeople, who were constantly approaching us. One guy even took notes while Jake educated him about a particular model. But I was disgusted with their too obvious tactics.

In the end, I was exhausted and Jake was frustrated because I couldn't commit to buying anything, and I was at a loss to understand how a car could mean that much to anyone.

It's funny. Now, I see it so clearly. It wasn't about the car. It was about who he is. I mean it's what he knows and loves, and there I was with sort of the attitude "This isn't that important." I could kick myself every time I think about it. It was such a simple thing to understand.

When we got home—back to Jake's—Ray was nowhere to be found. I fell onto the sofa, spreading myself on it like peanut butter on bread. Jake walked into the kitchen to get a glass of iced tea.

I hadn't rested for a minute when my cell phone rang. I sat up and pulled the phone out of my purse, dropping it and then fumbling to open it—the brief release of muscles and my constant anxiousness about Ginny making me clumsy. By the time I'd gotten the phone to my ear and realized it was a call from the unit, Jake was back with his tea. He knew the tone of my voice when someone from the unit had called and he sat down close to me.

"This is Ginny's mother," I said.

It was Maria. She said, "We don't want to alarm you, but we did want to let you know Ginny was having difficulty breathing."

I sat up straighter. "What? Is she okay?" I demanded. "What happened?"

Jake put one arm around me.

Maria answered like a robot. "It's a typical response to one of her medications and we have it under control. We've administered some Benedryl and she should be fine."

"What if she isn't?" I asked, pushing Jake's arm away and standing up suddenly. "What if this happens again? What if she's sleeping? What if no one is there?" I was crying now, and my whole body was shaking. I called out, "Where is she? Where is my baby?"

Jake stood up and tried to put his arms around me, but I was pacing and crouching and sobbing hysterically. "I want to hear her talk!" I shouted. "Where is my baby?"

Maria answered calmly. She is right here Ms. Robbins, but I suggest you calm down before I put her on. Ginny..." she emphasized her name, "is fine now. You need to calm down."

I tried to stifle my sobs. My chest felt like it was cramping. Then I heard Ginny's soft distant voice.

"Mommy?...Hi, Are you okay?"

I couldn't stop crying, but I said, "I'm okay, baby, how are you? What happened?"

Ginny said, "I couldn't swallow. I was sitting on the couch after dinner and I couldn't swallow. The nurse saw me kind of turning blue, so she came over. But I'm okay now."

I felt like I would throw up. I caught my breath and was conscious suddenly of my own swallowing. Then I said, "Did they give you some medicine? Is that what made it better?"

Ginny answered, "They gave me a shot. Then in a minute I could swallow."

I let out a sigh. "Have they been with you all the time?"

There was a beat of silence, then Ginny said, "Yes...," like someone was telling her to say it. "Yes, they have been with me."

I said, "I want to come be with you, Ginny. I'm going to ask Maria if I can come stay with you tonight."

Ginny said to Maria, "Mommy wants to know if she can come stay with me tonight."

Maria must have taken the phone away from Ginny because she was on the other end in a second telling me, "That won't be necessary, Ms. Robbins. We have everything under control here. We were just calling you as a courtesy."

I choked out, "Courtesy? You've given my daughter medication that stops her breathing—so she has to have a shot to be able to breathe again, and you call me as a courtesy?"

Maria's voice became sterner. "I told you difficulty with swallowing is a common side effect of Ginny's medication and we have the situation under control. Now goodnight, Ms. Robbins."

I screamed, "Don't hang up! Where's Ginny? I want to talk to Ginny."

Maria answered, "We have already put her to bed."

I demanded, "Let me speak to her! I want to hear she is okay or I'm coming over there right now!"

"Ms. Robbins," Maria said, "there is no need for you to come here, and if you do, you will not be admitted. Now I have Ginny under twenty-four-hour observation. Someone will be with her at all times."

"But I'm her mother," I cried. "She's my baby. I want to be with her."

"I know you do," Maria acknowledged, briefly softening; then growing stiff again, she said, "but we have rules that must be followed. Now goodnight."

And before I could say anything more, Maria hung up.

Jake was standing in front of me, and I threw my arms around him, sobbing louder than ever. He held me close, every now and then "shushing" me and every so often kissing the top of my head.

"It'll be okay," he said. "It's going to be all right."

"It's not going to be all right," I mumbled into his chest. "My baby couldn't breathe." I cried harder.

"Shhhhh," Jake whispered. "I heard you say they gave her a shot. She's okay now. You need to calm down. It's okay."

I knew it wasn't okay. Nothing was okay anymore. But I had no energy left to fight. So I let Jake pick me up and carry me to his bed. There he undressed me, tucked me in, and kissed me good night. All I could think about was breathing and how I felt I had to breathe from now on, not just for me but for Ginny.

Chapter 27

H i d e   a n d   S e e k

Now I know the term for what Ginny experienced that night. I combed the index of a medical handbook looking for references to swallowing and breathing, turning the pages back and forth until I found the condition. It is called *dystonia*, a fancy way of saying that muscles are in spasm. Sometimes those muscles are in the region where you draw breath, so you can't get air. The so-called "standard" antipsychotics, such as were prescribed in large doses for Ginny while she was on the unit, are more often involved in episodes of dystonia than are the more recently marketed antipsychotics. Nothing I learned from my reading is reassuring, and though I never remember thinking about breathing before that horrific night on the unit, I have thought about it too much since. I believe it goes without saying that a parent's worst nightmare is that her child will stop breathing for any period of time. It is a life-changing event.

In fact, all that followed that night is altered by it—I am more conscious now of every rhythm. And of how it feels when rhythm is interrupted in ways we cannot control.

Before she came to the unit, one of the rhythms of Ginny's life familiar to anyone who knew her was her honesty. She was truthful to the point of being unsociable—

telling famly they had stayed too late on a school night when she had homework to do or a friend from school he didn't have the voice to try out for the lead in the musical, even telling a minister once, at a church she and Winnie had attended briefly for a school project, that she felt matters of faith were personal. "Mommy, they went around asking people to say how many times they had witnessed for Jesus since the last class," she told me on the Sunday the minister had asked her if she and Winnie enjoyed the church school lesson. "I just told him that was between me and Jesus."

So when I discovered Ginny had been lying to me during my visits to the unit, I felt blindsided again—the honesty that had seemed as natural to Ginny as three-four time to a waltz would suddenly be traded for stories my daughter thought I needed to hear. "Dr. Traynor says I can come home soon, Mommy. Probably next weekend."

Of course, I had no contact with Dr. Traynor and Ginny had no history of telling lies, so I did what any parent would do—I believed my child.

I began calling John every night to check on his progress with his move, and I started spending evenings at my home, rearranging the rooms so that he would fit in. I even decorated our screened in patio with silk purple irises and long strands of vines, dotting each window sill with vanilla citronella candles. I bought a couple more patio chairs to make the porch more comfortable, and the night before Ginny announced she would definitely be coming home, added a corner-full of exotic potted plants. On the way out of the garden store, I had noticed some fairytale-looking insects, with little marbled bodies and wire legs and wings, and I carefully chose the ones I knew Ginny would like best. Later I would find a way of attaching them to the plants for a touch of whimsy. I could hear Ginny's laughter. The way it used to be. When the mystery in her life had to do with something either she or I or both of us together had created. Not the way her mind works.

I planted all new flowers beside the walkway to the front door of the condo. Pink impatiens. Lavendar. Sage. Butterfly bushes—anything I thought would remind Ginny of our home on the mountain. I told Jake and Maeve and Ted, "Ginny is coming home!" I even called Whispering Pines to notify the school she'd be returning soon.

Ginny's tennis coach called me back as soon as she got word. She invited us to the athletic banquet where Ginny was to receive a letter and pin and recognition as the player who had the best win-loss record on the team. Everything, I thought, was falling into place. But, of course, the homecoming was a fantasy Ginny had made for me, not without reason and certainly as substantial to her as the gifts she made in craft class. She had no idea the preparations I found myself making daily to take care of her or how much I hoped her homecoming would mean…Ginny rediscovering herself.

Not only had Dr. Traynor never told Ginny she was being released, he was actually fighting the insurance companies not to demand her release. My company's insurance covered only thirty days at a time in a crisis unit. And Ginny's thirty days were running out.

Much later, I would discover that Dr. Traynor had added another medication to Ginny's regimen about the time she had begun creating stories about her release. Loxapine. Potential side effects: low blood pressure and—though none of the books admit to it, of course—additional terror, grief, and bewilderment for the mothers of children to whom it is prescribed.

This time, when the call came in from the unit, I was at work. The voice I heard when I answered my phone came in a whisper, and so the usual anxiousness I felt was elevated to alarm before I even heard the reason for the call. "It's Eric, Ms. Robbins—

from the unit." I remember wondering why Eric, one of the male nurses who frequently supervised recreational periods, was calling me instead of Maria and why he couldn't speak in a normal voice; I also remember that it seemed my hearing had grown so acute that his whispering was almost painful to listen to. I desperately wanted and didn't want to hear what Eric had to tell me, which was that Ginny had been transported to the emergency room at Willow Pond. "We were at the pool swimming," Eric told me, "well, not Ginny because she told me she didn't feel well. She was just standing on the side of the pool watching the others, when all of a sudden she fell over and hit her head on the concrete."

"What?" I cried out. "Is she bleeding? Is she conscious?"

"Please, Ms. Robbins," said Eric, still whispering. "I'm trying to tell you.... It happened a couple of hours ago. They didn't want me to call you. But I.... I knew I should. So I did."

I had already begun to assemble my things without thinking, instinctively hooking my purse over my free arm, flipping a light sweater I carried to restaurants over my shoulder, and tucking reports I took with me wherever I went between my arm and side as I repeated the questions Eric had not yet answered, trying not to panic, "Eric, was she bleeding? Unconscious? You've got to tell me now."

"No," Eric said. "I mean, yes, she was bleeding a little...her head and her arm... All the places that hit first. I think one knee is scraped pretty badly too and maybe a place on her stomach. But she was conscious when they left here and she was asking for you."

"Oh God," I said. "I can't believe this."

Eric said, "She'll be in the emergency room. I'm going over there right now. I'll be there with her. Don't you worry, Ms. Robbins. I won't leave her."

"Thank you, Eric. "Thank you," I said. I was trembling and sweating. "I'm leaving now. I'll be there as soon as I can." I said into the phone. I was already walking fast down the hall. "You tell her I'll be there and I love her, Eric. Tell her I love her with all my heart."

I stopped briefly at my sales coordinator Brianna's coral to let her know there'd been an emergency and I was leaving for the day but that I'd call her as soon as I knew anything.

I drove like a maniac, blowing my horn and weaving through the heavy traffic, the whole way to the hospital, forcing one motorist onto the curb and another into the median to avoid a collision with me. I'm thinking they must have seen the look on my face and knew that whatever lay between me and my daughter didn't matter to me. Only getting to her. When I'd parked my car in the hospital parking lot and was half running, half fast-walking the two blocks to the emergency room, my phone rang again. It was Maria. She said, "Ms. Robbins, I regret to tell you we had to take Ginny to the emergency room today. She…."

"Yes," I said, not letting her finish. I was conscious of my own voice, sharp enough to cut ice. "I know. I'm at the emergency room, and I have nothing to say to you except no one, not you, not Dr. Traynor, no one on your staff better come near me or my daughter without legal protection. I'm with her now," I said. "Though I realize I should never have brought her to this place, I'm with her now," I repeated, as much for myself as for her. "And if you try to get near her or me, trust me, it will be the last time you ever interfere in our lives." I jumped over a patch of neatly landscaped pansies. "What you and Dr. Traynor better do right now is pray. You better pray Ginny is going to be all right. You better spend every waking minute of your day doing just that. Because whatever little justice I can seek isn't half of what you face." I looked to my right then to my left and walked into the breezeway. "It is clear to me that none of you believe in God. But God is here, Maria. He's with Ginny and me. He sees everything that is happening and has happened. You don't need to worry about calling me. And you can tell Dr. Traynor the same. You two need to answer to someone else."

I clicked my phone off and walked into the packed emergency room, where I searched desperately for the face that would help me find my daughter. I was beginning to think I was somehow in the wrong place when I saw Eric. I almost tripped over a table getting to the sofa where Ginny was lying sideways, her back to the room, with her head in Eric's lap. I knelt down beside her and put my arms around her and she turned a little, moaning and trying to smile. Her forehead and left arm were badly scraped and bruised and her top lip was swollen so much it looked freakish. "I knu you cun," she said, unable to close her mouth to form the words.

I put my head down to kiss a small undamaged patch of skin on her forehead, careful not to touch the awful rawness all around it, and my tears spilled into her hair. "I'm here, baby," I said. I'm here. It's gonna be all right."

She smiled and relaxed her head against Eric again.

"I would have been here sooner, but they didn't call me when it happened, I said to her. Eric is the only one who called me."

Ginny spoke in a voice that sounded as if she was asleep, "I tol you he nishe," she said, struggling to make the words, and drooling. I gently wiped the spit off her chin.

"I know he is, sweetheart," I said, rubbing her back. "Don't try to talk anymore. You rest now, while I talk to Eric, okay?"

"Yeh," she said, "I gla yu here," she said softly and then repeated herself, trying harder to get the words out, "I glaad yur here." I rubbed her back again until Eric said, "You want to sit with her?" I nodded to Eric and whispered to Ginny, "I love you. I will always be here for you."

Eric and I changed places. "We've been here for more than an hour. They know she's here for a possible head injury, but she hasn't been called yet."

As I sat with Ginny, Eric tried to fill me in. He said she'd been resting without complaint, and when I asked him, he told me they'd checked her mouth at the unit for cracked teeth and there were none. He said the doctors in the emergency room had asked for Ginny's file so he'd had another staff member bring it to him. He pointed to a blue folder he'd been holding close to him since I first saw him sitting in the chair. It contained at least an inch of pink papers. I asked him if I could see it.

"Oh no, Ms. Robbins. I can't do that," he said, the alarm in his voice evident. "No, these files are for the doctors' use only."

"But," I said, "they're my daughter's, Eric. I'm her mother. Why can't I see them?"

"No," Eric said, his agitation growing. "I can't do that. They entrusted me with these. That's against the law, Ms. Robbins. Please understand."

"It's against the law for me to see my own daughter's medical records?" I asked.

"Yes," he answered and held the file even closer.

I rolled my eyes. "This is unbelievable," I said. "Who in their right mind would invent such a system?" and I was conscious in a beat of the language I had chosen with my daughter's head there in my lap. I remember her asking once a long time ago in the uncanny way she had of bringing the darkness into the light, "Don't you think we're all some crazy, Mommy?"

I turned my attention back to Eric, who was looking at me, still anxious and defensive. "So who is responsible for keeping medical records from parents?" I asked more gently, realizing I didn't need to blame Eric who had already risked a lot for me to be here and who clearly had nothing to do with it.

"HIPAA," is all he would say.

Fortunately nothing can keep a person from researching HIPAA. In the bookstore, I learned that it's an acronym for the Health Information Portability and Accountability Act instituted by the Department of Health and Human Services through the Office for Civil Rights. It's purpose is to preserve the rights of patients and their families with regard to disclosure of medical histories, but it is made impotent both by state laws and by physician's discretion.

What I want to know is how anyone can feel protected knowing their medical history can be locked away from them. And why would any good doctor want to conceal medical information? These are questions no one has been able to answer for me and they are questions I ask myself daily, as I ponder the irony of an act that was created to protect patients but that actually has terrible potential to harm them as well as their families.

In talking with John about the day in the emergency room, I learned that his brother and family tried for years to access his medical records, desperately seeking answers about his treatments and medications in an effort to find a better way to help him, to improve the quality of his life. But they were not given access to his records. I could hear the bitterness in John's voice when he explained, "The doctor just prescribes another bottle of Heldol for him, and we all wait for the next episode." Heldol is an antipsychotic with life-threatening side effects, I learned later from my reading. It is to be used only in the most severe cases of mental illness and for a short time until symptoms are under control. At the time, John's brothers' doctors had been prescribing Heldol for him for twenty years.

§

Recently, John's brother—Ginny's uncle—took his last prescription of anti-depressants and anti-psychotics. All of it.

He was forty-three, once an avid down-hill skier, who lived for challenges. A photographer—who captured the smallest surprises, the most gentle joys. Even after years of being medicated with mind-altering drugs, he was still his family's memory. Never forgetting the events that made their lives unique and recalling them to their delight.

Ginny's uncle was a remarkable man, who, in the end, acted like so many others with mental illness, he chose a quicker death, because all that was offered him was a slow and painful one. When what he truly wanted was to be well and to live.

§

After another hour of waiting to see a doctor, and me demanding, not once but five times, for Ginny to be seen, her name was finally called. We were given a semi-curtained room with a bed. Ginny was given another round of tests along with another CAT scan, and at nine that evening, we finally saw a doctor who told us there appeared to be no damage to the skull or the brain but that he would like to keep Ginny overnight for more observation and tests.

Ginny was actually released the next day at 6 p.m. and taken back to the unit. I had talked with Eric enough to know there was no choice for me about that, and I guessed Maria and Dr. Traynor must feel a wonderful sense of revenge for rages like mine, which they must surely be accustomed to, because they know parents are ultimately at the mercy of the system. I'd need a gun and the resignation to go to prison to have my daughter back without their say so; and of course that would make my time with her brief, just long enough for the authorities to catch up and wait for me to fall asleep. When I learned Ginny was going back to the unit, there was a brief moment when I wondered if I could pull it off. Escape with Ginny. Tuck her into my arms and run away. From a place where nightmares came with the rising of the sun. But I decided against it.

I did get to be with her during the twenty-eight hours we spent in emergency. I left her side four times—to go to the bathroom. I didn't eat or sleep or want to, which is why I figured I'd do fairly well in a stand-off with the law. When emergency was finally desperate to free up our room for another patient, they transported us to the children's wing, the one I learned later was where they kept terminal cases. There were teddy bears and balloons everywhere, brightly wall-papered halls and softly lit rooms. Ginny smiled and said, "Look, mommy, we're in a special place now. We must be very special."

All I could say was, "Yes, you are, sweetheart. Yes, you are."

When Ginny was released from the hospital, I took Eric's advice and signed the papers to have her readmitted to the unit; it occurred to me that the best thing about Ginny's readmission was that it used up her available crisis coverage, which meant she couldn't go back again once they released her. It was a policy that enabled the insurance companies to cut costs and increase their profits, but I saw it as an act of God.

On May 3, 2003, Ginny was released. A week after she'd fallen at the pool. Dr. Traynor never called me. We were given a referral for Ginny's ongoing psychiatric treatment in a message from the staff that Dr. Traynor already had too heavy a caseload. I would say that I thought the doctor's heavier load must be one of conscience, but what I really believe after our experience with him is that he has no conscience at all.

Chapter 28

G a r b a g e   I n ,   G a r b a g e   O u t

When I first accepted a job with Environmental, Blake, my family, and friends were very skeptical about how long a creative writing major could last in the waste management industry. I, of course, was less skeptical. Erring on the side of optimism always.

I was certain a Fortune 200 company would have a good training program and gained reassurance this was in fact the case in my interviewing process. And though I knew nothing of the waste management business, barely able at the time to recall exactly what a garbage truck looks like, I had complete confidence in my ability to sell or manage anything. So I signed on—at thirty-seven years old, a creative writing major, working mother, with a background in theater and marketing—for a new career in the waste management industry. Without a doubt in my mind I would be very successful. And so I was.

Not without help, though. Environmental is the number one waste management company in the nation for a variety of reasons— most importantly, they hire the cream of the crop to take care of their customers. Now when I say "cream of the crop," I don't mean the best educated or best dressed or those from the best homes. I mean they hire the best person for the job. And almost always ones who are honest, ethical, compassionate, practical, and even creative. This is the chief reason Environmental is number one.

The general manager of the local division I worked at, Ace Reddick, was a prime example of the cream of the crop, a former football coach and teacher, who when I started with Environmental had already been with the company some twenty plus years. Ace commuted a hundred miles one way to work every day over windy mountain roads so his wife and family could live in the home they built together in Tennessee.

He taught me as much about life as he did about the garbage industry, returning to work just a few weeks after quadruple bypass surgery, and working an average of ten hours every day. He told me once, while we were standing in the transfer station and he was checking to make sure our loader had been repaired properly, "We do our job, pick people up like they expect, on time, when we said we would, don't hurt anything or anybody, the boys up top can ask more of us, throw more reports our way, ask us to measure things better… but in the end, we can go home to our families feeling good. We can sleep at night. We're here to take care of our customers, Haley. And it's my job to see we do that right every day. You'll see. You listen to me. Sky's the limit for you. 'Cause you're smart. You got a good head on your shoulders. And a good heart. Just don't let them take you too far away from your family or your home. Cause it's not worth it. You stay close to the trash. Close enough where you can still smell it. And stay close to your family. You'll be all right. You'll do fine. " That's Ace. Part sage, part garbage man, part caretaker, part prophet. The best man for the job. And one of the best I've ever met in my life.

It wouldn't be fair to say picking up waste and disposing of it is one of the most difficult jobs there is because "difficult" doesn't really do justice to the reality of the task. One where there is no down time. Never a moment when someone isn't creating some kind of waste that has to be managed.

You've got waste of every different type and shape. And you've got employees who speak different languages and come from a wide variety of backgrounds. You've got customers of every different personality, educational background, and job title. You are operating heavy, temperamental equipment. You are making runs to transfer stations and landfills. Recycling materials. Reporting to a public who still mostly believes managing waste is as simple as throwing it in a place where they will no longer see it, and therefore expects no mistakes from the four biggest companies in the nation, the ones who almost single-handedly manage millions of people's garbage and recycling every day.

Managing waste is an every day gut wrenching, nerve wracking, mind boggling lesson in humility. It may not be brain surgery, but it's every bit as much needed and frankly, from the experience I've had with those in the medical profession versus those in the waste industry, there's no comparison in my mind which are more compassionate and capable people. It's who the public so blithely calls "garbage men." It's the men and women in waste management. Hands down.

I was simply one of the many working in the industry who work harder in one day than some in other industries work in a year. Only I was a little different. I was doing it as a single mother taking care of her mentally ill child. And working for Evergreen, with a company who was not only trying to succeed in a very difficult business but who was trying to do so without the necessary resources.

There are several things you learn quickly when you work in the waste management industry. Number one—nothing else matters if you don't pick up the trash; number two—whoever owns the hole is king. The hole meaning a landfill.

Evergreen had no municipal solid waste landfill in central Florida. What it had was old trucks and a very limited inventory of containers and compactors. And—the kicker—a negative ebit due to some large, unprofitable residential and commercial franchises bid on and acquired before they hired me.

Prior to me becoming central Florida sales manager, they'd gone through five other sales managers in three years. One who they'd promoted to their national sales manager, who couldn't make a dent in the negative numbers attached to the hauling companies in central Florida.

So I had my work cut out for me. No doubt about it. And the only positive things in my favor were my own abilities as well as my experience and training at Environmental.

In spite of all that, and my ongoing days dealing with Ginny's care and recovery, I felt I was up to the task of turning Evergreen into a successful waste management company in Florida.

Before I took over as sales manager, they had no training program, no sales staff to speak of, no decent equipment, an outdated data base, no marketing campaigns, no price increase program or module, no retention programs, no auditing process, a ridiculous budget tied to nothing tangible that actually had happened or could occur, no affiliations with business groups, no relationship with brokers, no presence at all in the communities where they had divisions, and—maybe more important than all of that—no heart in the building.

I helped turn Evergreen around. Brought over a million dollars of revenue to their bottom line—my first year. Increased density on the routes. Reduced the weight of the trash. Increased the quality of our revenue. Hired, trained, and shaped a sales team that could compete even without a landfill and good equipment. While caring for my ill daughter.

My daily thanks for this was an occasional head nod from the men in management as they left the building for another in a series of two-hour lunches. Leaving me to help our customer service answer all of the calls about missed pick-ups and price increases, while still managing my sales team. Keeping the saying "a woman should know her place" alive and well.

And the truth has several parts. As I pointed out, most men and women who work in the waste management industry work very hard and smart. But there are always exceptions. And the waste management companies that are the least successful have those exceptions in management. I was an anomaly at Evergreen.

Second part to the truth. I have always given my best at any job I've ever worked. From winning the golden fry award for serving the most french fries an hour when I was fifteen at my first job at McDonald's to managing four sales divisions for Evergreen. No matter what the job was or what was going on in my personal life, I have always given my best.

Third part. I had no choice. And...I am no exception—to the millions of single working mothers who can never leave their jobs and their responsibilities. Or take two-hour lunches.

Chapter 29

D a i l y   N i g h t m a r e

John didn't arrive until two weeks after Ginny had come home form the crisis unit. Initially, when we were making plans for Ginny's care, I thought I
might have to bring her in to work with me after I picked her up from school
a couple of times, and though I knew under most circumstances, bringing
your child to work with you could be grounds for dismissal, I was hoping,
considering the fact I had only taken one day off the entire time my daughter
was having a crisis, my coworkers and other management would understand
I had no options.

But the fact is John's delayed arrival forced me to bring Ginny into work
with me ten days, not two, and each time I was greeted with more and more
raised eyebrows, hostile whispering, as Ginny and I walked toward my office,
and I felt keenly that in my most desperate state, others at my company outside my sales staff actually imagined I was taking advantage of them.

Ginny and I would leave our home every morning at 6:30. After I dropped
her off at school, I would head into work. I would work through the morning
and three shifts of all the other employees eating lunch—then at 2 o'clock

in the afternoon, I'd spend my allotted lunch time driving to Ginny's school to pick her up and bring her back into work with me. There she would sleep for hours in the makeshift bed I'd made for her underneath my desk, occasionally wrapping a warm hand around one of my ankles and murmuring, "Mommy here."

I worked late every day, trying to overcompensate for having my child with me at work. Racked with guilt I wasn't at home with her, listening to her day (still living in the past, believing Ginny would soon talk to me again) or fixing her a hot meal, dancing with her.

Around seven in the evening, two hours after my staff and the other management had gone home, Ginny and I would pack up our belongings. I'd turn out the lights and lock up the building, and we'd head for my car, waving goodbye to the nightshift mechanics. On good nights with no accidents in our path, it would take us another hour to get home; then I'd cook our dinner, and we'd eat in silence, both staring past each other at the framed pictures of family gatherings I'd hung all over the dining room walls.

After dinner, Ginny would get ready for bed. I'd give her her medication; then I'd start on the dishes. When I'd finished the dishes I'd do laundry, then assemble both our outfits and pack Ginny's lunch for the next day. I would usually get in bed around 11 in the evening for what purpose I began to wonder. My sleeping had become sort of a dream to me ever since the night Ginny stopped breathing. Like something I knew could happen and believed would happen again, but I just wasn't sure when.

There are many days now when I stay up writing until 3 or 4 in the morning. Actually doing something with all the thoughts and feelings I have bottled up inside me. Then I wake at 9 or 10 in the morning, fix breakfast for Ginny and my mother and me. Drink big mugs of coffee. Talk and laugh with them. Because I can. I've even taken a few naps. Not many. But a few. Something I have never done before in my life. Not as a child. Not as a pregnant wife. A new mother. Never. But I do now. Because I can. And I treasure this time. Which might seem confining or even boring to others. As a chance to reconnect with all I love and almost lost.

§

Just before Ginny was released from the unit, I spent whole days and nights planning how I would keep her alive. How, on my watch, no harm would ever come to her. The truth is, if someone wants to kill themselves and they have the will to do it, you can't stop them. Lock them in a bare room with rubber walls, ceiling, and floor. They will bounce themselves to death. But living with a loved one who has a death wish makes it hard to face the truth. That life is only given once. After that, you must want it.

So I emptied every cabinet, closet, and drawer in my condominium of any chemicals, medicine, sharp objects, and anything you could hang yourself with. The crisis unit had nothing on me. In fact, I made their safety precautions look like child's play. Tossing belts, ribbons, hair clamps, scarves, bandannas, bracelets, chokers into a plastic bag. Then gathering every knife, fork, corkscrew, cake divider, and skewer and placing them in a shoebox. Matches, lighter fluid, glue, bleach, scouring powder, razors, ant spray, roach killer, and boric acid went into various other plastic containers. All of this went into the trunk of my car.

I hid Ginny's medication under the mattress of my side of the bed and wrote emergency numbers on sticky notes, placing them in every room of our condo.

But I also decorated for her homecoming, softening the rooms with clusters of pink and purple balloons. Hanging "Welcome Home" posters with pictures of family and friends that I'd pasted on before hiding the glue. And setting up times for both John and Blake and then other family members to call Ginny, welcoming her home.

Ginny's second day home and back in school, I received a call from Jodi, her tennis coach. She was also Ginny's history teacher. Jodi told me Ginny was talking loudly to the voices in class. And that while some of the students were just laughing about it, other seemed very disturbed by her behavior. Even frightened.

I told Jodi I would speak to Ginny and her doctor about the problem and see if I couldn't make things better. The doctor never returned my phone calls, and when I talked with Ginny, she told me she was fine. She said she'd just had a bad day and that it wouldn't happen again. Believing her seemed my only option, even though with each new episode, it was becoming harder to remember a time when me believing what Ginny told me did not require weighing of potential outcomes.

On Ginny's third day back in school, I received a call from her guidance counselor, telling me Ginny seemed to be confused where and when her classes were because she was continually showing up at the wrong one at the wrong time. I asked if she could be appointed a helper to walk her to her classes, and the guidance counselor hesitated only for a moment before saying it was a great suggestion and that she'd get one immediately.

I hung up the phone and burst into tears.

§

When Ginny and I were still living in Asheville, she was voted into a leadership program at her high school. It was an elite group of straight-A students who worked on service projects at the school and in the community. One of the projects was assisting students with mental and physical disabilities get to and from their classes. Ginny was head of this program. And many times when I would pop into her high school during the day to talk to her tennis coach or pick up a schedule or drop off goodies for her teachers, I would see Ginny helping guide a student to class.

§

Ginny's fourth day back from the unit, she was so groggy from the medication I could barely wake her to get dressed. It took her almost an hour to get showered and put her clothes on. She missed first period altogether, and I was late for work.

And so it went. A day never passed without a phone call from Ginny's school about her behavior, and I began to count myself lucky at work if I even made it through a morning. I had Faith's e-mails to keep my spirits up and Jake's love, but other than that I felt very alone. Living a nightmare.

When John did not arrive as promised, Faith offered to come help. It was like all of Faith's offers, totally selfless. She was teaching five philosophy courses, had committee work, was a mentor for two beginning instructors at her college—the deadlines she faced some weeks would have frightened Donald Trump. But she insisted. And I didn't refuse, because when you feel finally helpless, the sacrifices you and others make don't even seem like sacrifices—just the only thing to do.

The minute Faith arrived, with flowers and a bottle of my favorite chardonnay for me, pastels and sketch pads for Ginny, and hugs and kisses for us both, I saw Ginny light up again.

The first night we ate dinner together with Jake. I remember feeling so happy. For months, ever since I'd met Jake, I wanted him to meet my family, just as much as I wanted to meet his.

If you choose to marry someone your own age fairly young as I did, you've lived so little there are questions that never come up. Situations that can be completely avoided. I met John's parents soon after we'd begun dating in college. And his brother and sister. With very little planning. And throughout the years we were dating and engaged, we spent numerous occasions together with no questions asked about my past or our future together.

But with Jake, things were different. We were both adults when we met, with jobs and lives of our own. I had a teenaged daughter. We had the age difference factor, and just in general, the whole uncertainty of who we were to each other and who we might be.

While I wanted to bring Jake to Asheville to meet my family and we had talked about it several times, it never happened. With our work schedules and coping with Ginny's illness, we never made it a priority.

And while I'd talked to one of Jake's brothers on the phone for quite a while, his mother a few times, and could tell how much I could love them both, I'd never actually met anyone in Jake's family either.

This was harder on me than it was on Jake. I believe it's always harder for women. Not to have their whole family together. I think men just feel, "Hey, I got what I want. I'm not marrying the rest of 'em anyway. Hell, I may not even marry her." Something like that.

But that night, as far as I was concerned, I had my family together. And I couldn't have been happier.

It was pouring rain when we finished supper at the Italian restaurant where we were eating. Jake said he'd get the car and pull up in front for us. He did, then popped out, umbrella over head, running to retrieve Ginny, then Faith. Taking me last. As he tucked me into the car, he kissed me on the cheek and said, "You happy now?"

To anyone else, it might have sounded like Jake was boasting about what a gentleman he was being. But not to me. I know him. He was talking about how much it means to me to have family together. See, he knows me, too.

Faith stayed longer than she could. Cooking dinner for us every night, with Ginny by her side. She'd give her little jobs to do. Get the oil out of the pantry. Fold the napkins. And Ginny would smile each time she completed a task.

After dinner, Ginny would take Faith to her favorite spot. The gazebo next to the pond just outside our condominium. I'd chosen our unit based solely on this spot. You could see it from the upstairs bedroom window. The first time I looked out on to the misty green lily padded pond with the little white gazebo set on its mossy banks right between two weeping willows, I thought to myself, "Ginny will love it here.'

Faith would sit on one of the gazebo benches and read to Ginny from a journal of her poetry. And Ginny would stand on the bench beside her, first rising on tip toe, then pirouetting, then lifting herself toward the low rafters as if she were weightless. Dancing to Faith's words, as if they came from her own heart.

§

Every afternoon before Faith arrived and after she left, I'd spend my lunch hour driving to pick Ginny up from school, then I'd bring her back to my office. I'd arrive in the high school's parking lot relieved just to find her sitting on the front stairs. Ginny would rarely acknowledge me. Staring blankly into the parking lot. She'd stand straight up when I'd pull the car in front of her and walk like a robot to the passenger side. Throwing her books in the backseat with no recognition of how close she came to hitting my head.

When she'd first returned to school, there was talk she'd play on the tennis team again. Not from me. I never promised her coach anything, nor did Ginny's coach expect anything. But parents of Ginny's teammates called for a few evenings to ask about Ginny– "We sure do miss her," they'd say or "Doesn't seem the same without her." What they wanted to say was more like "It's not fair. That state championship will be out of reach for us if she doesn't come back." I don't know what they wanted me to say or do, but after Ginny had been back in school a couple of weeks, the calls stopped. It had become apparent to everyone at Whispering Pines that not only could Ginny not help the school win a state championship, she could barely help herself through a day of classes. And before long when we'd see her teammates after school— those whose parents had called thinking mainly of themselves and recognition for their daughters—they began to act as if Ginny were invisible.

On our drives back to my office, Ginny would alternate between staring at the dashboard, talking to the voices, laughing hysterically, sobbing inconsolably, and telling me the drugs were making her crazy. This for four-teen miles every day—in traffic thicker than peanut butter.

At least one night a week, usually when I had a manager's meeting the next day, Ginny would be up all night. She would go to bed at her usual time—9 o'clock, but around 11, just as I was crawling into bed, she'd sit straight up. Her facial expression would change instantly, from the blank calm of sleep to a mad hatter's grin. Then she'd burst into laughter and laugh for hours. And the laughter was not a child's laughter. More like a helpless, hopeless ache. Like I imagine an angel might sound being kicked out of heaven or like anyone might sound in the instant before being buried alive.

When I called Ginny's new psychiatrist to explain how concerned I was about her behavior and to schedule an earlier appointment than the one we'd been given when she left the unit, I was told by the receptionist that he was booked for months. When I said I felt this was an emergency, she asked me point blank, "Is you daughter suicidal?"

Now there's a question. Making all of my thought provoking "life questions" to Jake and Maeve and Ted seem hollow. "Is your daughter suicidal?" Gee, what are my options here. Yes? No? Maybe? How about—"Can I get back to you on that one...when I figure it out...next lifetime?" Or maybe this– "If I knew, I'd be in psychiatry, and I wouldn't be bothering you with changing an appointment"? What the hell? "Is your daughter suicidal?" And worse, she said it like, "Could you pass the butter?" Just like that.

"No," I answered, half way holding my breath—because, you know, what if I called it wrong? "No, she is *not* suicidal," I heard myself insisting—as if there were something here about preserving dignity while I silently begged this receptionist to change the appointment anyway, just in case. But the receptionist was scripted. She had not been asked to listen for degrees of desperation, to hear when a mother says *no* but really means *God only knows, and please don't make me gamble with my daughter's life.*

"Then she will have to wait for her scheduled appointment," the recep-tionist told me, and hung up before I could protest.

At work, when I brought Ginny there from school, Richard began clearing his throat, asking me behind closed doors when John was coming. I knew my job was on the line. That I was jeopardizing it every day by taking care of my daughter. As is the case with most working mothers, I found doing what was best for my job in direct conflict with doing what was best for my child. And while I still managed most days not to let worry overwhelm me, there were moments when I caught myself staring at a figure on a chart or a word in a memo, wondering how I would take care of Ginny at all if I lost my job.

John would call almost every night, updating me on his progress. I would thank him for rearranging his whole life to come help and assure him we would make it until he got there, but each night I felt less confident, and while I praised and comforted John, I was saying to myself—just get here soon, please…soon.

Jake was talking less and less. And when he did speak, it was usually with defiance. We'd be sitting in the living room after eating take-out Chinese, Ginny reading Jake her fortune, Jake holding me in his arms, and all of a sudden he'd mutter, "I think we're doing okay." He'd kiss me with a kind of fierceness on the top of my head and say, "I think you can call off the big rescue attempt from Mr. California. Yeh. I need that like I need a fuckin' hole in my head."

At night, lying next to Ginny in my bed, two things ran through my mind. One—that no matter how hard I'd struggled to keep my job, I'd wind up like all the other patients' parents I'd talked to, unable to keep it up. And two—that regardless of what Jake had told me initially about its being fine for John to come help, it really wasn't fine with him at all. It never had been and it never would be.

The mothers and fathers I'd talked to while Ginny was in the unit had told me two things about dealing with employers: tell them as little as possible, and when they find out your child is mentally ill (and they always do), let them know you have NAMI on your side and they better not try to pull any crap. Well, NAMI or no, they'd all lost jobs due to their children's mental illness. Most often the ones that could not hold on were single parents, too often mothers. They said it wasn't because they weren't doing their jobs but that their employers feared they wouldn't be able to do them. They said other employees could come and go from the building as they pleased, take extra breaks to smoke and pop mood enhancers, come in late and leave early—but the minute an employee with a mentally ill child asked for time to take care of an emergency, that was a problem. All of a sudden weeks, months, years of committed service were forgotten. And it was all about how management wasn't sure how well you were going to be able to do your job going forward. Like parents of mentally ill children have any choice. To be anything less than the best. When they are faced every waking minute with the worst. The chance they could outlive their child.

Finally, weeks after we'd initially planned, and just when Jake was convinced he wasn't going to show, John arrived with a car full of boxes and his dog Mischief. Overnight, my once immaculate, beautifully decorated home, filled with my new furniture, Jake's stereo and speakers, pictures of Jake, Ginny, me, Maeve, and Ted became transformed into a pseudo bachelor pad with fleas.

For the first few weeks of his stay, John focused on two things: telling me basically everything I'd done with our daughter up to that day was wrong and taking Ginny off her medication. In meetings with the counselor, he claimed in front of both me and Ginny that what Ginny was hearing was not "voices" at all. But one voice—mine. Criticizing and over-parenting every step of her life.

§

All my life, no matter what their differences, the men I've known have had one thing in common. They all hate drama. Jake is no exception. And while I was forced to deal with the drama of my present life, Jake could choose not to. And so he did.

In one month, we went from spending every waking minute we could together, to sharing our time together with Ginny, to seeing each other once a week, to seeing each other every other week, to calling occasionally to talk, and finally to not even calling.

Maeve told me, Ted told her, Jake told him—he was breaking up with me. I didn't know whether to laugh or cry. Here I was, forty-one years old. A mother. A regional sales manager. A woman who'd spent her entire adult life in two committed relationships, hearing from her best friend—queen of the one-night stands—that the man I thought was truly the love of my life was breaking up with me. I felt like I'd been cast in some horrific high school romance. Only I was twenty years too old for the part and the play had turned into reality.

But Jake did not "break up" with me. Instead, he called again one night after a long period of silence, and then for weeks we found ourselves in tight-lipped conversations full of painful pauses. Saying what we didn't mean. Feeling what we didn't say. And when we made love, it was desperate love making. Not like there were hundreds of people we could choose to be with and we chose to be with each other, but more like we had no options. Like we were the only two people on the planet.

Jake refused to come to my condominium. And when I went to his place, he'd complain about everything. From the fact that I was late to what I was wearing; then he'd ask if John had moved out yet.

It seemed all Ted's premonitions were coming true. It was every bit as difficult as he'd claimed it would be—living with John and loving Jake. I remember wanting so much during this time to tell Jake how I was feeling. To stop looking past him when we made love and to not let him look past me. To hold him once again, look deep into the blue of his eyes and let that blue calm me as it had so many times before. I wanted to tell him, "This is bigger than me. I wasn't expecting Ginny to become mentally ill. And I may be doing a terrible job while I'm trying to do the right thing. But it's all I know how to do. Love me anyway. Love me past this. Because I love you forever."

Chapter 30

This,   too,   Will   Pass

Two weeks after John moved in to "help make sure Ginny would be safe at all times and well taken care of"—his explanation to anyone who asked—Ginny tried to kill herself. We'd all been spending the afternoon at the pool swimming and resting in the sun. Ginny said she was going to the bathroom, got up, and walked inside.

When Jake had spent afternoons with us at the pool before John came and Ginny did this, he'd wait about two minutes after she left, then follow her. He'd stand outside the bathroom door, and if she stayed in longer than he considered a reasonable amount of time, he would come outside and get me to check on her. He didn't check his watch the second she left. He didn't yell or make a big scene. He didn't even say he was going to see if she was okay. He just tried to make sure she was always safe and that I had a little peace—could feel I didn't have to jump up every time Ginny was out of my sight, which he'd seen me do a hundred times since she came back from the unit—fixing dinner, or sitting at the table after a meal, or when the three of us were watching a rented movie together or just sitting quietly holding hands and Ginny would get up suddenly and leave the room.

But Jake no longer spent afternoons at the pool with us. And John was asleep in his chair. And after a few minutes of Ginny's being inside alone, I felt the familiar anxiousness mounting, my heart starting to beat fast, my muscles tensing and any impulse I had to give her a chance to show us she was able to be on her own ended instantly when a car backfired on the drive just outside the pool enclosure. I launched myself from the chair and ran barefoot over the hot pavement and through the rough grass to the screened porch, calling her name before she could possibly have heard me from inside. The porch door was stuck where it had warped from the damp, and I wrenched it open, dashing through the inside condo door that Ginny had left ajar, calling her again. There was no answer.

I ran straight for the bathroom, the door was open, and Ginny was not there. I screamed for her, turning and running back toward the living room—aware I hadn't even looked there as I was tearing through the condo. The kitchen was tucked into a recess just past the front door, part of it out of sight if you are moving down the hall to the bathroom and I had given no thought to Ginny's being there anyway, but when I rounded the corner from the bathroom hall running back toward the living room, I saw her. She was sitting on the floor of the kitchen with her back to the cabinets, her legs curled to one side—and she was holding a steak knife John had brought with him and insisted on keeping in a cabinet—"She'll never even know it's here," he'd said, "She doesn't fix anything for herself." I'd fought briefly, then given in. And now Ginny had the knife and had already slashed both of her nipples. Her head was down, her chin tucked into her chest, her free hand over her face, and she was delicately boring a hole in her stomach. All of this I saw in the instant of stepping through the kitchen door, and what happened in the next seconds between her having the knife and her not having it is clearer now to my body than to my mind, but as nearly as I can remember, I pulled up abruptly, thinking that if I startled her she could drive the knife in suddenly. Some days now I'll be sitting somewhere in my parents' condo and suddenly my toes will remember that day—the sensation of three tiptoe-ing steps toward her and my hand will recall clamping itself over hers and pulling the knife back—these are the images that stayed. If I said anything, I don't remember the words. I'm fairly certain I didn't scream again. The next memories are of taking the knife, which she let go of thankfully without a struggle. I hurled it into the sink, grabbing two kitchen towels and apply-ing pressure to the cuts she'd made. Blessedly, they were not deep. I recall thinking they could not begin to mirror her pain. But I felt them—the holes might as well have been in my heart as I held my little girl and rocked her and looked at her drops of blood all around me on the linoleum and felt my own tears stinging my shoulders where the sun had been just a short time ago. I felt what she was feeling. That whatever pain she had inflicted or could inflict on herself would not hurt her as much as her illness.

I wanted to call the doctor. I still believed he could help. But John insisted this was not a true suicide attempt, simply a cry for attention. Maeve insisted I look into putting Ginny into a long-term care facility. Ted insisted John should go back to California. Jake stopped calling. Faith was Faith—wanting to do something, admitting she had no answers. I remember her saying once a long time ago, "You know, Haley, I think I chose philosophy because I realized I'd never have any answers about the important things, and it's the one field where you can't lose your job for that." I had laughed then before realizing that Faith wasn't trying to be funny. The night I called her to tell her about Ginny, she said over and over, "Tell me what I can do?" But I didn't know. I didn't know what anyone could do. I asked her not to tell the others back home.

"They can't help and they'll just worry," I said. She agreed.

"Call me again, soon," she said.

"I will," I promised, but I don't remember exactly when I called Faith next because in the days that followed, I was too busy trying to hold onto to a life—any life—

for both Ginny and me.

One night, the very next week, when I was even later than usual getting home from work, Ginny found her medication, doubled her dosage, jumped in the pool with her clothes and shoes on just as I pulled into my parking space. John was in the bedroom I'd given him working on a business proposal for his company. I didn't even tell him. I knew what he'd say.

Two nights later, when Ginny and I had gone to dinner at Maeve's, Ginny, who'd been lying on the sofa near the hall saying she wasn't hungry, got up suddenly and ran to Maeve's bathroom. In the time it took Maeve and me to get up from the table and dash after her, she was standing with her back to the mirror over the sink, tickling her wrists with Maeve's razor. Maeve called me later that evening, insisting again that I institutionalize her. This time I asked Ginny to tell her father what she had done; it was something I hadn't tried. Maybe saying herself what she was trying to do to herself would make her see the horror of it and make John see she wasn't acting. But John insisted to me again that this was just another cry for attention. "If she was determined to hurt herself, she would do it, Haley," he said. I'd been certain all along that his advice was not wisdom, but I couldn't face what Maeve was demanding either. And I had begun to believe no matter what I did, I could not keep my daughter from harming herself or help her want to live.

During those days, I marked the passing of time not so much by days beginning and ending but by what Ginny had survived. One week—slashing and stabbing herself. Another, overdosing. Another, going at her wrists with a razor.

But there was one important day, I had marked on the calendar coming up with some of my old sense of hope. Ginny's sixteenth birthday. With my long days at work and all the "surprises" that greeted me when I arrived home—days Ginny was calmer, Mischief more than lived up to his name, dragging the contents of every wastebasket through the condo, including one with the bloody napkins and tissue from Ginny's period; another time strewing his food everywhere—I had not found time to shop for presents.

So two days before the big event, I drove into the teeth of a torrential rainstorm, looking for some gift that might brighten Ginny's days.

The winds were blowing, as had been predicted, between twenty and thirty miles an hour, strong enough to move my little car sideways on the road, while a steady rain pelted my windshield. I felt beside me for my cell phone where I'd laid it on the passenger seat. It took me several sweeps to find it, and by the time I'd finally palmed it, a little slacking of the rain gave me hope I was about to pass through the storm. I was moving my thumb across the plastic case to find the number to call John and Ginny and let them know I'd be late for dinner, when a truck drove past, covering my windshield with a heavy grey sheet of water from the road. I flicked my wipers on high speed to clear the windshield as quickly as I could, but they didn't work as fast as the engine going forty-five miles an hour, and I drove onto the median and straight into a metal pole.

I remember hearing the car crash first, then seeing the front of it fold, and in those first few seconds, I felt as if I was watching it happen —a bystander, not actually in the wreck. Then I remember feeling the pressure from the air bag pinning me between the seat and the wheel and hearing Jake's voice in my head telling me I had my seat too far forward. "I can't reach the pedals if I don't," I heard myself saying out loud, as if Jake were there. The thudding explosion startled me more than the initial impact—the sudden acrid smell of smoke mixed with what I would later learn was a chemical from the airbag that had ripped apart. In a few seconds more, the back of my left hand became the sole focus of my attention. It felt as if I was holding it to a burner turned on high.

A police car arrived in minutes, and two policemen stood in the pouring rain, prying me out of my totaled car. "Ma'm. You okay, ma'm?" one of them shouted through the window of the driver's door.

"Yep," I said to the remains of the air bag. I didn't have the energy to shout, and until they got the door open, they couldn't hear me, so they took turns yelling,

"Are you okay?"

"We'll have you out in a minute."

"Take it easy, ma'm."

When they finally got the door open, they both squatted down beside my seat and asked me at least ten times if I wanted them to call an ambulance.

"You look pretty shook up, ma'am," one said, and the other told me I needed to go to the hospital.

All I could think of was how thankful I was to be alive and then, for the rest of the night, what would happen to Ginny if something happened to me.

I had insurance—out the wahzoo as they say—and a will with explicit instructions for her care that Faith kept in a fire proof box. Everything from what Ginny had hoped for her own schooling, which I explained she should have the chance for whenever she felt well enough again, to what she would miss if someone didn't supply it in my absence—her favorite meals, an evening of baking cookies near Christmas, the shampoo she liked, the band-aids she used, to keep herself from biting her nails the week before her period, the only kind of socks she'd wear. And I'd written a letter that Faith kept too; in it I reminded my daughter that I would always be with her and that she must remember us laughing and singing and cooking and reading and running and dancing together and try to live well and love life and find her own way. I'd also given Faith a list of all the contact numbers: doctor, counselor, hospital, school. I'd made copies of my insurance policies, checking to be sure they were up to date. I had everything in order for me to die and for my daughter to live. But I couldn't stand the thought of being separated from her again—even for a night.

I told the officers I was fine. That there was absolutely no need for me to go to the hospital. I willed my voice to sound sure. One of them looked at my hand and winced. He said I had to promise to see a doctor. I told him I would.

They checked my license and registration and radioed the information, then told me a tow truck was on its way and I should remove any items I might need from the vehicle.

I walked around to the trunk and opened it, exposing the arsenal of hidden chemicals, knives, rope. The knowledge of these things packed away in my car was nothing startling to me by now, but when it occurred to me suddenly how such a collection would look to someone who knew nothing about my life, I glanced up at the officers standing over me to find their eyes wide and their mouths open.

I explained to them, while I picked up a set of knives and a shoebox with corkscrews and other sharp objects, "My daughter's going through a rough time right now." Two razors spilled out of the box and into the trunk. I set the knives and the box back down, picked the razors up and threw them back in where they had been. "I just have to make sure she's safe," I told them, grabbing a can of roach killer and adding it to the box before picking it and the knives up again. "Until she gets better," I added. I handed the set of knives to one officer and the shoebox to the other, then turned back to the trunk to retrieve a jump rope and sling it over my shoulder. "If you'll just take that stuff to your car, I'll get the rest and we'll be good to go," I said, realizing there was enough left for at least two more trips to the cruiser and trying to think what would be best to leave. By this time my hand was hurting so badly, I couldn't make choices, so I gathered what was closest, clutching a few small items in my hands and gathering as many other things as I could press against my chest before I turned and walked toward the police car.

The two officers appeared to be stone. So I smiled at them and said with all the cheeriness I could manage, "It's her sixteenth birthday on Sunday. I'm taking her to Cocoa Beach."

At that, both men seemed to revive a little. "Yes, ma'm," said the policeman who had made me promise to see a doctor.

Then I laughed. "Well, I guess not in this car."

Neither man answered me this time. Instead they both turned and walked back to their patrol car in silence and I followed them. I took a few steps and stopped, calling out, "I'll be there in a minute. I forgot to shut the trunk."

When we were all finally settled in their car, the officers drove me home. They didn't ask me any more questions. Even when I asked them to help me temporarily store the things I retrieved from my trunk, they followed me without a sound to the gazebo, where they watched as I tucked my belongings behind the shrubs that hugged the base of the little shelter and stood back to be sure they were well hidden—looking only once before turning toward the condo, to be sure that Ginny was not there dancing on the benches.

It is not describable. Both the guilt and the pain I feel about not having done more research earlier concerning the drugs Ginny's doctors so readily prescribed for her. I have no excuse. I am a well-educated woman with the resources to find any information I need. Instead, I bowed to medical experience and knowledge and my belief that the doctors in whose care I placed her knew what was best for her. Faith keeps telling me, I couldn't have found anything useful then anyway because the information that might have helped Ginny was not yet available to the public. And Jake always finds a way to let me know he feels I am a good mother. I thank them both for their comfort, but I am not comforted. All I know is that I should have known.

There are some truths we should not have to seek out. Some that we should know by virtue of our own human frailty. One is that doctors are not gods, the best of them are capable of gross error and the worst are no different from the worst in any other profession, except perhaps that their mistakes can more frequently mean the difference between life and death. At least some of them, may genuinely want to help, but they often want other things too—among them, I firmly believe now, is to appear more knowledgeable than they are about healing the mind. I acknowledge that it must be difficult to be a doctor and to have to admit that the best you can offer your patient amounts to an experiment, but my feeling is that if a doctor is too proud to admit his ignorance, he or she should find other work.

One of the medications Ginny was taking long after her initial trauma is an anti-depressant called Paxil. In the wake of recent news reports showing that children have committed, not just attempted, but committed suicide while taking this drug, the public finally has a chance to hear what the doctors who cared for those children have known since the children killed themselves. And I have confirmation of what I tell myself I must have known from the beginning. Why else did I repeatedly question the nurses in the unit? Why else did I keep writing to Faith about how I hated opening the medicine bottles, could smell the pills in my dreams?

In their internal documents, open to scrutiny in continuing litigation, Glaxco Smith Cline, the company who makes Paxil, records problems dating back to 1997 related to discontinuation of the drug, observing that as many as 62% of patients who stopped taking the drug had experienced problems. Current packaging of Paxil indicates 2% of users will have problems associated with discontinuing the drug.

As I write this, I remember sitting rigid in a chair in my parents' condo one evening not long ago listening to a prime time special in which all of this and more was aired. Ginny had gone to bed early, tired from a walk and doing dishes by herself, a task she has always liked but which is a struggle for her now. When the show came on and the subject was announced, I pressed the mute button quickly and walked down the hall to see if Ginny was asleep, almost tripping on an area rug in the hall, clumsy in my hurry to get back and in my dread of what might be revealed. What I heard, among other things, was compelling testimony from the parents of Julie Woodward, who hanged herself while on Paxil as well as from the parents of Jacob Steinburg, who killed himself after just one month on the drug. I closed my eyes from time to time. My parents had gone out for the evening and with each revelation from the television, I fought the urge to run to Ginny's bedroom to check on her again. Near the end of the special, I heard that Congressman Henry Waxman now leads an ongoing Congressional investigation into the use of Paxil and the possible efforts on the part of Glaxco Smith Cline not to disclose accurate information to the public both about the drug's side effects and about the problems associated with its discontinuation. And when I cut the television off at the end of the show, I sat in the quiet for several minutes—the faces of the strangers I had just seen, parents who had buried their children, still occupying the room. I tried to pray for them, but no words would come, and when I couldn't endure the despair in their eyes another moment, I tiptoed down the hall to Ginny's bedroom and sat beside her as she slept, watching her face serene in sleep and her graceful hands folded over her heart and the blanket beneath them, rising and falling.

Chapter 31

L e t t i n g   G o

At the time of my accident, I was upside down on many things, but most importantly, my car loan—since without my car I couldn't work and without work…well. Both my car and GAP insurance paid, I still owed three thousand dollars on a totaled car. Everyone at work and all of my friends told me I needed to fight. That I had plenty of insurance to cover everything and that I should never have to pay on a totaled car. Also that I could sue the car company for my air bag bursting.

I decided to be selective with my time and energy, not to sue a billion dollar company for what could easily have been life-altering injuries due to their defective equipment but to pursue my insurance companies for the money I was rightfully due.

For two months, I spent my lunch hour calling my insurance companies. Getting everything from a voice mail in Spanish to disconnected. Only actually speaking to two human beings in eight weeks, all said and done, losing ten pounds and not gaining one penny more from my insurance. And maybe it was good I was extra lean and actually able to run a marathon because it looked like I might have to—every day, back and forth to work— if I couldn't solve the car problem.

I'd been really practical too when I was choosing insurance options. I'd picked two of the most expensive policies money can buy but I'd drawn the line at paying an extra two dollars a month for car rental. So now I had monthly payments on a totaled car and a two hundred and forty dollar a week rental fee for a car I would never own. Oh, and of course insurance for the rental. Wouldn't want to forget that.

I can't remember which act of human kindness happened first. Whether John offered to loan me his car or my top salesperson, Carson, offered to teach me how to drive a stick and give me one of hers, or if Brianna, my sales coordinator, insisted she would take me anywhere I needed to go at any time. It all seemed to happen at once. It was as if my accident brought home to all those closest to me that I really was not coping very well. In fact, I was hardly coping at all.

Jake was one of the first to find out about my accident. Carson decided to call him and tell him about it. When we met, he took one look at my burned hand and groaned. With all my hassles with the insurance companies and making arrangements for transportation, I hadn't bothered to see a doctor. The skin no longer looked much like skin—more like old construction paper, flaking here and there and slicked in places with glue. If anger were a color, that was the color of the worst part of the burn where the chemicals had hit directly when the air bag burst. Further from the center of the wound, little scales and bubbles had formed. A few of the bubbles had begun to break, releasing a strange thin yellow fluid that felt by turns hot and cold. For days, I'd just been applying hand crème to what turned out to be second-degree burns. And the crème mixed with the fluid had produced a kind of paste. "Jesus," Jake said, guiding me to his kitchen sink and adjusting the water to warm. He held my burnt hand in his and washed it gently. I winced when the water blanketed my raw skin, but Jake kissed me and told me it was going to be all right, distracting me while he worked.

When he was satisfied my hand was clean, he bandaged it neatly with gauze then put his arms around me. He hugged me tight and told me, "It's okay," and I heard his voice crack for the first time since I'd met him. Jake put his head on my shoulder and I felt his tears running down my neck. He said, "I'm glad you're okay." Then he hugged me tighter and cleared his throat. We stood there for minutes in each other's arms. I could feel the mid-afternoon sun on my back and Jake's heartbeat near my throat.

After a little while, Jake stepped back, still holding me by the shoulders. "Actually," he said, trying to smile, "this is good. I hated that damn car any-way." Then he cupped my face in his hands. "But you know," he said, tilting my chin up and looking down into my eyes, "you didn't have to get rid of it that way."

I laughed a little then and said, "I know."

Jake drew me into him again, resting his chin on my head. He told me, "You need to see two doctors. "One for your hand..." he paused and kissed my curls, "and one for your head."

§

One of the things I love most about Jake is how he says what he means. Keeps things simple and direct. If you believe in opposites attracting, that people instinctively choose mates who balance and complete them, you believe in me and Jake.

Jake says I'm a miracle, that I came into this world talking. I tell him that's impossible and there are no records of it. He says I'm so old they've been lost.

When I protested once and told him on that day I was almost the same age as Brad Pitt, he said, "So? What's that supposed to mean? Are you gonna start growing a beard? Is Brad Pitt gonna kiss me?"

I remember this one time we were having dinner at TGI Friday's, sitting across from each other in a booth. I'd been rambling on about something for about five minutes and Jake had gone into his "tune her out" mode. I was determined to finish my story, so I kept right on talking, but for some reason, something else caught my attention and I glanced away from Jake. The second I did, he ducked under our table.

When I noticed he'd disappeared, I protested. "Jake! What are you doing?!"

I knew he couldn't have gotten far.

Immediately, he popped back up, grinning from ear to ear. Then he said, "It was a test. I was seeing if I disappeared if you'd go on talking to the walls." He laughed, then added, obviously delighted with himself, "And you did! You talked to the walls!"

I tried to act like I was mad, but I couldn't keep a straight face and next thing you know, I was laughing with Jake at myself.

§

My accident did have a few good side effects, not the least of which was it forced John and me to work together to help our daughter. John loaned me his car for weeks and began walking Ginny home from school. He signed her up to volunteer at the puppet theater around the corner from our condo and they began grocery shopping and cooking most of our dinners.

On Sundays, we went to church together and John enrolled Ginny and himself in a community service group that met Thursday nights at the church. On clear Saturdays, we drove to Cocoa Beach. Ginny and I rode the waves together and John played volleyball on the beach with her.

It wasn't as if I had this accident and everything was suddenly all right. We were all still struggling mightily. But at least we were doing it together.

Maeve was working days and nights, trying to make a sales manager's salary as a nurse. We'd still call each other every day. And she'd pop by occasionally with a new outfit she'd bought for Ginny or a dessert for me. But our friendship wasn't the same.

Maeve didn't like John or approve of the fact he didn't take a part-time job to help with the bills. She thought he should definitely get a place of his own and wondered out loud why I didn't demand this of him. And she was determined to convince me John's arrival had nothing to do with Jake's distancing himself from me. She told me I needed to come to terms with the reasons Jake was ever with me. And then she listed them. "One," she said, "you're a good lay. Two, you're drop-dead gorgeous. Three, you can support yourself. Period. The end." According to Maeve, there was no love involved. Never had been. Never would be.

We did manage to get together a couple of nights. And one of those nights, I called Jake. I have no idea why I did. I'm going to have to plead temporary insanity, I guess, because I knew better. Maeve didn't want me talking to Jake at all. Never mind when I was with her. So maybe, thinking about it again, I did it partly to spite her, though I don't remember seeing it that way at the time.

Anyway, when I called him, I told him I was with Maeve, so he'd know there were things we couldn't talk about. He asked me if I knew what he was doing. I had no idea what he was talking about. If he meant that moment or just in general. And after I didn't answer him immediately, he asked to speak to Maeve. I couldn't hear what he was saying, but I guessed he'd asked her the same question when she said, "No, and I don't' care either." She handed the phone back to me and for a moment I had the impulse to hang up, was sorry I'd called, but I put the phone back to my ear and said, "It's me again."

Jake's voice was cold. He might as well have still been talking to Maeve. He told me he'd started his own business. That he was selling tools to mechanics. What I heard was, "I didn't tell you about this because I've moved on."

I fought the tears and said, "That's great, honey. I'm really proud of you," desperately trying not to sound hurt and to be happy for him.

And I was happy for Jake. And proud of him. But in a painful way. The way that is the most unselfish. And the hardest. The way that always begins with hurt. Because it's not about sharing joy and achievement. It's about letting go.

Jake talked a little bit more about his business. Then suddenly he seemed aware that he'd said more than he'd intended. He told me he had a customer and had to go.

When I put my phone back in my purse, I glanced over at Maeve. She reached for my hand and squeezed it lightly. She didn't say a word.

Chapter 32

Moving   Forward

Ted still came over after church on Sundays to create Sauce Sundays. But the crowd had changed. Maeve worked almost every Sunday, so she almost never came anymore, and Jake was still boycotting the home I'd let my ex-husband live in.

I'd started inviting Brianna and Carson and a neighbor Maeve introduced to us at the pool. His name was Randy—a brilliant, handsome, twenty-five-year-old man who speaks like he's part scientist, part poet and whose heart is as good as his mind. He holds multiple degrees, has a variety of investments, is a partner in a ground-breaking business and talks to everyone he meets as if they matter more than he does. Flicking his politician's smile one way and his cigarette ashes the other, he gives you this feeling you might have just met the next President.

John, Ginny, and I bonded with Randy immediately. Spending most of our nights and weekends with him. Randy helped me enjoy cooking again. He told me his mother is a wonderful cook and that he grew up eating one great meal after the next. Then he'd compliment every part of the meals I made, never missing a detail.

John and I talked about everything with Randy. He seemed deeply interested in helping us find better ways to treat Ginny's illness. He'd studied psychology in school and knew that heavy medication is not the answer for mentally ill teenagers. In our dinner table and poolside discussions, we covered life from first loves to politics and every topic in between. I felt like I had a new family. And though I missed Jake more than ever, I was thankful for the patch on my heart.

Ted adapted to the new crowd immediately. He's like that. There are certain things Ted doesn't want to change: his mother's sauce, his drink. But with friends, he's always flexible. Always forgiving and welcoming more.

He talked to Randy about cars. Carson, about motorcycles. Brianna, about government. Then, when the sauce was simmering, he'd take me in his arms and we'd dance around the stove.

Carson fit right in, adding the missing element of Jake. Always seeing the world with salt in her eyes.

Carson and Jake are very much a like. I've often thought they must have been related in another life. And though she disapproved of my dating him, telling me several times she believes Jake is very jealous and resentful of my accomplishments and warning me more than once, "Puppies bite!" she actually liked Jake as a friend.

Carson's dad owned a couple of car dealerships and he'd taught Carson all about cars. She could drive motorcycles too. And had the most incredibly organized garage I've ever seen, with every tool imaginable in its exact place. She'd be the envy of any man. And *was* of the ones she dated.

Carson comes from horse country, straight out of Lexington, Kentucky, but she will always be a Texas beauty to me. I say that because I truly believe the most beautiful women in the world come from Texas.

She has this sense of what looks good on her. While other women squeeze themselves into pants that don't fit, whack their hair, and reveal the breasts they bought, Carson simply manages to look beautiful any time, every day. She wears her dark brown hair long and there's something in the way she looks at the world that says she's never even thought about bleaches or dyes, in spite of the fact that most of the women around her have chemically treated hair. And while most of the female population in America over the age of twenty-five desperately want their faces to look more natural, Carson lines her deep brown eyes with charcoal pencil, paints her lips ruby red, wears antique jewelry with her ten-gallon cowboy hat and makes it all look right.

When Carson was a teenager, she cut a few of her toes off mowing her lawn barefoot, and if you ask her about it, she'll grab a cold bud lite and casually tell you the whole story, down to her brother packing her toes in ice like she'd just spilled some milk and he was cleaning it up.

But despite her beauty, skills, common sense approach to life, and knack for organizing garages, Carson has no luck with men. Mondays she'd come into my office to drop off her weekly sales plan, and I'd ask her how Friday's date went. She'd reply simply, "Next toad."

Brianna and Carson get along like most sisters. They love each other, but not so you can tell it. Brianna is like water to Carson's fire. Her mere presence calms me. And she has this way of walking. Like she always knows where she's going. Like when she comes to a fork in the road she doesn't even see the fork, only the right path. She speaks with purpose. As if her every word will either stand alone or connect beautifully.

Carson is a doer. Words get in her way. She combines street smarts with Heloise's tips and a woman's intuition to make her way through this world.

And both women, in their very different ways, literally carried me through some of the darkest days of my life, seemingly effortlessly. As if I were a feather on one of their wings.

Carson became hell bent on helping me gain back my independence. While she appreciated the fact John moved his whole life to Florida to help care for his daughter, she felt my living situation was impossible and that, at the very least, I needed my own car. So, one morning, a few weeks after my accident, she marched into my office and announced, "Put the 'do not disturb' option on your phone, we are going for a drive." Then she walked me out to the employee parking lot where she'd parked her shiny red Mercury Capri convertible right in front of the entrance to the building.

"I'm taking you somewhere where you probably can't hit anything and even if you do, you'll be forgiven." Carson told me. Then she drove us across the street to a church and parked us in their lot while I tried not to laugh. Not that I wouldn't have been completely justified. I'd heard numerous stories about Carson's love-hate relationship with the Catholic Church—how when she either became old enough or wise enough or both to figure out the world would be a better place without Catholic confession, she'd not gone back, except for occasions like this one, where she decided the church's parking lot could serve a practical purpose. The way she'd said to me "you'll be forgiven," was like a retelling of the best of those stories about her abandoning the faith—about how she'd gotten up out of her pew and as she'd said, "without genuflecting or taking a hit off the holy water" had walked straight out into the real world and hadn't looked back.

So sitting in a parking space beside a cathedral, Carson told me, "There are two things to remember. First, keep your foot on the clutch when you're changing gears. And second, easy does it with the gas. When you let up on the clutch and press down on the accelerator, you gotta feel it. Now, go ahead," Carson said. "Press the clutch in."

We'd all already switched seats and I'd been sitting behind the wheel for a couple of minutes. But suddenly, after twenty some odd years of driving, I felt like I'd never been behind the wheel of a car. There's something about that extra pedal sticking up out of the floor like a taunting tongue. I put my foot on it and before I'd even exerted any pressure, I felt like things were already out of control. "Press it in," said Carson again. "Nothing'll happen. The car's in neutral." I had no idea what that meant, and I was pretty sure something *would* happen, but I finally managed to push. "Clear to the floor," said Carson. And I pushed harder. "Okay," Carson encouraged, "now shift into first, just the way you saw me do it."

Oh god, I thought, the kiss of death during any tutorials I've ever had. A teacher who thought I could take something in by seeing it. I know it's a percentage call. I think statistics show that about ninety percent of the population learns visually. But not me. No siree. I've got to hear it, smell it, talk about it, and, most important, feel it—the seeing is really a minor part of the experience for me. They call people like me kinesthetics. When I told Jake that once, he'd said, "You mean pathetics." It hadn't been funny then and it still wasn't, but it occurred to me that is the way I felt. My legs have always been strong and yet the one pressing the clutch felt suddenly palsied.

I focused my eyes on the gear shift and tried my best to shift into first per Carson's instructions. But it didn't happen, the thing felt like a stick in cement. On my fourth try, Carson could see I was losing patience. She said, "It's okay. First is the hardest. You get this, you got it made. Put it back in neutral."

"I thought that's where I was," I said.

"Well, not exactly," she said. "There's a little area of play, where you aren't quite anywhere."

"Sounds like my whole life," I said.

Carson ignored me and put her hand over mine, moving the gear back so I could feel it pop from where I'd had it, in no man's land, into neutral. Then she moved my hand and hers forward and slightly to the left until the shift stopped against something hard. "Now you try it again by yourself," she said. So I did what she told me. Three more times, trying to feel her hand still there. And finally, I got it in first. Second and third took half the time to learn, just as Carson had assured me, and within ten minutes, I'd started the car and was cruising around the church parking lot, grinning from ear to ear.

I told Carson, "Jake won't believe this!"

"Screw Jake," Carson said. "Forget about him. He's obviously forgotten about you."

I didn't say anything.

"Hey, and what about your captain friend? Maeve, is it? Where the hell has she been…missing in action?"

"She's been working really long hours," I said.

"Shit," Carson said. "She oughta try one of your days. Managing the sales revenue and staff for four divisions of a Fortune 200 company, then going home to take care of your mentally ill daughter. What the hell? She doesn't know what a long day is. Or..." Carson paused, "what true friendship is about."

I was circling the parking lot for the fifth time, shifting back and forth between second and third, a little smoother each time. I told Carson, "I can see how it seems to you like she really hasn't been there for me...but...."

"But nothing," Carson said. She hasn't even offered to give you a ride to work, has she?"

I cleared my throat, feeling sheepish but also in need of defending Maeve. "No. But I didn't ask her to take me." I said.

I could feel Carson smirk. "Like you needed to," she said. "Hell, she knew you wrecked your car. Yeh, I'd sure love to be under her charge." Out of the corner of my eye, I could see Carson pretending to salute. "Oh um, Captain Maeve," she said in a mock-fearful voice, "pardon me, but um...I got no wheels to get to work and a sick daughter to take care of . Think you could help me out?"

Carson dropped her hand and changed the tone of her voice to mimic Maeve as "the Captain." "Well, fuck me running. I don't think so, private. Hell, I've got three dates today." Carson sneered and returned to her normal voice. "Yeh, Jake's a damn prince next to her. Truth is I'll excuse Jake. But your little captain friend. Forget it. I mean your life is a little screwed up right now, and I can see where that wouldn't be very appealing to him."

"It isn't a little screwed up. It's totally screwed up. Plus," I added, before she could change her mind about excusing Jake, "he's trying to get his business off the ground. You know? He just can't keep going through one crisis after the next with me. He's got to focus."

Carson's laughed low in her throat. "Yeh," she said, "well he better start focusing on you, 'cause if he doesn't, I've got the answer for him. I know twenty men off the top of my head that would be more than happy to take you and all your worries away, just like that!" She snapped her fingers. "So your little puppy better stop pissing all over you because if he doesn't, I'm gonna send you an army of completely trained men. And missy, trust me, they'll be happy to wait on you hand and foot."

I laughed at Carson's drama though I have to admit, it felt good to have her defend me, but still I was all the more inclined to defend Jake. "I don't care what you say," I told her. "Jake is not a puppy. He's a grown man who loves me very much."

"Yeh?" Carson said. "Well, he needs to prove it."

I cruised the parking lot once more without answering, then Carson said, "You got this down." She adjusted herself in the seat as if to prepare for the next part of the lesson. "Okay," she said, "now we've got to knock out reverse then hit O.B.T. for fourth and fifth. That should do us."

O.B.T. stands for Orange Blossom Trail. It's a poorly maintained road that runs the length of central Florida, north to south. If you were Dale Earnhardt Jr. you'd have difficulty driving it with an automatic transmission during rush hour traffic—never mind me in a five-speed I was just learning.

But once again, my recent challenges with Ginny made any others seem relatively manageable, so I told Carson, "I'm ready if you are."

"Ready," Carson said. "Just do me one favor."

"What's that?" I asked.

"Don't back into the church. I haven't been in years and I don't want to go back in reverse."

Chapter 33

Hitting the Nail on the Head

The next day, Carson had another surprise for me. First thing in the morning, she popped into my office, face glowing, and announced, "I've found it! I've got the answer to all your problems. But…" She paused and looked at me, cocking her head to one side. "Before I tell you anymore, you have to promise me one thing."

"Anything," I answered fearlessly. "You have to do it," Carson said. "No matter what it is, you can't say no."

"Okay," I agreed.

Carson's eyes lit up, and she jumped straight up in the air, then pounded her fist on my desk. "I knew it!" she said. "I knew you'd do it! I don't care how crazy people think you are. You got guts, missy! God, I love your guts!"

And with that somewhat disturbing, however endearing, praise, Carson ran around my desk and hugged me like I was her favorite teddy bear, not her boss.

§

Though I'd be happy to give Carson full credit for anything she's done, I must admit, she's not the first to "love my guts," though most others who have expressed that idea have, as I remember, done it with some reservation—a little hesitation, maybe even a little bit of hysteria in their voices. "Love your...uh, well...uh your guts," Faith said, her face a little paler than usual when I told her I'd gone skydiving as my college graduation present to myself. Whereas, Carson's admiration that day she came to me with her proposal and made me promise I couldn't back out of whatever she was getting me into was complete.

I think there was a minute after I'd agreed to her plan without knowing what it was that I thought about my only fear—frogs, and though I didn't come even close to backing down, I did recall for just an instant the man-made pond on that mountain where nothing else had scared me but where I never got over jumping when I saw one of those primeval looking creatures perched on a lily pad, just waiting to spring at me.

Go ahead. Laugh. You wait and see. The time will come when you too must creep onto your patio late at night to recover something you left there and out of the darkness, before you can even blink, a slimy hypothyroid-eyed creature will hop at you, landing at your feet and croaking like Elvis with the hiccoughs. And just when you think you've gotten out of its way and that it's going to jump back into the darkness from whence it emerged, that's when it will give you the devastatingly quick headfake, then catapult right into your crotch.

So anyway, when Carson told me I couldn't back down, I had this frog moment, my thoughts springing in every direction. I imagined Jake discovering my frog phobia and the mileage he'd get out of that. How I'd lift the toilet lid one night, delighted that he'd remembered to put it down, only to have a frog spring into my open mouth. I remembered those horrid childhood stories about frogs turning into princes—or was it princes turning into frogs? Great, I said to myself. That's all I need. Some frog giving me a headfake and jumping into my lap and then turning into a man twice my size.

290

So I'm afraid of frogs, was the only kid in my biology class in high school who refused to dissect one, gave some excuse about not adding insult to death, but just really didn't want to look at the slimy, stretchy, bug-eyed things, let alone take a knife to one or touch its insides. Still, I think it's fair to say that among my family and friends, from the most timid to the most daring, I have generally been revered for my ability to live on the razor's edge and for my belief that the only things that can really kill anyone are worry and fear.

Public speaking and death—the two things at the top of most people's fear list—don't even bother me. I was doing monologues for guests at my parents' parties when I was five; my job in management has put me at a podium in front of three thousand people; and I once lived on five acres of woodland three miles up a mountain, where straight-line winds topped speeds of fifty miles an hour regularly in winter ice storms and where the forest just outside my door was alive with copperheads and recluse spiders in summer.

Anyway, the day after Carson waltzed into my office and announced she had the answer to my problems, she took me to an audition for a reality t.v. show called Dreamhouse. The show was to be filmed somewhere near Orlando, and the casting crew had spent the better part of a year traveling to every state before ending up in Florida to choose the final members of the cast.

When we arrived at the hotel where the audition was being held, we were told they expected thousands to audition for the three remaining spots. And though I didn't see thousands in the lobby, I thought maybe they were hiding them somewhere and that it was a mistake to have brought Ginny.

But as luck would have it, I was in the second group to audition. Carson stayed in the lobby with Ginny when I was called into the banquet room with ten others soon after we arrived. I winked over my shoulder at my friend and my daughter, who were both smiling hugely as I waltzed through the banquet room door, and as I think back at what happened after, I wish they'd come with me to see what happened next.

The standard rule in theater or show business of any type is not to make friends with your enemies—the others' auditioning. But I think I knew before the door closed that, true to form, I'd not be following that rule. In fact, before anyone could be called, I'd met three of the other people in my group: Jason, a voice student at a local college, who'd done a little Off-Broadway work; Pam, a carpenter with two children who both loved Rocky Road ice-cream; and Jerry, a professional actor, who told me he had already passed some preliminary qualifying for the show through his agent.

When we were brought into the audition room, we seated ourselves at a huge mahogany conference table with the panel of judges just across from us in wing chairs. We were told we would each have two minutes to speak and that we needed to tell everyone a little bit about ourselves, then why we wanted to be on the show.

The first two in our group took exactly their allotted time. And then there was me. I could hear Jake saying that I'd talk to the walls if he disappeared, but in my defense I really did try to keep what I had to say to two minutes. And after all, it could have been worse. I could easily have taken an hour or a day, because Jake's right about how much I love to talk, but the story I was telling had a natural ending at ten minutes, so ten it was.

I don't know if the others were outraged later when they realized how much time the judges let me have. But I can tell you while I was telling my story, I had the whole room holding their sides from laughing so hard.

I talked mostly about trash, the business of picking it up, which never fails both to fascinate and amuse people. I guess there is so much of it, and so few of us involved in hauling it away that the whole process seems like a giant comical mystery. I think part of it is they are laughing at themselves. At the scale of the mess they suddenly realize they've been making all along. And at how something so necessary in all of our lives is simply taken for granted.

Anyway, when I'd finished, the judges gave the last seven auditioners one minute a piece to speak, and I was convinced of two things when I left the room. One—I'd made it through the first round. And two—nothing, including the garbage industry, is as competitive as show business. I was right on both counts.

§

Prior to marrying John, I'd spent my life in the theater. I began performing when I was five years old. I acted in school plays, community theater productions, college shows, on commercials, in documentaries and in movies. My father was a community theater director and my uncle a famous character actor. Though I'd been out of performing for years, I was no stranger to the spotlight. And so the next round of auditions for Dreamhouse would be even more advantageous for me. Because this time, the spotlight actually was on us; our audition was being filmed.

While the other contestants seemed both frightened and preoccupied with the camera, I had other concerns. You see, our task was to hammer a nail into a board, and for me, well, they might as well have turned me upside down and asked me to touch the ceiling.

But I was determined to remember what the men in my life have taught me about hammering. Focus on the head. Cock your arm. Keep your wrist firm. Make quick, straight, short hits. I can remember thinking *this is good. It's all coming back to me.*

In the end, much to my surprise and delight, I hammered the nail straight into the board. Then I screamed. "I did it!" And I jumped and danced around the board while the camera man followed my every move. I sang some half-assed version of a song Henry Higgins sings in *My Fair Lady*—"You didn't think I'd do it, but I did it, I did it! And now that I've done it, I can't believe I did!"

The judges were all laughing and clapping, and before I could tell them how much fun it had all been and that I was just glad to have the chance to audition, they were handing me preliminary paperwork.

I caught a glimpse of Carson and Ginny, who'd been too curious to stay in the lobby and were standing in the door of the audition room just as I was being handed the papers. Ginny looked sleepy, but she was trying to smile, and Carson was holding her up with one arm and giving me thumbs up with her other hand.

On the way home, Carson invited us to eat Chinese, and we stopped at a restaurant in Winter Park. Carson reviewed the paperwork while Ginny and I gorged ourselves on the buffet. We fixed Carson a plate, but she let it sit while she read the five pages of tightly spaced small print. Finally she looked up, pushing the cold food away with one hand and putting the papers down in front of her. "You could win this, you know." Her voice seemed to anticipate that I wasn't taking her plan seriously, and she repeated her prediction slowly, "You could *win* this." The truth is I hadn't been very confident from the beginning, and though I planned to make good on my promise to Carson, advancing two rounds hadn't convinced me I had a shot at the big prize.

I told her, "Okay, let me get this straight, if I even get on the show, I have to help build a house with possibly the worst carpentry skills in the history of mankind—womankind too—beat all the other contestants and then I get the house?"

"Exactly," Carson said, ignoring my concerns. "And getting the house is great, but there is so much more."

I glanced across the table at Ginny, who'd finished her meal. She seemed to be listening to Carson, and she was smiling.

Carson continued, "Once you get this kind of exposure on national t.v., do you really think you are gonna have to be a sales manager for Evergreen? Come on. None of the people on these reality shows ever go back to their day jobs. Certainly none that look like you. They do commercials. Get on sitcoms. Write books about their experience. Do talk shows about the books. I'm telling you, this is only the beginning. You get on this show, you and Ginny will be set for life."

Ginny smiled again and I smiled back at her. Her smile got bigger, and I knew she had been hearing everything Carson said.

"So." Carson put her hands down on the papers in front of her. "Are you in?" she asked.

I swallowed my last mouthful of noodles, then said, "I already auditioned. I'm in the third round. What do you mean am I 'in'?"

Carson smiled, "Just checking. Okay, according to this," Carson picked up the paperwork again, "we have to make a video of you immediately. That's what it says here." She put the papers back down and found the part about the video and traced it with her finger. "And we have to mail it tout suite. That's next on the list."

"What?" I said. "I don't have a video camera. How are we going to do this? And I..."

"Just leave it to me," Carson jumped in, before I could finish protesting. "I'll find a camera, or borrow one— hell, I'll steal one if I have to. Don't worry about it. You just keep flashing that beautiful smile."

"Okay," I said, "but I have nothing to wear."

"Yeh, well doing that would make you a shoe-in, but I'm thinking we can come up with an outfit. No offense, but I thought I was gonna die when I saw what you were wearing today. What is this, your Daisy Mae look?" she said, taking hold of a dotted scarf I'd tied around my neck and looking up and down my long john shirt.

"Shut up," I said. "Yes, and as a matter of fact, that is just the look I was going for. You know, sort of rugged and sweet. Like I could build a house and do some housekeeping too."

Carson and Ginny burst out laughing together.

Then Carson said, "You couldn't build an outhouse, but trust me, missy, you haven't made it this far on your carpentry skills."

I protested, "I hammered that nail straight into that board."

"Yeh," Carson said, "Well, don't be pressing your luck. We don't need any black nails or broken fingers when we make this audition tape."

When we got back into Carson's car, she asked me if I'd told Jake about the audition.

"No," I said, "I haven't talked to him in weeks."

"Shit," Carson said. "Sorry, Ginny. But, shit." She pulled out of the parking lot and headed toward our condominium.

"What?" I said. I thought you'd be glad we aren't talking."

"I am," she said. "But that won't last. You need to tell him. He isn't gonna like it, but you need to tell him."

"Why are his feelings suddenly important to you?"

"Nothing to do with his feelings, missy. It's your feelings I'm worried about. I don't want him finding out when we've got this thing in the bag and putting you on a guilt trip that, if I know you, might make you decide to give it up!"

I shot back, "I'll tell him when I get on the show and not a minute before. Trust me it's better that way. Jake doesn't want to hear about the pregnancy. He just wants the baby."

Carson raised her eyebrows at me. "Yeh," she said, "Well, I'm gonna bet this is a baby he won't want."

"You don't know that," I said. "I think he'll be excited about it. He'll be excited," I repeated, trying to reassure myself and quiet Carson.

"Yeh," Carson sneered. "He'll be excited all right. Like nutso. I mean, you may as well face it, missy. They want you on this show for two reasons—one you're available, and two—you're cute as hell. It's about numbers with these guys. And your cute little smile and even cuter butt are gonna draw numbers. They are gonna have you in your underwear, your bikini, whatever they think will get the most viewers. And they will make you the target of all the men on the show and let it be known to all the viewers that you're completely available."

I glanced back at Ginny. She was lying down on the backseat and had fallen asleep.

"But I'm not." I protested. "Available," I added, for emphasis, when Carson didn't answer right away.

"Please," Carson said, drawing the word out to show her disgust. "Spare me. When I see a ring on your finger, I'll know you're not available. And not a second before."

I frowned, then said, "You're right. I don't have a ring. But I have had them. I've been engaged three times. Married twice. I had rings every time. Big, beautiful, expensive rings. But you know what means more to me?"

I could feel Carson rolling her eyes as she said, "Wait. Let me strap my boots on. Shits gettin' deep. Okay. What means more to you?"

"The men." I answered, ignoring her sarcasm. "Giving themselves to me. Sometimes…just the smallest part. A memory of them. Riding their dirt bike through orange groves. The first time they hit a tennis ball. The best video they ever made. Or something that hurt them. Their mother not coming to one of their games. Their father telling lies. Parents so different they didn't seem like blood. Their telling me things like that—things they wouldn't tell anyone else. That's the stuff that matters. When a man shares his life with you. That's what matters. Trust me. They don't care more about you because they've given you a ring. They give rings because it's expected. And, in the beginning, they resent the expectation, and in the end, the ring, because neither come from the heart."

"Okay," Carson said, briefly throwing her hands in the air, then returning them to the wheel. "You win. I'm out. Can't argue with a vet. But you know, missy. Rings are about a lot more than spending money. I mean, they do symbolize unity and tradition and they're an integral part of every wedding. It's not just about buying a gift. Giving a ring to someone is very significant."

I turned in my seat to face Carson and cleared my throat. "Have you checked out any pawn shops lately? 'Cause they're stocked full of those significant pieces."

Carson frowned. "You are jaded, missy," she said.

"I am not," I told her. "I'm anything but jaded. I've just learned."

Carson smirked and I turned back around, resting my head against the high seat. Carson said, "That's rich. Well, you know, missy, I could sell tickets to you telling men that."

I turned my head to look at her and she took one hand from the wheel, clenching her fist into a fake microphone, which she raised near her mouth.

"Ah, excuse me," she said, "all male shoppers out there. Beautiful chick for cheap on aisle four. Yessiree. No ring purchase necessary. Get your cheap chick right here."

"Not cheap," I corrected Carson. "Just can't be bought."

Chapter 34

The   Path   Less   Taken

I've been aware for a long time that I am not the typical parent of a mentally ill child. From the first, I didn't attend NAMI meetings or call parents in a similar situation. I had no psychologist or counselor for myself. Didn't go to group therapy.

I had my own way of dealing with the cards that had been dealt both Ginny and me. It had to do with connecting and reconnecting. Ginny to this beautiful world. Me to Ginny. I developed new routines for us. Routines that had nothing to do with discussing "the voices" or anything else about mental disorders. Life giving routines.

Every night after supper, we walked a trail in Winter Park called Daisy Way. All the locals knew about it and after Jake pointed it out to me, it became a place of revival.

Daisy Way is part exercise course, part fairy tale. It winds for six miles through the majestic neighborhoods of Winter Park, spilling into the rustic ones of Orlando. Joggers, walkers, bikers, and rollerbladers alike navigate it daily, uncounsiously cast in an un-choreographed ballet, temporarily escaping their jobs, love lives, and central Florida traffic.

It's teaming with every imaginable flower, shrub, and tree. Grapefruits hanging within reach, climatis climbing trellises to the sun. Wisteria and honeysuckle scenting the air. Willows blowing in the breeze. Sounds of life forming a canopy of comfort—water coolers gurgling, children laughing, wheels turning, feet touching the ground, wings waving in the sky. Daisy Way is more than a path. It is a celebration of life. And I took Ginny to it every day, expecting nothing, praying for a miracle. That somehow all that revives me would heal her.

On one of our walks that summer, Ginny surprised me by actually starting a conversation. Since the onset of her illness, I could count on one hand the number of conversations she'd actually initiated.

"Is Jake coming back?" Ginny asked me.

"He isn't gone, honey," I said. "What makes you think he's gone?"

"'Cause he is," Ginny said, matter-of-factly. "I haven't seen him in weeks."

I was staring at two bikers coming toward us and trying to think of a good answer. Finally, I said, "Well, I'm sorry about that, honey. I know we used to do a lot of things together, but, um, Jake's started his own business, and he's really busy right now."

"It's Daddy, isn't it?" Ginny said.

"That's part of it," I said. "I'm not going to lie to you, Ginny. Your dad being here. Not just being here, living with us, has made it tough on Jake and me. But I brought your dad here to help take care of you, Ginny. Because I can't be with you all the time. Because of my job. And I would do it again if it helps you at all. And the truth is, honey, if Jake loves me, though it's frustrating and annoying and just difficult, really difficult the situation we are living with, it won't keep him from being with me in the end. If you love someone, if you truly love someone, nothing else matters enough to keep you from spending your life with them. Nothing." We had stopped while I was talking, and Ginny looked at me and smiled. "Jake loves you, mommy. I know he does."

This caught me by surprise. Though it was not the first confirmation or denial I'd heard of Jake's love for me, it was one without an agenda. And other than Jake's telling me himself, the most important one to me. You see, all her life, my life, our life together, my daughter has had complete clarity with regard to my personal life. And, though, some of what she has told me has hurt beyond words, it has always been true.

I kissed Ginny on the top of her head and said, "Out of the mouths of babes. Out of the mouths of babes."

Chapter 35

Reconnecting

I decided even if I hadn't talked to Jake in weeks, I needed to tell him about the show. And it had nothing to do with Carson's insistence. It was that I could not forget how I felt when he told me he'd started his own business. So not included. So surprised in the worst way.

Although we had dreamed together, talked about me getting my first novel published and him having his own shop, he never said anything about a tool business. Without me, he'd chosen a name, gotten a business license, had business cards printed, made cold calls and appointments, and created a customer file.

I suppose I should have just seen this as a variation on the dream we discussed. But I didn't. And even knowing Jake is the kind of man who is all about doing, not about talking, I couldn't help feeling when he told me about starting his business that he was also starting a new life, one that didn't include me.

So I called Jake. I told him something important was going on and I wanted to talk to him about it. He told me to come over.

When the awkward time of his opening the door and our strained greetings were over, he motioned me to the couch in his living room, and I started telling him about the audition. He seemed to be listening with interest, so I continued talking about the specifics of the show. Then what I could win. And what opportunities the whole thing could lead to. And I thought everything was going just fine. Until I added the reason I was telling him all this. That I didn't want him to feel the way I did when he sprung the fact he'd started a business on me.

Jake has this big vein in his forehead that looks more like the branch of an oak when he's mad. It pops out of nowhere and pulses when he talks.

He told me, vein pulsing, "Don't compare this to me starting my own business without telling you first. First of all, you did know I wanted to start my own business. We did talk about it. And frankly," Jake lowered his eyes to mine, "I thought I was giving you a break. Seems to me, you've got all you can handle, what with feeding and housing your ex-husband and taking care of your daughter."

I scooted a little further away from Jake and swallowed the truth hard. "I guess I wasn't being fair," I told him. "But you hurt me. And I just...I just...I want us...I want you to be a part of everything in my life. I want to include you in everything."

"Well, don't," Jake told me. "Don't include me in this. What...I mean... come on. Have you lost your mind?" Jake leaned back and momentarily covered his face with his hands. Then he sat back up, faced me, and said, "You'll lose your job over this, you know. They won't let you do this show. They'll make you choose and even if you choose your job, they'll hold it against you." He paused, glanced briefly out the living room window, then back at me. "What about Ginny? Where does she fit into your grand scheme? You know if you get this, you'll be living on a set for weeks at a time. How's that gonna work? Don't tell me." Jake clenched his hands together into one big fist. "Don't even tell me you are leaving her with Mr. California. Jesus Christ!" Jake stood up, pacing in a tight circle. "I can't believe you, Haley. Here I think you are spending time with Ginny, taking care of your daughter, and

I'm trying to back off, trying to be considerate of the fact she's your number one priority, and this is what I get?" You—auditioning for some trashy reality show? I can't believe you." Jake sat back down and hung his head. "I really can't believe you."

I inched closer to him. "Honey," I said, "I know it's hard for you to understand."

"You're damn right it is," Jake said without looking at me.

"I know you don't like this type of show. And you know I don't like them either, but…"

"But what?" he demanded, staring straight at me suddenly. "You don't like them, so you're auditioning for one? God! You are driving me crazy. You know? Hell, by the time you get through with me, I'm gonna need the crisis unit." Jake clasped his hands together again, holding them in front of his face. "That isn't acting by the way. They're not hiring you for your ability to act…if you haven't figured that out."

"I know," I said.

"Well, then, why the hell are you doing this? I told you Ray knows lots of people around here in theater. If you want to act again, he'll introduce you to them. Jake pointed out the window. "There's a theater right up the street. I'll be glad to help out with Ginny. We can grab dinner. I know it's not Broadway, but you could act, and maybe she can help out back stage. That would be good for her to work on the sets. I don't know. But if you want to act again, that's fine. You know that's fine with me. Just don't lower yourself to this."

"Honey," I said, "That's incredibly sweet. And there is nothing I'd like more than to act again and have Ginny involved. And I'll never be able to tell you how much what you just said means to me…but…"

"Yeh, yeh, yeh, blah, blah, blah, but you're gonna do it anyway…"

"Yes," I sat up straight and stared at Jake. "Yes, I am. And whether you believe it or not, I'm doing it for all of us," I said.

Jake rolled his eyes.

"Yes I am," I repeated. "Do you know what this could mean for our future? Do you know what an incredible opportunity this is? The house alone is worth 250,000 dollars! And we'd own it clear. I'll have commercials and offers to be on sitcoms—interviews, God knows what all. I will never have to worry about taking care of Ginny financially again. And I'm not the only one who thinks that. Carson says this will definitely lead to something else."

"Yeh," Jake sneered. "Like what? V.D.? You know," Jake said, scooting a little closer to me, "they expect you to sleep with the guys on the show."

"Honey!" I protested. "You know I wouldn't do that."

Jake clenched his teeth. "I don't know anything about you anymore," he said.

I didn't know what to say. Every part of me was aching for Jake. We were sitting just inches apart, but in that moment, we might as well have been in different states.

And then something happened. His face was still telling me *don't get near me*, but his body was quiet, his knee almost touching mine. And he hadn't moved it away.

I gently placed one hand on his right thigh. Jake didn't budge. I glided it up to his waist, then turned toward him, pressing my breasts against his chest. I kissed him once on his forehead, happy to see the vein had vanished. Jake turned his head slightly, then nuzzled my neck with his cheek, softly kissing it.

I asked playfully, "You sure you don't know me?"

Jake groaned, then kissed me again. This time on the lips. "I'm sure," he said, then with a shy smile he added, "but I could get to know you."

Starved for each other, we undressed ourselves, kissing whatever part we bared as if it was a long lost treasure. Jake lay down on the sofa first. I was still standing next to him. He put his hands around my waist and lifted me on top of him. He was lying with his knees up, and he rested me against his thighs. I inched forward, sat straight up circled his stiff penis, with one hand and put the tip of it inside me. He felt so warm, pulsing with excitement, I came instantly and he slid inside me. Jake was moaning now. Low and soft. And his fingers gripped me tighter. I reached one hand behind my back, down between his legs and fondled his balls. This time he groaned and I felt the muscles in his strong thighs quivering against the soft place in my back. Jake held me by my hips and gently pushed me further down his penis, while he thrust it into me. Then he guided me up and down and around, easy at first, and then fast, harder, faster. Until hard turned to soft. Passion to tenderness, as Jake held me against his chest, running his fingers through my hair, whispering with a smile in his voice, "Maybe I do know you."

Chapter 36

Can't Let Go

Timing can be everything. I'd been married for years to a video producer, and now, when everything depended on making a video, I didn't even own a camera. And Carson and I had made a pact to tell no one at work about the show. At least not until I was cast. Not even Brianna. So we were on our own.

But Carson had a plan. Carson always has a plan. She'd decided we'd go to Value Video, buy a tape, ask a salesperson to borrow one of the store display cameras, then shoot the audition in the store.

I thought the plan was brilliant. Carson thought our success would depend on my ability to charm the salesperson, and she kept telling me we'd need to find a man. I told her she'd have to come up with a tougher challenge or I'd get bored.

The salesman, "victim" as Carson called him all the way to the store, was named Ryan. He was a student at a local private college, majoring—here, I thought, was some proof for the theory of synchronicity– majoring in film production. He was tall and thin, with sand-colored hair and eyes you could swim in. When I told Carson that, she said, "Yeh, well just take a dip, we got business to do."

After I spoke with Ryan, he gave us the most expensive camera in the store, the tape for half-off, loaded it for us, then kept the whole area we were shooting in free of traffic for half an hour. "Halfway through the process, when Ryan had gone behind a counter for a half-off sticker, Carson whispered in my ear, "Have you ever found a man who doesn't like you?"

"Yes," I told her without even thinking.

"Who?" Carson challenged me.

I told her, "Jake." Then added, "He loves me."

Carson rolled her eyes and said, "Poor bastard."

§

Carson did put together a support group for us—outside the office. It consisted of her current boyfriend, Ben, who looks half Greek, half Italian, with big brown eyes that could make the worst bedroom lines sound honest, a phone salesman by day and carpenter by night, then Jim, Ben and Carson's friend, who is a roofing salesman, Jaqueline and Jack, a couple she'd known for years—well, actually she'd known Jaqueline for years; Jack is one of those people who instantly makes you feel like you've known him for years.

We spent Sundays at Jacqueline and Jack's home. It is a haven for entertaining. They have a beautifully designed indoor pool, a den with (I'm not kidding) ten big screen t.v.'s, a huge galley kitchen, bedrooms and bathrooms enough to house the Brady Bunch, and they both act as if everyone they invite to their home is family.

Ginny loved them and their place. We would swim for hours in their pool. Then wander from room to room, sampling the different foods people brought. Jack grilled Ginny veggie burgers, while Jacqueline offered to paint her nails. It was like a vacation for us. One Carson made sure we had.

On Friday nights, Carson, Ginny, and I would meet Ben and Jim at a hole-in-the-wall Mexican restaurant in Winter Park, called Pedro's, Ginny's favorite.

At Pedro's, the chips and salsa are free and abundant, the waitresses all multi-taskers with earrings as big as their hearts, and the tables are carved with years of love stories. You can't hear the person next to you talking because the place is so small and the bar is so big, and the drinks are even bigger. Everyone in Pedro's sounds like they've had a bathtub of margaritas. And I think part of the reason Ginny loved it was for the noise—loud enough to drown out "the voices."

Ben sold me a cell phone for practically nothing, as Carson had warned him I could lose my job if I was cast in Dreamhouse, while Jim offered to run with me. Carson had literally surrounded us with people who cared about us, and of course she gave us her own special brand of Carson care too, liberally spiced with Carson humor.

I felt like my new family was growing, with at least one new member Maeve would love—Jim.

When Maeve saw Jim for the first time, I'd invited him to one of our now rare Sauce Sundays, along with Ben and Randy and Brianna and John, and, of course, Ted, the master of ceremonies. We were standing in my kitchen, sipping wine, staring into my dining room through the opening in the bar, when Maeve spotted him.

"Oh my God!" she said. "Who is that? Is it Andy Garcia's twin? Fuck me running! Who is that gorgeous man in your dining room?"

"What?" I said, turning around in a circle, knowing immediately who she was talking about and already prepared to tease her. "Is Jake here?" I asked. I tiptoed to look over Maeve's shoulder toward the door. "I didn't see him come in," I said.

Maeve stuck out her tongue and gave me a raspberry. "Shut up, you goof," she said. Then she pointed at Jim, who was talking to Carson. "You know who I'm talking about. Who is he?"

"Oh," I said, stretching my voice and my body in surprise toward Jim's figure in the dining room. "That gorgeous man. Yes, in fact he is Andy Garcia's twin. I had him imported especially for you."

Maeve giggled and blushed and punched me in the arm. "Shut up. You did not," she said. Then, as I predicted she would, she asked, "What's the deal on him? Is he single? Is he gay? Please don't tell me he's gay." Maeve glanced out at Jim again while I stayed silent on purpose to torment her a little. "Forget it," she said. "No way is he gay. Okay, what's his deal?" She swung her glass in Carson's direction and said, "Don't tell me that bitch is dating him."

I winced and took another sip of Chardonnay, thinking about Carson coaching me in the church parking lot and the audition and the video store. For a half second, I thought I was going to tell Maeve off, then realized how absurd that was. "Carson is not a bitch," I said finally and deliberately without any heat. "And yes, she used to date him," I added.

"And...?" Carson asked when I purposely didn't give her any more information immediately.

I waited a little longer, until I could feel Maeve's fuming and my own satisfaction at defending Carson quietly, then I said, "They are just friends now. She dates Ben. Did I introduce you to Ben?" I smiled to myself at this icing on the cake, a perfectly sociable question to delay a bit longer the introduction Maeve really wanted.

Maeve rolled her eyes. "Is it necessary?" Then unable to control her impatience any longer, she told me, "Listen, I'd love to be polite, but, um, the 'ol biological clock is ticking. Time's a wastin'. And all that. And though I'd love to meet Carson's new boyfriend, in another lifetime, right now, Andy Garcia's twin is standing in the next room, and I swear, if you don't introduce me to him right now, I'll...I'll..."

"You'll what?" I said.

"I'll call Jake and tell him you've fallen in love with another man," said Maeve.

I set my wine glass down on the counter and laughed. "Jake knows better," I said.

Later that night, Maeve and Jim salsa danced for all of us in the living room, putting on quite a show. Maeve flinging her wispy hair. Jim twining his body around hers. They looked sensational.

And after it was all over, Maeve asked me to walk outside on the porch so she could have a smoke. I told her to wait a minute and went to give Ginny her medication and see her safely into bed. Then I walked out on the porch where Maeve was already smoking. "Okay," she said, taking a long drag on her cigarette, her high cheekbones rising as she drew in comfort and falling as she blew the smoke sideways through her pursed lips. "That was fun," she said. Her voice was flat.

"What?" I said. "You looked like you were having a ball. Ginny loved watching you dance. And, hey, I didn't know you could salsa."

"Yeh," Maeve said, not trying to disguise her annoyance, "I have a lot of hidden talents." Then she glanced through the panes on the door at Jim, who was standing at the bar looking our way. I knew Maeve was upset about something, but it didn't add up after the scene I'd just witnessed.

"Your boy there seems enthralled with you," said Maeve.

"What?" I said. "You just got through dancing with him. What are you talking about?" I asked, Maeve's jealousy suddenly dawning on me but her reasoning still making no sense.

"That was one dance, babe," said Maeve. "And may I remind you, *I* asked *him*. I think he'd like to dance with you for the rest of the night."

"You're ridiculous," I said. And I meant it. "You're just tired and probably a little drunk too. It's the wine talking."

"No," Maeve said, shutting her beautiful green eyes half way, then slowly exhaling smoke she'd been holding in. "Actually, it's him," she said, her words mingling with the smoke. "He's talked about you all night. Asked me every question under the sun. Far as I know, by this time tomorrow, he will have proposed. And I'll be dancing alone at your wedding."

"Oh, my god!" I said and laughed loudly enough to startle Maeve, who had turned and was walking across the porch toward a lawn chair. "You have flipped," I said.

"Do me a favor and warn me if you're going to laugh like that again when I'm not paying attention," said Maeve. She'd stopped to scold me, but then walked on to the corner of the porch to grab a plastic chair, dragging it back toward me and scooting one near us close to it. She said, "You need to sit down. I have to tell you something."

I sat down next to Maeve. She stumped her cigarette out on the rock floor, then took my hands in hers. "This guy, Jim," she said, "really likes you, babe. He's an athlete, gorgeous black hair, brown eyes, tan, white teeth, the whole healthy package. He's a good salesman, a college graduate, he can build a future. And…" She paused and smiled, as if certain the last thing was best. "He dances like a dream," she added. Maeve waited for a moment, then stared into my eyes. "Don't be stupid," she said finally when I didn't speak. "Don't throw your chance away. This guy is incredible. And he wants you!"

I leaned back, dropping my hands out of Maeve's, then glanced out at the fence surrounding the pool. The fence Jake and I had climbed so many times together. I told Maeve, "Jim's a friend. And I'm…I'm sort of a novelty right now…with the show. That's all it is, Maeve. He likes who I can be, not who I am. He doesn't even know who I am." I smiled, thinking about what Jake had said when we made love after the Dreamhouse argument.

"Give him a chance," Maeve was pleading.

I sat straight up then and confronted Maeve. "Why do you do this?" I said. "Why do you keep on and on when you know I love Jake? It's not fair, Maeve. It's not fair to me or to him."

Maeve looked away from me. "Yeh, well, I don't give a damn about being fair to Jake."

"Why?" I demanded. "Because…" Maeve faced me and made me look in her eyes before she said, "he's not fair to you, babe. And that's the nicest way I can put it."

I didn't say anything. Part of me was exhausted from the long week and the long day and knowing I had a mess to clean up when everyone left. And the other part of me just didn't want to argue with anyone anymore about Jake. I was tired of defending him and me, us.

Maeve put one hand on my knee. "Ted and I saw him Friday night," she said. "At Spud's. We were there playing pool."

I didn't say a word.

"He walked in, sat down next to us at the bar. Even ordered us drinks. Told us about his trip to California. You know he went out there to visit his brother?"

"I know," I said. "I know he was in California."

Maeve got another cigarette out of the pack in her jeans, lit it, and inhaled. She said, "He stayed awhile, watched us shoot. When Ted asked him why you weren't with him, he told Ted he didn't want to talk about it. Then he said you aren't seeing each other any more. After he downed his drink, he said he had to go. Said he had a date. No," Maeve corrected herself, "said he had to meet someone."

"That's not a date," I told Maeve.

"Yeh?" she said. "Ted said it was. He said he knew who Jake was going to see. And it wasn't a friend."

"Really," I said. "So who is it? Did Ted say who it is?"

"No," Maeve said, "Just that she is not in your league. Not even close."

"Well," I said, taking a deep breath, then letting it out. "I guess I should be thankful." I stood up. "I mean for you guys. For friends who tell me who cares about me."

"Maeve stood up too. "I'm sorry, babe. But you would have found out. Soooner or later, you are going to have to face the truth."

I stood and faced Maeve. "What do you think that is?" I asked.

"That you're too good for him," she said quickly. Then added, "That he doesn't even know who he had. And that he doesn't care either." Maeve paused. The silence was thick but I was determined not to fill it. Finally she finished. "That you need to move on," she said.

I looked out at the fence again. I could see Jake and me climbing it. How when we first grabbed on to the boards, we were the same. Crouching there together, feet side by side, taking the first step. But Jake's stride is much longer than mine and he would always reach the top first, leaping to the ground on the other side, while I imagined him landing. And when I got to the top and looked over, he was there just as I had pictured him, and it couldn't have been clearer...who was falling. Or who would always be there to catch me.

Chapter 37

C o u r a g e

In that moment by the fence, watching Jake's feet and mine, I sometimes think I lived another lifetime, and though I would be angry with Maeve again, in one sense I think I forgave her that night—for always—for the comment about Carson and for all the attempts to talk me out of believing in Jake. She was, after all, just being Maeve, and it occurred to me more intensely that evening than it ever had in the days we were closest, how much of Maeve was about her boldness and how much of every friendship and every love and every individual courage— including the courage it takes to go to war or start a business or to love when love is not returned or to live with mental or physical illness or without a home or a mate or children, if you want them—how much of all of this courage goes unsung.

Ben and Jim turned out to be wonderful friends to me and Ginny. And Carson, when I told her how much I believe music helps heal Ginny, found jazz concerts at different parks for us all to attend. Brianna would prepare wonderful snacks: prosciutto with melon, barbequed shrimp with mango, roasted red pepper and goat cheese tarts, and hummus and pita for Ginny. Jim and I would pick up bottled water, wine and beer, and Ben and Carson would bring blankets, chairs, and a pillow for Ginny.

Jim even played tennis with me and Ginny. He's actually a soccer player, but obviously just a very good athlete. He had no problem volleying anything I hit, and though Ginny's pace on the balls was twice as fast as his and mine, his anticipation is so good, he even got to most of the balls she hit.

And Jim and I did start running together. At first just on weekends when John was either playing tennis with Ginny or swimming with her. But then on weeknights too, after work, before supper.

John and Ginny had developed a new routine of going to the gym to work out with Randy. And they all went to the service group meetings on Thursday at the church, as well as supper. I felt like things were beginning to settle down some. And though I still missed Jake terribly, I was trying not to think about him. Whatever I hadn't learned about men over the years, I did know this—when your memories outweigh the time you spend with them, you aren't so much a part of their lives as you are a part of their past.

One of the nights I was getting ready to run with Jim, Ted called. I hesitated about telling him I was rushing to get ready to run with Jim because my weekend runs with him had replaced Ted's Sauce Sundays. But when Ted asked me if I wanted to meet him at Duffy's for a drink, I had to tell him the truth.

Then Ted told me, "Baby, I don't want to burst your bubble, but this guy isn't really interested in running with you. And you know it's getting dark earlier now. I really don't think that's very safe."

"Oh come on!" I told Ted, slipping one shoe on. "Listen to you. All overprotective. That's really sweet. Thank you."

"So," he said, clearly missing my tone or choosing to ignore it, "How 'bout a drink? Ted's buying."

I slipped on my other shoe. "I'll take a rain check for sure," I said. "But I can't back out on Jim. I promised him."

"Yeh," Ted said, "that isn't all he's hoping you'll promise."

"Ted!" I said, hearing my impatience with him growing, "Cut it out. We're running together. Just running together."

Ted coughed, then said, "He wants to get down your pants, baby. I'm telling you."

I tugged at my tight running top and pulled at the crotch of the matching bottoms, where it was digging into me uncomfortably because I'd pulled the pants up too far in my rush to get dressed. Out of irritation with the suit and Ted, I almost told him that Jim would have some trouble getting down the particular pants I was wearing—one, because they fit like a second skin, and two, because after I'd been with Jake, I knew no man other than Jake would ever get down my pants again. But instead I said, "Ted, Jim and I are friends, that's all."

Ted said, "He's a man, isn't he?"

I protested, "What's that supposed to mean?"

"Men aren't friends with women, baby. Specially not women like you. Trust me. We're all alike. If we run with you or play tennis with you or take you to dinner, whatever it is—we're doing it to get what we want. And we all want the same thing."

I laughed, not bothering to razz him about what that meant in the moment, knowing he would be hurt and that he really was concerned about me. "Oh my god, you're ridiculous" was what I opted for, then laughed again.

Ted argued, "I may be ridiculous but I'm right. Have you seen *Harry Meets Sally?*"

"What does that have to do with anything?" I asked. "Yes, I've seen *Harry Meets Sally*," I said. "How clueless do you think I am? That orgasm scene is like—it's like a memorial to women's efforts through the years. What woman hasn't seen that?"

"Not that," Ted said, disgusted. "I'm not talking about that. Go rent the movie. I want you to see the part where Harry tells Sally about friendship. It's a classic."

"Okay," I said, "I will. Meantime I'm late. But...I'll take a raincheck, Ted."

"Get outta here," Ted said. "Just be careful."

"Aren't those two pieces of advice along the lines of an oxymoron?" I joked.

Ted laughed. "You're the moron," he said. "But a very cute one."

Chapter 38

J u s t   W o r d s

Funny thing about love. You can't measure or manage it. Though God knows I've tried. And I've seen hundreds of others do exactly the same thing.

We start by making lists. The pros and cons. The good and bads. What we have in common and what we don't. Our dreams and goals.

But the truth is, even though I thought I was in love when I made my lists, I wasn't really—ever. Because when you are in love, you don't try to measure or manage it. And you wouldn't even think about making lists. About figuring out ways to tell if you're right for each other. You just fit. Not even like this part goes in that one. No, there is nothing tangible or measurable or manageable about it.

True love, lifetime love is a gift from God. It never comes when you expect it, and it never goes away. It doesn't take into account age or color or religion or gender or geography or education or culture or wealth or poverty or even language. It only acknowledges two things—hearts and souls. Hearts and souls that are made to be together.

Now that doesn't always mean they are alike. Sometimes they are. Sometimes they aren't. And sometimes they're a mix. But when it's love, they fit. Not for one night. Or one season. Some brief period in your life. Forever.

And though Maeve and Ted would always have a special place in my heart, I had grown tired, more than once to the point of being angry, at both of them for measuring my love for Jake and his for me. Neither seemed to understand what I told both of them repeatedly. That they could say anything they wanted to about us—it would not change a thing. Not my feelings or Jake's. And certainly not what is meant to be.

I think I drove them both a little crazy. Because even though Jake and I were apart, and no one other than Ginny believed we would ever be together again, Maeve and Ted really didn't know for sure we wouldn't make it. They couldn't totally rule out the possibility we might. But they sure as hell tried.

One of Maeve and Ted's favorite anti-Jake conversations would always begin with one of them asking me if he'd told me lately he loved me. They asked the question knowing the answer.

Jake has only ever said he loves me once. That is it. It was the night we walked out on to the beach. Only just before. Ted and Jake and I were sitting in a shabby little dockside bar in Daytona Beach trying to order some supper. We'd been sipping our drinks, trying to get the one bartender/waiter/ manager's attention again so we could get some food.

For some reason, Ted asked me if I'd ever met Jake's mother. And though Jake and I had only been together three months, this was a sore spot with me.

Sitting in between Jake and Ted, I told Ted, "No, as a matter of fact, I haven't. I would love to. But I haven't. Not sure what that's about, Ted," I said then, after glancing at Jake and seeing him frown, I tried to lighten my tone. I even winked at Ted, then said, "See, where I come from…back in the sticks…if a man loves a woman he introduces her to his parents."

Jake wheeled toward me on his barstool and said, "I do love you."

322

And I smiled. First at Ted, then at Jake. Drinking his words in as if they were water. As if they would always be there for me simply because I needed them. And I haven't heard them since.

There is a part of me that believes I can't live without hearing him tell me he loves me, that wants so much for Jake to tell me he loves me as much as I tell him. It is the part of me I don't like. Because the part of me I love knows love doesn't change a man. Not who he is or how he does things. It just fits into his life. You can see it in his eyes, hear it in his voice, feel it by the way he touches you. If I never hear Jake say the words *I love you* again as long as I can still see or hear or touch him, I will know whether or not he loves me. The words are merely words. Calling attention for one brief moment to what goes on every day without them.

Chapter 39

Barefoot   and   Naked

All of Ginny's life, wherever we've lived, traveled to, whatever our circumstances were, we would discover together. At the beginning of her life, when we lived in Hickory, North Carolina, we found favorite places to walk in our neighborhood, and nearby parks to play in.

In one of those parks, Ginny fell in love with an old pale blue plastic horse resting on two huge rusty metal coils affixed to a concrete base. She called her horse "Boo" because when she first discovered him, she couldn't say "Blue," and she rode "Boo" all over the country. Or so it seemed to Ginny. Laughing out loud, throwing her head back, blonde curls bouncing off her shoulders, big eyes sparkling with delight in the midday sun.

And while Ginny rocked and rode, I would swing. As far out as I could on my favorite red swing, next to Boo, the one between the yellow and blue swing. The one I'd worn a hole in the ground beneath, pressing the earth as hard as I could, pushing myself into the afternoon sky.

But in Florida, our discoveries were of a different kind. Oddly linked and separate. Ginny learning how to live with the voices—me, learning how to live with my mentally ill daughter.

In the months before Ginny's arrival from North Carolina, I'd made elaborate plans. Found all kinds of places I planned to take Ginny where we could spend hours discovering parks and nature trails, little towns circling lakes, craft shows and fairs.

But when Ginny arrived and almost immediately became a total recluse, spending whole days curled up on our couch or sitting in the dark in the master bedroom closet, my enthusiasm and hope for our new life full of adventures waned. And finally, after living a couple of months with her deep depression, disappeared altogether.

But when Ginny was released from the unit, I became, once again, determined. Not so much to try to return to our former life filled with wonder— even my optimism didn't encompass that kind of unconditional faith and hope—but to find new ways to share experiences with my daughter.

This pursuit was wholly different than the ones of years past. Completely without judgment about what would afford us the most exercise or fun or education. It was a spontaneous pursuit. An every day search for ways I could connect with my daughter. For discoveries I'd previously ignored or shunned as common. Not worth our time.

Interesting. How for so long, when all was well in our world, how not well I was. How judgmental. And how it took my daughter becoming mentally ill for me to see that life itself is a discovery. Every part of it. And if you drink that message in and absorb it, your days will be full. Always.

Ginny and I discovered another new Florida activity one otherwise unremarkable day. Other than being able to wear t-shirts and flip flops and bathe in the sun all year round, swim outside into late October, walk on beautiful trails in shirt sleeves in January, have our pick of sun glasses and choice of ice-cream shops that were never "out of season," drive for thirty minutes any day of the week and feel the warm sand on our bare feet, we had identified a soothing, relatively inexpensive pastime beloved of the natives. The women that is. Getting manicures and pedicures.

Though I'd been in the business world for years, I had also spent the majority of my time in Asheville, where six months out of most years your feet and hands need to be covered and where on certain days exposing them can mean frost bite in minutes and the chance of losing fingers and toes. In Asheville, even the most conscientious, well-maintained ladies do not have weekly pedicures, and some don't even get manicures. One of my friends told me once, "If you need a place to fall apart, go to Asheville. Nobody gives a damn what you look like there."

I can't speak to other parts of Florida, but where we lived, in central Florida, the attitude about personal grooming is the polar opposite of my friend's description of Asheville's indifference. In central Florida, I've seen two-year-old girls with French manicures. Nearly any street you drive on has at least two or three nail shops to choose from. And you can get a pedicure and a manicure for the price of one manicure in Asheville.

So week after week, Ginny and I began treating ourselves to this unquestionable pleasure of a manicure and pedicure. I could never tell what Ginny liked most about it. She loves for me to hold her hand, and I would do this while we were having our feet massaged. She would smile at me, like when she was a little girl. And for a moment her eyes would be clear and bright. No confusion or pain in them at all.

But she also seemed to love the different voices of the nail technicians—some Chinese, some Vietnamese, some Japanese, some Filipino—each speaking their own languages as well as the language their hands spoke. Ginny would cock her head to one side, then whisper to me, "Can you guess what they're saying by the way they say it?" And the thing is, you could. And I began to think of all those times through the years when some question or observation of my daughter had inspired me to write.

I think now, looking back on our run of the nail shops, that the part Ginny liked most is being touched. And I believe there is a huge healing power in this alone.

Whenever I would get my nails done, I would feel so pretty. I mean the truth is, you can be blessed by God and parents with good looks, but the nail thing is different. Having your nails done makes you feel like the most beautifully wrapped present under the tree.

Jake was funny about my nails. I remember this one time, he was taking me out to his favorite Sushi restaurant in Orlando. I was a little late getting to his place and praying he wouldn't be upset. And when I told him Ginny and I had been getting our nails painted, he said, "Let me see them."

I held my hands out for him to inspect and he handled them as if they were lace. Then smiled like a little boy and told me, "They're pretty. Very pretty."

He is, however, quick to point out anytime I wear sandals how my toes are crooked. Now there is a reason for this. A perfectly good reason. Which I've never told Jake. Because for one thing, the first time he saw my toes and told me they are crooked, it hurt me. And the second and third and fourth time (you get the picture), it just made me madder than hell. Finally, whenever he brought the subject up, I just ignored him, treasuring the truth he doesn't know.

I love my toes. And actually only two of them on either foot are slightly bent. One of my toes has a birthmark on it. It is a half moon. When I was in college, I used to model shoes and sandals for the most expensive shoe store in Asheville. My feet are display size. A perfect six. And unlike most of the women in Asheville, I have always gotten pedicures.

I am also a runner, as I've said. So my feet and toes have taken me many places. Probably thousands of miles. They've run down Mount Haleakala in Maui and up Grandfather Mountain in North Carolina. They've run across the Golden Gate bridge in San Fransisco and through the streets of New York City. They've run the beaches of Monterey and Cape Cod. And over the Delaware River. Well, not literally. But you know what I mean.

I love my toes. One time, though, I did hurt them pretty badly. I was running in a marathon in Greensboro, North Carolina. It is the oldest marathon in the state.

It was November of 1992, and I woke up at four in the morning to do stretches in my motel room. I had a whole routine, complete with moves that relaxed every muscle in my body, from my neck to my feet. When I finished, I did my breathing exercises, focusing on one word—win. Then I turned on the t.v. to check the forecast and immediately shot to hell all of the past hour's attempts to get myself in the ideal state of mind and body to race.

The forecast called for sun, rain, sleet, and snow. Temperatures could vary, they thought, as much as twenty-five degrees during the course of the day.

There was only one thing to do. I had to run fast enough to avoid at least two changes in weather. And I made up my mind right then and there to do just that. And so I did. Winning my age division in the first marathon I ever ran in.

So I was and am really proud of my little feet and toes, though that day they were not so happy with me. Two days after the race, I noticed how sore my two big toes were. Really tender to my touch and swollen with puss. And then three days later, I had streaks running up my legs from blood poisoning.

I had to have both all of my toenails removed, and when I told the doctor that removed them I was going to continue to run marathons, he insisted that I get the roots burned so that the nails wouldn't grow back. Otherwise, he said, I could count on dealing with this again. So I took his advice.

I can't decide which part I liked better—his sticking a five-inch needle into my toes "to numb them," he told me, or the smell from the singeing procedure. But I do know this, the whole thing made childbirth seem like a piece of cake.

Anyway, all that said and in spite of what the doctor promised, my toenails did grow back. Yep. That's right. Except my big left toe nail. And I can't say I'm sorry, because I've got toenails for pedicures.

And of course you still don't know why my toes are "crooked," and that story is more dramatic—one I'd have probably enjoyed telling Jake if he hadn't teased me.

My toes are crooked because there wasn't enough room for me in my mother's womb. It's the truth. Not enough room in the inn. Perhaps it was a foreshadowing of my life sleeping with men—where I always seem to wind up on one small corner of the mattress, clinging to the corner of less than half a sheet.

Actually, it wasn't just my toes that were cramped; it was both my feet. I came into this world with both of them completely turned in.

That's okay, though. Do you know some of the fastest runners in the world are pigeon-toed? Of course, I'll have to admit, I kicked it up a notch. In the pictures I've seen, the outside ankle bones stared at the camera, and the tips of my toes on each foot looked like they were kissing each other.

The doctors gave my parents two options. They could wait until I learned to walk to fix them, or they could correct them immediately so the bones would grow properly. But I would have to be put in casts before I could walk.

My parents tell me they were torn. If they chose to let me learn to walk first, I'd be facing, to put it mildly, a greater challenge than most toddlers and I'd face it twice: once with crooked feet and once with straight. If they chose the immediate fix—essentially letting the doctors reposition my bones—I'd have to wear casts when most toddlers would be learning how to walk, which meant I'd be very late walking and who knew what other problems that might cause? Try to visualize it. They weren't just any casts; each was permanently affixed to a metal bar that held the plaster forms and my feet at just the right distance and in just the right position for the bones to learn their new direction, making any independent movement of my right and left legs impossible.

Anyway, my mother said she was standing there in the doctor's office holding me in her arms and looking into my eyes and they seemed to be telling her, "Bring it on. Go ahead. Put those casts on me. I'll walk anyway. Might even run marathons someday."

And so they did. And so I have.

Chapter 40

L e a d   M e   N o t

My runs with Jim were growing longer each day. We'd both wear our head-sets, sometimes running ten miles without speaking a word, just listening to our music and the gentle lap of our feet on the pavement. But sometimes we would talk too. Jim liked talking about ways to help Ginny. He'd compiled a list of organizations he thought she'd enjoy volunteering for. Both of us believing that feeling useful is a key element in wanting to live.

One day, after we'd been running for over an hour, me leading Jim on a course Jake designed for me to run, I realized I'd taken several wrong turns. I wasn't worried. I was actually relatively familiar with the neighborhood we were in. But I did realize if I wanted us to get back on Jake's course, we'd be running about seven miles more than usual. And I wondered if Jim was going to say anything.

It was funny. Really ironic. Me leading another man astray on a course Jake designed. I must say, though, even as clever as Jake is, I didn't think he'd made a course I would lead another man astray on. In fact, what I thought was what he told me— he was actually trying to make my life easier.

He'd mapped this particular course for me to get to his place easier. And, yes, I can see there was a mutual benefit in this. Since the path took ten minutes off the run, it meant I was with him sooner, and the route wound through the most beautiful neighborhoods of Winter Park, which brought me to his door in a kind of euphoria that made me believe running might be among the principal pleasures in heaven. Jake enjoyed seeing me arrive in that state, and he'd enjoyed teaching me the course.

The night he taught me, Maeve was over for supper. We were standing in the living room talking, when Jake walked up behind me, placed one hand on my hip, the other on my shoulder, and began telling me the streets on the course, turning my body in the direction I should go.

Maeve watched him for a few seconds, then burst out laughing. She told Jake, "You don't have to do that. Just tell her left or right."

Jake didn't take his hand off me. But he stared straight at Maeve and said, "You can tell her anything. She has to feel it to understand."

At first, Jim didn't say anything. I mean, after all, it was my course we were running. But after about an hour and a half, when I'd initially told him we were going for a short run, he asked, "Are you lost?"

"Always," I answered, simply, then laughed. "Always."

We'd run about twenty miles when the bottom dropped out of the afternoon sky. A wall of water hit us like a giant wave, soaking every part of our bodies.

The whole time I was living in Florida, I never got used to this. Because when you spend a lifetime living in the valleys beneath the Smokey Mountains, you don't get surprised by storms. If one is strong enough and big enough to get past those mountains and drop into the valley, you see it coming.

That day Jim and I got caught in the rain, I was wearing sunscreen, which immediately ran down into my eyes, causing them to burn as if I'd poured battery acid into them. Jim had the same problem—only worse, because he was

332

wearing contacts. In addition to this, my nose started running, and while I was trying to wipe it with a soaked sleeve, Jim reached the end of his willpower and pulled me into the nearest 7-eleven.

We stood there in the brightly lit refrigerated store, swiping at our eyes and noses, dripping a puddle onto the welcome mat, and Jim asked me, "Is this what you do to guys?"

"What?" I said, too uncomfortable between the sudden cold and the persistent stinging to joke with him and hearing some real annoyance in his voice.

He shook more rain out of his drooping raven hair and said, "Run them to death?"

I laughed then, though by that time my eyes were crying wildly from the sunscreen.

Then he said, "Cause that's probably the only reason you're still single. I mean, I'm guessing this little course of yours would wipe out most of the male population."

I watched Jim drip and listened to a voice that sounded only something like my own answering him. "Yes," it said, "Maybe that's what its designer had in mind."

Chapter 41

D r e a m   H o u s e

I've lived with men. I know the rules. What's mine is yours and what's his is his. But when Jake started asking for his belongings back, it hurt. Like the sticky part of a band-aid being pulled off an open sore. Every time he'd ask for something else of his, I'd remember when he brought it to a place we once shared. But, one by one, when he asked, I gave them back. And when I didn't have any more of his things, Jake disappeared too. Never even calling.

But the producer of Dreamhouse did call a couple of weeks after Carson had sent him the tape we made.

He said, "Haley?" and I thought I recognized the voice, but I couldn't place it.

I answered, "Yes."

He said, "Bob Larson," and if I hadn't been sitting down, my knees might have buckled because I knew this was a situation where consolation calls would be unlikely. And still I wasn't quite prepared when he said, "How would you like to be on Dreamhouse?"

I screamed first. Then thanked him. As soon as he hung up, I ran to tell Ginny and John. John smiled and said, "A star is reborn!"

Ginny put her arms around my waist and would not let go for minutes. She said, "You go, mommy. Finally!...You get to live your dreams." Then she walked over to the corner closet and pulled out one of the sketch pads and the pastels Faith had given her and sat down on the living room floor and began drawing for the first time in months.

She drew a picture of our dream house. She worked on it for hours while I cooked supper.

The front of the house was pink, and the roof was made of red tiles. You could see through one of the windows, there was a fireplace in the living room, bricked in yellow and alive with flames. There were purple petunias, spilling out of white planters over the rails of the front porch. And the grass in the front yard was the color of my eyes. Ginny had drawn three figures standing side by side on the front porch, holding hands. One was a man, one a woman, and one a little girl. When she'd finished her drawing, she ran into the kitchen and held it up for me to see. She said, "Look mommy! It's me and you and Jake in our new home!"

I kissed Ginny on the forehead, then smiled as big as I could smile. But when I couldn't hold back my tears, I opened the front door and stepped outside.

I wanted so much to be happy. I'd been chosen to be on the show. Ginny was proud of me and happy. We had a chance at a whole new life in a beautiful new home where Ginny could grow and heal, and I'd have gardens again. But I kept looking down at the rock-shell patio where Jake used to stand and kiss me good night, and I just couldn't feel any hope. Because I knew Ginny could color him into every one of her drawings, but if he didn't choose to be with us, they would always just be pictures of what might have been.

§

When I called Carson, she was ecstatic and immediately willing to help me formulate my next plan. I had to tell Richard about the show Monday morning and I needed to make sure what I had to say made sense for me and Evergreen. Carson volunteered to call Ben and Jim and tell them while I worked on my speech to Richard.

But just before she got off the phone, Carson warned me, "Don't let Jake ruin this for you."

At first I started to defend him. But I stopped myself and said, "It's okay. You have nothing to worry about. Jake doesn't give a damn about the show or me."

For a moment, Carson said nothing. Then I heard her sigh. She told me, "I hate to say this, but you leave me no choice. You know I have this sixth sense about people. I can tell what they're feeling, even if they don't show it."

I said, "Yes, I know. You've told me before."

"Well, as much as I hate to say it, missy, I hate worse seeing you discouraged, so I'm gonna tell you Jake doesn't give a damn about the show; you're right about that much. But...he does love you."

"Yeh?" I said, feeling a small flutter of hope returning. I wanted to hug Carson, but since I didn't have her "sixth sense" and the flutter was already fading, I just said, "Well, he sure has a strange way of showing it."

But Carson wasn't resigning herself to my sarcasm. She said, "Hey, haven't I taught you anything about men? All those crack-of-dawn Monday mornings before the opening bell for garbage sales—you and me beating the boys to the beginning of a new work week so they couldn't claim a lack of dedication on our part. Cranking the coffee pot up and talking about my disastrous love life for an hour before the first damn man walked through the door, and you haven't learned a damn thing about men, the way they work or the way they love?"

"Guess not," I said.

"He's letting go," Carson told me. "Let him let go," she said. "He knows you aren't meant to be here. He knows he just lucked out. And he knows he took a very big chance being with you. That he could have lost his heart and you. So he's letting go before anything worse happens."

"I would never leave Jake," I told Carson.

"Never is a long time, baby."

"I know," I said, "But I mean it."

Carson waited a second, then said, "I know you do. But your puppy's still learning. And he's a smart puppy. He'll learn. You just gotta give him time and space. Let him go for now. It's show time for you, girl."

Chapter 42

J u s t   T h i n k i n g

At the ripe old age of nearly forty-two, I had finally discovered a new way of being in the world. Actually, I'd been living it for nearly a year. Ever since I moved to central Florida. And I just could not have been any busier. Doing absolutely nothing.

Of course, I mean nothing of substance. Nothing that had anything to do with a purpose in life. Nothing that gave hope, brought light or life to this world, and nothing much beyond beautiful diversions, like walks on Daisy Way and manicures, to make my daughter's life brighter.

I knew this deep inside. And despite all my trials and tribulations at work, heartache for Ginny, turmoil with Jake, this—this absence of meaning—was what I couldn't live with. That I was not doing what I am here to do. No one can truly live without living their reason for being. Not for very long anyway. Certainly not for a lifetime.

I woke early that Saturday morning to fix Ginny her favorite breakfast, waffles made with 7-Up, hashbrowns from real potatoes, and fried tempeh. After she'd eaten and we'd washed the dishes together, I let her take Mischief for a walk around the condos, while I sat on the bench by the pond, sipping my hazelnut coffee.

John was at the gym working out. When he got back, he told me he'd be packing more of his things. He'd found a vacant unit, just across from ours and some of the investors in his company were going to help him afford the rent.

I knew I should be happy. At least happier. Ginny was back in school and doing better, and I had a good job. I'd landed a part on a t.v. show. I was surrounded by friends. We had a nice home and were soon to have more privacy. I should have been counting my blessings. I should have been thankful for every one of them.

And I tried to be. There, sitting on the bench by the pond, sun shining down on me in my pink cotton pajamas, I tried to be at peace. But I just couldn't.

My stomach was gurgling with anxiety, my head was tight with tension. My neck felt sore and my lower back strained. My jaw was even rigid, and I was aware for the first time that I was clenching my teeth together. My stomach and jaw muscles seemed to by vying for the cramping award.

After a few minutes of thinking about nothing but how uncomfortable I was, I decided I would focus on something other than myself. Divert my attention from my miserable state of being. So I began staring at a patch of pond just in front of me.

It was thick with lily pads and algae and smelled like soured milk. Just beneath it, there was dark flashy movement, tadpoles, I guessed, that looked like squirts of ink.

I watched their little show for a moment, and almost immediately they began gathering together in one big chorus of motion before darting full force into the muddy bank. Their impact caused some sort of earth-under-water explosion, brown prevailing over green, darkness covering light, with everything suddenly unclear in their world and in mine.

While I waited to see if the tadpoles had survived, I tried to sort things out. Why, why, why, why didn't I feel good? Was I some sort of nut case? Some sort of hormone-crazed forty-something female who was letting her love life take precedence over everything? Was I so exhausted and stressed about the last six months of my daughter's life that I couldn't see improvement in either of our lives? Was I so desperate, so uncharacteristically fearful that I really believed I would lose my job because of the show.

No, no, no. What then?

§

I realize this questioning everything is the opposite of what anyone in the world who has ever had a clue about achieving inner peace would advise someone seeking it to do. I've read my share of Kahlil Gibran and Julia Cameron. I studied the Eastern traditions in school. Buddhists, Taoists, New Agers, yoga teachers—none would recommend crunching detail after detail of personal life. Holding onto every little part of it. Analyzing everything to death.

They all believe you must let go of everything. Inner peace comes not from seeking or holding on but from letting go. So, at last, you are left only with your true self and then you will know your purpose.

But I believe, like so many others in our acquisitive culture, that if I just have one more cup of coffee and ask just one more question, I can solve not only my problems but the world's. Filled with just the right amount of caffeine and curiosity, I am nothing less than a prophet.

That the world is full of people just like me is no secret. Ask any coffee shop owner. Literally packing their establishments every day with caffeine addicts. And each one is a self-proclaimed miracle worker, who, after a few cups of his or her favorite blend and some lively conversation, is ready to work wonders. Thinking Jesus, Mohammed, and the Dalai Lama have nothing on them.

Meantime, the tadpoles return—having given no thought to anything, having merely lived in their wondrous gathering and sudden movement and the momentary muddiness and the return to light.

Then a car horn somewhere startled me, and I was back in my world. I strolled to my mailbox, resolved for the moment to slow down at least. I couldn't quite dismiss the dread of what the box would contain because it rarely contained much other than bills I couldn't pay. But what I found instead was a letter from Whispering Pines, actually a preliminary grade report of the first four weeks of school. Ginny was taking five college bound courses. And the report said she had A's in every one of them.

I clutched the paper to my chest, looked up at the sky, and smiled. "Thank you, God," I said. "Thank you."

I ran back to the condominium, holding the report like it was the most important document ever written. Full of hope and excitement and new-found energy. I burst through the front door, walked across the living room, and showed it to Ginny. She was sitting on the floor, petting Mischief. She looked up at me and frowned. "Mischief has two more fleas," she told me. "I'm telling daddy when he gets back from the gym. We'll have to get more powder." She glanced down at the report and rolled her eyes, and then, as if she were still talking about the fleas continued her speech, "And this isn't real. The voices told me. I got all F's. You paid the teachers off."

I sat down next to Ginny and put my arm around her back and told her, "Honey, I'm so proud of you. You should be proud too." I rubbed her back. "And you know what the voices are telling you isn't true. You just have to look at the facts. You've made A's on all your homework. I know, because you showed me all your papers. And when I called to check with your teachers to see if you were able to concentrate during your tests, they all told me you're doing fine." I held the paper up. "Better than fine, I'd say. Look—all A+'s!" I set the paper back down and continued to rub her back. She pulled away and fell over onto her side, ignoring Mischief who was whimpering for more attention.

I tried again. "I'm so proud of you, honey," I said. I kissed her cheek. "You are incredible."

Ginny had curled herself into an almost fetal like position and was staring ahead at the stairs. She said in a voice that sounded like it was trapped in an empty hallway, "I used to be a good student. I used to make straight A's. But now…when I try to study, the voices won't let me. Sometimes I read the same sentence a hundred times and I still can't remember what I've read. That report is a fake. I am a spy for the U.S. government. I'm investigating the behavior of teenage girls in the Florida school system."

Suddenly, Ginny looked at me, eyes glazed, face frozen with a "say cheese" smile, then burst into hysterical laughter, which lasted for a full minute until she glanced at Mischief, still waiting expectantly for her touch, then began sobbing, telling the dog through her tears, "I'm so sorry you have fleas. I hope they don't hurt you." Then she wiped her running nose with the back of her hand and moved closer to Mischief, speaking more softly into John's dog's eyes, "I don't want you to hurt."

And this is how it went. Hour to hour, day after day, trying to convince my daughter what she lives with is not what everyone else lives with. And that what everyone else lives with is considered real. And that the truth…well, I didn't bring up truth anymore. Because somewhere over the course of the past six months, I had lost any sense of it. I put both my arms around Ginny and cried, telling her, "I don't want you to hurt either, baby. And I'm trying to keep you from getting hurt. But I don't seem to always know how to do that anymore. You know? I can't…I can't put a band-aid over what's happened to you. And I can't kiss it away. I just, I can't seem to make things better for you. I'm trying, baby. God knows I'm trying. But I'm no good at this Ginny. I used to know you. I used to know everything about you, and I told those damn people at the crisis unit that. I told them they didn't know you and I did. But now, now it's like all I know is…is to love you. And it's not enough, Ginny. It's just not enough."

"It's okay," Ginny told me in a comforting tone, hugging me back. "It's okay, Mommy." Then she dropped both arms down at her sides, sat straight up, and said she thought she knew the solution for both of us: "We just need to get more flea powder."

Ginny was volunteering at the puppet theater that afternoon, so I had some time to work on my speech to Richard. And after I was satisfied with what I was going to say, I made calls to Ginny's psychiatrist and counselor to update them about the show and make certain there would be no hitches in Ginny's having prescriptions and regular therapy and that they would be in contact with me immediately should they have any concerns about Ginny's state of mind or well being. Then I began making lists for John—about medication, food, destructive patterns of behavior to look for, when Ginny's period was, what groceries and supplies to buy weekly, directions to the doctor, counselor, and hospital, emergency numbers, Faith's number.

I bought Ginny a cell phone so she could call me anytime, wrote letters to all her teachers, and reconfirmed with the director that I would be able to talk with Ginny every day and that they were still willing to make an exception to the no-visitors rule so that John could bring her once a week to see me.

I didn't call Jake.

Chapter 43

B r o k e n   H o m e

I'd typed a ten-week plan for the sales department at Evergreen, regarding every revenue, density, and marketing goal we were working on and I'd delegated each task to a specific member of the team. And I developed a marketing campaign associated with the show, which I also intended to pitch to Richard when I pitched my plan to be on Dreamhouse.

On Monday morning, Carson called me on my drive into work to pump me full of support. She told me, "Most people in your situation would have asked for a paid leave of absence. And you, missy, would have been completely justified in taking it. But not you. You came to work every day. And the sales team you hired and trained is ahead of budget. And what about all the incredible free publicity Evergreen will get out of this? They could never afford this kind of national advertising. It's great exposure for them. First of all, they'll get points for hiring a female sales manager in a male-dominated industry. Then a bonus for your being a single mom. And then when the viewers realize the company is supporting you living your dream—trying to win a beautiful home for you and your daughter… hell, every woman in

America will be calling them for trash service. You're doing them a favor. They should be paying you to be on the show."

I laughed. Inside, I felt very conflicted and nervous. But I laughed for Carson's sake. She wanted the dream house for me as much as I wanted it for Ginny. Who could want a better friend?

After I'd signed off on a couple service agreements, returned my messages and e-mails, and organized the bids I'd be working on later, I stopped by Richard's office and asked if I could speak with him. He welcomed me in.

I sat down in one of Richard's leather visitors' chairs and faced him across his huge desk. I began by telling him Ginny had found the audition, which is what Carson and I had agreed to—and that she'd encouraged me to go. I told him how much we both wanted to own a home in Florida but how we couldn't afford one with all the medical bills. Then I went on to tell him I was cast, a little about the show, my plan for the department in my absence, my plan for commnication with him, and ended with my pitch about the marketing campaign.

When I stopped speaking, Richard , who had kept a poker face during the whole time I was talking, sat back and smiled at me. Then he rocked forward in his chair, which protested his considerable weight. He put his elbows on his desk and leaned toward me, staring straight at me. "You have got to be kidding," he said in a voice that told me he knew I was as serious as a day without trash pickup. He raised both his thick grey eyebrows and asked, "Who do you think I am? Do you think I came out of retirement, moved my wife across the United States to get this company going in the right direction with a sales manager who isn't sure whether or not she wants to manage revenue and a sales team or her own career in television?" Richard snorted and pushed himself away from his desk. Then he said, "It's your choice, not mine. You want to be on the show? Be on the show. But you won't be working here."

I stood up and pushed back my chair, my heart doing a mad dance. "Thank you Richard," I said as calmly as I could, extending my hand. Richard stood up and shook my hand.

"So," he said, smiling. "What's it gonna be? Hollywood or Evergreen?"

"You leave me no choice," I said, wanting him to wonder for just a moment if he'd made a huge mistake, since unless I were to sell my soul I had no other power over him.

Richard said cheerfully, "Choice is yours."

And I wished then for myself and for Ginny that I hadn't delayed answering him. Because the delay meant nothing to him. "I choose to take care of my daughter," I said. I was hoping I could give her something we've both dreamed of. But it's clear to me now that isn't going to happen. So I choose to take care of my daughter."

"Good choice," Richard said, then he chuckled. "Thought for a minute there, you'd lost your mind."

"No," I answered him. "I've probably broken my daughter's heart again, but I haven't lost my mind."

§

I had to call Jake. I had to talk to him about what had happened. But I waited until I was driving home.

Listening to his phone ring, I prayed he would answer. And when he did, when I heard his voice for the first time in weeks, I knew I wouldn't be able to keep form crying.

I told him, "You were right. I got on the show. I told Richard today, and he didn't like it one bit. He said I had to choose and I told him I choose to take care of Ginny. He was smiling at the end but you were right. I probably cost myself my job and I'm not gonna be on the show. And worst of all, I've probably hurt Ginny. God, Jake what was I thinking?"

"You weren't," he said, then after a few seconds added, "Ginny'll be okay. Don't worry about that. Hell, she'll be a lot better off now that you won't be gone. She needs you there, with her, not on that damn show."

"I know," I said, crying. "I know. I didn't want to be away from her either. Everything just happened so fast and next thing you know we were both caught up in this dream, and I never wanted to leave her. You know I never wanted that."

"I know," Jake said softly. Then suddenly changed the tone of his voice to angry and told me, "You can tell Miss Carson, I said for her to stay the hell away from you with her grand schemes. You've got enough to deal with now. You don't need any of her brilliant ideas. You just need time to figure things out. And space. And you never have either thanks to those assholes you work for and Carson and Mr. California. Jesus, I can't do this anymore. I can't... Just do me one favor, okay? 'Cause I gotta go. You are getting me totally upset again about things I have absolutely no control over and I'm not...I'm not gonna let you do it anymore. Just take care of yourself and Ginny, okay? Just tell everybody else to go to hell. Will you do that for me?"

I was sobbing now. "Which one?" I said.

"All of 'em," Jake said.

"Okay," I said, "I promise. But who's gonna take care of you?"

"I can take care of myself. Don't' ever worry about that. I don't need anybody to take care of me."

I couldn't stop crying.

"What's the matter now?" Jake asked. "See, this is what I'm talking about. You drive me crazy. I'm trying to help you, but I guess I hurt you."

"You don't hurt me," I told Jake. "I just love you so much and I miss you so much..."

Jake stopped me. "I'm right here," he said. "You have my number. I'm not going anywhere. You just need to take care of yourself and Ginny. Don't worry about us."

"And what's that supposed to mean?"

Jake didn't say anything.

"Jake? Do you mean forget about us or don't worry about us because we will always be together?"

"What do you think?" Jake said.

I swallowed hard. "I think you mean don't worry because we'll always be together."

"Yeh?" Jake said. "That's your problem. You think too much when you already know the answer." Then he added, "I gotta go. Take care of Ginny. And tell her I think she's lucky she doesn't have to live in a house you built."

Chapter 44

B e i n g   R e a l

I'll never know what really happened that day in Richard's office. Whether I sealed my fate by creating a plan for my sales department to run without me. Or just planted a seed. Either way, I realized almost immediately after telling Mr. Larson I couldn't do the show that I never wanted to do it to begin with. While I was certain Evergreen would never be a company that I could feel proud working for and good about my future with, replacing my regional sales manager's position with a spot on a reality t.v. show was not a practical choice either.

I came to Evergreen from the top waste management company in the nation, Environmental. But here's what's more important. I came on my own. Environmental is literally the giant in the industry and typically when you meet someone working in the waste management business from another company you'll find they used to work for Environmental. More importantly, in my case, you'll find they didn't leave of their own volition.

Unfortunately for me at Evergreen, I was literally surrounded by people at work who were either cast-offs of Environmental or could never get hired by them to begin with. And I was incredibly naïve not to see this as a potential problem.

At Environmental, though I worked in possibly the most male-dominated industry there is and clearly one of the most conservative, my creativity was always encouraged. There, under Mario's direction, I helped him develop a regional 1-800 campaign. There I won the company's national contest to name their database. There I was nominated for Rookie of the Year. A member of their Circle of Excellence—the top ten sales reps in the Southeast. I won the contest to name their regional newsletter and contributed articles quarterly. I was chosen to be a part of their elite management training program.

At Environmental, my unique creative personable style of gaining business and taking care of customers was rewarded time and again. Not because I'm special. Not because I was made an exception. But because they are number one in the industry. And they got to that position because they value people. They take care of their customers and their employees.

When I came to Evergreen, I was confronted with possibly the most apathetic, unproductive sales staff I've ever seen in my life. Along with no goals. I replaced all of this with a sales staff who could run the country, never mind Evergreen Waste services. A well-written, well-implemented training program, consistent marketing campaigns, a complete scrubbing and upgrade of their database, as well as a daily maintenance program, tools for the sales reps, realistic but challenging goals, reports to track revenue, density, and quality of revenue, incentive programs, networking events, well-run sales meetings and an atmosphere that nurtured cooperation and growth.

I've done a good deal of reading over the years about what constitutes successful management. And this reading, coupled with my experience, leads me to believe the path to success is paved by surrounding yourself with people who make you better than you are. Who could do your job in a heartbeat. Maybe even better. But who for reasons of loyalty and other values and priorities choose to do their jobs, not yours, to the absolute best of their abilities. And this is exactly the style with which I managed at both Evergreen and Environmental. Only it elicited two very different responses from higher management. At Environmental, I was respected. At Evergreen, every move I made was second guessed.

I have worked for years now in the waste management industry with people too good to describe as jewels. At Environmental, I had a sales team I would take the bullet for. But at Evergreen, I had one that would take the bullet for me.

§

Carson and I never told anyone at work about the show. Carson was as loyal to me as she was to her own words. She just went right on, never missing an opportunity for a sale, working a territory where we had no disposal advantage, plugged with traffic thicker than mud, where some of our competition was pricing trash as recyclable cardboard then hauling it to a dirty manufacturers' recycling facility, and where there are possibly more franchises than in any other marketplace in the United States. And then, every day, no matter what, still making certain I was okay. That I was able and willing to face another one.

When John first moved in with me and Carson knew Jake's feeling about it, she would invite Jake and me and Ginny to her home to grill out, swim in her pool, play with her dogs. Anything she thought would bring me peace and happiness. She'd paint pictures for me and Ginny. Take us to craft shows and concerts. And even though she and Ben were becoming more involved every day, she never chose her boyfriend over her friend. She never forgot about me or Ginny. And while Maeve told me Carson would drop me like a hot potato after I decided not to do the show, Carson never left my side.

But she did tell me, while we were having one of our many conversations about life, lounging on her screened in patio in overstuffed cushions that pillowed Carson's furniture, sipping wine, nibbling fruit and cheese and crackers, listening to Ginny laughing and watching her throwing a Frisbee in Carson's backyard while her dogs chased it, "You pick impossible men on purpose."

"Why do you say that?" I asked, popping a grape in my mouth.

"Because you do. I haven't met husband number two, but I've met number one, and your current number one, and they are both clearly impossible men to love."

"I laughed. "They are not," I said. They are both just very strong-willed… okay, stubborn…but intelligent, fun, handsome, creative, resourceful men."

Carson frowned. "Hey, I didn't ask for a litany of virtues on the men you've loved…love. And I didn't say they aren't all that. But what I said is true. They are both impossible to love. And I would bet another toe that number two is too." Carson smiled and took another sip of her wine.

I told her, "You give up toes too easily. Bet's off."

Ginny squealed just then, as one of Carson's dogs, Skipper, jumped up on her thighs, trying to take the Frisbee out of her hand. Carson yelled, "Skipper, get down. Jesus Christ. Males. They are all the same. Dogs, men. Can't keep 'em out of your crotch."

I laughed, then said, "Well, for your information, I've had a lifetime of committed relationships, so if I've done it with impossible men, kudos to me." I raised my glass for a pretend toast, then brought it back down and took another sip of chardonnay.

"Why congratulate yourself for making your life harder than it needs to be?" Carson asked, dawning her signature smirk. "I think you're dumber than a box of rocks when it comes to men. And" Carson said, leaning forward, "you choose impossible ones because," she stopped and smiled and took a deep breath, then finished, "you really don't want a long-term relationship after all."

I sat up straight, protesting, "Right. That's why since the time I turned seventeen, I've been nothing but either engaged or married. Because I don't want to be in long term relationships." I frowned. "Come on Sigmund, I think your analysis skills took a holiday."

354

Carson smiled. "I wouldn't be so quick to judge, missy," she said. "The obvious is not always the truth. And correct me if I'm wrong, but I believe you did leave both your husbands?"

"It's not that simple," I told Carson.

"Spare me the gory details and stick to the point I'm trying to make. You may have been in committed relationships all your life. But that doesn't mean you really wanted to be in them. Or that they are all right for you. Look at the things you love most." Carson and I both glanced out at Ginny, who was laughing and racing Skipper to get to the Frisbee she'd thrown. "Okay, Ginny, number one. But for now, let's focus on just you as a person not as a mother." Carson drank her wine, apparently to give me time to think, but when I kept looking out the window she said, "You love to write and you love to run. Both solo activities. And then there's the other part of you. The part that likes to perform. Again, not an activity necessarily conducive to having a long-term relationship. It's just…it may not be obvious, but it's probably true. Subconsciously you do not want to be in a long-term relationship."

I said nothing for a few minutes, eating a cracker, some cheese, and two more grapes, while Carson picked up a fly swatter and swatted a fly that had been buzzing around the food.

Finally I told her, "I don't think I've ever told anyone this. So, bear with me. This is unrehearsed."

Carson rolled her eyes. "Hit it drama queen," she said, "before this wine makes me fall asleep.

"You're close," I said. "You're close to the truth.

Carson smiled and clenched her fist in the air. "I knew it," she said.

"Easy there, Freud Jr. Here me out," I said.

"Carson raised her eyebrows. "Go ahead. I'm all ears."

"You are right about the men, not me."

Carson frowned.

I smiled. "They are all pretty impossible. I vote John the most controlling, Blake the most stubborn, and Jake…well, easily the hardest to love. But

I also vote John the most romantic, Blake the most caring, and Jake the most passionate and...the most fun."

Carson interrupted, "You can't give Jake two votes, it's unfair."

"Yeh?" I said. "What do you know about love that's fair?"

Carson laughed. "You're right there, missy," she said.

"But about me. You're dead wrong. I'm all about commitment. And there isn't anything the matter with my track record—twenty some years of marriage and I'm friends with both my ex-husbands. Absolutely, totally, faithfully, unconditionally in love with one man for the rest of my life. Go ahead. Check Eharmony. See if you find a lot of examples of that. I doubt it. And since I've been here, I've never met so many people literally hopping from bed to bed. I'm telling you. They ought to try to make it profitable. Get some mattress company to sponsor them."

Carson laughed. "You're all right, missy. And we may not get out of this married or alive, but you sure as hell know how to make a girl laugh."

Chapter 45

Lakeside

October runs into November in central Florida. If you live there and don't work in retail or shop on a regular basis to see the holiday displays change, you have no idea the seasons are changing. The colors stay the same. The wind blows the same. The temperature stays the same.

Jake had not called in over a month, and every day I spent without him, I relied on my memory of us to boost my spirits. I remember running through the neighborhoods of Winter Park and Orlando, blooming with fruit and flowers, carrying a bittersweet feeling that life goes on when love doesn't.

Meantime, Jim and Ben were on a mission. Both good skiers, they were determined to rent a house on a lake. They wanted the perfect bachelor's pad. Complete with a deck to grill on, Jacuzzi, game room, bar, fireplace, and plenty of bedrooms.

They made a point of including my female opinion in their process of setting up housekeeping. After Ginny, John, and I had eaten supper and Ginny and I had walked, John would take over. He and Ginny would either work on homework or on returning e-mails from his customers, get a yogurt, and then watch television until she went to bed.

John and I were divorced when Ginny was five years old, and other than a few scattered visits, he had spent very little time with his daughter in the past eleven years. I was happy for them to have the chance to reconnect.

So, flashlight in hand, I'd jump in my little red car and head out to meet Jim and Ben for one of our nightly househunts.

You never really know what you're going to get when you are looking at lake properties. You could find one that had been well-maintained, one a family had just moved out of, or you could find one that was a second residence and hadn't been lived in for months, or one that had been lived in by several slobs who left their mess for someone else to clean up, or one whose owner had pretty much decided just to sell the land and had literally abandoned taking care of the property or the house. In our search for the perfect bachelor's pad, we found all of these. And something more. I'm quite certain, we found Ted Bundy's second home. His Florida residence.

But finally after about a month of nightly searches, we discovered the perfect bachelor's paradise. It had everything the guys wanted and more. Not only was there a deck off the back of it, the deck had two huge levels. And on the first level, oak trees sprung up through man holes, providing another touch of character.

I pretended to inspect the bathrooms and kitchen with a critical eye. Mainly because this is what guys expect women to do. But I knew if I'd said to them I didn't like either one, they would have argued the house's other good points. And truthfully, both the bathrooms and the kitchen were fine. Definitely needed cleaning and a woman's decorative touch. But they were fine.

So Ben signed the papers and began a new search—this one, for a third roommate. Quickly and luckily he found Greg. A single soccer playing father with a son named Jed and a cat called Pudding.

They were set. Between the three of them, they had enough sofas and recliners to furnish a large fraternity house. Beer mugs, corkscrews, and bottle openers galore. A pool table. Two refrigerators. A big-screen t.v. Three stereos. Two boats. A grill. I told them all they needed to do was make a big sign that read LADIES WELCOME, plant it in their front yard, and stock up on condoms.

Jim, Ben, Greg, and I became a pretty tight group. The guys took me on boat rides at sunset, taught me how to shoot a decent game of pool, grilled steaks while I fixed potatoes and other vegetables, and tried to teach me the game of football.

I kidded them a lot. Told them we had to have certain understandings. For instance, they could date anyone...with my approval. We established signals for when their dates were there. It was a sneeze if I liked them, a cough if I didn't. And if any of them got too noisy in the bedroom, I just kicked their door and told them to get a hotel room. And pretty quickly they were teasing each other about me. They started calling me "Miss Thing."

"Did you ask Miss Thing if you could wear those trunks?"

What I didn't expect was how much the guys would include Ginny and me together in their lives. Almost every weekend they invited us to ski, cook out, shoot pool, play darts, go for walks, watch football. Their place became our place.

I loved my days with the guys, who unknowingly created this wonderful nostalgia for me—filled with memories of my brothers, some of my best guy friends— and faith that no matter what I was going through, they'd be there for me.

Sauce Sundays became ski and sun days. The guys would start out early. They'd fuel the boats, then clean them inside out while I would waltz around the deck practicing songs for the concert I was singing in over the holidays, dancing with Ginny.

We'd spend the whole day on the boat, skiing—two of the guys guzzling beer and the "designated boat driver" enjoying the iced tea I made especially for him, while Ginny and I applied sunscreen and enjoyed the cool of the air rushing all around us as the boat skimmed over the water. At the end of the day, we'd come in, assess the groceries we needed for supper, and head to the store.

Eating on the deck, surrounded by citronella candles, listening to the occasional neighbor's boat passing by, we'd cover every topic I've ever discussed.

I remember one conversation Ben started. We'd just finished eating our steaks, refilling our wine and getting a few more cold beers from the fridge in the garage. It was just Ben and Jim and me sitting around the table on the deck that evening. John had taken Ginny with him to visit his parents who'd just moved to Ocala, and Greg was spending the day with Jed at the movies.

Ben said, "So tell me, you're a creative writing major, right?"

"Yes," I said. "And your point?" Then I added, "No let me just say this, if you're going to say something about how that isn't exactly what you would expect of a sales manager in the waste industry, don't go there. I've already had that conversation. A hundred times."

Ben chuckled. "Gotcha. But no, that isn't what I'm going to say. Now just listen before you jump to conclusions."

I didn't say anything while Jim swatted a gnat.

Ben took a swig of his beer while another neighbor cruised by in his ski boat and waved. Then he said, "If you could marry anyone, who would it be?"

I rolled my eyes, then said, "I can't believe this! Here I am in bachelor heaven and you're asking me a question like that? Totally out of character. The ultimate non sequitur with regards to your life. I'm out. No fair. Besides...you already know the answer, and it will never change, so it's not a good question anyway."

Ben put his beer on the table. "Forget that answer. Forget him. Fuck Jake. Guy's a card carrying commitment phobic." Ben picked his beer back up, took a sip, then said, "Hell, by now, by now...he shoulda had a ring on your finger and, excuse my graphic nature, but...planted his seed in you." I winced and turned red, while Ben belched and set his beer back down. "He shoulda taken care of his treasure is what I'm saying. But, instead, what does the guy do? He plays hide and seek with a gift from God." Ben stared down at me. "Fuck Jake. That guy is *not* your answer."

"I know who it is," Jim said.

"Who?" Ben asked, surprised.

Jim smiled. "It's Donald Trump."

Ben rocked forward in his chair and burst out laughing. "You gotta be kidding me."

Jim looked defensive. He said, "What? The guy's a brilliant business man. And I know she thinks that because she told me. Tell Ben the thing you told me about him. I don't want to screw it up."

"Which thing?" I asked. "We've talked about him a couple of times, and *The Apprentice* too. Which one are you talking about?"

Jim frowned. "See? You're gonna make me paraphrase and I'm gonna fuck up the impact. He looked frustrated and insisted, "You remember. The thing you said about experience."

The minute he said "experience," I knew what he wanted me to tell Ben. So I did.

"The thing, well, one of the things that separates Donald from the rest of us is the way he internalizes his experiences. The way he doesn't have to learn lessons twice. It's one of the many simple reasons why he's so successful. How he stays a step ahead. While most of us are making the same mistakes two and three times, learning nothing from our past, Donald learns once. It's like his experiences immediately become a part of him. What he does and who he is are inseparable."

Ben smiled. "Cool. Very cool. Now let me just go get my cell phone and call ol' Donald up. I bet none of the broads he's been with have ever told him anything like that. I'm thinking we got a surprising new marriage proposal in the making." Ben stood up, then added, "Just don't forget your friends."

I laughed. "You can sit back down. And don't call his wives 'broads.' I'm sure they are very bright women."

Jim told Ben, "There you go, offending Miss Thing. And it's just what she said. You've made the same mistake before because you haven't learned she doesn't like that word."

Ben put his head down and stuck out his lip in mock contrition. I winked at Jim and said, "Anyway, as I was saying, I wouldn't marry Donald if he asked me."

Ben's head popped back up. "Why not?" he asked, sitting back down.

Jim jumped in, "Yeh, why the hell not?"

"Because…" I said, taking a sip of wine and holding it in my mouth for a moment to hold them both in suspense. "Because, there's a dark side to all of Donald's abilities." I paused again and watched, enjoying the effect until Ben got impatient.

"And that would be?" he urged.

"He's only happy when he's challenged," I said. "And," I added, "he's rarely challenged."

Ben and Jim both considered this for a minute. Then simultaneously set their empty beer cans down, crushing them slightly.

Ben said, "Damn."

"What?" I said, in a tone of mock innocence.

"You're right again," he said.

"Of course," Jim chimed in, "she's…" Ben interrupted with a laugh, realizing what Jim was going to remind him of again.

And then both guys laughed and said in unison: "Miss Thing."

Chapter 46

R i d e s   a n d   S t r a n g e r s

Despite the perception we live in a completely mobile and mostly transient world, the reality is sixty-five percent of Americans spend their lives living in the place where they were born, and another ten percent return to live in their hometown after moving away. So, once again, I found myself in the minority. The lonely minority during the holiday season.

I'd spent a lifetime planning and preparing for special occasions. My home, a center for celebration. I'd cooked Thanksgiving, Christmas, Easter, birthday, and anniversary dinners for anywhere from six to forty people. And decorated my home for every season and holiday.

But my life in Florida was very different. It's pretty difficult to plan and create celebrations of life when your every day is a battle for survival. And soon after Ginny's breakdown, celebrations in my home became few and far apart. And never quite what they used to be. But I did still enjoy talking about wonderful memories of celebrations past, and Brianna and I spent many hours doing just that.

Brianna, who moved from Nicaragua to the United States when she was a little girl, grew up in a family where good food, good drink, and good company were staples. And until she got divorced, she carried on the tradition of festive Nicaraguan mealtimes with her husband and son.

Brianna has a passion for cooking. Many times Ginny and I stood by her side in her kitchen, watching her create some sauce from ingredients I'd never even thought about using but that when it was finished would taste like heaven.

She and I were a pair made in heaven, because while I love to cook, my specialty is baking. So while Brianna slipped a Patsy Cline CD into the stereo, Ginny and I would begin to organize my tools and ingredients: measuring cups, spoons, graters, ghiradelli chocolate, fresh nutmeg, and vanilla bean. Then Brianna would take her place on the other side of the counter and the top of the stove—her home—and Ginny and I would make the other side of the counter and the oven ours. And while Patsy fell deliciously "to pieces" and crooned about the blue moon of Kentucky and walkin' after midnight, Ginny would hand me ingredients, and Brianna and I would create meals as rich and memorable as Patsy's voice.

Brianna invited us all over for Thanksgiving that year my world was coming apart, and I could not have been more thankful. I did not have more than the actual day off from work, so visiting with my family in Asheville was not an option, and I hadn't spoken to Jake in weeks. So when Brianna asked for me and Ginny to come to her home, I threw my arms around her, feeling if we couldn't be with family, we'd be surrounded by love and laughter, and maybe Ginny would begin to feel we were home.

Brianna insisted that I should bring Jake, but I knew it wasn't the right thing to do. I figured when someone doesn't call you in over a month, he isn't looking to spend the holidays with you. So I sang along with Patsy and counted my blessings, which multiplied during the day.

Brianna invited Carson, Ben, Jim and Greg, along with another of her friends—Celie, and Celie brought her son. We made a table that should seat six, seat nine. And with Brianna's creative touches, it still looked beautiful and inviting.

She draped the table with white linen and red organza. Then splayed teardrop shaped glass beads around pearled candles, sprinkling the arrangement with gold leaf and holly berries. There were lifelike grapes in purples and reds and greens cascading from her bar topped with cream colored platters that held a variety of cheeses: a creamy dill Havarti, a red-skinned Gouda, a wedge of Stilton, and slices of Jarlsberg.

Her contemporary living room and dining room were alight with matching geometrically shaped candles dipped in shades of avocado, berry, and gold. And her home smelled like a combination of fresh oranges, cinnamon, and roasted turkey when Jim and Ginny and I arrived.

Brianna greeted us at the door. We could hear Patsy in the background singing "Crazy…" and Brianna looked at me apologetically, as if to say she was sorry for the coincidence, but Ginny just smiled and said, "Listen, Mommy, she's playing our song."

The others began arriving soon after we were settled, and we sipped apple flavored vodka in martini glasses the size of my face, laughed, and ate until we hurt. Ginny was having a good night. She'd joined in at least two conversations for a few minutes and helped with washing the dishes.

At the end of the evening, Ginny and I carried six different bowls filled with leftovers to the car. And when we packed them neatly in the floorboard of the backseat, we headed home. I had waited an hour later than usual to give Ginny her medications. I wanted so much for her to be able to enjoy the evening without falling asleep at 8 or 8:30 as she so often did. But by the time we were on the road, it was 9:30, and Ginny was yawning. When I glanced over at her from time to time, her big eyes were blinking open, then shut.

She told me between yawns, "It was a wonderful Thanksgiving, Mommy. Thank you for having me."

"I smiled at Ginny. "You mean tonight or just in general?"

Ginny said, "Both." Then smiled and put her seat in a reclining position.

I told her. "I love you, Ginny. I will always be with you."

She smiled again and closed her eyes.

A few miles down the road, I noticed we were almost out of gas, so I pulled into the nearest service station. Ginny had already fallen asleep, but she woke up when I stopped the car. When I looked over her eyes were wide and startled. I told her as I always did, "Everything's okay. We're almost home. I'll just be right outside the car." Then added, "Gotta fill up before work tomorrow. You sleep, baby."

Ginny smiled. Then all of a sudden she sat up, alert and energized, asking me, "Can we put the top down?"

I frowned at the thought of even trying and the thought of disappointing her after such a perfect night.

She said, "You told me Carson showed you how." Then she encouraged me, "Come on. You can do it. I'll help. I promise. We can do it."

I said, "What if it rains?"

Ginny smiled. "Then it rains, and we'll put the top back up. Come on! Nobody has a convertible and doesn't use it. Let's do it!"

So I gave in. I fueled my little red car up and pulled into a parking space. Then struggled for the next twenty minutes to get the top down without ripping some part of the old vinyl. But finally, much to Ginny's complete delight, I did it. And we rode into the warm star-studded night, giving thanks again.

After about two or three miles of sailing along in bliss, the soft night air kissing our faces, air touched with the scent of pine from all the roadside vendors selling Christmas trees, Ginny fell asleep once again. I knew it would be a struggle to wake her when we finally got home, but I didn't see the point in doing it then. In fact, I played with the idea of staying in the car when we got home, watching the sky, trying to name the constellations Jake had taught me, giving her a while longer to sleep. My daughter looks so peaceful when she sleeps, with no trace of the illness that plagues her every waking hour.

We were about five miles from home. I was glancing at the lots of Christmas trees, strung with bubble lights, multi-colored bulbs, fairy lights, and ones that twinkled. On my radio, Dolly Parton was singing "Hard Candy

Christmas," her voice sounding far away because I'd turned the volume down when Ginny fell asleep.

I remembered Christmases on the mountain. When we lived three miles up a winding dirt road and snow fell at our house first. I used to make wreaths from branches of the different evergreens on our land—white pine, frazier fir, hemlock—then decorate them with holly from the bushes around our house. I'd bake cookies for two weeks straight, every night after Thanksgiving, with Blake and Ginny sampling each kind. Then I'd layer them between wax paper circles and box them in Christmas tins. I usually made about twenty-five tins of cookies for family, friends, and neighbors. There were seven standard ones I always baked—linzer tortes, red and green M&M cookies (Ginny's favorite), wedding cookies, Hungarian keufles, iced sugar cookies, chocolate acorns cookies, and macaroons. Then, every year, I'd let Ginny choose a new kind and Blake choose a new kind, and if they turned out to be a hit, I'd add them to the repertoire. One year I added orange-glazed macadamia and coconut cookies. One year, chocolate date balls. One year, fruit cake cookies. One year, snicker-doodles. For two weeks out of every holiday season, I literally lived in the kitchen, but I loved it. And Ginny loved helping me.

Now we have six of the largest photo albums you can buy, filled with pictures of our life on the mountain. And there are whole sections devoted to cookie baking between Thanksgiving and Christmas.

When I first moved to Florida, before I met Maeve or Ted or Jake, I used to sit alone in my condominium, paging through the albums, walking backward through the years, and wondering how I could have ended up in Florida. I was totally aware of all the events and details that had brought me to this place, but looking at a part of my life so completely different from my current one, I was awed by the journey…suddenly conscious of a greater plan. Then, out of the corner of my eye, I'd catch a cockroach scurrying across my immaculate floor to some dark corner of the room. And once again I'd feel totally out of place. In complete disbelief that I was living where people take the presence of roaches in their homes for granted.

Ginny stirred in the seat beside me and I downshifted as I saw the light in front of me turning red. Then suddenly nervous in the unfamiliarity of having nothing between me and the night street, I glanced left and noticed a man with what appeared to be his life's belonging packed into a grocery cart next to him, standing in the median. His face, lit eerily by a streetlight a few yards away, had not been shaved for days and his eyes were ringed with burgundy circles. He was dressed in ripped jeans with big pockets, boots, and a t-shirt too small for him. His body looked young, but very tired, and the veins in his muscular arms were thick. He was holding a small cardboard sign that read I NEED HELP.

I pulled the car past him, up to the light, then glanced over at Ginny, who was still asleep. I felt terrible that I'd looked in this helpless man's direction, observed him closely enough to describe him in detail, and then driven by him. He looked bone tired and desperately hungry. And here I was with my stomach full, riding home in my car also full of food. On an impulse, I reached behind me to grab a casserole to give to him, and just as I did, I saw him running toward our car, an open pocket knife held straight up in his right hand.

I jerked around front again, didn't even look up at the light, working my feet on the pedals before I was settled in the seat again. The car lurched with too much clutch and almost stalled, then I shifted too soon to second and had to downshift for more power. I felt for a moment like I was in one of those nightmares where you know your life depends on moving fast, but you can only move in slow motion. Finally, and probably in much less time than it seemed to me then, I managed to get the clutch and gas in sync and moved through second and third and fourth and finally into fifth. Oddly, even then I was still anticipating feeling the weight of the man I'd left behind, swinging himself over the side of the car into the back seat, the point of his knife at my neck.

I never said a word. Was too terrified, in fact, even to make a sound. When I felt we were safe, I glanced over at Ginny. She was still asleep.

I knew I had to call the police as soon as we got home and I put her to bed, but for now, all I could do was say another prayer of thanks.

And just as I was doing that, Ginny woke up. She leaned forward and turned her head so that she was staring straight into my eyes and said, "Thank you for getting us home safe, Mommy."

I still couldn't speak, so I just hugged her.

After I put Ginny to bed, I called the police and gave them a description of the man and the street I'd encountered him on, telling them everything that happened. Then I checked to make sure every door and window in the condominium was locked. The dispatcher I spoke with said she'd be sending an officer to my home to patrol the area for the next few hours. And within minutes, one was at the door.

He was a nice man, early thirties, easy to talk with. In minutes, he'd pulled out pictures of his sons and his wife and while I fixed coffee, he talked about them briefly. Then he looked around the condo, carrying his cup with him and holding his hand under it as if to protect the carpet from spills, something I'd never seen a man do before.

He told me, "I don't mean any disrespect, but is their a man of the house?"

When I didn't answer him, he said, "Now I know a pretty woman like you has got to at least have a boyfriend and I'm thinking you need someone here tonight."

I said, "I do. But he wouldn't want to hear about this."

The officer looked surprised. He said, "You mean you didn't call him?"

I stared at my feet, "No," I said. "He would be furious."

The officer disagreed. "I doubt it ma'm," he said. "I think worried is more like it. And relieved nothin' happened to you."

I told the officer, "You don't know him. Ever since we met, he's been telling me I trust people too much. That I need to keep my doors locked. Watch where I walk. Pay attention to whose following me."

"He's right about that," the officer said. "He's absolutely right."

"I know," I said. "I used to tell him where I come from, you don't have to lock your doors."

"Well," the officer looked down at me with kind but stern eyes, "that certainly isn't here. In fact, I'm not sure it's anywhere anymore. I'm sorry ma'm but I've got to side with your boyfriend. You do need to be more careful. Probably should never go anywhere alone if you don't have to. And you really ought to call him. He might act like he's mad, but he's just covering. And he'll want to be keeping an especially clear eye out for you until we snag this guy. He'll be worried sick, but he'll be glad to know, so he can watch out."

"I know," I told the officer. I wanted to tell him that with Jake's feelings right now, telling him I'd been driving around at night with the top down was probably the last thing I needed to do, but he was finished with his coffee and I knew he didn't need another long story, so I just said again, "I know."

"All right then," the officer said, "you listen to him. He's a smart man, and he's just tryin' to protect you."

"Okay," I told him, my eyes watering a little from his kindness and from memories of Jake. "I promise."

Chapter 47

F i r e s i d e   T a l k s

Christmas was in the air, and the guys were determined to dethrone Martha Stewart as the master of decorating. It was funny—their behavior, adorable and heart warming really. Ben, Jim, and Greg are all big men with thick necks, broad shoulders, muscular thighs, and sexy Adam's apples. They talk like men. They eat like men. They belch like men. But they do Christmas like little boys. You see it in their eyes.

They remind me of my brothers. Waxing the runners of their sleds, then striking out headfirst down the steepest snow-covered hill in our neighborhood. Daring the other kids to do it half as good.

Greg and Jim strung over twenty strands of white fairy lights around the deck and in the trees, while Ben brought home a ten-foot Christmas tree. Greg and Jed made stockings for everyone and Jim bought the guys Santa hats. It amazed me how they'd all saved boxes of decorations from their homes. Ornaments they'd made or their sisters had made for them.

But then I realized it was a sign. They'd all been loved. No matter how grown up they were or how far away they'd moved from their families, these men had been loved. And I knew someday each of them would bring that love to a new family.

On the evening given to most of the decorating, Ginny and Jed and I made a gingerbread house. Then after John picked Ginny up for their "together time," Ben and Greg and Jim and I built a fire and sat around it, toasting marshmallows on kabob skewers.

I was determined not to ask them any deep questions of the Sauce Sunday variety. I had made up my mind just to fit in that evening. Whatever they wanted to talk about was fine with me. I wouldn't change the subject.

And they chose love. These big, strong guys, with their deep-throated voices and chiseled chins, already showing heavy stubble after a day without shaving, wanted to talk about love. And I just smiled from the inside out.

Ben started first, telling us about his parents. How his mother died when he was just turning into a man and how his father had never remarried. Ben talked about his one sister, also not married. What he didn't talk about that evening but that came out in other conversations and in other ways was that Ben and his sister have been looking their whole lives for what their parents had.

Jim talked about the woman he moved to Florida for. How they'd shared a home together, bought furniture together, taken care of each other in good times and bad. Then when they moved to Florida, both of them transferred by their companies, she first and further south, she just stopped calling. He said at first he just blamed it on her new job. Said both of their new jobs were stressful. But after a few months of her never calling, of him always initiating the calls, he decided placing blame wasn't the answer. Moving on was. Jim had talked to me before about this woman. Actually, several times on our runs. So while I'd never met Sara, I knew her, by the look in his eyes.

She was his dream. His love. All he wanted and needed. And though I did not know her, I knew from Jim's stories what she didn't feel for him.

Greg talked about his son Jed. How no matter what he'd had to endure with Jed's mother, it was worth it to have his son. How nothing mattered more to him than Jed's happiness. Nothing.

I listened to the men talk while I tried to solve the problem with my marshmallows. I couldn't get them browned the way I like because my arms are too short. I like them a light golden brown, and if you like them that way, you either have to be very quick and observant, twirling them over the hottest part of the fire, or you have to move your stick where there are just embers and hold it there for awhile. I could only reach the hot part of the fire, and my quickness and observation skills were failing me.

Ben said nothing, he just took over. Handing me his perfectly golden brown marshmallow and saying, "Here you go, little one, I like mine well done." I smiled and thanked him, then gulped his marshmallow down.

Ben told us all, "Here's the thing about relationships. There are the people you date and the people you marry. It's a cliché but it's also the damn truth," he said, waving his free hand in the air. "And it's no mystery. You know within five minutes of meeting them which they are. So there's no excuse for these people who waste other people's time."

I started to laugh, but I tried not to do it loudly because when I looked over at Jim, who was sitting just across from me, he looked distressed. He was holding his skewer over Ben's and he said, "That's harsh."

Greg smirked. "True, but, yeh, harsh."

I didn't comment.

Jim said, "You know it's not always that easy. I mean sometimes you grow to love someone."

"Yeh, but you know," Ben said. "You know when you meet them, they're the one."

Jim cocked his head sideways, considering this. Then he said, "Yeh, and sometimes you're wrong. Or...well, things don't work out like you plan."

Greg agreed. "You got my life down. Yeh, I'm all about thinking I have a plan."

"Well, we all think that, Jim said, his voice taking on a conciliatory tone. "And sometimes...most of the time, actually, 'the bigger plan' wipes out your plan." He popped his toasted marshmallow in his mouth then licked his fingers. "I mean I thought Sara and I would get married. Definitely, I thought that. I mean, sure, I took a job here...but I really moved to Florida to be with her. We went through everything together. I lost my job, and she supported us. She lost her job, and I supported us. We did the hard stuff. The 'for worse' part. And then..." Jim took a deep breath and let it out. "Then, she calls me one time in the first three weeks I'm here, and she talks to me like... like a stranger. No, it was more like a high school friend. Like I was her girl-friend. She told me about this guy she danced with all night. And she was all...I don't know...her voice was all high and light and excited. Like it used to be when she'd see me. God, what the hell is that? I mean what does she think? What...I suddenly have no feelings for her? You know, we took on new jobs, not new personalities. I just don't get it." Jim put his head down. "Let's stop talking about this," he said. "It's making me sick. God, she really fucked me over."

Ben made an attempt to lighten things up. He patted Jim on the back. "It's the marshmallows, buddy. Lighten up on your marshmallow consumption. It's going to your head."

We all laughed.

I said, "Well, here's one for you. You know how in high school your senior year—how you get everyone to sign your yearbook?"

The guys all nodded.

"Well, I had seventeen guys sign mine, and five of them wrote they wanted to marry me."

Ben burst out laughing. "Good god, woman!" he said, "That's got to be some kind of a record. Not one I'd want to have...but definitely a record."

Greg and Jim were both chuckling, and Ben went on, trying to talk me into confessing I was just telling a good story for laughs. He said, "I mean five, what...seventeen... eighteen-year-old guys wanting to marry you? Come on! Guys don't want to get married at that age. Hell, most of us don't want to get married at any age." Somewhere in the middle of the speech, he seemed to realize I wasn't exaggerating for some fun, and finally he stopped and cocked his head to one side and said, "Well...I think this deserves a marshmallow toast." He looked around at Greg and Jim and added, "Gentlemen?"

Ben stuck his newly skewered marshmallow up in the air, and Greg and Jim joined him with theirs.

"To Haley," Ben said, raising his skewer higher, for her uncanny ability to gain marriage proposals from seventeen-year-old boys!"

"To Miss Thing," said Greg and Jim. And they all laughed.

I'd been laughing the whole time, so much my eyes were tearing up and when the guys lowered their sticks over the fire, I decided the time was perfect for telling the rest of the story. "Well," I said, "I wish it had stopped there, but the tradition continued."

Ben glanced up from his work over the fire. He was wide-eyed, "No!" he said. "You didn't get more? I mean we know you were married twice, but there were more?"

"Way more," I nodded. "I think twenty total. Maybe twenty-one. Oh, who cares?" I added. "There were too many."

Ben wheeled around on one heal and lunged in front of me, kneeling down on one knee. "Will you marry me?" he asked, his voice mock-passionate.

I pushed him away playfully, laughing.

"Stop," I said. "Cut it out."

Ben laughed, "Sorry. Just couldn't resist. You have that effect on men."

I kept laughing for a minute, but then something struck me. I remembered vaguely how one of those yearbook letters had said something about my lipstick: through all the changes in lip-painting over the years, I'd always worn what I thought looked the least like paint, even when the darkest shades were in fashion, and a thought occurred. "Maybe it's my lipstick?" I offered, feeling suddenly a little let down. "Maybe that's what's been attracting them all along."

All three men looked at me at the same time, winked, and said, "Yeh, that's it. It's your lipstick."

Chapter 48

In the Shadows

When Ginny came home from the crisis unit and returned to school, I walked with her to her first class. I realize this is not a cool thing for a high school student's parent to do. Not that I cared. Then or ever.

Even when I was in high school, I didn't care about being cool. I hung out with everyone, from nerds to football players. I was in "drama," and that was something of a clique, but I also was a cheerleader, ran for vice-president of the student government, sang in the choir, and played on the basketball and tennis teams. But I never cared about being cool. There were subjects I did well in and subjects I didn't, and I didn't succeed or fail in anything in order to impress a particular person or group of people. What I did, I did for the joy of doing it.

When Ginny started high school in North Carolina, I walked right in to her classes with her several times. Spoke to teachers that taught me. Spoke with her classmates. Talked with her coach. Volunteered. Ginny never minded. In fact, when some of the boys in her class made up a rap song about me, Ginny made a point of learning it, and when she brought her tennis bags

to the car after practice every afternoon, she'd open the door and start dancing to the words in obvious delight:

"'You can call her Mrs. R., but don't go too far

Cause she really Mrs. Robbins

And she know who you are.

She the queen of parent stop-ins

Mrs. R., Mrs. Robbins,

And she ain't nobody's fool, Mrs. R.

Talkin' fine and sweet and tight

Loves her daughter, yeh, uh huh, with all her might

Mrs. R., lady cool, what a sight

Rockin Robbins, Mrs. Robbins, Mrs. R. that's right!'"

The boys had it right about the love, and since Ginny was born , I've been
called both a MILF (mother I'd like to fuck) and "one hot mama." But truth
be told, I didn't feel like the queen of anything on Ginny's first day back at
Whispering Pines. And the best I could do was focus with all my might on
what I thought the people at the school would need to know. I spoke with the
school nurse about Ginny's medications and dosages and the side effects—the
ones we'd already experienced and the ones that might show up. I checked
to make sure Ginny's teachers and her guidance counselor had my correct
phone numbers, then distributed a letter to her teachers' mailboxes about
behaviors they might notice, adding several reassurances about my support.

As I think back on that day, I recall how the rap song from Ginny's old
school played in my ears while I walked around Whispering Pines. If the boys
who wrote the song had been there, I'd probably have confessed I wasn't sure
I'd ever known who anyone was, but on this particular day, everyone seemed
to be a stranger, and my talking was neither fine nor sweet—just the desperate
effort of a mother to control in any small way she could what was really well
beyond her control.

Before Ginny came home, I had checked out other available options for
schooling. I found Florida is one of the few states with a home schooling

program on the Internet. And we also had the option of a phone-in class-room situation, offered through the government for disabled children. But that would have involved my qualifying Ginny as disabled. And, of course, the various learning centers and private schools were there, most prohibitive because of the expense. Even so, there were quite a variety of options.

I offered them all, even the most expensive ones, thinking I'd find a way. Ginny didn't want to hear about any of them. She was determined to return to Whispering Pines. And, as always, I was determined to support her.

But standing there with her in the main hallway of her high school that housed over two thousand students, I could not imagine how she would cope. Her classes were spread into five separate huge buildings, and she would have to negotiate over twenty different hallways and paths to get to them.

Before her breakdown she'd been taking five college-prep courses, and she insisted on continuing with them. And while she was trying to deal with all of this, she'd be surrounded by hundreds of teenaged voices, along with the twenty others in her head. It was overwhelming to me. And the only voice I heard was my own telling me, "This will never work."

§

Now, on our walks, we talk about Ginny's return to school The way it truly was. Beyond what she pretended.

She tells me, "Some days, I'd be walking to one of my classes and I'd forget where I was. I don't mean which building I was in, I mean everything. Other times I'd be sitting in class trying to focus on what the teacher was saying, trying to block out the voices, and my vision would blur. Then I guess I'd black out, because the next thing I knew was someone would be calling my name, asking if I could hear them."

What Ginny was experiencing, disorientation and blurred vision, I now know were the side effects of her medications—not part of the illness. They were two of many such effects associated with anti-psychotics. They are the reason that people taking them are not allowed to drive. And the truth is, if you get a certain amount of those medications in you, you can't even hold your head up.

§

Every night when I got home from work, I would find Ginny in the dining room "studying." I would walk over to her, kiss her, and ask her how her day had been, and every night she'd give me this frozen smile and her stock response, "Fine, just fine."

When I tried to discuss her day with her or ask if I could help with homework, she would refuse to let me. And usually, while I was preparing dinner and she was "studying," she would have at least one episode of fury. Slamming her book shut, she'd stand up and storm outside, screaming loudly at the voices I couldn't hear. "Leave me alone!" or "I won't listen to you anymore" or "Stop it right now!" she'd yell at a pitch that made me wonder if she would have any voice left before long.

Her counselor told me that this was a good thing—the nightly screaming episodes. She said it was a very good sign that Ginny was fighting with the voices instead of letting them try to control her. And while I wanted to see her point, I had also to worry about complaints from the neighbors. Emptying the trash once, I had stopped just before tipping the can into the dumpster, drawn up short by the conversation of a couple walking their dog on the grass just across the drive:

"Myrtle Ormond told me she's crazy."

"Hardly need Myrtle to tell us that. Have you seen her eyes?"

"I know. And did you hear her tonight?"

"Something about how it wasn't her idea?"

"Yeh, and then she screamed over and over, 'Get off my back!'"

"What I worry about, though, is her drowning in the pool."

Beyond being pierced by hearing others talk about Ginny that way, I had to be concerned about how long they would wait before going to the management. And so whenever Ginny would storm outside, I'd run after her, trying to keep her from screaming. As a matter of fact, I got so used to this nightly routine, I'd developed a plan of action, always waiting until the very last minutes of my meal preparation to broil or boil anything. And when I did, I made certain Ginny was in the kitchen with me.

But during the episodes, after about a half hour, sometimes longer, of my sitting her down on our patio talking her through whatever the current crisis was—the voices telling her she had bad breath and so shouldn't breathe anymore, the voices telling her the utensils I was using to cook with had been dipped in poison, the voices telling her I was slipping more medication into her food so she shouldn't eat, the voices telling her it was a good night to die—we would go back inside together and eat in silence.

Jake is right about me. I think I may have come into this world talking. I just love to talk. But after so many long days at work trying to keep my staff's spirit alive and so many long evenings preparing meals while trying to keep my daughter from killing herself, I didn't have much to say. Actually, I preferred not to talk at all.

About half way through the fall semester of her junior year, Ginny insisted that she was no longer going to take any medication. She told John and me it was making her dizzy, blurring her vision, zapping her energy, causing her to gain weight, and not getting rid of the voices. And she was right.

Months before Ginny started her campaign, John and I had convinced her psychiatrist to take her off Paxil, John citing numerous articles he had read about the drug's dangerous side effects and me having seen more than I wanted to already of what it did and didn't do. We had switched her to Prozac, a much more widely used anti-depressant. And though I'd read a few articles that suggested this alternative might be more effective for men than women, I was willing to give anything else a try for awhile. With the psychiatrist's approval, we'd weaned her off Clonipan as well. But she was still taking 600 milligrams of Seroquil a day.

Alone, John and I discussed Ginny's determination to stop all medication. By that time we'd determined that the Prozac was doing her no good at all. In fact, it seemed to have caused her behavior to be slightly more aggressive, her outbursts of temper more violent. So we decided to wean her from that drug too, the psychiatrist agreeing with some pressure that since we'd observed no improvement in mood, we might see if she could manage on the Seroquil alone. He spoke of Ginny's taking the Seroquil by itself as if the drug would be scarcely more potent than aspirin, yet she was taking what would be for an adult a moderately high dosage of the antipsychotic. Seroquil is one of those "wonder drugs" the pharmaceutical companies are touting as if they were a cure—one of four antipsychotics, along with Clozaril and Rispiradol and Geodon, which are reputed to eliminate voices. The truth is that they set off chemical reactions in the brain, in layman's terms a series of little explosions that temporarily deaden both normal as well as abnormal brain activity. *Labotomizing* is the word you might hear from a psychiatrist describing the effect—if he or she were honest.

If my daughter had gotten a more popular disease, there's little doubt there'd be more research in how to treat it, but my strong feeling is that the most helpful health-conscious treatment for any mental condition will not be discovered until research is funded by sources other than drug companies. I mean how naïve can we be to think that drug companies are going to invest in research that indicates the need for long-term counseling, well-balanced meals, exercising, artistic development, faith-based healing, and family love and support in the treatment of mental illness?

When you have the "opportunity" to walk in the shadows of life, as Ginny and I both have for these past two years, you see things from a different viewpoint. For instance, there are many types of terrorists in this world. And how they are not always labeled terrorists rarely strikes us until we are victims of their treachery. But what would you call individuals who willingly and knowingly manufacture and distribute drugs that cause children, in the best cases, to lose control of their bodily functions and, in the worst, to kill themselves? On reflection, *terrorist* may not be a harsh enough word since terrorists often genuinely believe they have a righteous cause for what they destroy, so the word can't conjure, at least for the generous thinker, the type of person who for the sake of money alone does irreparable harm to an innocent population of people who cannot help themselves and who merely want to feel like living.

I know the truth of my daughter's feelings and words. I know it like I know the beat of my own heart. What she lives with makes fear of the common sort seem tame. And I know what we have been told not by one but by numbers of mental health "experts"—that she would not have to live with the voices. Because of the "advancements," according to them that have been made in medications. We've been told more times than I can count that the voices can be eliminated. Well, bullshit!

I call "bullshit" from the passenger and the driver's seat. And on those days I realize that no amount of swearing will likely change the world of "legitimate drug makers," I ask myself what is left for me to do? And the answer is always the same. If I can work one miracle with my voice before I die, it will be to convince others who care about people with Ginny's illness—you, if you recognize yourself in Ginny—not to live this lie. We have already lived it for you.

In the end, after hours of discussion alone and with Ginny, John and I had no reasonable argument to keep her on the medication. And so, after speaking with her doctor once again about our concerns and receiving no reasonable explanation for her to continue taking a drug with a myriad of harmful side effects—a drug that was not eliminating the voices, we stopped giving it to her, sure we were doing what was best for her.

At first, rather amazingly considering what I now know, Ginny seemed much better. Her mood became a little more upbeat. Her energy higher. She was talking more, actually interested in her day to day life.

But then, about a week after she'd stopped taking the Seroquil cold turkey, Ginny began to exhibit flu-like symptoms: aching, sweating, and vomiting through the nights. After that, her thoughts became more jumbled, her behavior erratic. My phone rang constantly with calls from either the school nurse, her counselor, or her teachers. And once again, I felt I'd made another bad choice by taking Ginny off the Seroquil, yet I had no idea how to help my daughter.

The truth is, Ginny's doctors in Florida, so-called experts in their field, and I, as Ginny's mother, both made bad choices. But unless you have a vested interest in the pharmaceutical company or have never been a parent, I think it is pretty easy to see how I made my decision and pretty difficult to understand Ginny's doctors.

Both doctors overmedicated Ginny, increasing medications that were not working for her to begin with. Neither were honest about their treatments or Ginny's prognosis. John and I acted out of concern and love for our daughter. Looking back, I shiver at the thought of the harm we might have unknowingly caused her, and my heart aches for both of us and for other parents like us—parents who start out feeling around in the dark, taking hold of extended hands out of desperation, sure that others' knowledge can take us back to light and safety and the life we remember, knowing nothing of the way children with mental illness are treated in our current mental health care system.

I have since learned. And I pray what I have learned will help others.

I've learned that when anti-psychotics are abruptly discontinued, the episodic mild tremors and seizures that these medicines are capable of producing anyway can escalate—could even be fatal. I've learned that there is no cure for schizophrenia, no medication that eliminates voices. None. The only medications currently available to treat the illness come with a laundry list of side-effects, some life-threatening—a hard reality of all strong drugs.

And from Ginny's valiant but naïve determination to go without her medicine, I've learned what comes down to this: if you try to quit anti-psychotics all at once, the quality of your life will not improve; in the worst case, in fact, you might not care to live at all.

Chapter 49

R e v e l a t i o n s

More advice. If you feel your child's psychiatrist is a person you can't trust, trust the feeling. Fresh off the experience of having one psychiatrist over-medicate my daughter, causing her to pass out and hit her head on concrete, I was observing yet another one take equally poor care of her.

Month after month, I would go to Ginny's doctor's appointments with her, and we would wait sometimes hours to see her doctor for ten minutes. Never during any of her appointments with her doctor do I remember him looking me or my daughter in the eye. Never in the ten-minute sessions we had with him did he ever give us his undivided attention. He answered phone calls and let his staff parade in and out of the office to tell him he'd forgotten to sign a form or that he had a lunch date or needed to return a call, while Ginny and I waited patiently for him to care for her for one moment.

Instead, he ducked his head, grabbed his pad, and hastily wrote prescriptions for medications in script I'm pretty sure could be easily analyzed as that of a guilt ridden man who knew the answers to Ginny's problems weren't on these papers. Who knew we have no good answers to treating or curing schizophrenia—at least not yet. Who knew. Who knew.

And though Ginny's doctor spent so little time caring for her, he did take the time to call social services on me. It seems John's and my opposition to heavily medicating our daughter was of much more concern to him than her actual state of health.

§

I was cooking dinner one evening, and Ginny was helping me. The doorbell rang, and John, who'd come over for dinner, answered it. I wasn't expecting company, so I walked over to the door to see who might be visiting. A nicely dressed black woman greeted John and me with a warm smile, then told us she was from the Department of Social Services and wondered if we'd mind answering a few questions.

I invited her in, even asked her to stay for dinner, but she would only accept a glass of water. Mischief sat on the rug beside her heels, trying to lick her panty hose while John scolded him. Ginny danced back and forth from the kitchen to the dining room singing "Wouldn't It Be Loverly" from *My Fair Lady*, another one of God's little touches, I thought to myself. Up until that night, I hadn't heard Ginny sing in over a year.

When the woman finished asking both John and me a series of questions about Ginny's illness, her treatment, my work, our marital status, she stood up and showed herself to the door. I followed right behind her, asking again if she wouldn't like to stay and eat.

She glanced over at Ginny, who was still singing and folding napkins, then into our kitchen. She took a deep breath of my vegetarian lasagna, smiled and said, "You have a lovely home, Ms. Robbins. I wish I *could* stay for supper. But," she said, glancing again at Ginny, "looks like you got good company and plenty of care without me. Sorry to have bothered you."

And that's the last we heard from social services.

Chapter 50

W i n g s   a n d   P r a y e r s

The counselors at Whispering Pines phoned me just before the holidays to ask me if I'd like to qualify Ginny for the 504 Accomodation Plan with the Orange County Public Schools. It is a plan which offers three types of accommodations for students with a wide variety of "challenges": extended time on tests and assignments, alternative locations for quiet testing, and visits—essentially any time the student feels the need—to the school's clinic. I told them "yes" and immediately scheduled a time to come to the school and fill out the paperwork so everything would be in place for Ginny to have a less stressful second semester.

But Ginny had a different plan, and when school let out for Christmas vacation, she began a campaign, which would continue through the holidays in Asheville. She not only wanted to spend Christmas in Asheville, she wanted to stay there, claiming she had never wanted to go to Florida.

I told her that while I'd arranged for us to spend Christmas with my family in Asheville, we would have to return to Florida where I had a good job and we had a home. Where she was in school and had a doctor and a counselor. And where her father had moved to help take care of her.

Once again, as it had been for me since the onset of Ginny's illness, I was brutally aware of how much more difficult our life would be without the income and insurance my job provided. However, what the insurance didn't cover was Ginny's counseling. The one element of her treatment I believed was helping her. Ginny met with her counselor twice a week at one hundred dollars a session, something I could not afford for her to do in Asheville.

Every month I had a stack of medical bills that would frighten someone with three times my income, rent higher than most mortgage payments, and a payment on a totaled car. But it was Christmas. And once again, I led with my heart. Throwing rational, practical thinking to the curb and driving as headily as if I'd just gotten word of an inheritance, to the Christmas store to buy a cartload of decorations, everything Ginny wanted.

She wanted to create an old-fashioned theme. So we bought wooden cranberry-colored beads and plastic creamy-colored popcorn, strands of white fairy lights and a quilted patchwork tree skirt. Ginny found three matching stockings with teddy bears on the front of them, and I bought spools of cranberry and crème-colored satin ribbon, throwing four vanilla and burgundy candles on top.

On the way home, we bought our tree and stand. It was a little Frazier fir, about five-feet tall. A film student from the school next door sold it to us. He strapped it to the top of our convertible while telling me his life story, ending with him graduating in June and moving to L.A. When I paid him for the tree, he said he had to go back to his tent to get my change, and when he returned with it, he was holding a piece of paper and a pen. He wrote his phone number on the paper and told me to call him anytime, that he'd like to see me again.

When we were driving away, Ginny asked me, "How do you do that?"

"Do what?" I said.

"You know—attract men like that."

I told her. "He's not a man, Ginny. I will bet you that guy isn't a day over twenty-two."

"That's a man," Ginny protested.

I smiled, then said, "I know. You're right. But the reality is, I could be his mother."

Ginny rolled her eyes and told me, "I don't think that's what he had in mind."

§

At home, we decorated like busy elves. John helped put the tree in the stand, while Ginny and I unpacked the decorations. We slipped Christmas CD's in our jambox and munched on bowls of popcorn. Together we worked all evening—laughing, singing, forgetting about everything except the joy Christmas brings.

Mischief loved the tree. She would sit at the edge of the skirt, staring up at the lights as if she too understood how special this time of year is—and how temporary.

Every night before Ginny and I left for Asheville and after she'd gone to bed, I would blanket myself with the afghan Faith crocheted for me and lie on the sofa staring at our tree. Thinking about Jake.

Sometimes, I would picture him sitting right in front of our tree, wrapping presents in newspaper and sipping a beer. Other times, I'd picture us together picking out our own tree, then decorating it. And sometimes I'd just get lost in a feeling he'd given me. That I was once loved beyond words.

I ended every one of these nights with a prayer. That the new year would bring better health for my daughter. That the voices truly would go away. And that I would spend it with the two loves of my life—Ginny and Jake. Then I would unplug the Christmas tree lights. And face the darkness that surrounded me.

Chapter 51

T o a s t

Ginny and I stayed with Faith and Glen over the holidays and spent them celebrating with my family, none of whom have ever been divorced, all of whom have grown accustomed to the absence of a man in my life.

Christmas at my sister's is part magic, part melody, part sensual bliss. All created by her. Faith is an artist with paper, ink, oil, and clay, food, watercolor, music, and thread, wire, yarn, charcoal, and berries, hair, jewels, flowers, leaves, glass, cloth, wood, and words. An ocean of imagination, filled with compassion and waves of fire. A true artist.

We all take what she gives us for granted. This is how it is with quiet beauty. We applaud loud accomplishments: Trump Towers, the Super Bowl, fireworks on the Fourth of July; and we miss spring's first violet.

At Faith's, my family sat around her table, softened by a centerpiece made with dried hydrangea, stems of red berries, and long needle pine, eating casseroles filled with the flavor of comfort and listening to an old recording of all of us singing "The Twelve-Days of Christmas." Well, let's be honest, some of us were singing.

It snowed twice the week Ginny and I spent in Asheville. Not big snows like I was used to as a child, but big enough for Ginny and me to make snowmen and snow angels. And that was enough for us. I even had to admit, though I love Florida, Christmas to someone born in the Blue Ridge means pine trees and snow, not palm trees and sunshine.

§

We returned to Florida just in time to celebrate the arrival of the new year. However, neither Ginny nor I was in a very celebratory mood. She'd spent the plane ride home trying to convince me once again we should move back to Asheville. And I spent it nervously munching miniature bags of pretzels, wondering how in the hell I expected us to have a good year when I was literally dragging my daughter back to a place where she didn't want to live.

Fortunately, when we arrived home, John was in a very festive mood and had made elaborate plans for himself and Ginny to enjoy bringing in the new year while I returned to work, immersing myself in filing year-end reports.

I stayed in the office hours after everyone in the building had left. Creating new plans and programs, analyzing revenue, phoning potential customers, making retention calls. Anything but dealing with my personal life.

Maeve called on New Year's Eve, just at my breaking point. I'd worked three fourteen-hour days, preparing for the new sales year and had not heard a word from Jake. I'd called him a couple different times over the holidays, hoping to talk, wish him a merry Christmas. But he never picked up the phone. And I'd given up believing he would ever return one of my calls.

Maeve invited me to join her at the last place on earth I wanted to be—Duffy's. I could just imagine what it would be like standing on the dance floor without Jake's arms around me, not knowing how to move without him.

I wanted to tell her, "No, absolutely not, no way." But I hadn't seen Maeve in over a month. Carson was out of town. Jim was sick. Ben had a date. Brianna was having some old friends over and John thought he was doing something special for me and Ginny, treating us both to a night out.

So I told her I'd meet her at Duffy's when I got off work. Maeve laughed and said, "Get out of there. Do you think anyone gives a damn you're there?"

I wanted to answer, "No, I don't. I don't really believe anyone gives a damn where I am." But I just let it go. I told Maeve, "I'll get there as soon as I can."

She said, "Okay, babes. See you there."

But it was Ted, not Maeve, who greeted me at the door of Duffy's. I hugged him without kissing under the mistletoe. Ted stepped back, holding me in his arms.

"How you doin?" he asked, giving me his best Joey Tribbianni impression. I forced a smile and said, "Good."

He hugged me again and said, "No, you're not. I know you. You miss him bad."

I turned my head away, fighting back tears, then said, "I'm fine," and wiped away a tear that had just escaped. "I just need a drink."

Ted yelled at the bartender, "You hear that? Lady needs a drink. Get her a chardonnay on me."

I said, "Thank you," and both of us sat down at the bar under a strand of blinking multi-colored bubble lights.

The bartender handed Ted his captain and coke, me my chardonnay, and Ted raised his glass to mine. "To one hell of a year," he said. Then he smiled and sighed. "May we never have another like it," he added.

We toasted, then sipped our drinks. I tipped my head back and shook my hair; feeling its life against my skin gave me a confidence I hadn't felt all day. Then I said, "I don't know. It wasn't all bad."

Ted frowned, "You got a short memory, then. I mean, I don't know, but I think if I was you, I'd say it was definitely the worst year of my life."

"Yeh," I conceded, "it had some worst moments."

Ted raised his thick eyebrows. "Some? Hell, baby, it was full of the worst. Look it, first off you start seeing that jack ass who has all but ripped your heart out, then…you're daughter gets sick, your asshole ex moves in with you and your asshole boyfriend walks out on you. I mean I'm telling you baby, it doesn't get much worse than that." Ted took a sip of his drink, and then his face brightened suddenly. He smiled and said, "Wait...yes, it does. I forgot about your wreck."

I laughed. "Well, don't sound so happy about it."

Ted laughed too. "I'm just saying, how can you not call this the worst year ever, may it rest in peace."

Ted clinked my glass. "Here. Here."

And we both took man-sized drinks, swallowing hard, as Maeve walked in the back entrance for staff and regulars—dazzling.

Maeve was wearing an off-white sweater with a sweetheart neckline, gold hoops dangling from her ears, her tightest jeans, and sling backs. She looked like a young Angie Dickinson. Only her smile was twice as pretty.

Maeve hugged me, then Ted and told us both she had a date. Ted and I both knew who it was. He was a regular at Duffy's, who Maeve had actually fallen for over a year ago. Unbelievably she'd confided to me earlier, "I'd like it to be like you and Jake, but it's not even close. I mean you guys are serious. Way serious. And we're just...I don't know—there for each other, I guess." It was the first time Maeve had ever acknowledged Jake's and my relationship in this way, and it was so out of character and so after the fact I couldn't even respond.

Maeve sat down on the vacant barstool on the other side of mine and ordered a glass of white zinfandel, while Ted pulled his barstool closer to me. He said, "Hey, you know a guy from that show you were supposed to be on brought his car into the shop. When he told me what he was doing here, I told him I had a friend who was supposed to be on the show. And he asked, 'Who?' and I told him your name. Then you know what he said?"

"What did he say?" I asked.

"He said he'd never heard the name. He said no Haley Robbins was ever cast on the show."

Maeve giggled and touched my shoulder. "It's okay, baby," she said. "It doesn't matter. It's all over now."

I glanced back and forth at both of them. Then said, "What? Are you kidding me?"

"No," Ted said. "Swear on my mother's grave. The guy said he'd never heard your name. No way were you ever cast on that show."

Maeve buried her face in her glass and took a long drink, while I stood up between her barstool and Ted's, putting my glass on the bar.

I said, "I was cast on the show!"

Maeve cleared her throat and swiveled away from me on her stool, while Ted put one hand over his mouth.

"Do you want me to go home and get the paperwork? I'll go right now. And I'll show you everything from the first forms they gave me about sending them an audition video up to the contract I signed, even my wardrobe sheet, where I had to give all my measurements and sizes. I have copies of all of them."

Ted rolled his eyes, then said, "Hey, settle down. Why are you getting so upset? We don't care if you never really got on the show. We're your friends." He leaned toward me. "It doesn't matter to us. You don't have to lie to impress us. We like you anyway."

I glanced at Maeve, who was now staring down at her painted toenails, then grabbed my purse and told them both, "Yeh, I can see that, Ted. I can see how much you like me. Don't trust a damn thing I say, but you like me. That's nice." I looked at Maeve. "I'll remember that," I said to her. I took a couple of steps toward the back exit and told them both, "Here's a thought. Why don't you start the new year fresh. Clear your head and heart of all the times we've spent together. Everything we've shared. And start listening to strangers. Let them tell you I never had a dream come true. Never chose taking care of my daughter over living that dream. Just keep listening to strangers. See where that gets you. I'm guessing you keep that up for a while and pretty soon that's all you'll have to listen to. Hey and just a heads up—friends don't make a bad year worse."

I didn't wait for Ted or Maeve to answer me. Just walked straight out the back door to my car, took one look up at the full moon and one down at my watch. It was 9:30 p.m. Three hours until midnight, and I couldn't decide which I was looking forward to more—the ending of the worst year I'd ever lived or the beginning of anything different.

Chapter 52

Decisions

The beginning of 2004 shot holes straight through my hope and faith. No matter how much I prayed they would go away, the voices stayed with Ginny and no matter how much I prayed he would come back, Jake didn't. I found myself living through whole weeks unable to remember a single day or even wanting to. Except for one.

One Sunday in January, John had taken Ginny to Ocala to see his parents new home, and I took off for a run. It was one in the afternoon when I started running through Winter Park toward Altamonte Springs. After I'd gotten through Altamonte Springs, I went through Longview. And after that, Winter Springs, and after that Oviedo, then I turned around and ran home. I got home at seven o'clock. Then drove over to the track at the high school, where I ran sprints.

That's what I do when I have a lot on my mind and heart. I run for a while. I had told Jim about my run and he said, "That's awesome! You could probably run a hundred miles if you had to."

I told him, "Probably...depends on how many issues I had that day."

§

Like every business, Evergreen began the new year reviewing the old one. There were staff meeting and managers meetings, business reviews and forecasting, and one goal set in the first managers' meeting of the year—to reduce RISK. We were told by Richard, we had had a very good year in 2003, with the sales department bringing 1.5 million dollars worth of revenue to the bottom line and if we had just run a safer operation, kept our accidents to a minimum, we would have had an excellent year. Our goal for 2004, according to Richard, was to keep accidents to a minimum, thereby reducing our costs. He said if we did that and maintained the same level of performance from the sales and maintenance departments, we would easily make budget and possibly exceed it.

The meeting was the equivalent of getting an A+ on my report card. My department had not only managed existing revenues and retained them, we'd brought in the new revenue expected. I knew this as well as anyone in the company, but it is always a wonderful moment when your team's accomplishments are acknowledged.

It was January twelfth. The beginning of a new year, and I was newly filled with hope. Ready for challenges. Except one, the one I faced next.

On Friday, January sixteenth at four o'clock, Richard called me into his office. It was Brianna's birthday, so I assumed he was going to give me the okay to take the sales staff out for a little celebration. He greeted me warmly and welcomed me in, then shut the door. Walking over to his desk chair, he sat down and leaned back, folding his hands in front of him. The welcoming smile I'd gotten at the door was gone, and he wasted no time telling me, "We've decided to take the company in a new direction, Haley. Your position has been terminated—effective immediately."

§

My contract with Evergreen did not expire until October 20, 2004. The company offered me a severance package tied to a noncompete (no work in garbage with another company in a two-hundred mile radius for a two-year term). At the time, I was counting on ten more months of salary and benefits. The package included one.

I was devastated. And completely incredulous. Even knowing sales management is one of the riskiest jobs you could ever have. That you are as good as you are on the day, sometimes in the moment. That you have no tenure, no job security at all. I was devastated.

I had given Evergreen everything I had. Relocated myself and my family. Created a self-sustaining revenue-producing sales staff out of rubble. Hired and trained the best sales team in the company. Developed programs, established relationships with clients, brokers, and local government. Cleaned up and expanded the database. Updated the files. Created marketing campaigns, tools to measure revenue.

And my reward? One hour to say goodbye to my team and remove myself and my personal effects from the building.

I had two more months of an expensive condominium lease to make payments on. COBRA medical insurance bills. Ginny's counseling services to take care of. Car insurance. More payments on my totaled car. Food for three. Gas. Electricity. Cable. Internet Services. And a growing balance on nine months of medical bills. On top of which my only source of income was tied to an agreement which would force me to work outside of my field of expertise in a place I'd recently relocated to.

I had to reevaluate—my career plans, where we could live, how I would take care of Ginny, everything. And like most people forced into change because they do not make changes when they are needed, I found the truth inescapable.

The truth is—years ago—I did not choose to work in the waste management industry. I chose to work for a man named Mario DeMarco, who happened to be a regional sales manager for Environmental.

Mario is a bear of a man with eyes like a newborn...seeing this world filled with possibilities. He is one of the few people I've ever met in the business world who takes care of his loved ones as well as he does the company he works for. He manages people and revenue with integrity, purpose, and attention to detail. And his passion for life is matched only by his sense of humor. I knew the moment I met him I could work for this man. That if he'd been master of ceremonies for a circus, I'd have auditioned to be the opening act.

Mario and I worked together for three years at Environmental. Under his mentorship, I rose form a territory account manager to a district sales supervisor. And Environmental benefited greatly from both of our work ethics, our visions, our leadership, and our loyalty.

Okay, that is part of the truth. The other part, the painful part precedes my career in waste management.

Eight months prior to interviewing with Environmental, after years of working in the sales and advertising industry, I made the decision to take a year off to pursue my lifelong dream of writing professionally. I wrote my first novel At the Calling of Our Hearts in six months. Faith spent a month typing and editing it. And we spent a month querying targeted literary agents. Ten out of ten of the agents we approached asked either for excerpts of the manuscript or a full manuscript, and one made an offer to represent me. If you don't know anything about the literary world, let me just say, I'd made a pretty good start.

It is difficult now for me to describe the feeling I had then, writing my first novel. Though I've had scores of friends and family ask me to do it. And I watch this one station where they interview published authors, often asking them questions about the first novel they wrote. How it felt. What it was like. Their answers always shame me. Usually well thought out and deeply inspiring.

I can't do that. I can't give you that. But if you could just see me now, look into my eyes, you'd find how I feel about it.

400

It was like walking home with my brother after school. In Autumn. Spotting a tree's whole wealth of leaves fallen and raked into a hugely mounded drift on the side of a curb. Sprinting for it, like I was on fire and it was a pool. School books flying out of my arms, diving head first while my brother yelled, "Stop! You don't know what's in there!" Too late. I could barely hear him trying to protect me. Buried in the must mystery of so many still soft leaves. I'd stay covered for a minute, breathing them in, surrounded by the comfort of being so close to life—earth and worms, fallen limbs edged with leaves. Then I'd spring straight up toward the sky, laughing and shaking my head. Punching my tiny fists into the air. Screaming, "No guts, no glory!"

Guts or not, after eight months of me bringing in no income, Blake and I were faced with a mounting stack of bills. Debt two good incomes would be hard pressed to eliminate and enough stress to end a marriage. And so I banana-clipped my hair, brushed on some blush and gloss, slipped back into my suits and stiletto heels, and headed back to the business world. Where I spent the next two weeks interviewing with three Fortune 200 companies, gaining offers from each one—finally choosing to work for Mario, which I'd known would be my choice the moment I met him.

And years later, long after we stopped picking up trash together, we still manage to lift each other's spirits.

§

It goes without saying one of the worst feelings you can have is driving home from work to tell your loved ones, the ones you're supposed to be supporting, "I was fired." But, once again, by making choices, I'd reduced my options. And no matter how far I can run, there was only one place I needed to go. Home. To face Ginny and John. And tell them, no matter how Richard phrased it, "I was fired."

But after a couple of hours of struggling with both past and future, I found myself squarely in the present. With one person on my mind. Jake.

Just about that time, ten minutes from pulling into my parking space at home, my personal cell phone rang. It was Jake's aunt, trying to get in touch with Jake.

Turns out, his brother in California had been badly injured. Fell eighty-some feet from a scaffold while he was working. She was trying to find out if Jake was flying out to be with him. And she had my number.

I told her how sorry I was. That I'd say prayers for Jake's brother. And where I thought she could reach Jake.

Then I pulled into my parking space. Took a deep breath. And went inside to deliver my news.

Ginny and John were wonderful. Totally supportive. Irate about how I'd been treated. Fluffing pillows for me. Fixing dinner. Even rubbing the feet I'd have to hit the pavement with tomorrow.

Later that night, I walked outside to sit by the pond and call Jake. He didn't pick up, so I left a message telling him, as I'd told his aunt, how I'd be praying for his brother. I was about to press the disconnect when something in my voice broke, and I added softly, "I lost my job today, honey."

A few days later, we finally spoke. Jake had flown to California. He was busy taking care of his brother and our connection was bad. But we were talking again.

I didn't feel like asking him when he'd be home, and I didn't want to assume anything. Not that he was coming back to Florida or me.

But a week after we'd talked for the first time in months, Jake did come home. And he called me. Telling me to meet him at a restaurant called Legs and Wings, just down the street.

I told him I'd be there in a minute, pressed the end button and screamed, "Yes! Yes! Thank you God, thank you! Thank you! Thank you!" Scaling the stairs to my bedroom like a long jumper.

I tried on five different shirts and three pairs of jeans and when I finally settled on a little white peasant top and my favorite jeans, I nearly spilled lipgloss all over both. Ginny sat on the edge of our bed watching me and laughing, while John called from downstairs, "You better hurry up; the prince might turn into a frog."

Then I rushed out the front door blowing kisses, while Ginny and John both sat on the sofa, holding their sides from laughing.

§

Jake looked incredible. He was wearing one of his Marlon Brando white muscle shirts with a button-down western shirt that clung tightly to his broad shoulders. And jeans I love. He'd changed his cologne to Hugo Boss, and it smelled wonderful on him.

I wanted to slide my arms around his waist, press my jeans into his. Kiss him like he'd just made love to me. Instead, I sat next to him in the rose-colored light from the bar, sipping a beer and acting like I was ready for change.

We talked for awhile, drinking each other in. Jake told me about his flights and I told him about getting fired. After awhile, we decided we wanted food. Oysters, actually. At Henry's.

We dropped Jake's car off at my place and drove together, Jake telling me my car reminded him of a match box and asking me who *didn't* teach me how to drive a stick.

At Henry's, we sat at the bar, fed each other oysters and crackers, while Jake tried to teach me how to whistle. I was blowing crumbs everywhere, Jake laughing so hard he almost fell off his stool.

But back in the car, it was different. No joking around. Or talking like old friends. It was all too familiar.

The way he touches me. How his kisses make my whole body tingle. The way I can't breathe when any part of him is in me.

I'd been in Florida for over a year then. Seen night after night of the fireworks from Disney. Only to know they had nothing on Jake. Shooting passion and light deep inside me. Making me tremble with his magic.

Chapter 53

See, Saw

I'm trying to decide whether having hindsight makes living any easier. Today, I'm sitting outside the bookstore café, observing this flannel-shirted, blue-capped woman, who is also sitting on the patio. She has her Jack Russell terrier on a leash at her feet, and he's jumping at every car that passes by.

Every time he does it, she pulls his chain and tells him, "Bad boy, Largo." I have no doubt they've done this before. Largo jumps. Blue cap jerks his chain and scolds him. Largo jumps again. Blue cap jerks his chain again and scolds him.

Largo has great hind legs. But no hindsight. So he just keeps jumping. And getting jerked around.

But I have hindsight. And sometimes it's worse than getting jerked around. Sometimes, it's pure torture.

§

Over the holidays, Ginny didn't tell me once she wanted to stay in Asheville, live with my parents, be homeschooled by them. She told me a dozen times.

So what was I expecting when I brought her back to Florida? That she'd fly the state flag out her window? Suddenly have a miraculous recovery in a place where she didn't want to be?

Not quite. That is not quite what happened. What did happen is after we returned to the Sunshine State, Ginny became as stubborn as a Tar Heel. Doggedly determined in her own way to get back to the state where she was born. A place she truly believed she would no longer hear "the voices" or be confronted with the heartbreak and challenges she had faced the past year in our new home, Florida.

She began her campaign to return to the mountains by e-mailing Faith. When Ginny first told me she was writing Faith, I was thrilled. Since she'd come home from the crisis unit, I'd been encouraging her to reconnect with her family in Asheville and with her friend Winnie. Hoping against hope that this connection, however distant, would be another kind of support system for her.

But Ginny did not reconnect with our family or Winnie. In fact, despite my encouragement, pleading with her to write or call her family and her friend, she remained disconnected from the rest of the world.

Then one day when I came home from work, I found her sitting in front of her computer busily typing away, and when I asked what she was doing, she actually smiled at me. Told me she was e-mailing Faith and asked me when she finished to make sure her spelling was correct.

I smiled back at Ginny. Told her I'd be happy to check her spelling. And when she did finish, I slipped easily into her chair, facing her written words for the first time since she'd had her breakdown.

Dear Aunt Faith

The weather is reported nice here even though it is January but not June in Asheville. But I will go back soon. After Mommy talks to my teachers and we return the books. I can still help my dad with his company because I will have my computer there and I will get a job to help pay for the Internet. Mommy is going to marry Jake and have a baby. He loves her a lot more than my dads did and she really loves him. You don't have to worry the baby won't be like me. Mommy isn't crazy. That isn't where the voices are. They come from me and my dad's family. That is what the doctor said. He likes the way Mommy dresses but she doesn't see. Jake is in her eyes.

I'll be home soon. We can bake biscuits considering we haven't done that since Christmas and I can't find the recipe. I can't go outside without sunscreen and we have to turn the oven off Mommy says. We can write it down so we won't forget. I can't wait to get back in Asheville. There won't be any voices there. They don't have a cell phone and I am going to make sure my underwear is clean before I pack them so they can't say anything about that.

See if you can find a site on the Internet where I can volunteer for the army. I meant to ask you earlier (considering I have a lot to do here every day but that is going to change). Maeve told Mommy a long time ago they need more volunteers and when after I go to college I am available. I want to help. I will write again before I leave but I want you to send me your recipes so I can practice them. Write down how much each item costs so I can ask Mommy for money. She gives me and Daddy grocery money and I like to be responsible because she works hard. I think they will cost more here because Mommy is always worried about money but write it down for me and I will research it.

Love,

Ginny

"Did I misspell anything?" Ginny asked, standing beside me, staring down at the monitor. When I turned to look at her, her pupils were larger than ever, her forehead furrowed with intensity. "I don't want Aunt Faith to think I can't spell."

"No sweetheart," I said, touching one of her hands. "No, it's perfect. Aunt Faith will be so happy to hear from you."

Never mind hindsight, those days, I didn't seem to have much vision at all. One minute, everything I did, every action I took, word I spoke, came straight from my heart. And the next, I'd be totally rational. Completely focused on being practical. A human seesaw of approaches to living. Straight from my heart, I'd tell John, "We have to take her back to Asheville. We've tried to make it work here, but it just isn't working. We have to drag her to school. She doesn't want to do her homework. The voices are getting worse not better. She doesn't want to be here. We have to give her a chance to rebuild her life somewhere she'll be happy."

Then, on another day, I'd tell Ginny in my most practical tone, "I need to be in a place where I can get a good job. Your father moved across the country to help take care of you. This is Jake's home and I love him. I have commitments here. Responsibilities I need to take care of. We have to work together to build a life here." Ginny would always sit for these lectures expressionless.

One day out of exasperation, I said, "You can't just pick up and move every time things get tough. Life doesn't work that way!" and Ginny came out of her trance to ask, "How does it *work*, mommy?"

Startled, I stared at her for a moment. Then recovering, I said, "I mean the reality is, Ginny. Everywhere you go, there you'll be."

"That's what Buckaroo Banzai says, Mommy! What does it mean?"

"Never mind," I said, not sure what amazed me most about this conversation.

"Anyway," Ginny added, "I don't care what Buckaroo Banzai says, or you either, I want to go back to Asheville."

And the next day I was back to telling John, "We've got to take her where she wants to be."

Back and forth I went. Thinking I could manage someone else's life when I couldn't even manage my own. Until the first week in February, when it became quite apparent I couldn't manage either.

I was driving to a job interview in downtown Orlando when my cell phone rang. It was the school nurse. Asking me to pick Ginny up.

She said they'd had a fire drill earlier that morning and when Ginny returned to her class, she began ranting and raving about how she was responsible for the "bomb threat." Her teacher brought Ginny to the nurse. And when the nurse couldn't calm her down, she called me.

"I'm sorry, Ms. Robbins," she told me. "I wish there was something I could do, but I think you just need to come get her. She seems really upset. Worse than ever."

I headed for the school. Went straight to the nurse's office, where I found the nurse and Ginny, Ginny sitting with her hands gripping her head, claiming she planned to bomb the school. I put my arms around her, and she burst into tears, telling me, "You don't understand. They told me to do it. And now I've got to stop them."

The nurse helped me gather Ginny's bookbag and purse. Then opened the door to her office. I lifted Ginny up and guided her down the main hallway. I thought everything was going to be okay. That we could make a clean escape. I thought wrong.

The minute we stepped outside, Ginny shoved me to the concrete and started to run back inside. "Get away from me! I've got to save them," she screamed. "I've got to find the bomb."

About that time, two large men dressed in security uniforms appeared from behind the cafeteria doors. They walked over to Ginny and me and asked if I could use some help.

"Just a little," I told them. "I'm not as good as I used to be at carrying her."

"Shoo," one of the big guards told me, while holding Ginny in place with one hand, "You couldn't carry a baby, never mind a grown girl." Then he said to Ginny, "Your mama looks like Tinkerbell."

I smiled. "Thanks for helping me," I said. "I just need to get her home."

The guards walked Ginny to our car. I trailed them with my skinned knees burning in the fresh air. Once inside the car with Ginny, I thanked the guards again, then shut my doors and drove away in silence. The ride home took only five minutes, but it was amazing how it transformed Ginny. By the time we got home, she seemed completely calm, even smiled at me as we were walking up our sidewalk asking, "Can I go back to Asheville now?"

§

Part of the problem dealing with teenagers who are experiencing some sort of mental breakdown is that they are teenagers first. And a good deal of their behavior is related as much to their age as to their problems. Making it difficult, sometimes impossible, to separate the two.

John and I spent the afternoon trying to reason with Ginny. But after hours of debate and tears, we both began to accept that despite both our efforts to make a good life for Ginny in Florida, she didn't want to be there.

And trying to keep her there against her will would not make any of our lives better.

That night, I called my parents, updating them on what we were going through. They insisted, once again, that we bring Ginny back to Asheville. So after ironing out a few more details, speaking with her doctor and counselor, and withdrawing her from school, John and I spent the next two days packing Ginny's things. Then we loaded John's car up and headed for Asheville, hoping once again that a new direction would help our daughter.

I returned to Florida with several things on my mind: finding a job so I could take better care of Ginny, finding a new place to live, saving money, and spending more time with Jake.

I had several good interviews with potential employers but found a national sales manager's job with a local financial seminar company the most attractive. I'd have to travel nationally as well as internationally four days a week. But the pay appeared to be very good. In three months, I'd have full benefits and the truth was, I was glad to take a break from waste management.

I talked with Jake about my options. I'd also been offered a couple of other sales manager jobs where I'd be traveling quite a bit. We decided the one with the seminar company was my best option. That it definitely had the most income potential. And we were going to make the best of our time apart. Treat our time together like a honeymoon.

I talked with Ginny and my parents every night, and when I told them about the job, Ginny seemed very excited. She said, "Oh, Mommy, this is perfect for you. You love to travel! Send me postcards from everywhere you go."

And so I did. To this day, our bureau is covered with postcards from Calgary, New York, Detroit, Tampa, Seattle, Vancouver, Salt Lake City, Atlanta, Charlotte, Las Vegas, Pittsburgh, and Richmond. I wrote Ginny e-mails and letters, sent souvenirs and t-shirts. It was not like being with her, hearing her breathe at night, seeing her sleeping in peace, catching the few moments in a day where her mind seems clear, her eyes bright. But we'd found a way to

§

Up until I was eighteen years old, I had lived a life without flying. Literally, I mean—in a plane. The first time I ever flew, John was taking me to visit his parents in Massachusetts. And I fell in love. With being in the clouds.

Through the years we were together, John and I flew a great deal. He didn't like it so much. Had problems with his sinuses. But I never tired of it. Always ready to hop on a plane.

In this respect, my new job was a dream for me. I love to see new places, just like Ginny said. To explore history, geography, and culture. And my job at the financial seminar company afforded me that opportunity. One week in Calgary, sitting in a restaurant across from one of the Olympic sites, eating nachos and listening to a group of French Canadians cheer loudly for their hockey team, then glancing outside to find snow falling in May. Another in Seattle, running through the fish market, watching cherry blossoms bloom. Yet another in New York, walking through a spring rain, treading lightly Ground Zero.

Jake would call every day, and we'd talk for hours. When I flew home, he would be there, waiting to pick me up.

I'd decided to pursue a career with the seminar company as one of their seminar speakers. I'd heard the pay tripled what I was making and that I'd have control over my schedule. Also, I'd get to speak to large audiences—just my style. I looked forward to the chance to educate myself better about the financial world. The option of being based out of any city and having great benefits for me and my family. It was a no-brainer. And I knew I'd be great at it.

Jake was totally supportive. He knew how much I loved to speak in public. Anywhere, really, but especially in public. And how I love to travel. And that I was excited again about learning and work. Truly interested in what I was doing.

He wasn't thrilled about the actual flying part or me spending most of my days either in airports or airplanes. And I noticed each time he'd bring me to the airport or come to pick me up, he would hug me a little tighter, cradle my head in his neck so I could feel his pulse quickening in his throat. He didn't change his style. All of a sudden gushing with lines like "I'll miss you or I missed you or I love you so much." Not Jake. But whenever he talked, which was less than ever, when he was driving me to the airport, he would look over at me when we were stopped at a light and his eyes would search mine, and every now and then, no matter what he was saying, I would hear a little quaver in his voice. Like something in his heart breaking loose, causing him to lose just a little control.

It was on these airport drives that we started talking about growing his business, then maybe even selling it. Buying a home on a lake. Putting Ginny in a local college. Nothing earth-shattering. Just a few little dreams. Something to hope for and believe in again.

On our weekends together, Jake would take me to look at different houses, showing me the styles of architecture he's attracted to, while I would look for potential garden spots. We'd cruise the neighborhoods of Orlando, Jake pointing to his favorite house on each street.

I don't know why, considering how strong our connection is, but it always amazed me how Jake would like the same houses I like. Without my saying a word, we'd be driving down a street thick with homes on either side and he'd pick my favorite every time. I wouldn't say anything. I don't know why this recurring experience rendered me speechless. I can only believe I was a little awestruck by a plan I couldn't see. A plan slightly greater than a house's design.

As soon as I had spoken with Jake about pursuing a speaker's position and we'd agreed it was a good plan, I approached management with my goals. And much to my surprise presented them to an audience of raised eyebrows. Though I had done my research about the scope of the position, planned a timeline and program for the training I'd need, considered how the change would affect me and my family, I never once thought about the fact the company had never had a female speaker.

Part of this omission of thought about living in a male-dominated world comes naturally to me. I grew up with not just one but two big brothers. Have a very dominating father. To this day, most of my best friends are men. And most of my favorite teachers and mentors have been men. My entire life has been full of men calling the shots. But I've managed to take a few. And every time I've gotten the chance, I've scored. That's what matters to me.

Also, I was coming from the waste management industry. A primary example of a male-dominated industry and one I'd succeeded in. So, the fact that this fairly new company had no history of female speakers didn't bother me at all. Was a non factor as far as I was concerned.

So after gaining some very reserved approval from management, I made my goals known. Most especially to my team leaders.

The team leaders of this company, at least ninety-five percent of them, were also men. All between the ages of twenty-five and thirty-five. All who had worked their way up through sales. All who also had the speaker's position as their primary goal.

And oddly, soon after word got out I was training to become a speaker, these leaders found some new tasks for me, like carrying all the heaviest equipment from the van to our servicing room. Or smoothing over relations with the hotel management they'd just cussed out. Also, suddenly, they became unable to synchronize their watches with mine. Telling me I was either too early or too late, depending on when they arrived to set up.

And while all of what the company referred to as their "road warriors" had to endure occasional red eyes, I somehow managed to be scheduled for four in a row.

But I tried, even in the face of the ongoing harassment, to remain positive. Even when my commission checks were continually wrong and late. My expense reimbursements, nowhere to be found. I had invested a lot of money and time into this new sales position, and I had a goal for a much better one.

I wanted to talk with Jake about what I was going through. I needed his support. But at the time, he was in the midst of going back to work for a dealership as well as still running his own business, and I really didn't want to bring up the fact that my job wasn't working out very well. That it looked like our dreams were on hold once again.

But the red eyes began to take their toll. Along with the continual verbal abuse from my "leaders," the whole thing was becoming a nightmare.

I tried to talk with a few of the other female salespeople in the company about the leaders, but they just laughed, telling me, "You mean you didn't know they were little dictators? Come on. That's all they hire. And you, with your plans to become a speaker. You're a prime target for them." One of the women said, "Trust me, if they have anything to do with it, you'll never see the spotlight. I bet you have the worst evaluations in the company. Get over it. Either love what you've got, or leave it." Another told me, "Just enjoy the ride. Forget about a freakin' career. That's for men."

I was two days away from gaining full insurance benefits for Ginny and me. Packed full of dreams for me and my family. And I knew exactly what I had to do. I would address my issues with the leaders in front of management and see what their reaction was. If they were apologetic and eager to make necessary changes, I would stay. But if they were running the kind of company that both disables and discourages women, I would leave.

So I met with them. Then I drove home to page through the classifieds.

I was forty-two years old. Had worked full time since I was fifteen. Through high school, college, marriages, pregnancy, moves, illness. And within the course of six months had somehow managed to be unemployed twice.

To say I was at a low point would be an understatement. To say I was completely lost would have been much more accurate. And I can't think of a person I know who faced with the same circumstances wouldn't have moved back to where their family was. Where they would be surrounded by those who would love and support them.

But not me. No. Not me. I was determined to succeed in the place I loved. Make a good salary. Have good benefits. Help heal my daughter. Stand by my man. Conquer any obstacles. Climb any mountain.

Only problem is, where I was, there were no mountains. Only an insurmountable stack of bills for me to pay. Rent overdue. And no income in sight.

The financial seminar company's irregular and incorrect checks had cost me dearly. I was three weeks late paying my rent, and when I drove home that day after meeting with management, I was greeted by a bright yellow eviction notice taped to my door.

I realize sometimes while I'm writing that reading this most people will be thinking "what next?" All I can say is that living it was totally different. Had sort of a mind-numbing effect. I got to the point where I felt like saying, "Go ahead. Cut deeper. Stick me harder. See if I'll give. See? I can't even feel it. Can't feel a thing anymore."

One more thing I forgot to mention. Right when I got the job at the seminar company, when I was adjusting to flying four days a week—in and out of different time zones—dealing with different currencies, having actually only one day during the work week when I was in town to take care of bills and correspondence, my credit/debit card was stolen.

It took me over ten weeks, fifty-two phone calls to customer service and the recovery department, ten faxes, two fed ex's, six face-to-face meetings with local management, and one final phone call, for the greatest bank in America to put my money back in my account. The phone call was to the president. Of the company. Not the United States. Though he was next on my list.

So, with late payments and missing money, I thought I had a pretty good case for the condominium management to consider. During the past nineteen months, I'd paid them over twenty-two thousand in rent and fees. I was bringing them my last payment with the late fee and presenting, in a civilized manner, two valid reasons I couldn't pay my rent on time. But in spite of all that, management considered my predicament unworthy of any special consideration and completely and quickly dismissed it with one sentence. "We make no exceptions."

The long and short of it then was that after renting for over a year and a half and literally disposing of twenty-two thousand dollars of income, I found myself being treated like a cockroach. Actually, not that well. Management didn't bother the cockroaches. In fact, let them live there for free.

And in one day, I found myself out of a job and a home with only one thing to do. Have a yard sale. The ultimate irony was that I had no yard— the front of the condo was a walk with my garden—soon to be management's garden—on either side; the back was a little strip of sandy dirt between the screened porch and the pool fence.

Chapter 54

S t u f f

So I opened the doors and made the house a yard. I thought advertising items in the paper would be the best way to go, so I took out an ad in the classifieds. But a week later, when I'd gotten no response, I abandoned that strategy and followed Jake's advice—to make posters and tack them to telephone poles on the main street outside our complex. "If you do that, you'll sell everything in a day," he said confidently. And he was right.

People came. From all over central Florida, word of the posters spreading, I guess. Hundreds of them arrived at my door, some wanting the strangest things. Asking questions like, "Do you have a king-sized bed with a queen sized frame?"

"Sure," I thought to myself. "I've got any combination you want. Just step right in here to my factory." What in the hell? What is the matter with people? But never mind. If they were buying, what did I care if they couldn't reason.

I told myself just to enjoy the questions and observations, and there was no shortage of them. Like the one for the entertainment center. Not uncommon, right? Unless it had to be made out of glass tiles and marble, which is what one man wanted. This topped only by the couples who had apparently been waiting most of their married lives to furnish their homes from my sale. Circling the pieces of furniture like cats after a ball of yarn, pointing at one thing and then another, they'd ask, "Does this end table really go with that chair, or did you just put it there?"

I wanted to tell them, "You're right. It's a game. I stayed up all night rearranging my furniture to trick you into buying pieces that don't match."

I couldn't believe it! The people this sale attracted. And I couldn't have been happier I was evicted. Certain I'd never feel the same way about my home after they'd been in it.

One guy I'll always remember went over behind the corner of my sectional sofa and lifted it up, only to discover a squashed roach. He turned and stared at me, then announced loudly to all the potential buyers in the room, "Lady, you got bugs."

I just stared back at him and said, "Yeh, but there's no charge for them."

Several women and two couples left after that exchange, and the new arrivals had stopped, leaving just the guy who wanted to buy "the box." Now "the box" was not for sale, something I'd been telling him in between other conversations. It was a big cardboard container filled with pictures and memorabilia from my life. I was planning to take it to the storage unit John had rented for after the sale. And I'd put it in the living room so I wouldn't forget it. But in the end, this last customer, who had yellow teeth and a Grateful Dead t-shirt, started acting as if it had belonged to him all along and he couldn't part with it.

He kept rummaging through its contents, picking up pictures of me and smiling this nasty smile, like he'd just jerked off.

Then John, who'd been helping me all morning with the sale, came through the room and saw what he was doing. He lunged at him, yelling, "Hey, leave those alone! Get your hands out of there!"

Yellow teeth looked frightened and immediately dropped the pictures into the box. But he hadn't given up entirely. "I'll give you fifty for the box," he offered.

John stood over him, hands on his belt, fuming. "You can have the damn box," he said, "just keep your hands off her pictures and get the hell out of here."

And for some reason, I started to laugh. Not loud. Just a little. I mean it was so ridiculous. One man's perversion, topped only by another one's territorial hang up.

John heard me laughing and frowned. Then he told yellow teeth again, "Come on, get out of here."

The man stood up to face John, only it didn't work, because he was five inches shorter. He gulped hard and said with a shaky voice, "How about seventy-five? I'll pay you seventy-five in cash for all the stuff in the box."

"Jesus!" John said, inching up to the guy. "What the hell is the matter with you? I said get out of here. I'm telling you, buddy. One more word out of your nasty mouth and I'm gonna rearrange your face to cover those teeth. Now get out of here."

The man took one more long look at the box. Then another up at John. Then walked out of the condominium like a whipped dog, shutting the door behind him.

I looked up at John.

"What?" he said, then added, "Do you think I should get his license plate?"

"No." I laughed. "I was gonna say take the seventy five. It's the best offer I've had in awhile."

But John didn't laugh. He just walked over to the sofa and sat down, looking completely disgusted with me while staring at "the box."

John is like that. When I called him to ask if he would come help me take care of Ginny, he packed up his life and his dog and drove three thousand miles across the country to be with us. When he arrived, Ginny and I helped him unload twenty-four cardboard boxes from his backseat and trunk, only to find that ten of them were filled with nothing but memorabilia from our lives: Ginny's first pair of shoes, cast in porcelain, head shots of me when I modeled, Ginny's first tennis racquet, reviews from productions I'd been in, trophies of Ginny's, short stories I'd written. Whatever I can't remember, John has saved.

It is amazing to me how we lived together for years. Complete opposites. Ah, what we choose to keep in our lives. While I have either given or thrown way almost every award I've ever won, believing you are as good as you are on the day, John treasures the past. He has spent a small fortune over the years renting storage units, while I decided long ago that it costs less to move on.

Someone should cash in on our live comedy. U-Haul, for instance. Build a campaign around it. They could start with a commercial. Pan around one of their storage units. Then focus in on John, neatly stacking memorabilia in one of them. And the next shot could be me, driving away in one of their trucks. The tag could read, "U-Haul—for your past, present, and future." Something like that.

I'd paid eight thousand dollars for four rooms of new furniture a year and a half before our yard sale. We sold it all in one day for two thousand. And two things were clear. I wasn't as good in used furniture sales as in garbage. And a lot of the furniture you buy, the minute it leaves the showroom floor, will have about the same value as garbage has to everyone—except, of course, the big waste companies.

Nevertheless, as has been the case my entire life, God was with me. This time, tapping me on the shoulder, telling me, "You got your direction mixed up again. I said, 'dig out, not in deeper.' Come on now. Get with the program. Put those pretty little painted nails to work and dig. Dig. Out of this mess."

And just to make sure I would do it, he sent me another of his angels. This time it was Brianna.

She called me the day after the sale, insisting I move in with her. She had been planning for months to move back to California and her condominium was on the market, but until it sold she wouldn't hear of me living anywhere else.

I wanted to cry. Instead, I just thanked her. Telling her, "You're my angel."

Then Brianna told me, " I know, baby. But you're gonna need more than that to turn your life around."

422

"I know," I said. "But I can do it. And I will. Just wait and see."

Brianna said, "I know you will, baby. I just hope you take an easier path this time. It wears me out just watching you."

I laughed. "Yeh?" I said. "You're not the only one who's said that. But just close your eyes and believe in me."

"I do, baby," she told me. "I do."

So in a matter of forty-eight hours after the sale, John found a room he and Mischief could live in, a rental in a beautiful home in Winter Park. We moved all my dishes, glasses, cooking, baking, and entertaining supplies into storage. I packed fifty pairs of shoes (one thing I never gave away or sold, probably because of that special relationship with my feet I talked about before) and two closets of clothes into my Capri and drove away from yet another home. This time, with no desire to ever return.

Chapter 55

M i x e d   M e s s a g e s

There are two kinds of good-byes. The ones you sense and the ones you simply hear or see. Sometimes, goodbyes catch you off guard. Hit you like a coke bottle on the back of the head. Other times, they come as softened blows. A packed suitcase on an unmade bed.

If you live any time at all, you'll experience good-byes. I house enough of the "hear-or-see" variety in my memory to make a fortune if I could sell them. Doors shutting. Cars driving away. Planes taking off. Papers signed. Belongings divided. Hands letting go. Heartbeats stopping. Breath ending.

And I have sensed even more. Where there were no words written or voiced. An empty seat at parents' night. A Valentine's Day with no candy or flowers. Calls for help unreturned. A vacant home with no forwarding address.

Or simply a series of events where you find your timing is off, when nothing falls into place, and no one around you seems to notice. Because the message to say goodbye and "move on" is only meant for you.

Ginny was doing well. Best she'd been in months. She was actually looking forward to her seventeenth birthday and to John and me spending it with her.

Her doctor had introduced a different medication into her treatment. Risperadol. Another anti-psychotic. And Ginny seemed to think it was helping reduce the number of voices she hears.

She sounded wonderful when I talked to her on the phone, telling me about her spinning classes and voice lessons, talking about chapters she'd read in *The Great Gatsby*.

We stayed away from the subject of the future. Sort of an unspoken understanding. Ginny knew I was struggling to find a good job but that history showed I've always been able to get what we needed. And she believed as much as I did that she was healing. That we'd soon be together again, that was the missing piece.

Our unspoken plan for being together included Ginny continuing to heal. Me finding a good job in Florida and a new doctor for Ginny as good as the one she had in Asheville. We wanted a home on a lake with a pool. Ginny to go to a local college. And, of course, Jake with us.

I felt the whole plan was contingent on two things: Ginny healing and me getting a good job. And that Ginny and Jake and I were well on our way to starting a new life together.

And while I was busy planning for my career, my new home, and my new family, Jake was equally focused. On something a little different. Buying a truck, to be exact.

The truth is, we both needed new cars. But neither of us bought one for very different reasons. First, I would almost rather buy anything than a car. That's not true. There is one car I've wanted most of my adult life—a Mustang, and if I can't have it, I'm really not interested. Jake, on the other hand, loves cars. But he's very picky. Really that's not strong enough. He's incredibly picky. No he's off-the-charts picky. You get the idea. I think, too, mechanics have a thing about buying new cars. Almost goes against their grain not to have to "fix" something.

I remember my brother—the one who knows auto-mechanics inside out—telling me one time, "Don't ever trust a mechanic who drives a new car." When I asked him why not, he said, "Cause it means he can't fix his own damn car, never mind yours." Good point.

But Jake can fix his car. And any other. And though he refuses to admit it, I think he enjoys torturing car salespeople.

I loved looking for trucks, or I would have if Jake had been able to relax. There was something wonderful about opening their big, heavy, shiny doors, then stepping up into their cabs, surrounding myself with the smell of new leather. Surveying the dash. Pressing all the buttons. Tapping my feet on the paper dealership mats. It's fun. So much fun, I bet a lot of people are just like me. I bet they go car shopping just for the fun of it.

But not Jake. Jake is serious about cars. And being a salesperson myself, I feel sort of a special empathy for the ones who approach him in the car lots and showrooms. Like I should post his picture and a brief description on some general automotive sales website. Just a warning. It could read something like this.

> See this man? Avoid him. If he comes on to your lot, busy yourself with other customers. Do not attempt to tell him anything about a vehicle. And for god's sake, don't try to sell him one.

I mean, I love Jake, but I'm also a compassionate person. And it was just pitiful the way salesman after salesman would tag along after him. Trying to remember what he was telling them. Learning what they were supposed to be doing for a living from a customer.

One day, when we were out "truck hunting," Jake called up his best friend Brent to meet us for lunch. We hadn't seen Brent since he and Lisa had gotten married, which is a whole other can of worms, I intended to open another day.

When Jake and I were not seeing each other, he received an invitation to their wedding with an R.S.V.P. asking whether or not he'd be bring a guest.

He responded no. But when Brent and Lisa actually did get married, Jake and I were back together. Had been for months. And Jake did nothing to change his response.

Now I don't know about you, but where I come from, if you are invited to a wedding and have an option to bring a guest, and you are seeing someone seriously, you bring that person. And if you were broken up temporarily when you responded and the groom was one of your best friends, you'd ask him if you could change your response. Now that I think about it, the more I think about it, this would hold true anywhere in civilized society.

And the truth is, while everyone knows most single people attend weddings to meet a future spouse, Jake is not most people. In fact, I can rarely think of a generalization that fits him. And certainly not this one.

No, the truth is, in the past couple of years almost all of Jake's friends have gotten married. And I believe he is in total conflict about it. Part of him wants to point directly to the statistics that indicate very convincingly most love is not "for better or for worse," while the other part of him knows how deeply and truly I love him and how good that kind of love feels and wants to feel that good for a lifetime. But until he resolves in his own mind whether or not he wants to be married, Jake is not about to be with me at any wedding.

Anyway, I couldn't have been happier to eat lunch with Brent. He is my favorite of Jake's friends. Warm and funny and genuinely a good person. And I wished both him and Lisa a lifetime of happiness.

As for Jake, well, I had something in store for him. Like all women, I waste no ammunition. And this little wedding incident went right into my "ammo" box. Along with a few other little grenades I plan to use later. Just if it's necessary. If there is a lull in an argument. A need for something a little more explosive.

Like when I'm being falsely accused of misplacing our keys, when we're already late for a movie. Or of not answering my phone. Slip it in there somewhere. Just like, "And, no, I was nowhere near my phone. I could not have heard it ring, but you (clip down, spring engaged, ready, set—KABOOM!) you could have changed your R.S.V.P."

And there you have it. Another man caught off guard. Another in a long history of unsuspected female attacks. And they say we're not meant for combat.

During lunch, Brent invited us to dinner. Told us to come on out to their house after we'd finished our afternoon "truck hunting." And so we did.

If you didn't know Lisa and Brent were just married, you *would*, the moment you stepped into their living room. It is a gallery of wedding photographs and memorabilia.

Their home, like their marriage, was brand new. New floors, new walls, new paint, new countertops. No scuffs. No scrapes. No rust. No "for worse."

Jake and I sat on separate barstools around the tiled island in their kitchen, while Brent concocted his specialty—mai tai's and Lisa hers—chicken cacciatore. They were a picture of marital bliss, stepping around, then into each other. Kissing like magnets. Showing us their new china, talking about wine glasses they want, then glancing into each other's eyes and laughing about something unspoken, something that made them kiss again.

Jake was drinking Brent's mai tai's like water and clearing his throat each time they kissed, while I just took it all in from the viewpoint of someone who had been married and single longer than anyone in the room and who knew just a little about both.

Jake was trying to tell Lisa and Brent about our "truck hunting" experience in between their stories about picking out china, when the other couple they'd invited arrived, Burt and Elie, newly married also, and pregnant.

I think it was about this time Jake escalated his mood enhancing, chasing his mai tai's with Coors lights, while I could hardly keep from laughing watching him. Even though it did get to be a little predictable, his behavior. I think it was one mai tai for every wedding story and two beers for every one about having babies.

Meantime, I'd stopped drinking after my second mai tai, realizing I'd be the one driving Jake and me home.

I couldn't help but think, poor Jake. The hangover he would have. After a whole evening with these couples. Their knowing looks and touches. Their harmless squabbles. Their sharing of dreams. Preferring a vice grip on his head to a ring on his finger.

No matter what I feel or what Jake feels, he says he doesn't believe in marriage. And while I live every day loving him, believing in both commitment and marriage, Jake hopes I'll get over this. Not him. The marriage part.

But despite our seemingly opposite approaches to living and loving, Jake is no mystery to me. I grew up in a home filled with non believers. And they all have one thing in common. They are some of the most sensitive people you'll ever know.

It has been well said, "Life is a tragedy to those who feel, a comedy to those who think." And I would add only, "Those who won't believe are those who wanted to believe most."

After we'd eaten, and I was a little relieved Jake now had at least twenty percent food to what had previously been one hundred percent alcohol in him, we decided to go dancing. Well, really just up the street to the local watering hole with a live band and live gators, but I was always happy for the chance to dance.

The band played "I Like My Women Just a Little on the Trashy Side," while Jake laughed and winked at me, claiming to Brent, "That's my song." Then later, sitting next to me at the bar, untying the ribbon on my blouse, singing with the band, "Stroke it to the east, stroke it to the west, stroke it to the woman I love best," while gyrating his hard penis into me. Once again, proving himself the exception to every man—the rest do one of three things when they get drunk: they either fuck up, throw up, or can't get it up.

But not Jake. No siree. And he seems to have no clue that his hard-on is not the norm in such situations.

You'd think he would know. That somewhere in some locker room or maybe on a break at work, he'd have heard guys talking about when they can't get it up. But then, on second thought, maybe not. Maybe they only ever talk about when they can.

Anyway, later that night, when we got home, Jake made good on his words. Having no problem stroking me in every direction. All night long.

And even the next morning, when I was getting ready to leave, and you'd have thought he'd have had the hangover from hell, he pulled me back into bed with him. And started all over again. Bending my softness into his hardness. Touching me like he had me memorized. Finding ways to make it all new.

Bending me so far back one time, I think my legs popped up instinctively, trying to keep from breaking off, while I laughed so hard I cried.

Jake just sat up, putting his arms around me. Looking amazed. Like no matter how much he didn't want to believe in us, there was no denying it. How we fit. Paling "for better or worse" with "meant to be."

Chapter 56

What is Said and Done

John and I drove to Asheville together for Ginny's seventeenth birthday. Finding her twenty pounds heavier. With large patches of acne covering her once clear skin, varicose veins, and stretch marks on her formerly beautifully toned legs—her now oversized breasts actually lactating during her period. The latest side effects of the newest medication. And while devastating to any teenaged girl, much less harmful than some of the other terrible side effects of the new medications, like diabetes and tardive dyskenesia.

I called Ginny's doctor and counselor immediately, expressing my concern about both the weight gain and the acne. Saying that I was certain these were only mild external indicators of a body being traumatized by a drug that was obviously having negative effects on Ginny's hormones, central nervous and digestive systems.

And her doctor told me we have to weigh the good with the bad. Posing the question, was Ginny's appearance really more important than getting rid of the voices?

Once again, I felt surrounded by darkness. My stars of hope fading fast. And let's face it, I'm an easy mark. Having been given more than my share of good looks and athletic ability, any argument I have concerning my daughter's health could be misconstrued as some sort of preoccupation with appearance. When nothing could be further from the truth. When Ginny was born, unlike most parents, I didn't even count her fingers and toes. Figuring if she was alive, healthy and happy, that was all that mattered. And to this day, that is all that matters to me. I don't give a damn what any of her doctors think. It's not my mind or heart in question here, it's that we need to get a brain scan and pulse count on people who regularly prescribe life-threatening drugs. And lock those who create them out of the labs. Put them away in solitary confinement. Where they can take all the time they need to get rid of the one voice they may finally hear. Their own conscience.

Despite my heated conversations with her doctor and counselor, John and Ginny and I had a wonderful birthday weekend together. Faith prepared another special birthday meal, complete with flowers and vanilla cake, sprinkled with Ginny's favorite colors, pink and purple.

We watched movies. Attended church. Took walks. Drove on the parkway. Played scrabble. But after the weekend, John had to head back to his job, and I stayed on for two more weeks. Spending every bit of the time I had before starting my new job with the person I always wanted to be with, my daughter.

I did call Jake a couple of times. Left messages for him. And of course I missed him—every day. He did not return any of my calls. But I knew I'd be back soon. And we'd be together again.

We'd talked a couple of times before I left. Saw each other once. Actually, had sort of a big argument. But the last time we spoke, he seemed okay. Saying, when he was hanging up, how he'd talk to me later.

And here's where I learned another lesson. How "later" is a relative term. While I generally think of "later" in the context of the same day, some don't. Most specifically, Jake. Who really meant nine weeks when he said "later."

Chapter 57

F a c i n g   t h e   T r u t h

Assuming I knew Jake's definition of "later," well—that was one bad mistake. But it wasn't the only one I made that summer. No, at that time, I was into super sizing. Lots of mistakes. Couldn't just make one wrong turn. Had to make several. Until I came to the end of the road.

As I said, I went to work for yet another waste management company. Literally working my way down both the line-up of the top four waste management companies in the nation and the career ladder. And my first day riding the front load truck to learn my territory, observe its "lack of density" so I could "sell the gaps," my driver and I had a blow out—that is to say, a tire blew and my driver and I hung on the edge of disaster together for what seemed like an eternity. We were on one of the major arteries in central Florida. Fully loaded. Headed to the landfill and driving in the fast lane.

Unbelievably, he managed to get us, in a hair-raising, hurtling series of maneuvers, safely across three lanes of traffic without hitting anyone or turning the truck over. Gears screamed so loudly that if I was screaming too—and I can't think why I wouldn't have been—no one could have heard me. But the driver's negotiations during those potentially deadly moments weren't my biggest surprise.

After we'd climbed down out of the truck, called our maintenance shop for help, and were surveying the damage, he told me, "Damn retreads. I told 'em to give me at least two new tires."

I couldn't believe what I'd heard—retreads? On a truck that weighs tons? Carries tons every day? In the Florida heat! At highway speeds! For hours!

But that is exactly what I heard. And definitely what we were riding on. What all my drivers were riding on—every day. Literally risking their lives to pick up someone else's trash.

And the company's cost cutting measures, I quickly learned in the weeks to follow, didn't stop there. They also did not pay for maintenance or tires for their sales reps' vehicles. Expecting all six of us to average driving over two hundred miles a day in some of the worst traffic in America with frayed belts and bald tires.

Now I'll admit management did their part to help with cost cutting. All leaving every day around four. Coming in late the next morning. Checking out at noon on Friday. To conserve energy and resources, of course.

Anyway, once again, I found myself faced with the truth. That I had once worked for the best waste management company in the nation. And anything less than that was much less than that.

And there was a bit of revelation too—that maybe, just maybe, someone who at the age of seven wrote a fifty page novella for her brother's birthday gift might just not be meant for waste management.

Chapter 58

I t   G e t s   P r e t t y   S i m p l e

Jake or no Jake, it turns out, I did need a mechanic. Sooner. Not later.

My first day back working in sales in the waste industry, I hit I-4 early, trying to avoid the seven-thirty morning rush. I was cruising along in fifth, going about sixty-five miles an hour when I saw the smoke. In a few moments it surrounded me like a cloud. At the next exit ramp, I eased the car off the road and onto the shoulder. I spotted a service station about two hundred yards in front of me and decided to keep going. Swearing like a sailor. Praying like I was on death row. "Sweet Jesus, just another minute, please!" And I figure he must have been listening, because a minute later, I coasted into the station.

I had to wait a while for the mechanic to get to me. But I was used to that. I found an old cracked plastic chair missing two of its rubber feet and pulled it onto the concrete ledge just outside the station, sitting in the last patch of shade.

Just then, an older black man pulled up in a rusty blue 280-Z. He got out and spoke to the mechanic. Then he walked over to me, sat down on the hood of his car, and told me it looked like we were both gonna have a little wait.

I laughed and said, "Perfect. My first day at work. Great. Well, at least it's consistent. It's getting so I can just count on things being bad…every day."

The man looked down at me, his bright eyes widening and his chin tucking, gently scornful. He said, "Now what's a beautiful woman like you doing saying something like that? Things can't be that bad."

"Want to bet?" I said. Then pointed to my car parked next to his, its hood up, still smoking. "That's my car," I told him. "Overheated just a few minutes ago on I-4. It's my first day at a new job. I've got ten more miles before I even get there. The mechanic says I've got at least a half an hour wait before he can look at it. And…" I looked down at my wrist watch, "it's seven thirty already."

The old black man chuckled as if I'd told a joke and wiped the sweat off his forehead. Then he frowned in sympathy. "Yeh," he said, mmhm, that don't sound good. But…it'll be all right. You got anyone you could call to help you?"

I rolled my eyes. "Yeh," I said. "My boyfriend. He's a mechanic."

The man brightened again, "Well, there you go now. Why don't you call him? He'll surely come help you."

"Don't be so sure," I said. "He's not talking to me."

The man raised his eyebrows. "Oh?" he said. "Little lover's quarrel?"

I shook my head. "More like a big lover's quarrel."

The man smiled broadly and said, "Well, now I don't know what any man could argue with you about for long. Unless…" He paused for a minute and his smile faded. Then he went on. "Unless he idn't being honest with you," he said.

"What do you mean?" I asked.

"I mean he idn't in it for the long run. Not here for the rough parts. A lot of men like that you know. Spineless. Mmhmm. Nothing but muscle and hormone."

438

I smiled. "Yeh. I've known a few of those," I told him. "But Jake is not like that. He's a good man. And we've been through hell and back together. He just...he doesn't like it when things go wrong. He likes to think he's in control."

"Mmhmm..." The man said. "Don't we all?"

"Yes," I said. "We do. But Jake is worse. He's...I don't know, he really has to believe he's in control. And when it comes to me...well, he just believes the man should be in control of the relationship. And even though he knows I respect him and love him, he gets very frustrated when everything isn't in his control."

"Yeh?" he said. "So how long you been with this mechanic who don't take care of your car or you?"

I smiled again. "Oh, he takes care of me...when he's around."

The man said. "I see. Trying to make it all up to you in the bedroom?"

I blushed.

He said, "Pardon me now for getting so personal, but I got to tell you this. They'll come a time when he can't do that so good. I mean, you take me and my wife. We been married thirty-seven years. And to me, she still just as fresh as a daisy. And so warm. Lord, she warm. And passionate. Mmhmm. But me...well, let's face it. The tools don't quite work like they used to." He was silent for a moment, folding his hands in front of him. Then he said, "Happen to the best of us. And it'll happen to your man too. And when that happen, if you still 'round, he be thanking his lucky stars he got this beautiful woman with a car he don't fix. And a whole bunch of love he can't do nothing 'bout."

I'd been staring at this unassuming sage for minutes. Unaware my shade was gone. That the June sun had surrounded me. And there was no escaping. The heat. Or the truth of his words.

§

I had a leaking water hose. At least that was one of my problems. One that could be readily identified. The mechanic didn't have the particular hose for my car, so he jerry-rigged a fuel line in its place. Telling me it would hold up much better. To me, the fuel line looked much thicker than its predecessor. Less pliable. And even more likely to crack. But what did I know about damage control of any kind? So I just thanked the mechanic who was there for me and paid him.

Within a couple of hours, I was back at work. Finding more garbage to pick up. Until six o'clock, when I headed home in bumper to bumper traffic.

I was creeping along I-4, a tractor trailer on my rear, just a few miles from home when the clutch went out. Heart in my throat, mind racing, I managed to get the car off the road safely once again. Then vowed to do two things. One, tell Jake I'm a way better driver than he gives me credit for being and two, get rid of the car he so aptly named "a piece of shit."

And the next day, I did one of the two. I traded my car. For a pick-up truck.

My credit was shot, badly affected by the eviction, unpaid medical bills, late payments. And then there was the other negative factor—me just starting my job. All that taken into consideration, I was still able to get the truck. From a shark. For a hundred dollar a week payments. For two years.

He was a nice shark, though. Gave me fifteen hundred dollars on my Capri. And only asked for another thousand down payment.

I signed twenty pages of finely printed conditions and swung up into the cab. I told myself I was fine. I had a beautiful Carolina blue truck, with low mileage and good tires. I could pick up a lot of garbage in it. Accounts, that is.

What I didn't have was any furniture. Brianna had moved to California. And while she had no problem with letting me live in her place until she sold it, she did need to take her furniture with her. And what I hadn't sold of mine, I'd given to John. The rest was with Blake in Asheville. Interesting. Two houseloads of furniture and not a stick of it in my possession. You gotta love consistency. I was either standing by the man I love or giving the ones I'd lived with something to sit on.

Well, I've never pined for a lot of fancy things—discount stores have always suited me fine, but standing in the Walmart checkout line with my new bed under my arm—a five dollar child's raft, I found myself longing just a little bit for a few of the finer comforts in life—like a mattress I could lie on without sticking to.

Chapter 59

A   B i g g e r   P l a n

It was late June in central Florida. Code for torrential rainstorms. I drove through them every day. On my way to work. All day, taking care of customers. On my way home every night.

One night, inching my way through one of them, halfway up I-4, traveling east, the steady, hard rain even turned into pellets of ice, then back to translucent blankets of water. Huge blue-black clouds covered the early evening sky, hovering over my truck, making me feel like I was trapped in my own mobile car wash, a closet of water on wheels. When suddenly, with no warning at all, my windshield wipers stopped working. Wouldn't move at all.

I turned the wiper switch up and down. Rolled it to the right and left. Pulled it in and out. Then, noticed my windows fogging up. I switched the defogger on, but I still couldn't see a foot in front of me driving in rush hour traffic.

I kept my right hand on the wheel and rolled my window down with my left, then tried to grab the left windshield wiper to see if I could make it move. But once again, I found what I needed was just out of my reach.

I rolled my window back up, trying to focus on the road I couldn't see. I flipped my hazard lights on and prayed. Just then, the rain let up, for one instant. I could see a downtown exit directly in front on me, and I turned off onto it, drove down the ramp and pulled off until my tires hit rougher pavement that told me I must be on the shoulder, shutting the engine off.

I remember feeling very cold, my forehead damp. The palms of my hands were so moist they slipped off the steering wheel. Then I remember being dizzy, like all the contents of my head had been sucked out. Seeing only pins of light, and, finally, darkness.

I woke to pounding. On my window. A man's fist, framed in glass. I'd fallen over in my seat, and I tried now to sit up. But I did it too quickly, and immediately I felt nauseated. Gripping the seat, I took a deep breath and tried not to swallow, feeling instinctively that I was on the verge of throwing up and wondering vaguely what I had to lose—I couldn't remember when I'd eaten last.

My eyes were fixed on the dash when I heard the pounding again, and I forced my eyes to the window where a handsome face was now peering in, worried—his voice muffled by the glass but the words unmistakable: "Are you all right?" Later, he told me he had been shouting.

While I could see the man was big, about six feet tall with huge biceps, he didn't look threatening. For one thing, he was dressed in light green hospital scrubs, an unlikely outfit, I thought, for someone up to no good.

It had stopped raining and his face was anxious and other than start up the truck and ungraciously drive away, I didn't see that I had many options, so I rolled down the window, cleared my throat, and said, "I'm fine."

I actually still felt like I might throw up, but I decided quickly that wasn't the best way to start a conversation and so willed my stomach to be still.

The handsome stranger's deep blue eyes were unconvinced and concerned. He said, "You sure? You look really pale. Did you pass out?"

I said, "Yeh, I guess I did. But I'm okay now. Thanks for checking."

He said, "No offense, but...you don't look okay. I mean. I didn't mean that. You just...I don't know. You look um...really pale."

I tried to smile. "I'm Scottish," I said. We tend to be pale."

He smiled and said, "How about crazy?" Then added, "Listen, you need to move your truck, and I don't care what you tell me, you are not fine. At least not to drive. And you obviously have no idea where to park."

I tried to laugh, but I couldn't. Instead, I told him, "My windshield wipers quit working during the storm. That's why I pulled over. And...well I couldn't really see where I was—just tried to get out of traffic."

"Okay," he said. "Well, you didn't quite make it. You're still a little on the ramp. "But that's one mystery solved. And the windshield wiper thing can be fixed pretty easily. But you, you're a whole other mystery. One I'm guessing is not so easy to solve." He kept looking around anxiously, I guessed keeping an eye out for cars, but none came and he stayed by the window.

I looked at his scrubs again and asked him, "Are you a doctor?"

"No," he said, and his face was a question as if something in my tone had told him I didn't like doctors.

He looked down the ramp again, then back at me. He smiled and said, "I'm not that dangerous yet. Just an intern."

"Oh," I said. "Good. Maybe there's still some hope you'll learn something before you try to save anyone."

The handsome stranger stepped back then, holding his hands in the air. Then dropped them, moving back to the window and glancing nervously down the ramp—as if he'd momentarily forgotten about traffic. He said, "What are you like with the men who don't try to help you?" When I didn't answer immediately he said, "You *do need* help."

His face was bewildered, and remembering his hands up in surrender, I discovered I could laugh again; the dizziness was subsiding finally. I laughed louder, discovering the laughter made me feel better and better.

He said, "I'm gonna take that as a 'yes' before I hear a 'no.'" And with that, he checked traffic once more and then opened my door. I scooted over and he tried to tuck his big frame into the cab. "What in the name of...?" he said, pulling himself out again and looking at the seat. "Do you always drive like this?"

"Like what?" I asked, genuinely puzzled.

"With your seat a foot from the steering column?" he asked.

I laughed again, and he looked me up and down, his face seeming suddenly to register my size. He laughed then too, and quickly located the seat release, sliding the seat back to where he could fold himself into the cab—still not comfortably but with room to breathe. He looked around the console, trying to acquaint himself with the unfamiliar arrangement of buttons and gears and finally started the truck, glanced into the rearview mirror—adjusting it to accommodate for the new distance of the seat—then pulled onto the road, heading for downtown Orlando.

When he was up to thirty miles an hour, he said, "I'm Matt. What's your name?"

I told him, "Haley."

He said, "Haley? I thought you said you were Scottish? That name is Irish."

"I know, I said, but how on earth did you know that?"

"Did you know the name means 'ingenious?'" he asked, ignoring my question.

"No," I said, and smiled a little at that revelation before I added, "in fact, the only way I knew it was Irish is that Maeve, a…well…an old friend of mine, told me. But since we're on the subject, how many people do you think name their children based on their ancestry?"

"Probably more than you think," he said. "Anyway, to answer your other question, I went through a period of fascination with the whole idea of naming, and I must have read a hundred books about it."

"Yeh?... well, what does your name mean?" I asked.

"Matthew is Hebrew," he said. "Means 'a gift of God.'"

We road for awhile in silence then. I thought about names—wondering why I'd never given much thought before to their origins and meanings. I was about to ask Matt about his ancestry when we pulled up behind a brand new silver BMW parked in one of the spaces by Lake Eola. "Here we are," he said.

446

"Where's your car?" I asked, pretty sure I was looking at it.

"It's right in front of us," he said.

"Any chance you want to trade?" I asked. "I mean I know that would make me feel better."

Matt laughed. "No chance. I have a thing about working windshield wipers. Speaking of which," he said, "why don't we try yours again. Just for kicks?"

I said, "Fine, go ahead."

Matt flicked the windshield wiper switch and instantly the wipers began to move.

I faced him and said, "Oh sure," throwing my hands in the air. "Now they work," I said, "but not earlier, not when I was on I-4, surrounded by darkness, driving through a cave of blue-black clouds into a waterfall; no, by all means, not then—that would be like me living happily ever after, my prince getting through forests of thorns, scaling the walls of the tower, kissing me awake, finding a way to get us both back down to safety, back to his castle, where nothing could ever threaten us again, and it's just not gonna happen, just not meant to be…"

"Whooo!" Matt said. "Did you take a breath and I missed it, or can you just say that much without breathing?"

"I'm a runner," I told him.

"And a talker," he added.

"And a singer," I said.

"And ingenious," I added.

He laughed and turned the engine off.

"I'm not so sure about that last," he said, "I mean, come on, parking a car on an exit ramp?"

"I passed out!" I protested.

Matt smiled, "I know, he said, just checking your reflexes. Your color is coming back, by the way. Hey, how about a change of atmosphere? Do you have plans for dinner?"

I squirmed a little in my seat, then said, "No but…"

"But what?" Matt asked.

"I'm dating someone," I told him looking away. I'd pulled my cell phone out of my purse on an impulse, not even sure who I wanted to call.

"Yeh?" he said, skeptically, looking at the phone, "must be that prince you were speaking about earlier? Although I don't know about that happily ever after stuff if he's not even wondering where you are this late on a Friday night."

I didn't say anything and put the phone back in my purse, looking out the passenger window, fighting tears and the memory of half a summer with not even one call from Jake.

Matt lightened his tone. "Hey, forget I said that," he said. "It's none of my business. The guy could have a really good reason for not being here to help you."

I kept my head turned away, trying to stay composed, and said, "He doesn't even know what happened." Then I decided I didn't care if Matt saw me crying. I turned back and looked him in the eye. "Okay? That's all," I said.

Matt put his hand up to his mouth and pulled at his face, stretching his lips into a grimace. He said, "Okay, so he didn't leave you stranded." He dropped his hand and added, "just alone on a Friday night with no dinner plans."

I rolled my eyes.

Matt said, "If it'll make you feel better, call him. Tell him I'm taking you to dinner."

I laughed. "Yeh, right. That'll go over well."

"Okay," Matt said. "Suit yourself. Don't call him. But," he paused. "I'm taking you to dinner. And if anyone finds out, we'll just say I'm a doctor and I saw you faint and I insisted you needed food."

I smiled at Matt. "You got a deal," I said. But as he was opening his door, I added, "On one condition."

"What?" asked Matt.

I told him, "You agree my wipers weren't working."

Matt looked at me for a long time, then smiled and said, "God, stubborn and beautiful. What a combo."

I said, "Flattery will get you nowhere. Agree I was right. My wipers weren't working. Or the deal's off."

Matt got out of the truck and offered his hand through the door he'd left open. He said, "All right, Miss Haley. You are so right."

And I pushed the door open further and swung my feet out, jumping to the ground without taking his hand.

§

Lake Eola is yet another piece of heaven. Fitting neatly into a few of the mossy banks of Orlando. Complete with little wooden boats carved into white swans. Lanterned walkways covered by sprawling oak and willow trees, with firefly-size white lights and dark green canopies gracing the fronts of cafés and wine bars scattered around one curve in the lake.

It had become one of my favorite running spots that summer, as I was trying to avoid all the courses Jake had laid out for me. I couldn't stand running on them and thinking about him. Like I was desperately clinging to the past. Feet touching the ground Jake laid out for me. Head in the clouds.

I wanted something new and hopeful. Something that didn't resemble the patterns in my life. Two years of Jake coming and going. Appearing in flame to light my candle, only to burn me when I held him too long.

Matt chose my favorite restaurant at the edge of the water. The storm had moved on. He picked a table outside under the lights. Our waiter poured water, lit the candle on the table, and asked if we'd like something from the bar.

I told Matt I'd better start with ginger ale. He leaned forward, one lock of his curly dark brown hair falling forward on his forehead. He reached up to sweep it back, and said, "That bad, huh?"

I tried to smile. "I'll be all right," I said. "Just need to take it easy. And I don't need any alcohol. I haven't felt very good lately and today with this passing out thing…well, let's just say it hasn't been one of my better days."

Matt lifted his water glass and said, "To a better evening."

I lifted mine to his, "Absolutely," I said. "To a better evening,"

The waiter brought us black leather-bound menus embossed in gold. And though all of the entrees and appetizers looked wonderful, I found myself without an appetite, deciding on a very plain dish with roasted chicken that I thought I could keep down, while Matt ordered crown royal and a coke for him and a blackened rib-eye.

We talked like old friends. Thoughts matching, sentences overlapping. Truths easily told. Silences going unnoticed.

Matt told me he'd graduated from Emory and that he'd been interning at Willow Pond South since January. I told him why there was I chance we could have met before.

Matt seemed genuinely interested in hearing about Ginny, telling me his younger brother suffers with similar problems. We talked, while we waited for our food, about our different and similar experiences living with mental illness. Agreeing medication is not the answer, agreeing that beyond that, we'd learned a lot and still knew so little.

After that, we moved on to what we like to do. Matt is a biker. I reminded him I'm a runner. We shared stories about different races, trails we've trained on. He told me he used to run. Was on a cross-country team in high school, actually. But he said he hurt his knees running too much and hasn't done it since. Then he asked me if I mostly dated runners. And I laughed.

Matt said, "What? What's so funny? I mean don't most runners meet other runners? Don't people like to date people who enjoy doing the same things?"

I answered, "Yes. Absolutely they do. Both of those things. But," I said, "There is also the old deal of opposites attracting. And people finding mates who complete them more than mirror them."

Matt raised his thick eyebrows, thought for a moment, then said, "I guess you have a point." The waiter set our drinks down, then walked away. "And so," Matt continued, "I guess I can assume the men in your life have not been runners."

"You can," I said. "And they weren't." I took a sip of my ginger ale. "Not that they aren't all in good shape. I mean they all look like they could run with me."

Matt lifted his glass and winked at me. "But the truth is, they can't."

I lifted mind to his. "Touché," I said, smiling, and clinked my glass to his.

Then Matt pushed his chair back and stood up saying he needed to excuse himself for a minute. I nodded and sipped my ginger ale again. I was glad for the time alone. To sort my thoughts.

A slight breeze brushed my hair into my face, which I shook back. The glass fairy-lights clinked together, sounding like tiny teeth chattering. Couples walked in front of me on the sidewalk that circles the lake. Some holding hands. Others talking. A few pressing their lips together lightly but passionately, like they wanted to do more…later. After the storm, it was a perfect night. To be with someone you love.

Quietly Matt reappeared and sat down. Then he cleared his throat and said, "So…how long have you been running?"

I looked at him for a second misreading the question, then smiled and said, "Since I was twelve."

Matt looked surprised. The waiter brought our food and left and we were silent for a few minutes, Matt arranging his napkin again and then cutting into his steak. He chewed several bites thoughtfully.

In a few minutes the waiter reappeared asking if everything was all right and if we needed anything. He looked at my chicken, which I hadn't touched, and Matt looked at me. "I'm fine I said; just need to wait a few minutes." "We're fine," Matt reassured the waiter, who looked once more at my chicken and then reluctantly left.

"Tell me more about your running," said Matt.

"One of my brothers was a coach at the private school I attended," I said. "He designed this running course through the woods that surrounded the school. I think it was about three miles. Not very long considering my later runs. But I loved it. The trail wound up and down little hills of red clay, crossed over a stream full of fallen leaves that gleamed in the sun, wet with color. And though I remember the sun touching every part of it, it was shaded too by tall spindly pines, thick-bellied oaks, delicate dogwoods. Running it, you could hear squirrels chewing nuts, horses neighing in the nearby stable, birds in flight. And whoever was in p.e. class behind you, which, in my case, was everyone—you could hear them crunching tiny branches, tripping on roots, sucking wind."

Matt laughed.

"Even the boys," I said. "I never saw them do it, but I swear they would trip themselves on purpose. Hobble back to the campus saying they'd sprained an ankle." I shook my head. "They saw running the course as some form of punishment, while I...I used to run it just praying...it would never end."

Matt wiped his mouth and put his napkin down. He'd mostly finished his dinner. He leaned back and smiled at me, clasping his hands behind his head. Then he said, "You talk like a writer. Ever think about writing?"

I didn't answer him.

Matt said, "Don't you think you could eat a little now? You really need to eat something. You eat and I'll talk. Um, but first. I just have to say this..."

"What?" I asked.

Matt said, "Your company...the way you talk. Well, it completely makes up for your lack of driving skills."

I laughed, then said, "You sure about that?"

"Yes," he said. "I'm sure. Hell, if you were mine, I'd just have you chauffered around."

"Or tell me to run?" I added.

Matt laughed. "I hadn't thought about that. You probably can run all over Orlando."

I said, "Can and have. Do, actually—every day."

"Obviously," Matt said, looking me up and down again, then adding, "Eat."

I looked at him, frowning.

"Or not," he said, smiling.

I smiled back, then took a small bite of chicken. It tasted wonderful. I scooped up some potatoes, and before long was eating in earnest.

Matt watched me, and when I looked up from time to time, it seemed his face was genuinely relieved. He took one or two more bites of his steak before pushing his plate away. He wiped his mouth, took a drink of water, then said, "Okay, here's what I've got to ask. I mean I know it's not polite. Bad form. And all of that. But…here goes." Matt sat up tall and took a deep breath. Then he said, "Why are you alone? I mean…why are you with a guy who leaves you alone? Why?"

I said, "I thought you were going to ask something difficult," I said. "That's easy. I love him."

Matt took a longer drink of water, then a sip of his crown royal before asking, "Why?"

I told him, "There you go. That's the why I can't answer."

Matt said, "You have to. You can't really love him if you can't say why. Unless you just don't want to tell me."

"No," I said, "That's not it. If I knew I would tell you. Be glad to tell you. I'd give you a whole list of reasons. Maybe way too much information. But now…now…I'm just down to the feeling, without the explanation."

Matt pursed his lips, opening his blue eyes wider. He'd been playing with his fork, and he set it down. "Well, you got me there," he said. I mean that's pretty strong. You love him beyond explanation. Like he's too good for words."

I said, "Not exactly. Just, I don't know, Matt. I had a friend tell me once it would happen to me. That one day I'd find someone who stops me talking. But I never believed it. I mean I hoped, but truth be told, I never really believed. But I'm telling you, when it happens, when it really happens to you—you'll know it. You may not be able to explain it—but you'll know it."

Matt said, "You know what this reminds me of?"

"What?" I asked.

"I saw this special, I can't remember what station, on Faith Hill and Tim McGraw. Do you know anything about them?"

I laughed. "Yes, I know who Faith Hill and Tim McGraw are."

Matt looked annoyed. "I know you know who they are. I mean I didn't know if you follow country music. I'm a huge fan. So, I just didn't know if you knew their story."

I said, "Trust me. I know it. I'm also a huge country music fan. Listen to it all day. Every day."

Matt smiled. "See? Another thing we have in common."

I said, "Jake's got you there. He knows more about country music than either you or me. Loves it. Not just country, though. He knows music. Big buff."

Matt said, "Okay. Two points for Jake. But back to the thing I saw. And you need to start eating again; you were doing well there for awhile."

I'd put down my fork, but I picked it up again and speared another bite of chicken. "I'm eating." I said. "And you're talking." I really wanted to hear what he knew about Faith Hill and Tim McGraw and why he thought I needed to know their "story."

"Okay," Matt said, seeming satisfied that I was on my way to cleaning my plate, "The channel—whoever they were— had this deal on, like a couple's special. They were interviewing Faith Hill and Tim McGraw. And they were just so…I don't know. You could see it in them. The love in their eyes. But they really couldn't explain it very well. Or at least they didn't on the show I saw."

I said, "Yeh, well Jake would cringe if he heard you comparing us to Faith and Tim."

"Why?" Matt asked.

I said, "Well, don't get me wrong, Jake likes Tim's music. Actually is a big fan, but he says Faith left her first husband, the one who launched her career, for Tim. He thinks that's terrible."

Matt said, "What do you think?"

"I think I don't really know what happened. But if she didn't love him and she left him for Tim, the guy's better off. I mean who wants to be with someone who doesn't love you? You know?   They're not doing you any favors."

Matt smiled. "You're right."

"And," I added, "I think Tim needs to buy some false eyelashes, but he's a good singer and actor, and Faith is a beautiful wife and mother and singer, and their love is both real and inspiring. So, there you have it." I took a last bite of chicken, put my fork down, and wiped my mouth.

Matt laughed. "Don't hold back on my account," he said, smiling—then, "So, back to...Jake, is it?"

"What about him?"

"Why does he leave you alone? Why isn't he calling you right now?"

The waiter walked up. Matt motioned for him to remove our plates, then asked him for another crown and coke, while I leaned back in my chair debating what to tell him.

"You want anything else to drink?" Matt asked.

"Just more water," I said. The waiter left and I said, "There is something I haven't told you. Something I'd really like your opinion on that happened between me and Jake. But I feel like telling you would be an invasion of his privacy."

"Okay," Matt said. "What if I guess it?"

I laughed. "You won't guess this," I said. "Jake and I are anything but predictable."

Matt didn't say anything, but he looked disgusted.

"Anyway," I said. "Maybe I should just leave it alone. Let's talk about something else."

Matt said, "When's the last time you talked to him?"

I was stunned. No one asks me that. The people that know me and Jake, except for Maeve and Ted, who I hadn't talked to in months, just don't ask. They know Jake's patterns. And how much I was hurting. It just wasn't brought up. And now, faced with the thought of how long it had actually been, I felt paralyzed. I should have been angry too. However much at ease Matt and I had been, it wasn't a question to be asking someone you've known for less than a full day. But oddly, I felt no anger—just sadness. Finally, I said very softly, "Five weeks ago."

Matt winced then said, "You know the saying don't you? How it takes three weeks to break a habit?"

I stared straight into the blue of his eyes, leaned forward and put my right hand on the table. I was angry now. "I am not a habit," I told him.

Matt put his hands up in the air. "Sorry. God. Easy there." He put his hands back down, then smiled at me. "But if you were, you'd be a good one," he said.

I looked away, in no mood to be flirted with. A couple had rented one of the swans. They were floating toward us. Cutting through the black water softly.

Matt prodded on, "What did he say the last time you talked?"

I gave Matt a sarcastic smile. "He said, 'I'll talk to you later.'"

Matt chuckled. "Yeh, well I guess we all have our different concepts of *later*. Me—I'd have thought he meant later that day."

"I did too," I said, looking back at the floating swan and the couple, who were leaning into each other. I turned back to Matt, then lowered my head. "But after about a week," I said to my lap, "I started getting the message."

Matt said, "And what is that?"

I looked up at him and said, "I don't know." I paused, thinking I might not be able to hear myself talk anymore out loud about the man I wanted to be with so much at that very moment— "That this is not what I believe it is," I finally said. "That Jake really doesn't love me. That a lot of what I think of as our incredible journey this past year and a half, the way we've been there for each other through so much and learned and loved and just lived a lifetime in less than two years, that, you know, it didn't mean all that to him."

Matt said, "Unbelievable."

"What?" I asked.

"It makes no sense," he said. "It's like something's missing."

I sat up straighter, took a deep breath, exhaled, and said, "Because there is. I told you what Jake said the last time we talked. But I didn't tell you what happened the last time we were together."

"What?" Matt said. "Were you arguing?"

"Yes," I said.

"What?" he said. "What were you fighting about?"

"Senseless stuff at first," I said. Then I didn't say anything for awhile, thinking again of how little time I'd known Matt. One part of me feeling I'd known him longer. Sometimes I was sure that everything and everyone you met were in the stars and that resisting in moments like this one was an act of arrogance. What did you stand to gain by not sharing. What might you lose? And even though I felt like voicing the conflict somehow made it more real and harder to overcome, suddenly I wanted so much to tell someone, anyone what had happened. To get a second opinion.

I was about to speak, when Matt said, "He didn't hurt you, did he?" Then he clenched his perfect white teeth together. "Because if he did, if that son of a bitch laid one hand…"

I stopped him. "No. No," I said. "It wasn't like that. Jake would never hurt me. Not that way. No. Stop. Calm down. He is very protective of me and very gentle."

Matt was breathing hard, but he seemed to be settling down.

"No, listen, I said," still struggling with my need to talk about Jake and my need to keep our recent quarrel in the realm of memory, "listen…I got off track thinking about things. Let me start over. You see, the evening we had the fight, I'd brought him dinner. He didn't ask me to. I called him and offered to bring him some because I was having a casual dinner meeting with a potential employer at a diner right down from his house. At first he said no, that he had to run some errands after work, but then he called back and told me he wanted a gyro. So I ordered one and brought it to him. I didn't check to see if it was made the way it should have been, which is my fault because my waitress appeared to be from another planet and she hadn't gotten any of my order right. But, somehow, I thought she would—his. When I brought Jake his dinner, he opened the Styrofoam box, and found they'd put steak on his gyro, not lamb. And he was not a happy camper. I kept thinking he should just have been grateful I'd brought him dinner. But Jake wasn't grateful. No, he actually seemed angry or frustrated and angry, and he told me several times how I can't get anything right. That should have been my cue to leave. Bill Engvall's voice should have sounded in my head, 'Here's your sign. He's not in a good mood. You tried to do something nice, but he isn't in the mood for nice, so just go.' But, of course, there was no sign and no voice of reason and I stayed. And Jake's mood got worse. Before I could stop myself, I was crying for some unknown reason, all of a sudden admitting to him I hadn't been completely honest, that I'd told him just recently having another child didn't really matter to me and I didn't need to get married again but that the truth was I did want to marry him and I still wanted us to at least consider having a baby."

Matt cleared his throat, then took a long drink of his crown royal. He set his glass down heavily and said, "Yeh, you should probably have left after the gyro thing."

I laughed. Not a big laugh. Just one to break the tension.

Matt smiled.

"So," I said. Dr. Freud or is it Intern Freud, what do you make of that?"

Matt said, "What did he say?"

I rolled my eyes. "He said...he said a bunch of things. First, he said, because somewhere in that whole thing I forgot to tell you I asked him if he loved me...anyway, he said, 'If I have to answer you right now, the answer is no.' Then he said, 'You know how I hate being forced into making decisions.' And finally he said, 'I think you should just do what is best for you.'"

"You have a good memory," Matt said.

"Some things are hard to forget," I said.

We sat in silence for what seemed like half an hour, Matt cracking his knuckles and me fiddling with my dress. The waiter came and asked if we wanted dessert. We said "No thanks" together. Then Matt said, "Just the check."

When the waiter left, Matt sat up straight in his chair and leaned across the table. He said to me, "You still want an unbiased opinion?"

I said, "Yes, yes I do."

458

He said, "Well, first of all, a disclaimer. Because it won't be unbiased." He lifted his index finger into the air. "Number one, I'm a guy." Then he put his middle finger up beside it, "And number two, I like you. But…" He cleared his throat, then went on, "I can give you an honest one if you still want that."

"I do, and the wait is seriously about to kill me," I said, getting a little of my humor back and genuinely curious now.

"Okay," Matt said, smiling, "here goes." He leaned back in his chair and I leaned forward. "The guy…" he began.

"Jake," I said.

Matt rolled his eyes. "Okay, Jake, sorry. I should say his name. Anyway. Jake loves you."

My heart started racing like I was running a sprint and my face turned red. I'm sure Matt noticed but he ignored it.

"I'm not telling you this because you want to hear it. I'm telling you this because I know it. I'm a guy. And when a guy does not love a woman and she asks him if he loves her, he has only one answer. 'I do not love you.' Not 'If I have to answer you now…' No. If he doesn't love her, it is always the standard five-word reply. 'I do not love you.' That's it. It's ingrained in us. It's in our DNA. We come into this world knowing it. I mean, we may not know much, but we do know one thing and that is—when it comes to love—you don't leave things up to interpretation by a woman. No, trust me, if a guy doesn't love you, that is exactly what he will tell you. 'I do not love you.' Ten out of ten times. But, if you just pissed him off, or confused him so much he can't think straight, and you ask him right then if he loves you, he's gonna mess with you. Which is exactly what Jake did. Doesn't mean he doesn't love you. Just means he isn't getting what he wants, so he's gonna make damn sure you don't get what you want."

"What does he want?" I demanded.

"Well…." Matt leaned toward me and smiled. "For starters, lamb on his gyro."

I had to laugh.

"Wait, wait," I'm not finished. You said, he said, 'you know I don't like being forced into making decisions…something like that? All right. Right there, you have part of your answer. He feels like you're putting pressure on him. And let me tell you, if you haven't already figured this out, there is nothing we hate worse."

"I know," I said, glancing shamefully into my lap.

"Okay," Matt said, putting his hands on the table, "Now the last thing he said is the key to this whole thing. What's going on with you two."

My eyes started to water. "I know," I said, wiping a tear. "It's like he was telling me without telling me—it's over."

"What?" Matt asked incredulously. "You know," I said. "When guys say one thing and mean another."

Matt looked outraged. "No," he said. "No, I don't. And you know why?"

"Why?" I asked, a little frightened.

"Cause we don't do that! Women say one thing and mean another. Not men. Not ever." Matt shook his head. "Okay. Okay. Let me give you an example. We've only known each other for what—like two hours?"

I nodded.

"Okay, you've already done it once and I just met you. Remember when I asked you if Jake hurt you?"

I didn't understand what Matt was getting at, and I was quietly getting very angry he was insinuating that Jake would hurt me. I said in a low voice between clenched teeth, "Yes?"

I could see Matt hadn't picked up on my feelings, because he blurted out, "You said he is gentle, when what you meant is that he's good in bed."

I blushed.

Matt smiled, half laughing. "See, I'm right. Admit it. I'm one hundred percent dead right."

I smiled and said bashfully, "Okay, so you're right. Once."

Matt smiled. "Thank you. I rest my case. It's women, not men, who say one thing and mean another."

I smiled again. "Okay," I said. "You win."

"That's right," Matt agreed. "Anyway, back to what we were talking about."

"I know," I said. "But still, even with what you say, and you have a point, but it's like he was telling me without telling me—it's over."

Matt groaned and rolled his eyes. "God," he said, "I'm starting to feel sorry for the guy."

"What?" I said.

Matt leaned back, as if he were giving up. Then he leaned forward again and looked straight into my eyes. "You are without a doubt the most stubborn woman I have ever met."

I laughed.

"Don't laugh," he said. "It's not an attractive quality. And I'm sorry to sound so sexist but it is not an attractive quality in a woman."

I narrowed my eyes. "Oh," I said. "And it is in a man?"

"No," Matt said, "I didn't say that. I said it isn't an attractive quality for a woman to have. Unusual. But not attractive. And for you and Jake. Well, it just sounds to me like two bulls in one relationship. I mean, one of you needs to learn to back down. And let me just tell you—it isn't going to be Jake."

"So," I said. "Is it over? Is that what Jake was saying?"

Matt winced and pounded his fist on the table. "God you're stubborn. Or deaf, one. What did I just tell you? What little male secret did I just let you in on?"

"I don't know," I said. "I mean you said that guys say what they mean… but…."

"That's it!" Matt jumped up. "Now, you're getting it! There may be hope for you yet." The waiter arrived with the check.

I smiled.

Matt sat back down. "What he said—the last thing Jake said was, 'I think you should do what is best for you.' Right?"

I nodded my head.

"Haley," Matt softened his voice, "that is exactly what he meant."

For a couple of minutes, neither of us said anything. Then Matt took a sip of his water and said, "Want to go for a walk?"

I was grateful for the suggestion. I needed to move, even if it meant snaking around couples in love. I told him that would be great. And Matt paid the check.

We walked out on to the path around the lake and headed to the right. Matt said, "You told me about your acting and about that t.v. show, what was that, Dreamhouse? The one you auditioned for?"

"Yeh. Dreamhouse," I said, rolling my eyes.

"Yeh." he said. "And I've tried to tell you, you don't talk like other people. I mean beyond the fact you seem to be able to do it for minutes without breathing."

I stopped walking and turned to look up at Matt raising my eyebrows. He stopped with me and raised his eyebrows in answer, and we both laughed. Then I said, "No, seriously, what do you mean?"

"I'm as serious as I can be. The best I can explain is that you talk like you're writing."

I didn't say anything. And we started walking again.

"Don't get me wrong," he said. "I think it's cool. Really cool. But it's not normal. The way you remember things. The way you describe them. I had an aunt like you."

Matt grew silent. And I was almost afraid to ask what happened to her. But I said, "You said, 'had.' Did something happen to her?"

"Yeh," Matt said, stopping to stare out at the lake.

I stopped beside him and waited.

"She killed herself," he said after a long time. "Tied herself to a block of concrete, then tipped herself into the pool when no one was at home."

I swallowed hard. Matt put a hand on his forehead.

I said, "I'm so sorry, Matt."

He let out a deep breath. "I was a kid," he said. "I was actually thirteen. She was my favorite aunt. Really my favorite relative, my dad's sister. I think my dad didn't know what to do. How to tell me. So he had my mom do it."

Matt sighed again. "Which was a big mistake," he said. "See, my mom, well, I love my mom, but we're different. She's the one I get my ability to be a doctor from. She's aces in science and math. Anything practical. But I get my heart from my dad. He's what you might call a romantic." Matt paused for a minute.

I smiled up at him.

He went on, "Yeh, but, um, he couldn't take telling me about Aunt Kate, so he just, he let mom do it, and for years I never forgave him."

"What did she do? I mean, what did she tell you?" I asked.

Matt looked down at me. He said, "She sat me down on my bed one afternoon after school and said, 'Something has happened, Matt, that's not altogether a surprise to your father or me. Your Aunt Kate killed herself.'"

I put my hands to my face. "She didn't say it that way," I protested, "that it wasn't altogether a surprise?"

Matt nodded. "She did. That's exactly what she said. I'll never forget it." He was silent for a minute, then added. "I thought Aunt Kate loved life. That of all the people I'd ever met…she got it. And that she would never let it go."

Matt started to cry. And I reached up and tried to put one arm around this big hulk of a man. But it didn't fit. And when I could feel I was being no comfort I let it drop, and we just stood there in the light of a street lamp until he stopped crying. He wiped his tears off on the sleeve of his scrubs. Then he cleared his throat. "Well," he said. "So much for being the big tough guy. Blew that image all to hell, didn't I?"

I told him, "Not to worry. I've already got a tough guy in my life."

Matt tried to smile. "Okay," he said, walking again. "Enough of me. Back to you. So, I was saying, I think you're really a writer in disguise. Or an artist. An actress. Something. You're not a garbage dumpster salesperson, I know that for sure. And that is all Jake was saying. Only he said exactly what he meant. Do what's best for you. That's it."

"Not—without me? He wasn't saying, without me?"

"Did he say that?" Matt asked.

"No," I said, "But…."

"But nothing!" Matt almost shouted. Then he turned his head towards me. "Haley, I'm probably stepping over the line here. And I'm sorry about that. But I gotta tell you the truth." Matt paused and I couldn't help wondering what in the world he was going to tell me next. Then he just blurted out very matter of factly, "Men are dogs."

I couldn't help laughing.

Matt smiled, but then he got serious again. "Don't laugh," he warned me. "We are. All of us." He stopped to face me. "Do you know what I thought when I found you tonight?"

I swallowed hard, not really wanting to hear the truth, but said, "What?"

Matt went on, "I thought, 'Hot damn,' the Good Samaritan finally gets his reward."

I laughed, then said, "No, you didn't."

"The hell I didn't," Matt said. "I mean, I would have helped you anyway, you know, even if you weren't beautiful. I didn't know what you'd look like when I stopped, but when I saw you were—how shall I say it, knock down dead gorgeous, yes, that's it—let me tell you, I'm thinking, 'All right, Matt, my man, Christmas early.'"

"All right," I said and laughed. "Stop it. You've made your point. Sort of single handedly painting two biblical events in a different light for me."

Matt said, "You know, I know you've been with men. You told me you were married. But you really...I'm not trying to hurt you. I mean this in a good way.... You really don't know much about men. You're like. I don't know." Matt paused, but then it came to him. "Like the girl next door. Like... like that 'Stand by Your Man' woman. The real deal."

I looked up at Matt.

"You know?" he said to me. "Do you even know you're the real deal?" Two parents walked by us with their little boy holding a handful of colored balloons. I knew Matt was trying to be sweet. And he was. But the whole night was getting to me. I covered my mouth so I wouldn't hurt Matt, who was looking at me through very confused, hurt eyes, asking, "What? What's so funny?"

"Everything," I said, trying to stop laughing. "Life. This night." I looked up at Matt. "I'm sorry. What you said was incredibly sweet. I'm not laughing at that. Or you. I'm laughing at what Maeve said."

"Who's Maeve?" Matt asked annoyed. Then remembered—"Oh, that friend who told you your name was Irish."

"That's it!" I said excited. "That's all you know about her. But you told me the very same thing she told me—not the Irish name thing, the 'Stand By Your Man' thing. And…and…your brother hears voices like my daughter. And…and, I think things aren't working out, and I don't understand what is happening and then it storms and my windshield wipers stop working and I pass out and you save me. Then you tell me about my name and the very same other thing a friend told me months ago…and…and…" I caught my breath, then went on. "It's all connected." I jumped up and down. "I get it!" I said. I get it now. I mean it may not be my plan, but there is a plan." I looked up into the stars. "There is a plan."

"Yeh," Matt said, smiling down at me. "Right back at cha."

I laughed.

Matt said, "Back to what Jake said. That part about do what is best for you?"

"Yes?" I said.

"He's right. You know I don't know you like he does. I'm sure he knows what you do best."

I blushed.

"Not that," Matt said. "All right, that. But other than that. He knows you. He knows, just like I do, you weren't made to sell garbage dumpsters. But more than that. He knows what I can only guess at. But that's not important, Haley. It makes no difference what we do or don't know about you. All that matters is that you know it. God, if I could tell you only one more thing. If this is it. If I never get to spend another minute with you, if Jake wins, I'd still tell you the same thing."

"What?" I said.

Matt stopped and took my face in his hands. Then he said, "Be yourself. Be who you are. Stop masquerading as some garbage salesperson. It's ridiculous. And it isn't you. And why wouldn't you want to be you? There's no risk in being you. Hell, you've taken all the risks. Being who you aren't.

And look what it's cost you. Just look. I mean your daughter is sick. You are stressing yourself out so bad, you're passing out on the road. And what for? Do you think that garbage company you work for gives a damn about any of that? Do you?"

"No," I said.

Matt lifted his hands into the air. "Hell, no, they don't. They don't give a damn about you. But I do, Haley. I may not know you very well, and I know you told me you love Jake, but I care about you. So much I can't even believe it."

I smiled a little, but just as I did, I thought about Jake and how much I missed him and something snapped and I started to cry.

Matt put his arms around me. We stood in the path out of the light for what seemed like minutes. Finally, I looked up, just when a flock of colored balloons floated over our heads.

"Look," I said, pointing up at them. "Color filled with breath, daring the night to be so dark."

"Yeh," Matt said, smiling down at me, "That's just what I was gonna say."

And then we both laughed, warm, bright, hope-filled bursts of laughter—just like balloons.

Chapter 60

S u r v i v i n g

My truck was a '97 Chevy S-10. And that year, all Chevy S-10's were installed with defective modules. In layman's terms, these are the doohickeys that control your wipers. Anyway, you would think General Motors would have been more thorough. Screened potential buyers more carefully. Had some sort of test to gauge their sense of reality. Like if you can't face the truth, you may not also own, if you live in a hurricane state, a vehicle with defective windshield wipers.

Summer days are long anywhere. But this past summer in Florida, my days felt both long and pointless. I somehow managed to keep a flicker of hope in my heart that Jake would come back to me. Looking back on it now, I know that flicker was my faith alone and my spirit.

Though I had long ago stopped running the courses he'd mapped out for me, I did run by his house one day, only to find he and Ray had both moved out and no one had moved in. So even if I'd had the nerve to ask when the former tenants had moved out, there was no one there to answer.

I was twelve miles from Brianna's when I discovered Jake had moved without telling me. And I cried the whole way home.

It's funny, though. The spirit I was given—how it will not let me give up. On anything. Dreams. Love. Life. And my imagination always working overtime, my ability to see past the truth and create a world I can live with. So I invented this little story to take me through my days and nights. Making Jake the hero, of course.

I decided he'd moved back in with his mother. To help her take better care of her house and property. And to save rent money. For our future together. He'd have a much longer commute to work and back home, but that wouldn't matter to Jake. He has always been a good son. He was focused on work, doing a good job at the dealership and developing his business on the side. All the while saving to surprise me. Just waiting until he had enough money to come back to me and say, "I always wanted to spend the rest of my life with you, but you know me, I wasn't going to do it without a plan."

The truth is, I had a phone with Jake's number in it and the waste management company I worked for was five minutes from the dealership where Jake worked. But I never called Jake, and I didn't stop by his work place to find out where he'd moved or anything else.

There was a part of me, a part I was daily reducing to almost nothing, my heart and soul, that told me Jake is just like me. That he can live with pain a lot more easily than he can observe another in pain. And I was definitely in pain. And I definitely needed to find a way to heal myself. But the thought of that just hurt more.

So I lived the dream I created—all summer. The one where Jake was a hero. And I was not a lost soul but the lady of his dreams. I lived it. Relived it. Added to it. So much so, it became both an escape and the truth to me. One I never questioned.

I was lucky to be in the waste industry, in spite of what Matt had said. Still with the technical revolution in fifth gear, it's a very high touch industry. Where my customers and prospective customers cared as much about me as I did about them. Where we took care of each other.

There was Maleeva at the Spanish bakery she and her husband Raul owned and operated. Who baked me fresh coconut bread and pleaded with me, "Eat, eat! You are too thin. Si, flaca. Thin. You look like una ave with broken wings."

And Maleeva was right. I needed to eat. At least something good for me. Sort of a pseudo health freak all my life, always drinking eight glasses of water a day, eating good fresh food, never smoking, taking no drugs, never doing more than the occasional social drinking, sleeping eight hours a day—I found myself rarely sleeping more than four hours a night, drinking as little water as possible so I wouldn't have to stop between sales calls to go to the bathroom, and my eating was either optional or consisted of very cheap fast food.

Part of my efforts to turn my life around, heal Ginny, get out of debt, and buy a home for Jake and Ginny and me consisted of a high interest payment plan to a debt consolidation company. When I went in for my first consultation with the company, my counselor advised me, after hearing about my debts and current income, to make one hundred dollar payments a month. But I didn't see how this would help me even put a dent in my debt. So with literally no objections from him, I devised a more aggressive payment plan. To the tune of four hundred dollars a week. Add that to my shark's truck payment of one hundred dollars (fortunately, my company did pay for gas and tolls and gave me a phone) I had roughly twenty-four dollars a week to live on.

So I became the queen of value meals. I could spot dollar-or-less specials from a mile away. There was Wendy's junior cheeseburger. Taco Bell's bean burrito. Crystal's baby burgers. And, of course, canned beans. Those were my good days. My bad days involved bananas. I would drive to the nearest discount grocer and buy the biggest banana I could find. Buy it. Peel it. Freeze it. Then I'd suck on it for a day or two or three, depending on the week's other needs. Now there's an ad for Eharmony I'm guessing would get more than a few hits. "Can suck a big banana for three days at a time."

Once again, I found my life filled with irony. With my concern for healing Ginny, seemingly insurmountable debt, and a heart like a well inside me filled with tears from missing Jake, I felt like I was carrying the weight of the world. But the truth is, I was losing more weight than I was carrying. And some days, after so many nights of not hearing from Jake, I remember literally feeling like I was disappearing. Then I would pinch myself. Feel the pressure of my own touch. Know I was still here. And that I had no one to pull me through. Except myself.

But even if I did feel like I was disappearing, I had my customers. And I loved them.

There was Manny, the grocer, with a handlebar mustache, who taught me about tropical fruits. He would pick up a mango as if it were his baby, hold it in his huge hands, smiling like a proud father, then say to me, "It is just right, this mango," handing it to me as though it were a Faberge egg. I would take the mango from him and hold it nervously. While he'd tell me, "Touch it. Feel it. This is the only way to learn. Your eyes will always deceive you."

I spent days with these wonderful customers: Raymond at the mattress store, whose wife refused to sleep with him. Alex, at the carpet place, who lost an eye in the first Gulf War. Cambria, in her flower shop, designing arrangements for the wealthiest of the residents in Winter Park, her hands riddled with arthritis, heart broken by some man who never sent her flowers.

I'd make certain they weren't missed in our pick-ups. That their lids were on, their dumpsters in tact. That our trucks weren't leaking oil or leachate on their property. That their bills were correct. I managed their waste. So they could manage their businesses.

It wasn't like running the sales department for four divisions of a Fortune 200 company. No—where I was, back on the streets, you couldn't complicate the business. Where I was, it was completely clear what it is about. Picking up trash. And...if you don't do that well, nothing else matters. If you can't do right by your customers, you can't generate enough rapport to cover your ass.

At the end of one of my ten-hour work days, I came home to lie down on my raft, only to find the new owner of Brianna's condominium standing in the kitchen unpacking. Brianna's father was very ill, and with her move, his illness, and selling her home long distance, she'd forgotten to call and tell me the new owner was moving in.

But as luck or God would have it, I'd spent the weekend before giving away most of the clothes and other possessions I had left to Goodwill. At the time, I was down to one closet of clothes and shoes and a couple of boxes of other stuff. In one weekend, I whittled that to a quarter of a closet and one box.

Much to the amazement of the new owner, I packed in fifteen minutes. Loaded my truck. Handed her my key. And drove away. From yet another home. Without anywhere to go. Later, I would realize that in my haste, I'd forgotten my raft. But I decided to be philosophical about that—told myself there wasn't anything left for me to stick to anymore.

Chapter 61

H o o k s

You've heard the saying "Timing is everything"? Well, almost. That and a little help from the big guy, who, you would have thought had had enough of me at this point. On top of the fact, it was his busiest season. Summer time. When everyone from the ages of thirty to sixty is busy trying to kill themselves, reliving their younger days. Men drinking until they can't stand up, never mind driving a Harley on I-4. Women, twenty-five pounds overweight, running in the Florida heat. Both of them frying themselves in the sun like catfish on a hot grill. Hoping, I guess, if they just get red enough, you won't see their wrinkles. Be blinded by the beauty of their Rudolph noses and necks.

§

You would have thought this would have been the time for me to admit to myself, apart from my dream, I did at least know where Jake was Monday through Friday from 7 a.m. to 6 p.m. and that I could at least call him or go by his place of work and ask for help. But not me. No way. I decided this was my mess and I didn't need to concern Jake with it. Just needed to clean it up myself while Jake was busy building our future. There. Dream in tact. Rose colored glasses securely on. I would be fine.

So, there I was, driving up Route 436, thinking I'd go to John's. Formulate a plan from there. When my cell phone rang. It was Jill, a new friend I'd made when my credit card was stolen. Jill was my personal banker, the day I discovered what had happened. And more than that, she was a friend, from the moment I met her.

When I told Jill what had happened about Brianna's condo, she insisted I move in with her. Right then. No questions asked. And because I was a woman without a home, without even a raft, I accepted. Thanking her and the big guy...once again.

Jill is one of those women whose intuition and heart carry them far beyond their experience. She is eighteen years younger than I am, with the face of Snow White, the body of a dancer, and the energy level of a two-year-old on a heavy diet of candy. And she has this incredible sense of how to take care of things and others. Like a carpenter of souls.

Jill not only let me live in her home, she made it her mission for me to enjoy what turned out to be my last summer in Orlando. Conjuring peace, laughter, warmth, new friends, space, and sunlight to take me through so many days that could so easily have been filled with a darkness beyond night. A darkness that levels black, with the painfully slow unveiling of a life where I couldn't heal my own child.

Jill loved to go downtown to socialize. She had scores of high school and college friends who'd moved back to the beauty of Orlando and anyone she didn't know tended to become her friend after being graced with one evening of her presence.

And one Friday night, when we'd both come home from jogging, she called up one of her friends to join us. Lucy. Lucy is a morning glory of a woman. Part spring and part petal. With a smile that would make Judas loyal.

Lucy arrived an hour later. Driving up in a shiny black VW convertible, then taking us off into the Orlando night.

I rode in the back seat. With two views. Either the back of Lucy and Jill's heads or the sky. I chose the stars. Hanging lower than usual that evening, whispering to me, "Enjoy this. It is short lived. You won't be here much longer."

We drove in silence for miles. Then laughed inside out for the same unspoken reason. That we'd all three spent countless days and nights searching for the right man. Only to keep rediscovering we feel happiest in the company of women who are our friends.

Once in Orlando, we ambled down narrow streets lit by neon orange, green, and yellow script announcing the different bars and collection of eclectic cafés. Music was bleeding into the summer night air, while the conversations of different passers-by muted notes here and there, making strange rhythms. Girls in stacked sandals, tight jeans, and backless chenille smocks dodged stares from boys by ducking their heads and whispering into cell phones. While boys and men walked with a slow saunter seemingly having to drag their torsos along. As if all had penises the size of bucks' in mating season, or at least imagined they did.

I walked in between Jill and Lucy, both very petite women. And I was still the smallest and shortest, adding to the Lilliputian visual effect of the group.

I told them, "Jake and I hardly ever went downtown. He really doesn't like to go downtown."

Lucy turned toward me, looking disgusted, while Jill smacked my forehead lightly with the heel of her right hand, saying, "Be healed!" She smacked me again. "No more Jake!" Then they both laughed.

Lucy said, "Yeh, forget him. Who loves you now, baby?"

And they laughed again.

I told them, "You guys!"

Lucy broke into song. "Wherever we go, whatever we do," and Jill and I joined her, wrapping our arms around each other, singing, "We're gonna go through it together." Then all three of us burst into laughter. Heart healing laughter.

We wound up in one of Jill's favorite spots, a bar on Orange Avenue called The Moose. It looks like a Bavarian ski lodge, with its dark wood walls decorated in moose, elk, and deer heads. Wrought-iron chandeliers hang from thick wooden beams, while strands of multi-colored lights lend color to the stairwell. All over the bar, carved pedestals, shelving—there are blinking Christmas decorations that stay blinking year round. There's a stone fireplace tucked into one corner of the room with plump purple couches surrounding it. And really no dance floor to speak of. If you want to dance at the Moose, you just have to find your own little patch of wood or stair or perhaps toilet to stand on. And, of course, have very good balance.

The Moose is always packed with people. You never just enter the Moose. Best case scenario, middle of the week, rainy night, you might only have to stand in line for five or ten minutes.

That night, after we'd made our way in, Lucy, Jill, and I wound our way through the couples, single guys, and groups of friends. Jill made it through first, heading for the bar, and bought our first round.

Lucy and I snagged one purple couch and waited for our drinks. In just a few minutes Jill came toward us, having arranged our three drinks in sort of a tripod she'd made of her fingers. I was having ginger ale, while Jill and Lucy drank beer.

We sat there on the couch for a few moments, just taking it all in, the music from the 80s playing in the background, the alcohol-inspired conversations and laughter, the outfits—the range of Peacock's colors—worn especially to attract attention.

Another girlfriend of Jill's, by the name of Rosalind, made her way to our couch. Gliding through the crowd like a belly dancer, throwing her thick auburn hair back and laughing like you can't die from living. Rosalind introduced Lucy and me to Sam and Steve, who were also friends of Jill. I remembered hearing Jill talk about Steve.

According to Jill, Steve was the confirmed bachelor in the group. The one who had never fallen for any girl he'd dated but had had many fall for him. Upon meeting Steve, I could see his appeal. He had nice features, nothing alarming about his appearance, but like so many men women find attractive, his looks weren't his strong suit. Steve's playing cards were his boyish charm and his quick wit. Both of which were greatly diminished on this particular evening by his consumption of the Moose's entire inventory of Guiness.

From the moment we met, Steve began insisting that I dance with him, while I began politely putting him off. But after I'd observed him dancing with both Jill and Lucy, bumping and grinding his pelvis into any part of their bodies they dared to get near him, I became more defensive. I hadn't had to use my right hook on him yet, but I definitely had it warmed up. Just in case.

§

You think I'm kidding. That this pint-sized woman you've been reading about wouldn't have a mean bone in her body. Never mind a right hook.

Think again.

I can thank only one person for giving me this gift, and it is a gift, because I don't ever have to cower in the company of the Steve's of this world or shrink from going where I want to, even though I came to realize long ago that there will always be at least one Steve at every gathering in life where anything stronger than V-8 is available.

Raz Guifford was the boy's name. Raz was the bully of my neighborhood, thirty years ago in my hometown. And though I have no idea where he is now, whether or not he taught his kids what he taught me, I will always praise Raz for giving me my right hook.

I was a favorite of Raz's though I was four years younger. I think he liked my spirit. The kids in my neighborhood used to play kickball nearly every night of the summer, and Raz would always pick me to be on his team.

And though all the girls in the neighborhood seemed in awe of his attraction to me, I took it for granted. Really didn't care about it at all. In fact, I was very selective about the guys in my life. Waiting until time to get married, start a home and family, to pick "bad boys," the ones I have continually chosen to be with for the rest of my life.

So anyway, back to Raz and the day we taught each other a lesson.

We were playing kickball in the field up the street from my house. And Raz had, once again, picked me to be on his team. It was his turn to kick. And my brother, who was the "pitcher" on the other team, rolled the ball to Raz. Raz took one step back from homeplate, hauled off and kicked the shit out of the red rubber ball, right into my brother's face.

As far as I was concerned, that meant one thing. I'd been standing behind Raz, next in line to kick, so I only had to take a couple of steps before I could throw myself on him, which is exactly what I did. Holding Raz in a full body tackle. At least for a few seconds. Until he threw me off his back with one arm, then stood straight up over me, straddling my crumpled body and unwittingly placing his crotch in direct line of fire, squarely in front of my right foot.

At this point, I had only one thought on my mind—to help my brother, who was kneeling behind Raz, moaning and holding his bleeding nose and mouth. And the fact of the matter was—Raz was in my way. So this time, I cocked my leg and kicked Raz as hard as I could. You know where. (Come to think of it…maybe Raz can't have kids.)

Anyway, Raz got out of my way. And I helped my brother home, where iced cloths and my mother's tender care were enough to heal his wounds. And where, a couple of hours later, there was a phone call. From Raz. For me. He said he wanted to apologize. That he didn't mean to kick the ball at my brother. Then asked if I'd meet him up in the field. Said he had something to give me.

My mother was still busy making sure my brother didn't have a broken nose, so I slipped out of the house unnoticed. And though it probably was not the best idea to have a private meeting with a guy I'd nearly neutered a few hours before, I was fearless.

I found Raz standing straight up in the field. Apparently totally recovered. He motioned me over to him.

I walked over, keeping what I thought was a safe distance between us—enough to give me a good head start in a run for my life if it came to that.

He said, looking down at me with his steely blue eyes, "I wanna teach you something."

I told him, "Yeh, I'm thinking it was the other way around, a little while ago."

Raz smiled, "Yeh, well, um, that's part of me teaching you. See, um, I kinda like you and um you oughta know that isn't the way to treat a guy."

I said, "You're right. It isn't the way to treat a guy. I've got brothers. I know that. But you kicked my brother in the face. You deserved it."

Raz put his hands on his narrow hips and said, "I told you…I didn't mean it. I wasn't trying to kick the ball in your brother's face. Hell, if I wanted to hurt him, I'd just punch him."

"Yeh?" I said, "You do that and I'll…"

"You'll what?" Raz challenged me.

"I'll kill you." I said. Meaning it.

Raz took one step toward me. "You don't mean that," he said.

I told him, "Try me."

Raz smiled. "Okay, mighty mouse. Listen up. I'm gonna teach you something today you're never gonna forget. And after you learn it, you won't need to threaten anybody by running your little mouth."

And so he did. And an hour and a half later, I had the meanest right hook in the neighborhood. Next to Raz's.

I was getting ready to thank him. Go home for supper. When Raz took my face in his hands, closed his eyes, and gave me my first french kiss. I was ten years old. And hooked. For life. On bad boys.

Now, thirty years later, I'm constantly amazed. At the adult population who spend half what they earn on some psychologist. Trying to figure out what Raz Guifford taught me at ten. That true passion is always worth the pain.

§

Lucky for him and me, Steve found another victim. And Sam sat down on the couch next to me. Sam is a dead ringer for John Stamos. A younger John Stamos. And after you recover from his boyish handsome good looks, it's his voice you notice. A combination of a man singing a love song and one telling you his dreams—honest, warm, introspective, like the telescope to his soul. Sam was wearing one of the ultimate female turn-ons. A light blue button-down shirt. Second only to a white button-down. And grey pants. Giving him this clean, hot look that every girl in The Moose seemed to prefer to the one the rest of the men were wearing—bowling shirts and tight jeans.

Sam and I talked for a little while. Then I danced with Jill. And Lucy. And after a while, Sam asked me to dance.

We moved through the crowd of drinkers talking to their various partners as if they needed hearing aids, our hips nudging their hips, feet lifting over sandaled toes. We found a space to dance in an alcove by the bar. And I learned very quickly I had a good partner.

The Moose was playing "Brickhouse," and I couldn't keep from laughing, wondering if Sam even knew what Top 40 hit meant when I was in college dancing to this song.

Like all good dancers, Sam has incredible rhythm. The music gets into his blood. That's how it is with born dancers. It's not so much that they are listening to the music then moving to it as they are one with the music. Like their bodies are instruments. Consumed by the beat. Riding rhythms that sound like their hearts.

After we danced to "Brickhouse" and three more songs, we were both breathing like we'd been running wind-sprints, and John asked me if I wanted some water. I nodded, "Yes," and went over to the couch to sit down.

Unfortunately, I didn't notice Steve with his back to me and managed to sit down right next to him. Steve immediately stood up in front of me, grinning from ear to ear and said, "Hey, you. I saw you over there. Dancing your cute little ass off. You come to daddy." Steve jutted his pelvis toward me. "Yeh," he said. "You think Sam can dance. Daddy's gonna rock your world."

Just then, Sam appeared with my water and said to Steve, "Daddy better sit his ass down before I beat it."

And I laughed out loud. As did Lucy and Jill, who'd been standing nearby watching Steve's little performance.

Sam sat down next to me and said, "I made them pour you bottled water. I don't trust the tap in this place."

I laughed again and said, "You're right. I'm sure the only thing you want out of the tap here is beer. Thank you for the water." And I took a drink.

Sam asked, "How is it?"

And I said, "Perfect. Fixed it just right."

Then Sam and I both laughed.

Though I didn't know it at the time, that would be the last night I spent in downtown Orlando that summer as I began to fill all my evenings with running at a track near Jill's apartment.

It was actually a park with a track and soccer field. And different soccer teams practiced there every night of the week. Having grown up with both my brothers playing soccer, I loved the atmosphere. Watching the boys running for the ball, trapping, kicking, heading, and throwing it. It felt like home to me.

I'd run around the track for over an hour. Listening to my favorite country singers—Martina McBride, Kenny Chesney, Toby Keith, Gretchen Wilson, and Lonestar.

I'd even sing the words sometimes, when the soccer players were yelling so loud I thought no one could hear me. "Let's be us again," I'd sing, tears pooling in my eyes, remembering Jake with me.

And sometimes, for a few minutes, those singers I love would take me away. To a place where life is as easy as taking one step at a time with the one you love.

Chapter 62

L a u g h i n g   M a t t e r

There are no more nights for me at The Moose. I spend my evenings with Ginny, either curled up on my parents' couch watching our favorite sitcoms, taking walks around the neighborhood, or dancing with her in the kitchen while we bake our favorite cookies.

Our life is very simple now. We share one bedroom, one bed, one dresser, one nightstand, and one closet. And after all we've been through, all of our possessions combined don't fill our small space up.

It amazes me. How I spent years doing what I don't do best. Buying thing after thing we never really needed. To finally be faced with the truth. If you are with the ones you love and you are doing what you are here to do, nothing else matters.

Except, I have to admit, it is nice to have a working t.v. And it was no small deal to any of us when my parents' t.v. kicked the bucket.

Not that I didn't appreciate its exit. No lingering in a semi-functional state. Causing everyone around it to take notice. Nope. Not our t.v. It gave us no warning at all. Just one day went from light to dark. Not even giving us time to call for help.

My mother did call a local appliance store she thought picked up appliances. When she got off the phone, she said, "Well, I just don't understand. They asked me if the t.v. works. Why would I be calling them to pick up a t.v. that still works?"

"What did they say when you told them no?" I asked.

"They said they only pick up working t.v.'s. I just don't understand," she repeated, incredulous. "But here's what's even stranger. I was curious enough to ask what they'd pay me to pick up the t.v. if it *were* working. And do you know what they said," she asked me indignantly?

"No clue," I said.

"They told me I'd have to pay them and it would be according to the size of the t.v. I just don't understand," she said once more.

Well, here's my question. Can a t.v. that doesn't work collect unemployment? Seems to me no stranger than that you should pay someone to take your working t.v. away. But I'm thinking about trying out that kind of business for myself. Just make a few trial calls at least. "Hello, this is Haley Robbins' No Hassle Appliance Pick-up. We're running a special today. I can come pick up your washer, dryer, refrigerator, stove, and t.v. for a flat fee of three-hundred if all are in good working order." I told Faith about my idea, and she said that years ago she had paid someone to come pick up a sofa-recliner simply because it was too heavy and bulky for her and Glen to move by themselves and they really had no choice because it wouldn't fit in the small house they were moving to. So there you have it. My idea may not be that far-fetched.

Fortunately, the very next day, my brother and his wife bought us a new t.v., and I couldn't have been more grateful. I mean there is only so much I can take, and missing re-runs of "Friends" is not one of them.

We did have to miss one night, though. Before we got our new t.v. And Ginny and I spent it entertaining my mother and father. Trying on our collection of Halloween costumes, one of the treasures I'd saved through all our moves by using one of those bags that you pump the air out of to pack twenty sweaters in a space the size of a shoe box. We paraded around the condominium singing Halloween songs my mother taught me thirty-five years ago. "Witches on brooms with cats and bats, fly round after dark in their funny black hats…." We danced, sang, and changed from one costume to the other—all of us laughing until we hurt. At midnight, we both collapsed on our bed, fully costumed still—Ginny in a fairy's dress and me in a footed cow suit with a head and five rubber udders on the front that looked like several small penises.

At 12:44 p.m. by the little lighted clock on the nightstand, I heard a loud cranking noise coming from the parking lot just outside our window. I looked out and saw the shark's "legal team," two men in a red and white pick up truck, towing my little blue truck.

With no job, I'd fallen a few weeks behind on payments, so I borrowed money from Faith and mailed the shark the payments I owed. I sent them registered mail, then called to confirm I'd sent them and to say I'd try to make my future weekly payments on time. That's when I was told the matter had been turned over to the "legal team," who I was now staring at, the guys in the tow truck.

So I quietly padded outside to address them. The driver, a big burly man with hair on every part of his body, including his teeth, stepped out of the truck, looked at me like he was seeing a ghost—not a cow—and said, "Look ma'm, we don't want no trouble."

Then his partner climbed down out of his side of the cab, looking wild-eyed and a little scared.

I glanced back and forth from one man to the other, took hold of two of the little udder-penises on the front of my costume and gave them a significant twist, turning my head to one side and setting my teeth together in a maniacal grimace, then shouted, "Trick or treat!!"

The driver's partner yelled "Shiiit! Let's get the hell outta here, man. She's crazy."

And I laughed my cow's head off.

Chapter 63

Navigating

I have no job. No house. And no car—or truck. But finally, at the age of forty-three, an idea of where I'm going. And just who I want to be with me on the rest of my incredible journey.

As you have read, a great deal of the positive direction in my life comes form one source. God. And in Asheville, Ginny and I have found one of God's houses downtown, a place called Celebration—led by a minister named Red River.

Red is part modern-day saint, part well-meaning father, and part Saturday Night Live comedian. A romantic philosopher, who delivers God's messages better than Elvis sings a ballad.

When we first started attending his services, I wasn't very sure I was going to be able to come out of them unscathed. Because at the beginning of all of them, the congregation calls the Holy One from the four directions.

Now, I've already shared with you how directionally challenged I am. So when Red announced at the first service Ginny and I attended we needed to face East, you should not be surprised I was the only one in the church who

faced west. Fortunately, though, I can learn to follow. And the whole congregation does do this "facing the directions" in unison: two-year-olds, blind
people, my daughter who hears voices. And after about ten weeks, I'm happy
to report, I'm about to get the hang of it.

Together, working with Ginny's counselor and psychiatrist, who both seem a bit enlightened by our struggle
and are actually listening to both Ginny and me, we have reduced her medication from a collective nineteen
hundred milligrams of anti-psychotics, anti-depressants, and anxiety inhibitors to two hundred milligrams of
one anti-psychotic, and one milligram of another, with dosages of the vitamin Niacin, which Dr. Abram Hoffer
began successfully treating schizophrenics with some forty years ago.[22]

Since a friend gave me the web address for Hoffer's Home Page, I've
been hungrily researching connections between mental health and nutrition.
As with any research, what you find on the way to looking for one thing may
be as enlightening as the thing you first set out to discover. In this case, everything I've found has been intriguing but so much of it disheartening. Not
that the vitamin link doesn't seem promising—it does. But what I've mainly
begun to see with a terrible clarity is that if you are the parent of a mentally ill
child, you need to be one of two other things—filthy rich or destitute. If you
are filthy rich, you can probably afford to send your child, for example, to a
place called Soteria House in Berne, Switzerland. Soteria House was developed by psychiatrist Loren Mosher and described by Peter Breggin as "a haven
for individuals undergoing their first 'schizophrenic' crisis." [23]

I read about Soteria House with longing, knowing Ginny needs such a
place and, with it, time to heal on her own, to grow, to mature. It's not likely
she'll ever see anything like Soteria, though sometimes since reading about it,
I have prayed for a miracle—some angel at the door saying, "Haley, you and
your daughter have been chosen...."

Anyway, according to Peter Breggin, when Mosher opened a Soteria
House in California he "chose a home on a busy residential street. For the staff, he sought people

who had sincere interest in listening to the seemingly irrational communications of the patients. They [the staff] were egalitarian and non-authoritarian individuals who didn't seek a hierarchy in which to feel superior and who didn't insist on artificial distinctions between themselves and their clients." [24] Soteria was "by almost any standard," according to Breggin, "a success story." [25]

To make a long story short, Breggin explains, " NIMH decided not to continue funding it and the Department of Health of California would not pick up the tab." [26] Breggin goes on to say that "health insurance companies—oriented to hospital treatment and the medical model—would not reimburse Soteria patients for the cost of treatment [and]…the drug companies—who support almost everything in psychiatry—did not offer any help." [27]

Over and over, Breggin mentions that "creative alternatives" to antipsychotic drug treatments for mental illness will continue to be difficult to find "as long as the psychiatric and medical monopoly controls the delivery of mental health services…." [28] Still my heart leaps when I read that this good doctor thinks places like Soteria House and other residential treatment options such as Burch House in Littleton New Hampshire and Spring Lake Ranch in Cuttingsville, Vermont are, among treatment alternatives, "the least expensive and most effective." [29] Though my reality is that I cannot afford any of these places for Ginny, I am glad for the few who can benefit by them.

Some days I remember a recent past in which I was among the top six percent of women wage earners. But, oh, how I've fallen. And Ginny and I really are now what most people in this country would consider destitute. At rock bottom, I am now finally eligible for help, though not the help I would choose. The Soterias and Burches and Spring Lakes are still out of my reach. And so…there is niacin and there is love, and there is always, I tell Ginny in her worst hours, hope.

Recently, hope has come through a government-based program. Ginny has a part-time mentor, who is teaching her how to paint and encouraging her drawing.

And Ginny and I exercise every day together. We've taken up memorizing poetry of the Romantics, learning and singing songs from our favorite Broadway musicals.

Ginny volunteers once a week at the Humane Society's shelter, cleaning up after the animals and taking them for walks and, as I heard her tell Faith one day, "loving them until they find a home here or in heaven."

At night, we still take walks, catching up on the past two years. Talking about how this time has reshaped both our lives. And after our walks, we stand in a kitchen filled with sharp objects, cooking dinner together, listening to Keith, Tim, and Shania. Dancing around the knives.

Chapter 64

Missed   Chances   and   Direct   Hits

I didn't see Matt again that summer. On purpose. But he did not forget me. A couple of weeks after we met, I walked out to my truck after work and found the bed of it filled with long stemmed red roses. And a note from Matt pinned under one of my wipers read,

Hope you at least got your wipers fixed. I see you didn't quit selling dumpsters, just as you didn't let me follow you home the night we met, or kiss you, or have your number. You are a true lady, Haley, in love with a fool. But I may be a bigger fool for believing your heart might change. But I will keep on believing. I can't forget you. You are on my mind every day and I have to hope I am on yours. Jake has had all the time in the world to learn what I did in two hours. That you are the kind of woman men dream of spending a lifetime with. And he walked away from you. I'm here, Haley. Give me a chance. I miss you every minute of every day.

Unsung

Love,

Matt

P.S.   *Just in case Jake decides to pitch the roses, I left
the thorns on them.*

Now, I'm not a gambler, but I'd bet my life any woman I know would have driven straight to the hospital to find Matt. But not me. I wrote him a note, and had a friend at work deliver it to him. It was part thank you for having rescued me and part confession of my steadfast love for Jake. The friend told me he read it without blinking. Then crumpled it into a ball and threw it into the nearest waste basket.

* * *

While my every day was filled with a prevailing and foreboding sense of good-bye, all of central Florida was focused on the arrival of Charlie. The worst hurricane to hit Orlando in twelve years.

Anywhere you went, you'd hear people talking about the impending storm: at the gas station, the grocery store, the mall, the movie theater. All the d.j.'s on the radio were discussing it. The prediction was that the eye of the storm would hit Orlando. And the prediction was right.

Days before, I stocked Jill's apartment with batteries, an ice chest, ice, a portable radio, candles, and non-perishable food. But the day of the storm when the forecast for damaging winds and heavy rain became more alarming and real, Jill's parents insisted we stay with them at their home in Maitland.

So we packed up our supplies and headed for their home where we spent the night cooking Italian, drinking wine, and watching the storm gather.

492

Jill's family is Italian. You don't hear any "Do you know what I mean's" at their dinner table. When they say something, you know what they mean. And you can see in their eyes how this has shaped all their lives. Making things easier for some and for others incredibly painful.

We lost power around 9 p.m. Our light source changing from lamps to candlelight and our entertainment from television to story-telling. At one point, we did walk outside. The rain blew a thousand flicks of water into our faces, sharp and light, stinging us like a swarming of sweat bees.

Jill's brother and father seemed very excited by the storm. Walking up and down the street, pointing to bowed trees, downed power lines, pitching fallen limbs to the curb. While Jill, her mother, and I were more quieted by it. Watching them from just inside the opened garage. Mesmerized by the power of the winds on an edge of the storm.

Charlie raged on all night. Doing millions of dollars worth of damage to central Florida, ironically not touching me or anything I owned. Almost as if it knew, unlike most of the residents of central Florida, it had not been twelve years since I had to survive a storm.

The next morning, I woke up, assessed the clear roads in the neighborhood, thanked Jill and her parents, and headed for my church's morning service. There were no working lights. Those driving had to navigate roads with downed trees and power lines. But actually, considering the chaotic state we were all in, the residents seemed pretty calm. And once again I found myself witnessing first-hand how crisis and even tragedy brings out the best in people.

When I arrived at church, I found the steeple in the sanctuary. And the service moved to a building without power. And later, I learned that over half the congregation had been devastated by the storm.

There were those whose life-support systems had temporarily shut down, others whose homes had been demolished, and still others who'd passed away, unable to deal with the natural disaster. And once again, I thanked God. For the strength he'd given me. To help myself and others. And I volunteered to join one of the teams we were assembling to help rebuild homes and, in some cases, lives.

My team met in the church parking lot, a couple of hours later their jeeps and trucks were loaded with bricks, tarps, chainsaws, water, coolers, ropes, hammers, nails, and garbage bags. We headed for the home of an angel, a singer in our choir, by the name of Melanie, whose home in Winter Park had been christened by an eighty-foot oak.

We found Melanie standing in her front yard, her beautiful smile untouched by the pain of having her home partially destroyed. Kindly greeting each of the helpers as though she'd invited us to a party. And though I knew nothing of this woman but her lovely voice and current trouble from the storm, I could sense she is a survivor.

You can feel this when she sings. Her voice, part baby's breath, part butterfly wings. A touch of flame and an unbroken fall. I have lost track of the times a single song from her carried me through a week. Until I could hear her sing again. And feel hope.

We worked all afternoon in the pouring rain, trying to remove the tree and its limbs from where they had fallen. Most of the pieces of limbs I carried to the curb were bigger than my own body. And after about three hours of lifting and carrying them through the pouring rain, I found myself mostly pulling and dragging them through foot-deep puddles, while the men continued to saw all day on the trunk that would rival some redwoods I've seen.

By six in the evening, we all found ourselves soaked and completely exhausted and after we tarped the holes in Melanie's roof and weighted the tarps with bricks, we headed back to church for a huge bonfire and cook-out. And to say thank you to God. For giving us all the strength and faith and hope we need at any time to carry on.

I should have left Florida the next morning. After such a blessing of a day. But...how does the song go? "Like a fool I went and stayed too long..." So true.

Much too long.

After nine weeks of not speaking to Jake, I had spent another one without a call from him. The week Charlie hit. And while Jill and her family couldn't stop talking, anger and disbelief filling their voices, about how Jake hadn't called to check on me, I was finally silenced.

Because I knew Jake knew, better than anyone, I had no family or home in Florida. And would have had to assume, since we had not spoken all summer, I was alone when the worst storm to hit central Florida in twelve years touched down in Orlando.

I was silenced. With a hurt beyond words.

And I had another choice to make. I could choose to be angry with Jake, judge him, and never forgive or forget when he was not there for me. Or…I could choose to remember all the times he has been there for me, that Jake is human, that we all do things we wish we hadn't and don't do things we could have. And that the best choice any of us can ever make is to love and to forgive. And that is exactly what I chose to do—love and forgive Jake.

I was working twelve-hour days, helping my company with the part it played in the storm clean-up, but the first moment I could, I called Jake to make sure he and his family were all right.

He answered my call on the second ring, and his voice scared me. For one thing, I hadn't heard it in months, and I really wasn't expecting him to answer. I'd called around lunch time on a week day when Jake was working. And he sounded both annoyed and angry.

I apologized for calling him at work. Then asked if he and his mother and brother were all right. He said, "I'm fine. We're fine," like a door slightly cracked, shutting. I told him how I was sorry that I hadn't called, how I'd been busy at work, then said I was glad everyone was fine and how I'd just wait for him to call me. He mumbled, "Okay," And we both clicked END, the instant of silence I heard telling me he had been first by a breath to disconnect us, and that I shouldn't hold mine waiting for him to call.

I called to make certain Jake and his family were all right after the storm. But I also wanted to tell him how much I missed him. That I love him. And always will. But after hearing the tone of his voice and the few words he had to say after so much distance and silence between us, my heart stopped me. It had had enough. Of showing everyone how resilient it can be. Was struggling to beat at all.

Chapter 65

Wheels Turnin'

A week after my phone call to Jake, I finally did leave Orlando. Because I finally did realize it was time for me to go and because I was fired.

It is sort of funny. In the end as it was in the beginning with the waste management company I'd gone to work for, it was all about tires. Or how they did not want to buy them.

It turns out the tires on my truck were not new. Two were actually plugged. And in one week, I had both a flat and a blow out. Not really surprising if you consider I was averaging driving two hundred miles a day.

What I did not have was a wreck. And though I was greatly inconvenienced two times in a row, I couldn't help smiling. Just thinking about how what Jake calls my "terribly inadequate driving skills" had managed to save me not once but twice—again.

When I was hired on, I was told by the management that the gas card I was given also had a maintenance allowance. So I phoned the proper officials and found out what that was. It turns out it was only two-hundred fifty dollars for the year. But, fortunately for me, enough to buy two tires. I went to get the tires immediately, wanting to avoid having an accident while working. The tire company phoned my company to ask for verification on the maintenance allowance. It was readily given. So I got two new tires. Drove straight to work on them. To be fired.

I know I should have been outraged. Found some sort of connection between this and a member of management's asking me a few days before if my daughter is, in fact, mentally ill. Coincidentally, a couple of weeks later, I would have earned full-time benefits for myself and Ginny. I should have run to the phone right then and there to call NAMI. But, the fact is, I hadn't lost perspective. I'd finally gained it.

I'd been working for a company who cares nothing about the safety of its own employees, never mind others. Not only not helping heal my daughter but endangering me and everyone I encountered on the road as well. And it finally hit me. Why I got the new tires. To go home.

§

It took me fifteen minutes the next morning to pack up my life, write a thank you to Jill, and hit the road. I had one stop to make before I drove out of town. And I headed in that direction. To Carson's. To say goodbye.

On the way there I called Jake. This time, he did not answer. I left a message on his voice mail. Something about how I was going back to Asheville to take care of Ginny, but I hung up before I was even finished when I realized I could keep on talking into a recorder, Jake wasn't listening.

I found Carson standing on her patio, dressed in a t-shirt, jean shorts, and her cowboy hat, wearing open-toed sandals.

I walked up to her and looked down at her toes, then said, "I hope you weren't planning to mow the grass in those."

Carson laughed and gave me a playful shove. "No, missy," she said, "unlike you, I learn from my mistakes."

I laughed.

Carson said, "Speaking of your mistakes, where's puppy dog? 'Ol Jakey boy?"

I ducked my head out of the sun and said, "You tell me and we'll both know."

Carson smiled half way then pressed her lips together and said, "Oooo, that's pretty harsh coming from you, missy."

I told her, "Don't get too excited. Nothing's changed. For me, that is. I still love him. But...um...well, it's not fair for me to assume things..."

Carson cut in, "Not fair? Not fair? Shit! You don't even know how to be unfair. Trust me. There's all kinds of unfair in your life, but it ain't comin' from you."

I didn't say anything, while Carson walked over to one of her planters hanging from the railing around the patio and started savagely deadheading a bunch of yellow mums.

She told me, "Mark this down in the record books. The first time I've ever been wrong." Then she looked up at me, holding the heads of several mums, "Yep," she said, "mark it down. 'Cause I'd have bet my last dollar that son of a bitch is too smart to let you go. But," she added, "tossing the dead heads into the yard, "guess I was wrong. And," she said, staring straight at me, "if I were you, missy, while he has his head turned or up his ass or wherever it is, I'd run like hell. And..." She winked at me. "I wouldn't look back."

"Well," I said, throwing up my hands. "I guess that's what I'm gonna do. I mean leave. Guess I'm outa here."

Carson looked me straight in the eyes. Then she glanced out at my truck. And back at me. She said, "I knew you'd tear the clutch up."

And we both laughed.

"Hey," she said, "Get outa here."

I was trying to think of something memorable to say. To tell her how much her friendship means to me and thank her for being so sweet to Ginny, when she interrupted my thoughts.

"I got another job, you know," Carson told me. "It's good, too. I like it. Couldn't have gotten it without that recommendation you wrote me. You're one hell of a writer."

I dug the toe of my shoe into some dirt. "That's good,' I told Carson. "I'm happy for you," I said, looking up at her. "You deserve it."

She told me, "Yeh, well it doesn't take too much to stand out here. Hell, this place is full of average. I show up at work and I'm a damn hero." Carson tilted the brim on her ten-gallon hat to keep her eyes out of the sun. "Whole place is packed with thirty-year-old drop-outs who spend whole days at the beach drinking an ocean of beer, then stumble back to Orlando to go downtown and drink all night. But you girl," Carson pointed at me, "you got something special. You don't belong here.'

I rolled my eyes.

Carson said, "It's true. I told you. I may live in Loserville now, but I come from horse country. And I know a thoroughbred when I see one. Hell, I'd bet on you to win every time. Every damn time."

I tried to smile.

Carson's voice cracked a little bit, and I could see tears forming in her eyes when she said, "Damn pollen," and wiped the tears now rolling down her cheeks, adding, "Makes my eyes water." Carson wiped her nose with the back of her hand and said, "Me, Ben, Jim, Jake—we're just average racehorses. Showing up at the race track and grinding it out every day. Getting slower and slower. Making our way to hell. We're not stupid, you know," Carson said, "that would be too lucky. No, God made us all just average enough to never really be good at anything and smart enough to know it. Yeh," she said, then smiled, "but he did give us beer. And liquor. And wine. What ever we need to drown our sorrows. And so we do. Every day. Drinking like there's no tomorrow."

I didn't know what to say. I wanted to defend Carson. I wanted to defend them all. But before I could speak, Carson walked over to where I was standing and hugged me tight. Then she took a step back and said, "Get outa here. Go make all our tomorrows brighter," she said, taking my hands in hers. "Put these little hands to work. Writing." Then Carson let go of my hands and looked at me, as if I could be the answer to her prayer, saying, "You got something to say, missy, and you need to say it. God didn't give you that girl and that talent for no reason. Now go. Write. Tell people about the hell you've both lived through," she said through tears. "Make things better. You can, you know." She told me, staring straight up and wiping her eyes. Then she said, "You be the dream. Be the dream."

I hugged Carson. For all the words that wouldn't come to me. I hugged her. And then I turned and walked straight to my truck. Never looking back.

§

It's a ten-hour drive from Orlando to Asheville. Nine, if you can pee in a cup and don't need to eat or stretch. Eight and a half if you don't need to pee or eat or stretch. And that day, I did it in seven.

Don't ask me how. I don't remember. Not the interstates I traveled on or the bridges I crossed. No landmarks. No side roads. It was almost like I slept the whole way. Like something else drove my truck and me home.

Chapter 66

G i f t s

When Ginny was a baby in my arms, I began telling her the story of her birth. How she was born in a brand new maternity ward in a beautiful room with pink and blue flowered wallpaper and a brass bed. It took one, two, three pushes and she was out into this world. The clock read 7:07 in the morning. From that day on, I told her, 7:07 means "Magic Time."

All her life, I kept telling her the story and for years, up until her breakdown, about once a week, our eyes would meet on a clock at our home, in our car, at an office, in school—a clock that read 7:07, and together we would say, "Magic Time!"

We decided to get up early on election day, hoping not to have to stand in too long a line to vote. I set the alarm for 7 a.m., but when it rang, I just shut it off and covered my head with the comforter. The next thing I knew, Ginny ran into our bedroom, jumped on the bed, and squealed, "It's 7:07!" And together once again, we said, "Magic Time!"

§

Brianna used to tell me my memory is God sent. That it is a true blessing because without it, Ginny would have been completely lost these past two years. But I believe all parents try to fill the empty spaces in their children's lives. It is often all we have to give them when they are in pain. Recalling some time in their life when things were easier for them, when they could see how they are loved.

But Brianna is right about my memory. It is God sent. Along with many other gifts I've been given. And I have been given many.

It didn't take me very long to notice how gifts can disconnect you as much as connect you to others. How good can be viewed as bad. Light as dark. How in this world the majority's perception is often valued more than the presence of one who is different.

One of the gifts I've been given, which separates me from others, is an ability to listen to more than one person at a time and still take in everything I hear. I actually didn't discover this ability. My parents did.

I thought it was perfectly normal to be able to listen to four different conversations at one time and remember them verbatim. But one night, when I was a child, we were driving home from a restaurant we'd eaten supper at, and I began telling my parents the different conversations I'd overheard at the tables around ours. They were both silent for minutes. You would have thought I'd told them I was dying or something worse. Anyway, finally, my father cleared his throat and said to my mother as if I wasn't in the car, "Do you think she's making that up?"

My mother looked over at my father, "Bill," she told him, "She's six years old. She doesn't even know what an abortion is. And what was that she said that man said? That thing about his manager's goals and his goals being mutually exclusive? Where would she get that from? How could she make that up?"

I could see my father's profile from my seat in back. He did not look proud. Or even amazed. No, I remember exactly how he looked. Like a man who'd just discovered his little girl just might not fit very well into this world. It's the look I've owned for two years.

But the truth is, even though I didn't make up those conversations, I easily could have.

When I was seven years old, I wrote a ten-page story to the editor of a local newspaper. It was Christmas, and I was trying to win a contest they were having. I wanted to be able to buy my family a Christmas tree and first prize was twenty dollars. I still have a copy of the story I sent. It is riddled with misplaced modifiers, sentences that ended with prepositions and began with conjunctions. And all the verbs are in the wrong tense. But the voice, the voice was clear. And it was mine. Filled with a deep appreciation for all of life. From the creak in my parents' worn stairs to Faith's artistic touch.

I won first place, bought a beautiful white pine. But what meant the most to me that Christmas was the note I got from the editor who told me very simply, "Write on! Write on!"

I often think about how I've passed these gifts on to my daughter. And how much she would like to give all of them back. How my gift for feeling at the deepest level, remembering every last little detail, may have hurt her beyond words. And my ability to hear any number of voices I choose to hear transferred into a paralyzing mental illness in her.

And while others who have children with mental illness search for any source but themselves, I readily admit what flows through me may have almost stopped my daughter's breath.

Though I've had moments of fury with the medical community, I also do not believe any of my daughter's doctors, counselors, or the staff who cared for her at the crisis unit meant to harm Ginny, nor do I believe they mean to harm others. They are simply misguided. Yielding to the pressures of a powerful pharmaceutical industry, who would have us all popping pills instead of trying to make positive changes in our lives.

And there is a mentally ill population in our country who definitely needs medication. Who literally cannot live without it. And for those people, I am thankful we have medicine.

But I am not thankful it is being misused to treat the masses, especially children who may recover from adolescent stresses.

Every time I turn on the t.v. and some mood-altering drug is being advertised, I think to myself, "There is no hope in the form of a pill. No love. No spirit. No faith. No forgiveness." All of these, however, are present in health care professionals, most of whom chose their field for the sole purpose of healing others.

But when the pharmaceutical companies fund medical research, doctors have few good choices. And these bright, gifted, loving, caring people turn into druggists. Mass distributors of harmful medications. Glorified pill passers.

I believe we must, we simply must find more and better financial resources than these companies to fund mental health research. We must begin to train and retrain all mental health care professionals to discover the workings of the mind and heart. To listen with compassion and open minds to their patients so we can truly learn how to help them. So we may positively connect troubled people to this world, not disconnect them with numbing medication.

This is my prayer every day.

Another of the gifts I've been given is the ability both to observe life and to live it at the same time. All writers have this. Rarely does a moment pass that I'm not both a part of and separate from at the very same time. This, like all gifts, has both advantages and disadvantages.

While it definitely makes for better perspective and more powerful writing, it has a tendency to piss some people off.

I tell all my readers, everything I write is part truth, part fact, part memory, part imagination, and part luck, but no matter what I say they usually see it differently. Their responses vary from surprise to denial and include every reaction in between.

"How could you?" "What were you thinking?" "I knew that's what you were thinking!" "Is that what you were thinking?" "You think that's what I was doing?" "So that's what you were doing." "I never said that!" "We did not do that!" "That is not what I was thinking." "You have no idea how I feel." "Why didn't you use my name?" "You used my name? I'm gonna sue your sorry ass." "I always thought you had talent."

It's been said, "If you are happy with where you are, don't question the path." But if I had to do it again, I'm not sure I would be able to spend six years working in the garbage industry. But having survived it, I do know I wouldn't have missed the experience for the world.

Every job has a saying that goes with it at the end of the day. If you're in theater it's "The show must go on." If you're in garbage, it's "Did we get everyone picked up?"

Riding around my hometown these days, the one thing that makes me still feel a part of it is seeing the dumpsters I sold. They're everywhere. This is less a tribute to my sales skills than it is to the driving skills of the men in green and gold who service them every day. Simply the best in the industry.

I see my drivers from time to time. We pass each other on the road. Wave. I give them a thumbs up. I will never forget any of them. And the incredible part of my journey with them.

Years ago, when I started with Environmental, Mario and my general manager, Ace Reddick, put me through a training program designed to make even a creative writing major and expert in garbage. It worked. Because both these men are experts themselves and because they care about their people.

My first day of training, I had to wake up at 2 a.m. to make it to the transfer station on time. I was scheduled to ride on a front-load truck, and my driver started his route at 3 a.m.

At the time, I was living three miles up on a mountain. And the fog was pea-soup thick. Driving my Honda Passport, I snaked down my dirt road like a criminal escaping in the middle of the night, thinking, "What in the hell am I doing?"

When I pulled into the transfer station, my watch read 3:15 a.m. "Damn it," I thought. "Late, my first day."

My front-load driver, Harold, saw me walking toward his truck. He glanced down at his watch, then up to me and frowned.

Harold told me, "Get in, hot stuff. You're late. And this is my heavy day."

We pulled out of the transfer station and headed for downtown Asheville. Straight through the charcoal morning. Harold told me I could crack my window just slightly while we were driving but before he picked up a box, I'd have to roll it up because a rat could fall into the cab.

I could tell Harold was still annoyed with me. He kept glancing down at his watch. But I was busy taking in Asheville at three thirty in the morning.

The streets were bare except for the other garbage truck drivers, and the streetlights made the puddles on the road look like wells of ink.

All the stores' windows were dark, their parking lots empty. And the air, through the little crack in the window Harold allowed me, smelled like snow tastes. Like crisp nothingness.

The first can we came to, I rolled the window up fast, not wanting to annoy Harold further. He lowered the forks on the truck, guided them into the box sleeves, lifted it, shook it, then frowned and set the box back down. He shut the engine off and got out of the truck. Just as he was stepping to the ground, a bleary eyed, ashen-faced man popped out of one side of the can, shaking a fist.

He yelled at Harold, "You're late! I thought you weren't coming and I went back to sleep."

Harold, who has the voice of a preacher, told him, "Sorry, man." Then he pointed up through the cab's window at me. "Got a new one. She's training. She made me late."

The man in the box looked up through the cab window at me, completely horrified. Then, voice shaking, he asked Harold, "She's not taking over your route is she?"

Harold smirked and said, "Hell, no. She cain't even get to work on time."

Even though I'd taken a job in the garbage industry and had had many others through the years in sales, I'd spent my life writing. Believing I understood the importance of timing and paying attention to details. But that morning, my first day picking up garbage, Harold taught me—I have a lot to learn.

§

This past year, the color lingered in Asheville. Well into November, there were still patches of it everywhere. Golds strategizing with pinks to hang on longer than the reds. All conspiring to stave off the browns and greys of winter. So, even with the imminent cold pressing closer every day, I still felt surrounded by warmth.

Ironically, the sunshine state, home in my heart, had one of its coolest falls. I've talked to all my friends there since I moved back to Asheville, and they all say I took the sunshine with me.

Ben, Jim, and Greg are busy at work, then at home, and they did their usual "killer" decorating for the holidays. Ben told me it wasn't the same this past Christmas without Ginny and me.

Sam spent a couple of weeks in Greece. He's flying to Las Vegas next. Then to Boston to see an aunt. Sam loves to travel as much as I do, dancing in and out of the clouds.

Lucy is replacing all her kitchen cabinets. Says her whole house is a wreck. One room's contents spilling into the next. Dish-racks on top of coffee tables. Cannisters on the t.v.

And Jill bought a condominium with two other friends.

Brianna had a summer to test a saint. After she'd sold her home in Florida and moved to Los Angeles, her father, who was living in Nicaragua, became very ill. So she flew him to Los Angeles for better treatment. And he died. Then the love of her life, her son, who she lives with, announced he's moving to China with his girlfriend. But typical Brianna-style she tells me, "I'm where I want to be. Where I've wanted to be for years. Everything will work out. Maybe not in the time frame I expected, but in this lifetime. I'm home now. You need to find yours. It's not where you are now. Asheville is just a place for you to rest. You need to find your home. And you will. You will."

John has a new job selling time shares and Randy's latest investments are doing well.

Carson still likes her new job and says she thinks she'll stay in Florida. She advises me to move on from Asheville, says it's my past. She doesn't think I should move back to Florida, though, telling me, "I'm sure as hell glad you were here, missy. Hate to think about what life would be like without meeting you. But this place isn't for you. You ought to try New York. You won't have to drive there."

I even talked to Ted the other day. I called him. He told me Maeve is based in Texas now, serving in the reserves, and that she is getting married. He said the guy is way younger than Maeve, thirty, which I could tell Ted was skeptical about, but he said Maeve sounded very "in love" and happy.

I smiled, then told Ted, "That's wonderful. Give her my best when you talk to her. Tell her I am very happy for her."

There was a moment of silence between us. Of forgiveness between all of us. Then Ted said, with his voice quavering, "You deserve to be happy, too, baby. More than any of us, you deserve to be happy." There was another moment of silence, and I started to tell Ted that I am happy, but he pulled himself together and continued. "I want you to know I'm sorry… and Maeve is too…for not…for not…believing in you." Ted paused. "You're just so, I don't know, baby—off the map. I mean we love you, you know that. You gotta know that, but come on, I mean, a creative writing major managing a garbage company…and…and…your daughter gets diagnosed mentally ill, and you go get cast on a reality t.v. show to make sure you guys have a home? I don't know, baby. You're just too much, you know? Maeve and me and, hell, I hate to bring him up, but Jake…you know…we're just like average grunts. We, uh…we work with our hands. We fix things. We put plugs in, take catheters out. We don't know what it's like to live dreams. And…and…you don't know limits. We just…we didn't mean to hurt you." Ted sounded like he might be crying. "We didn't mean to doubt you. It's just all we know to do."

This was a lot, even for me to take in. But I knew it had taken a lot for Ted to say it. So I tried to lift some weight off his shoulders. I gave him my best Hugh Grant, Mickey Blue Eyes imitation. "Furgeda boud id," I said.

Ted laughed. Through tears, Ted laughed. Then he told me Charlie took a chunk out of the side of his house, and these days he uses our sauce pot to catch water. We talked for a little while longer, then he asked if Jake had called. If we were still together.

I knew Ted was just asking to make conversation and because he was a little curious to know how things worked out with Jake and me, so I didn't get too deep. I didn't tell him what I know of "together"—that all my life, I've loved without a safety net. A trapeze artist of the heart. But this time with Jake, it's different.

When we were "together" in Florida, I never really knew if it was fate or chance or habit. But now that we're apart, when he calls, I can feel what it is.

You can tell each other "I love you" 'til the cows come home. And you can do "I love you" day and night if the chemistry is right. But to feel "I love you" is life-changing. Like a sliver of forever.

And Jake does call. And when he does, we talk for hours, losing track of time and distance. He tells me about jobs he is working on: turning the rotors on brakes, replacing a clutch, flushing out a transmission, rotating tires. And I tell him about my writing. How I can't live without it. We talk about Ginny, how she's doing, what her plans are. Then movies, music, hurricanes, the economy, philosophy, my hair.

I'm not going to pretend these calls replace being together. But I am learning to appreciate this time apart. How no matter the distance between us, Jake still manages to get to me.

Like the night when he called and he'd just gotten home from work. He asked me to take a shower with him. At first, I blushed. Then laughed a little. But seconds later, he had me in his dream. Guiding me over him, him into me. Feeling beyond touch.

§

I have a picture of Jake and me on my nightstand. A pair of his swimming trunks he left one night after we swam at Brianna's. And every night before I go to bed, I slip into a t-shirt and his trunks, kiss him and pray. I pray that Jake will always be with me to dream and create, to live with me and love me and someday soon sleep by my side, once again.

I've been lucky enough to hitch two rides to Florida to visit him. There, in the place where I first met Jake and fell in love with him, we raced each other down the moonlit street in front of his apartment, then fell laughing into each other's arms. He told me he loved me for the second time, and that as soon as he buys the truck he wants, he'll come to see me. We even planned to buy land, build a log cabin together.

The last time I went to Florida, Jasmine took me and Ginny there. Jasmine was my top salesperson at Environmental, and though I was once her boss, we have always been friends. Since I returned to Asheville, she has made a time in my life which could have been a waking nightmare, a revival of my spirit. She is a dark-headed dose of heaven, who believes in me and my writing—beyond words.

And the last day we spent in Florida, John and Ginny, Ben, Jasmine, Jake and me had breakfast together at one of my favorite cafés in Winter Park. Ginny was struggling with the voices, having a difficult time dealing with them, listening to the conversation at the table, then trying to order. Jake came to the rescue, quietly telling the waiter what Ginny wanted but couldn't make him understand in her nearly whispered speech that comes always when the voices are strongest.

Later, when Ginny and I were alone, she told me, "He's good for you, Mommy. He's a good man. He helps you."

I just smiled and kissed the top of Ginny's head, but I wanted to do something else.

I am not a vengeful person, and most who know me would argue I have an ego the size of a pinhead and a sense of humor about myself the size of the Taj Mahal. I live with few regrets, and I try always to forgive. And I know my friends truly want what is best for me.

But then, in that moment, with the memory of Jake fresh on my mind—Ginny noticing, once again, what I see in Jake. That he is not only a good man, he is a good man who loves me. In that moment, I wanted to whip out my cell phone. Call Maeve, Ted, Ben, Jill, Ray, and tell them all, "See? I am right. And you are wrong. Jake is a good man. He does not just want to 'fuck my brains out.' He loves me. I know he does. You don't know him. And I do. Inside out."

But I didn't call them. Instead, I savored the memory of the day before, when Jake and I were together.

§

Every time Jake and I are together, it is part faith, part passion, part magic, part miracle. Wholly new each time, with all those elements. But this time—the sky-diver, climber of mountains, keeper of dreams, all of me, gave in. Finally, unable to keep even one small part of me separate from Jake. Admitting to myself, as he made his way into me, that the man I always want, is the man I need.

§

After breakfast, Jasmine drove Ginny and me out of Winter Park, and before we even reached the interstate, Jake called. He said he wanted to see me again before we left. (Well, he said something else, but that was the general idea.) Anyway, I blushed and my heart started racing, but I managed to control myself in front of Ginny, cupping my cell phone to my chin and whispering to Jake, "I can't, honey, I can't ask them to stop and ...you know...," my face was turning redder, "to wait." There was a long moment of silence, then Jake's voice, sounding like the hurt I feel every night I spend without him, saying simply, "Okay."

I told him it would be a long trip and we'd get in late, but I'd call him again before it got too late. Then I clicked END, squeezed Ginny's hand and felt Jake's love.

We drove the whole way from Florida to South Carolina surrounded by drivers who apparently had never driven with even one drop of rain falling—accelerating in fog, changing lanes without signaling, slamming on their brakes at the crack of lightning. Then we hit pelting belts of sleet. And finally, nearing the mountains, we forged ahead into a winter wilderness. Buttons of snow every imaginable size and shape. Ginny's eyes were fastened to them as they fell.

At the top of Saluda Mountain, the frosty drape of sky falling to pillowed slopes of snow on either side of us, all the air white with silence, our seemingly endless journey home came to an abrupt halt at midnight. And we waited for four hours for several drivers who had crashed into this cathartic night to be flown away.

Ginny stretched out in the back seat and quickly fell asleep, while Jasmine listened to the country music station I'd turned to, singing along to the songs. I stepped outside into the falling snow and flung myself into the nearest bank of white, wildly sweeping my arms and legs out to my sides, making two snow angels—Jake and me—wings overlapping, touching, even in flight.

When I got back in the car, I glanced out the window at my creation. Jasmine was singing with George Strait, "...in all the world, you'll never find, a love as true as mine." And I burst into tears.

Ginny woke immediately and tapped Jasmine on her shoulder. She told her, "We have to go back. I don't think she can live...anymore...without him."

§

Jake has not called since the day we drove out of Florida without stopping. But I've called him. He always answers. And we talk. Sometimes for hours, our voices filled with tenderness. Other times, for minutes, whatever words we manage to put together, our thoughts of separation sound. The tension in our voices telling the same story we've lived for two years. One of broken dreams, with only brief glimpses, flickers of fire and light, of the passion and peace to come.

But we keep on talking. Because it is all we have of time together. And we can't look into each other's eyes, so our timing is off. One reaching out while the other is pulling back. But we keep trying to touch.

Jasmine and I go out to dinner about once a week. It's a holiday for us. We could be eating at Burger King; it wouldn't matter. Time spent with Jasmine is like a bubble prismed with color. Like floating joy.

We talk a lot about Jake and me, and she told me during one of our dinners right after we'd gotten back from Orlando—the now infamous rain, sleet, snow-angel trip, "I've never seen anything like it. The way you look at each other. It's like your eyes are holding hands."

I smiled. A deep warm smile that felt like Jake touching me.

Jasmine sighed and sort of melted into her chair. Then, all at once she sat straight up and leaned across the table, looking straight into my eyes. "That's it," she said. "His face touched yours."

I rolled my eyes.

"It did!" Jasmine protested. "You know it did. It does!"

I blushed. My cheeks paling crimson. But Jasmine kept talking. "When he talks and laughs, he leans into you and his face touches yours."

I whispered, still smiling, "I know."

Jasmine said, "But he isn't like that, you know. You wouldn't have had to tell me anything about him, and I would have sensed when I met him. Jake is not a touchy, feely kind of guy. No," Jasmine said, "as a matter of fact, he seems distant, a little aloof, actually. Definitely not cold...he has a beautiful, warm smile. But he doesn't seem," Jasmine thought a minute, then said, "I don't know. He's not a hugger. He's not affectionate. Not open like you. He definitely strikes me as a loner. And somebody who doesn't trust anyone.... But...he trusts you."

I didn't say anything.

Jasmine jumped up in her seat and lightly pounded her fist on our table. "Oo, oo, I know what I was going to tell you."

I raised my eyebrows, wondering if what Jasmine had to tell me would be connected to her comments about Jake and me.

She said, "I read this article. I think… in USA Today—the weekend thing they do. Anyway, it was about couples…how they relate to each other physically in a relationship, and it said, '…the ones who look into each others' eyes, who *touch faces*…'" she slowed down and looked at me with a kind of wonder, then finished the line she'd remembered, "'they are the ones who are truly in love.'"

For a minute, I couldn't tell you where I was. What I did. How I reacted to what Jasmine said. For a minute.

After that, I was bathing in her words. Letting them cleanse me. Wash away all the dark spots Maeve and Ted and Ray had pocked my heart with when they talked about Jake and me.

I wanted to reach across the table and hug Jasmine. Answer her with love. Tell her how much she meant to me.

Instead, I just sat there trembling. From her quiet recognition of all I feel and know to be true. But all I said was, "Thanks…for noticing."

§

Since I came back to Asheville, Ginny and I have spent lots of time in the kitchen. Cooking comforts me, and though Sauce Sundays seem in one way a lifetime ago, there are certain rhythms of stirring and chopping, sounds and scents that bring back the unique beauty of those hours in another place I love.

Ginny likes to read and write while I cook. Sometimes she makes notes, long pages recording ideas from the books she studies—by preference, mostly alone. And even though Faith is just across town now and visits often, there are days when Ginny seems to need that old connection, something between the two of them—quiet soul to quiet soul. And Ginny still wants me to read what she's written before she sends it, so, ready-or-not, I have learned with each line from Ginny to Faith how a bright mind's grasp of language changes when it is at the mercy of mental illness.

A few nights ago, while I stood over a pan of frying okra, Ginny handed me this to read:

Hello Aunt Faith

Today I thank you for not taking into account that I have seen you sometime recently. Since six weeks after I came back to Florida the voices have never stopped. Actually coming back many times to Asheville also in all the rooms and even when we are walking. Now I am planning to go down there and make a schedule of work laps outlines and studying about Beethoven.

I also am helping many people by collecting things that are essential considering that I know there are problems. Sometimes Haley (your sister) and I are thinking about building a home on the mountain again with Jake (not that the voices will laugh there too).

I am walking Mr. Bojangles and there I am peaceful. Some days I am improving. Do you think we could have a discussion about making a tool box for us to take to Jake when we go to Florida? When I am not needing the medication, he will be coming here. I have made a commitment to chart my progress before school starts. This is a summary of what I have told you. Maybe we can talk about all your ideas next time.

I give the letter back to Ginny, smiling. "It's beautiful," I tell her. And I mean it. And still it's hard for a writer not to notice the struggle with putting words together. Harder still for a mother to read her child's desperate effort to envision a life that must seem always just beyond her grasp, to reanimate what were once her abiding themes—hard work toward cherished goals, concern for the world, a shepherd's feeling for animals, a sixth sense about others and, most of all, the yearning for beauty and the love we have always had in common.

§

Some years more than others, winter likes to linger. After a deceptive few days of thaw in March, the locals in-the-know have warned there will be more than a few evenings of late hard frost this year; the kind of spring when gardeners who are too ambitious too early have to cover their tender plants over and over to protect them.

Longing for warmth, I called Jake last night, just to talk. In the wake of Terry Schiavo's tragedy, I'd rewritten my will and made a living one, making certain, for Terry, her suffering was not in vain. And with hope filling my heart that Jake and Ginny and I will soon be together, I went to my doctor and got not just a clean bill of health but an excellent report card. I told Jake all this. And Jake told me he didn't want to talk, then said, "Never call me again."

I clutched the cell phone as if I were holding on to him, then doubled over, trying to protect my heart, to keep it from breaking. But when I was finally able to breathe, I became even more protective, and I asked Jake a question I know the answer to better than the sound of my own voice. I asked him if there was someone else. Jake's voice pounded the air between us like a fist, "No," he said, "there is no one else." Then he repeated, "Never call me again."

But I did call Jake. All night—crying until my tears had nowhere to run. And they had to stay inside me.

Then I stopped calling—his number, his name, our love… "meant to be."

I walked outside. The blue-black, star-slung sky spread its nightly spectacle before me. And I was surrounded by just another of God's miracles. It was midnight. A time for change.

The new day was April 3, 2005. Exactly two years to the day of Ginny's breakdown. Spring *is* here. A time for rebirth. My angels have melted.

The Bartlett pear trees are replacing the beauty of the snow with their own little show of blossoming white. And in an ultimate work of synchronicity and compassion, the wind blew forty miles an hour. Making it easier to let go.

And when I did, I saw clearly for the first time what happens. When sunrise and sunset come together, like the break of dawn sprinkled with night's new stars. When opposites attract…Jake and me.

When—one who can fix anything falls in love with one who can live with questions. When one who has a keen sense of direction falls in love with a rider of winds. When one who keeps everything locked up falls in love with one whose life is an open book.

It is a struggle. Minds search for answers. Hearts strain to find a rhythm. A way to love without fear. To believe.

§

Ginny and I have the privilege of living with a love story. My parents. On December 21, they celebrated their sixtieth wedding anniversary.

Years ago, when they met, as officers in the army, serving during World War II, my father was thirty years old. A poor Southern gentleman. My mother, twenty-four, a socialite from the North, who'd torn more than a few hearts up at Penn State.

My mother saw my father first. He was pitching a softball game—officers versus the enlisted men on the base where they were stationed in Texas. She tells Ginny and me he was the best player on either team. Striking out the enlisted men like they'd never swung a bat.

Later that evening, they met at an officers' ball. My mother had been giving my father the eye all night. My father had been waiting for a slow dance. Thing is—my mother dances like a dream. And my father, well, he knows how to hold her. And so he did. And they did learn how to move together. And sixty years later, they still do.

A few years ago, my mother fell. She did something to the sciatic nerve in her back and since then she has lived with chronic pain. Now it is hard for her to stand for a long period of time, never mind dance. When she showers, my father gently brushes back the curtain and, standing right beside the tub, holds her in his arms.

Surrounded by such love, Ginny and I are both healing. Ginny has a few hours each day now without hearing multiple voices. And me, I just keep listening to mine. It tells me, "Keep being who you are, and you'll do what you're here to do." So I am. Just now catching my second wind.

End Notes

1. Breggin, Peter M.D. Toxic Psychiatry (New York, N.Y.: St. Martin's Press, 1991) pg.367
2. Ibid, pg.367
3. Ibid, pg.367
4. Breggin, Peter M.D., Cohen, David Ph. D (Philadelphia, Pennsylvania, Da Capo Press a member of the Perseus Book Group,1999) pg. 77
5. 4. Breggin, Peter M.D. Toxic Psychiatry (New York, N.Y.: St. Martin's Press, 1991) pg.25
6. Ibid pgs. 361-362
7. Ibid pgs. 344-345
8. Ibid pg. 345
9. Ibid pg. 345
10. Ibid pgs. 358-359
11. Ibid pg. 354
12. Ibid pg. 354
13. Ibid pg. 354
14. Ibid pg. 354
15. Ibid pg. 354
16. Ibid pg. 354
17. Ibid pg. 354
18. Ibid pg. 11
19. Ibid pg. 363
20. Ibid pg. 363
21. Ibid pg. 9

22. Hoffer, Abram, M.D. (The Healing Journal, thehealingjournal.com, posted February 28th, 2009)
23. Breggin, Peter M.D. Toxic Psychiatry (New York, N.Y.: St. Martin's Press, 1991)
pg. 384
24. Ibid pg. 384
25. Ibid pg. 386
26. Ibid pg. 386
27. Ibid pg. 386
28. Ibid pg. 388
29. Ibid pg. 388

Where to find information, places I have found helpful

Books

The Conscience of Psychiatry: The Reform Work of Peter R. Breggin, M.D.
Dr. Peter Breggin, 2009

Medication Madness
The Role of Psychiatric Drugs in Cases of Violence, Suicide and Murder
Dr. Peter Breggin, 2008

Your Drug May Be Your Problem: How and Why to Stop Taking Psychiatric Medications
Dr. Peter Breggin and Dr. David Cohen, 2000

Toxic Psychiatry
Dr. Peter Breggin, 1991

His Bright Light: The Story of Nick Traina
Danielle Steel, 1998

Autobiography of a Schizophrenic Girl: The Story of "Renee"
Marguerite Sechehaye, Grace-Robin-Rabson, and Frank Conroy, 1994

Websites

www.breggin.com
www.empathictherapy.org

Places for treatment and healing

www.cooperiis.org
www.skylandtrail.org

Epilogue

In the years following writing *Unsung*, the author, Heather Hamilton, continued to research and find better treatments for her daughter, Melissa, while working as a regional sales manager in the waste and recycling industry. She is currently working on projects related to *Unsung* and finding the best medical research center for schizophrenia to donate a portion of the book's proceeds to. The author's daughter, Melissa, continues to defy all the odds against her, living courageously with schizophrenia. She is taking classes in general studies to gain her GED. She works daily at a clubhouse which supports mentally ill people in her community, doing administrative activities and helping with cooking, baking, and maintenance. She walks, swims, takes tennis lessons, writes in her journal and reads, attends her church, Jubilee, and takes voice lessons on a regular basis. Through her mother's constant research and efforts working with medical professionals, she currently has some the best treatment available today. Heather and Melissa treasure their time together. Their love for each other sustains them.

Author's Biography

Heather Hamilton wrote her first novella at the age of seven. She is a graduate of the Creative Writing program at the University of North Carolina at Asheville and a recipient of the Thomas Wolfe Memorial Award for Fiction. She is an avid runner, who lives in Bayport, New York. Her daughter Melissa's courageous struggle with schizophrenia provided Heather with her inspiration for *Unsung*. You can get in touch with Heather at heatherannehamilton@gmail.com or follow her blog http://www.facebook.com.2012Unsung